Critical Essays on
F. Scott Fitzgerald's
The Great Gatsby

Critical Essays on
F. Scott Fitzgerald's
The Great Gatsby

Scott Donaldson

G. K. Hall & Co. • **Boston, Massachusetts**

Library of Congress Cataloging in Publication Data

Main entry under title:

Critical essays on The Great Gatsby.

(Critical essays on American literature)
Includes index.
1. Fitzgerald, F. Scott (Francis Scott), 1896–1940.
Great Gatsby—Addresses, essays, lectures. I. Donaldson,
Scott.   II. Series.
PS3511.I9G832   1984   813'.52   83–18646
ISBN 0–8161–8679–0

CRITICAL ESSAYS ON AMERICAN LITERATURE

This series seeks to anthologize the most important criticism on a wide variety of topics and writers in American literature. Our readers will find in various volumes not only a generous selection of reprinted articles and reviews but original essays, bibliographies, manuscript sections, and other materials brought to public attention for the first time. Scott Donaldson's volume on F. Scott Fitzgerald's *The Great Gatsby* is a welcome addition to our list in that it is the most substantial collection of scholarship ever published on this classic American novel. Among the twenty-three essays are reprinted articles and chapters from books by Lionel Trilling, Norman Holmes Pearson, James E. Miller, Jr., Richard D. Lehan, and Kenneth E. Eble. In addition, there is a lengthy introduction by Scott Donaldson and five original essays written specifically for this volume by Jackson R. Bryer, Alan Margolies, Ross Posnock, Robert Roulston, and Professor Donaldson. Finally, there is a section of Fitzgerald's letters relating to his most famous novel. We are confident that this collection will make a permanent and significant contribution to American literary study.

JAMES NAGEL, GENERAL EDITOR

Northeastern University

CONTENTS

INTRODUCTION

From the beginning Fitzgerald aimed for the skies in *The Great Gatsby*. As the book was beginning to take shape in his mind, he confessed his ambitions to Maxwell Perkins, his editor at Scribner's: "I want to write something *new*, something extraordinary and beautiful and simple and intricately patterned."[1] That he managed to do so was the result, in good part, of two significant changes in his creative approach. The subject matter of his earlier novels—*This Side of Paradise* and *The Beautiful and Damned*—had been drawn almost entirely from his personal experience, but most of what happened in *Gatsby* was invented, based on "purely creative work."[2] In addition, he devised a new way of telling his story. By letting Nick Carraway, who is clearly not a carbon copy of himself, serve as narrator, he achieved a distance and an authority his first novels had lacked. Once he began the actual writing, Fitzgerald felt a surge of "enormous power." He immersed himself in the novel during the spring and summer of 1924. Then, after the thorough process of revision outlined in his correspondence with Perkins (see pp. 260–64), he awaited its publication with confidence. He had turned out some "horrible junk" in the form of stories during the past year, he wrote John Peale Bishop a few days before *Gatsby* was published on 10 April 1925. "But the novel I'm sure of. It's marvelous."[3]

Marvelous it was, though not everyone realized it. Sales were disappointing: during Fitzgerald's lifetime *Gatsby* sold fewer than 24,000 copies in the Scribner's edition, somewhat more than *Tender Is the Night* but less than half the totals for *Paradise* or *Damned*. The initial critical reaction was mixed. Generally the first reviewers failed to divine the remarkable merit of the novel. As G. Thomas Tanselle and Jackson R. Bryer observe in "*The Great Gatsby*: A Study in Literary Reputation," "it is difficult for a contemporary commentator to detect a future masterpiece. . . ."[4] The *New York World* attacked the novel as a "dud"; the *Saturday Review* called it "an absurd story"; the *New York Herald Tribune Book Review* found it a "trifle . . . neither profound nor durable." Worst of all, H. L. Mencken in the *Baltimore Evening Sun*, while acknowledging the "fine texture" of the writing, characterized the plot of *Gatsby* as "no more than a glorified anecdote." The novel was "certainly

1

not to be put on the same shelf with, say, 'This Side of Paradise,'" Mencken concluded; the author seemed more interested in maintaining suspense than in getting under the skins of his characters.[5] These judgments would have hurt less had not Fitzgerald respected Mencken so much.

Balanced against such negative assessments was an admiring chorus which pointed to the author's "admirable mastery of his medium" in permitting "not one accidental phrase" to be printed in a work as distinct from his earlier novels "as experience is from innocence."[6] The praise came primarily from thoughtful reviewers in the better periodicals, yet only a few seemed to recognize the significance of Fitzgerald's accomplishment. One was Gilbert Seldes, whose August 1925 review in the *Dial* (pp. 271–73) stressed the novel's "artistic integrity and passionate feeling" and exhorted the author to continue in this vein. Another was T. S. Eliot, who sent a 31 December 1925 letter from London (p. 268) referring to *Gatsby* as "the first step that American fiction has taken since Henry James," a cryptic compliment brilliantly decoded in the essay by James E. Miller, Jr., included in this volume (pp. 242–58).

Apparently sensing the importance of *The Great Gatsby* to his reputation, Fitzgerald repeatedly sought a wider audience for the novel. In 1932 he wrote Perkins that he intended to lobby for an inexpensive Modern Library edition of the book. Though Modern Library books emanated from Random House and not Scribner's, he badly wanted the exposure of the popular new imprint. "*Gatsby* is constantly mentioned among memorable books but the man who asks for it in a store . . . does not ask twice . . . and there is a whole new generation who cannot obtain it," he argued. His plan, he told Perkins the following year, was to issue the Modern Library *Gatsby* a few weeks after the publication of *Tender Is the Night* by Scribner's in 1934. Perkins should not worry about adverse effect on sales of *Tender*, since "people who buy the Modern Library are not at all the people who buy the new books."[7] In the end the *Gatsby* reprint appeared five months after *Tender*, and Fitzgerald wrote a new introduction for the occasion.

In his introduction Fitzgerald chose to attack "the critics among us." Though he professed that he had no personal axe to grind, since if "Jack (who liked my last book) didn't like this one—well then John (who despised my last book) *did* like it," he nonetheless accused the critical fraternity of lacking courage and intelligence. In the case of *Gatsby* he excoriated one reviewer, hardly capable of writing "a coherent letter in English," who had called his masterpiece "a book that one reads only as one goes to the movies around the corner." That trivializing struck close to home, and Fitzgerald took the opportunity to stress how hard he'd worked on the novel. "Now that this book is being reissued, the author would like to say that never before did one try to keep his artistic conscience as pure as during the ten months put into doing it. . . . What I

cut out of it both physically and emotionally would make another novel!"[8]
More than anything else, he wanted his work taken seriously, yet he was
bedeviled during his lifetime—and after—by his image as a Jazz Age
chronicler who recorded the inconsequential adventures of youthful flap-
pers and sheiks.

Gatsby, he knew, did not fit that image, and when the Modern Library edition subsided after one printing of 5,000 copies, Fitzgerald once
again importuned Perkins for some sort of reissue. Upon going to Hollywood in 1937, he was especially worried that his name might "sink out of
sight." Perkins had mentioned the possibility of an omnibus volume containing Paradise, Gatsby, and Tender. "How remote is that idea, and why
must we forget it?" he asked his editor in April 1938. Two years later, he
had yet another question. Cheap paperbacks were just coming on the
market, and he wondered if Gatsby might not make a fresh start in this
form. "Would the 25-cent press keep Gatsby in the public eye—or is the
book unpopular? Has it had its chance? Would a popular reissue in that
series with a preface not by me but by one of its admirers—I can maybe
pick one—make it a favorite with classrooms, profs, lovers of English
prose—anybody? But to die, so completely and unjustly after having
given so much! Even now there is little published in American fiction
that doesn't slightly bear my stamp—in a small way I was an original."
Read nearly half a century later, when the sales of Gatsby run to 300,000
copies a year for those "classrooms, profs, lovers of English prose"
Fitzgerald rightly conceived of as his eventual market, his May 1940
letter seems sadly ironic.[9]

When he died in December 1940, the obituaries concentrated on the
Jazz Age author and ignored the serious novelist. Time magazine mentioned his first two novels but said nothing of Gatsby or Tender. The
New York Times, in an editorial, regretted that Fitzgerald had never
grown up.[10] His literary reputation was never lower, yet within little
more than a decade Fitzgerald and his greatest work were to be established in the canon of American literature.

Edmund Wilson had a good deal to do with the restoration. In 1941
he brought out The Last Tycoon, the novel about Hollywood that Fitzgerald had left unfinished, with a laudatory introduction. Then in 1945,
Wilson collected a number of Fitzgerald's best nonfiction pieces, together
with essays and letters of praise from others, in The Crack-Up. The
appearance of that volume inspired Lional Trilling and William Troy to
compose influential articles reassessing Fitzgerald's stature. All three
critics emphasized the gravity of his accomplishment and the heights
for which he had reached. Here was no frivolous storyteller but an artist
with a handhold on Olympus. Trilling's article connected Fitzgerald
with Shakespeare and Dickens, with Voltaire and Balzac, with Goethe
and Stendhal, with James and Yeats. The apparent disproportion would
not seem large, he pointed out, to those who knew Fitzgerald's mature

work and especially *Gatsby*, a novel which had "gained in weight and relevance" since its publication twenty years earlier. The essays by Trilling and Troy also altered previous perspectives on *Gatsby* by seeing the title figure as "a symbolic or even allegorical figure . . . standing for America itself," as "one of the few truly mythological creations in our literature."[11] And in 1945 the public at large could judge for itself: Bantam brought out the first paperback edition of *Gatsby* in that year.

In 1951 Fitzgerald's ascending reputation skyrocketed after the publication of Budd Schulberg's novel *The Disenchanted*, whose alcoholic protagonist was modeled on Fitzgerald of the Hollywood period, and of Arthur Mizener's prize-winning biography, *The Far Side of Paradise*. Two volumes edited by Malcolm Cowley, *The Stories of F. Scott Fitzgerald* and an amended *Tender Is the Night*, also emerged that year, as did Alfred Kazin's collection of essays on *F. Scott Fitzgerald: The Man and His Work*. Clearly, though, it was the man and not his work that interested the average reader. Schulberg's novel and Mizener's biography stayed on the best-seller list for months; *The Stories*, containing all of Fitzgerald's best short fiction, sold only 1,671 copies during the first year after publication. The legend of Fitzgerald as burnt-out case, doomed lover, and tragic figure seized the public imagination, and to some degree militated against sensible and lasting appreciation of his work.

Still, his very notoriety demanded critical attention, and almost everyone who read his work (for whatever reason) was struck by the enduring power of *The Great Gatsby*. In 1951 the *Times Literary Supplement* (London) called it "one of the best—if not the best—American novels of the past 50 years,"[12] a statement which seemed extravagant then but is a commonplace now. During the intervening three decades more than 300 essays have addressed themselves to this novel. For an extremely valuable survey of the history of Gatsby criticism and listing of the best articles and books, see the beginning of Jackson R. Bryer's "Style as Meaning in *The Great Gatsby*: Notes Toward a New Approach" (pp. 117–29). As Bryer establishes, the first critics tended with Trilling and Troy to concentrate on the novel's themes, regarding it as a social and moral document embodying a criticism of America. In the 1960s the focus shifted to comparative studies, dissections of the major characters, and examination of symbol clusters. Matthew J. Bruccoli's bibliographical and textual work then led the way to studies on the artistry behind the novel: its patterning and structure, its style and language. Such essays have demonstrated beyond doubt that there was nothing accidental or haphazard about the composition of *The Great Gatsby*. Fitzgerald knew what he was doing, and why.

In the last fifteen years, a new generation of critics have built upon the groundwork established by their predecessors to produce much of the best writing about *The Great Gatsby*: the best informed, most scholarly, and most interesting. Accordingly this collection is an unusually modern one. Of the 22 essays that follow, one was written in the 1940s, two in the 1950s, four in the 1960s, nine in the 1970s, and six—five of them composed especially for this volume[13]—in the 1980s. Only a few essays that have been reprinted elsewhere—classics in the field—are included.

Critical Essays on The Great Gatsby is divided into four sections called Overviews, the Artist at Work, Fresh Approaches, and History-Myth-Meaning. The first section contains Trilling's landmark evaluation, two general essays on the novel, one on the books which may have influenced Fitzgerald as he wrote it, and another on more personal sources. Besides placing the author in the company of the great, Trilling (p. 13–20) locates the strength of his book in the "power of love"—the warmth and tenderness—that pervades it and in its awareness of the effect of social class on its characters. But the magic of *Gatsby*, Norman Holmes Pearson contends (pp. 21–31), begins in style, in voice, in the control of language by which Fitzgerald manages to imply at least as much as is stated. Pearson also subsumes or anticipates most other avenues of approach by dealing with dramatic structure, narrative point of view, and the mythic quality of its protagonist's dream. The novel does not depict the glamorous 1920s of the mass media, he points out, but "a time of illness and disease." Yet "Gatsby's dream . . . becomes . . . our dream too."

F. H. Langman (pp. 31–53), like Pearson, stresses the special appeal of language, by which he does not mean patches of elegant writing so much as the economy which makes it "a highly poetic novel." Word recurrence, patterning of scenes, echoes of motifs: all contribute to *Gatsby's* "taut professionalism." But Langman also recognizes that the book is "radiant with feeling," feeling implied rather than expressed, feeling communicated through a nearly Eliotic objective correlative. Gatsby himself he sees as a mythic figure who gains universality since what drives him is, basically, only an extreme example of the forces driving everyone else in the novel.

Robert Roulston's thorough and witty review (pp. 54–66) of the literary influences which are supposed to have shaped Fitzgerald's novel should disabuse anyone still inclined to view the author as an original genius who more or less intuitively happened to create a masterpiece.[14] Joseph Conrad is the writer most often credited with influencing *Gatsby*, but as Roulston argues, the sensibilities and values of the two men differed substantially. Moreover, "an undue concentration upon the influence of any single author on *The Great Gatsby* can obscure . . . the multi-faceted quality of the novel"—facets which when taken together represent originality and not imitation. *Gatsby*, Roulston concludes, is *sui generis*, not an eclectic hodgepodge nor a clever reworking of any source. Richard D. Lehan's exploration of actual biographical sources (pp. 66–74) uncovers the origin of some of the principal characters, and almost all of the feelings, that infuse the novel with life.

W. J. Harvey's important article (pp. 75–84) introduces the second section on the craftsmanship, the "astonishing accession of technical power and skill," that went into the making of *The Great Gatsby*. Harvey illustrates the novel's command of language in a brilliant analysis of a passage taken from *Gatsby's* first party. Beneath a comic surface, he shows, Fitzgerald not only revealed the kind of people who came to those parties but also adumbrated "the central themes and dominant moral attitudes expressed in the book." The author was "applying a light but insistent moral pressure" throughout; the novel combined "an extreme density of texture" with its economy, clarity, and force.

Working from the surviving manuscript draft, Kenneth Eble (pp. 85–94) explores the artistry in the revisions Fitzgerald made. Deletions, additions, and moving of scenes account for *Gatsby's* excellence, Eble believes: "the distance Fitzgerald traveled from *This Side of Paradise* and *The Beautiful and Damned* to *The Great Gatsby* is in the rewriting of the novel." As but one example, Eble considers how Fitzgerald fleshed out the portrait of Gatsby during the late revision by emphasizing his smile, "a characteristic that could give Gatsby substance without destroying his necessary insubstantiality."

Victor Doyno also works with manuscript and galley in his essay (pp. 94–105) on the intricate patterning of *The Great Gatsby*. These patterns—careless driving, restlessness, parties, love affairs—function to deepen character and to establish attitudes toward events and themes. Thus the "sheer idealization of Gatsby's love" is tempered by way of contrast to Tom and Myrtle's lust, Nick and Jordan's coolness. Positioning, too, produces certain effects: at the end of Chapter V, Gatsby holds Daisy's hand in rapture, at the end of Chapter VI Tom casually covers that same hand as he and Daisy plot to evade responsibility.

Confining his analysis to the first three chapters, Robert Emmet Long (pp. 105–12) illustrates how Fitzgerald creates three different worlds in the parties at East Egg, 158th Street, and West Egg—worlds which are separated from each other both socially and ethically. Yet all three gatherings, which proceed from late afternoon to evening to night, and so serve as dark foreshadowing, are knitted together by a common atmosphere of confusion. While Long takes up the opening chapters, Christiane Johnson (pp. 112–17) finds the whole novel "and more" implicit on the last page through suggestion and allusion and echo. Initially, Fitzgerald had planned to use the rhapsodic Dutch sailor passage at the end of Chapter I. In revision he did more than simply move it to the end of the book, however; he also made it more sweeping and universal in its implications by generalizing the pronouns from "I" to "he" and "we" and by fusing past, present, and future time in the penultimate sentence.

Beginning with a review of previous Gatsby criticism, Jackson R. Bryer (pp. 117–29) proceeds to an account of the way in which "the smallest units" of language—brief descriptive phrases, witty juxtapositions, evocative similes—"metaphorically encapsulate" the meanings of the novel. Such linguistic concision, Bryer believes, "is at the heart of the achievement" of the novel. For Fitzgerald, style and meaning were inseparable, as he made clear in letters to his daughter Scottie.

The interpretations by Harvey, Eble, Doyno, Long, Johnson, and Bryer look at Fitzgerald's novel with the kind of attention ordinarily devoted only to poetry. This is as it should be. *The Great Gatsby* is a beautifully crafted work, and repays the closest possible reading. Moreover, the novel is so dense and suggestive—again, like many poems—as to encourage widely varying reactions. A number of such elucidations, all published since 1977, make up the third section of this volume.

No technical question about *Gatsby* has been more belabored than that of Nick Carraway's appropriateness and trustworthiness as narrator. My essay on the subject (pp. 131–39) attempts to find a common ground of agreement between those who think that adopting Nick's point of view was a master stroke and those who, objecting to his apparent amorality and air of superiority, find him unreliable. Basically, my argument is that Nick Carraway is the perfect narrator for this novel *because* of his personal imperfections. If even Nick, a rather sarcastic snob who disapproves of Gatsby from beginning to end, can eventually come down on his side, how can the rest of us fail to do so?

Maintaining that we have "read over" scenes we should instead "read through," Keath Fraser (pp. 140–53) takes little-noticed incidents like that in McKee's bedroom and descriptions of Tom's powerful body and Jordan's curiously androgynous one as evidence that *Gatsby* contains "a cultivated ambiguity . . . which flirts with, but never answers the question of Nick Carraway's sexuality." Fraser's provocative interpretation derives some support, as he demonstrates, from cuts made in the surviving manuscript.

Sarah Beebe Fryer (pp. 153–66) also adopts a controversial stance toward one of the novel's major characters. Bolstered by reference to Fitzgerald's own remarks on the subject and fine close reading of the text, Fryer's article offers the ablest defense so far of the much-maligned Daisy Buchanan. To regard Daisy as morally irresponsible is to minimize the complicated nature of her personality, Fryer believes. Both Nick and Gatsby are confused about her behavior, because they do not recognize that her facade of artificiality serves as a shield against the strong emotions she fears but cannot help feeling. In the end Daisy is torn between her romantic love for Gatsby and her simultaneous craving for stability; as the "victim of a complex network of needs and desires," she deserves more pity than blame. Even Tom Buchanan is accorded a measure of understanding in W. T. Lhamon, Jr.'s, essay (pp. 166–75). Tom and Gatsby are basically alike in seeking to control their environment, Lhamon asserts. The difference is that Tom *can* master time and space—he reverses the flow of time, for instance, by turning a garage into a stable—while Gatsby cannot.

Photography is viewed in Lawrence Jay Dessner's article (pp. 175–86) as an attempt to freeze time. In this sense Henry Gatz and his son are both Platonists for whom the ideal is more real than the merely tangible. Thus the picture of his son's mansion means far more to Mr. Gatz than the actual place. Dessner also comments on Fitzgerald's photographic, often cinematic, sensibility in description: Gatsby stretching his arms into the night, Tom and Daisy at the kitchen table. The failure of the three films and one play based on *Gatsby*, Alan Margolies concludes in his enlightening survey of these attempts (pp. 187–200), can be attributed more to inferior productions than to any lack of dramatic potential in the novel.

In an original and challenging essay, Ross Posnock (pp. 201–13) maintains that Marx's critique of capitalist society, and particularly of "commodity fetishism," is "assimilated into the novel's imaginative life." This interpretation derives substantial support from the pages of the novel: mere objects, after all, take on an ideal glow in the eyes of Gatsby himself, until they are finally dulled to materiality. Only someone capable of holding "two opposed ideas in the mind at the same time," while retaining the ability to function—the test, as Fitzgerald put it, of "a first-rate intelligence"—could properly understand the capacity of money to alter and confuse our perceptions. Such an interpretation does not make Fitzgerald a doctrinaire radical, but neither does it countenance regarding him as an intellectual naif.

The final section of this volume consists of three major articles on the wider significance of *The Great Gatsby*. Building on earlier interpretations of Gatsby as a mythic character who in his inability to distinguish between reality and illusion embodies the romantic American vision, Kermit W. Moyer detects a circularity of structure in the novel (pp. 215–28) that "reiterates [its] perspective on American history." The Buchanans stand at a historical dead end, their backs to the wall. The promise of American life has reached a cul-de-sac. Boats can make no headway against the currents of corruption and materialism. Where Moyer's essay combines perceptive readings of key scenes in *Gatsby* with a historical perspective, Giles Gunn (pp. 228–42) brings an ethical sensibility to bear on the same material. In accounting for the novel's extraordinary capacity to reorder "the mental, emotional and spiritual furniture of our lives," Gunn traces its continuing appeal to Gatsby's "poetry of desire, his imagination of wonder." Buchanan and Gatsby virtually divide the American past between them, he feels. "Decadent and wholly self-serving" yet lacking the ability to feel anything but pity for himself, Tom is the child of the robber barons. "Ebullient and wholly self-effacing" yet without the ability to temper his feelings, Gatsby is the child of those early settlers who once, before they were betrayed by their own acquisitiveness, hoped to build a city on a hill. Contaminated though his dream may have been, however, it is Gatsby who triumphs, even in death. Those who think present reality too horrendous to contemplate can still admire Gatsby's capacity for wonder. We would even emulate it, if we could.

James E. Miller, Jr.'s, article (pp. 242–58) or Gatsby's "meaning, its themes, its moral implications" is organized around Eliot's characterization of the novel as "the first step . . . since Henry James." Two things Eliot probably had in mind, Miller writes, were Fitzgerald's rendering of the "deeper psychology" and his presentation of America and the modern age, each communicated "not through direct proclamation" but by dramatization and a sequence of "powerful, pervasive, and devastating images" not unlike those in The Waste Land. Eliot's poem reverberates in other ways in Gatsby, too: in its evocative images of death and in its depiction of the corruption of the times. It was not only the period that had turned sour, but the American dream itself which seduced Gatsby (even before he knew Daisy) into the worshipful "service of a vast, vulgar, and meretricious beauty." Gatsby was as much the victim of his American heritage as of Tom or Daisy or George Wilson. Yet, Miller concludes, The Great Gatsby "is still something more—something reaching out beyond its time and beyond its place" to express the simple basic human yearning "to snatch something precious" and "preserve it outside the ravages of time."

In constructing a collection of essays like this one, certain decisions had to be made. A relatively easy one was to regularize all references to conform to the Scribner library edition of the novel, by far the most widely available text. Much more difficult was deciding what to leave out. Though as it stands Critical Essays on The Great Gatsby is the most comprehensive critical volume ever assembled, nonetheless it can hardly encompass all the major work within its covers. Regretfully omitted are articles by Marius Bewley, A. E. Dyson, Edwin S. Fussell, John Henry Raleigh, R. W. Stallman, and William Troy, as well as sections of books by Miller, Sergio Perosa, Henry Dan Piper, Robert Sklar, and Brian Way.[15] But what is included here is very valuable, and much of it is new. As long ago as 1966 John W. Aldridge suggested that it might be time to stop writing about The Great Gatsby. Gatsby, he feared, was a "work of art particularly prone to being confused with its meanings" and too much emphasis on such an approach might damage a novel which was "above all . . . to be directly experienced and responded to."[16]

With that last observation one can only agree, but *Gatsby* has proved less fragile than Aldridge feared. Neither this nor any other collection can offer any last words on the subject. *The Great Gatsby* is a novel that criticism cannot exhaust.

Scott Donaldson
Bellagio and Williamsburg, 1982

Notes

1. F. Scott Fitzgerald to Maxwell Perkins, July 1922, *The Letters of F. Scott Fitzgerald*, ed. Andrew Turnbull (New York: Scribner's, 1962), p. 146.
2. F. Scott Fitzgerald to Maxwell Perkins, before 6 April 1924, *Letters*, p. 163.
3. F. Scott Fitzgerald to John Peale Bishop, April 1925, *Letters*, p. 356.
4. I am indebted to Tanselle and Bryer's article, which appeared in *New Mexico Quarterly*, 33 (Winter 1963–64), 409–25, for much of the information that follows.
5. H. L. Mencken, "The Great Gatsby," *Baltimore Evening Sun*, 2 May 1925, p. 9. For a comprehensive gathering of reviews see Jackson R. Bryer, ed., *F. Scott Fitzgerald: The Critical Reception* (New York: Burt Franklin, 1978).
6. Quotations from three separate reviews mentioned in Tanselle and Bryer, pp. 413–14.
7. F. Scott Fitzgerald to Maxwell Perkins, before 2 May 1932 and 25 September 1933, *Letters*, pp. 227–28 and 232.
8. F. Scott Fitzgerald, Introduction, *The Great Gatsby* (New York: Random House, 1934), pp. vii–xi.
9. F. Scott Fitzgerald to Maxwell Perkins, 23 April 1938 and 20 May 1940, *Letters*, pp. 278 and 288.
10. *Time*, 30 December 1940; "Not Wholly 'Lost,'" *New York Times*, 24 December 1940.
11. Trilling, pp. 13–20; William Troy, "Scott Fitzgerald–The Authority of Failure," *Accent*, 6 (1945), 56–60.
12. Quoted in Tanselle and Bryer, p. 421.
13. The five essays commissioned for this volume are Jackson R. Bryer, "Style as Meaning in *The Great Gatsby*: Notes Toward a New Approach"; Scott Donaldson, "The Trouble with Nick"; Alan Margolies, "Novel to Play to Film: Four Versions of *The Great Gatsby*"; Ross Posnock, "'A New World, Material Without Being Real': Fitzgerald's Critique of Capitalism in *The Great Gatsby*"; and Robert Roulston, "Something Borrowed, Something New: A Discussion of Literary Influences on *The Great Gatsby*."
14. As R. W. Stallman pointed out in "Conrad and *The Great Gatsby*," *Twentieth Century Literature*, 1 (1955), 5–12, Mizener's biography referred to Fitzgerald's "intuitive way of working" and assumed that he was not generally "aware of his literary sources."
15. Marius Bewley, "Scott Fitzgerald's Criticism of America," *Sewanee Review*, 62 (1954), 223–46; A. E. Dyson, "*The Great Gatsby*: Thirty-Six Years After," *Modern Fiction Studies*, 7 (1961), 37–48; Edwin S. Fussell, "Fitzgerald's Brave New World," *English Literary History*, 19 (1952), 291–306; John Henry Raleigh, "F. Scott Fitzgerald's *The Great Gatsby*–Legendary Bases and Allegorical Significances," *University of Kansas City Review*, 24 (1957), 55–58; R. W. Stallman,

"Conrad . . ." and "Gatsby and the Hole in Time," *Modern Fiction Studies*, 1 (1955), 2–16; Troy; James E. Miller, Jr., *F. Scott Fitzgerald: His Art and His Technique* (New York Univ. Press, 1964); Sergio Perosa, *The Art of F. Scott Fitzgerald* (Ann Arbor: Univ. of Michigan Press, 1965); Henry Dan Piper, *F. Scott Fitzgerald—A Critical Portrait* (New York: Holt, Rinehart and Winston, 1965); Robert Sklar, *F. Scott Fitzgerald: The Last Laocoön* (New York: Oxford Univ. Press, 1967), and Brian Way, *F. Scott Fitzgerald and the Art of Social Fiction* (New York: St. Martin's Press, 1980).

16. John W. Aldridge, "The Life of *Gatsby*: A Preamble," *The Devil in the Fire: Retrospective Essays on American Literature and Culture 1951–1971* (New York: Harper's Magazine Press, 1971), pp. 101–2.

Overviews

F. Scott Fitzgerald

Lionel Trilling*

" 'So be it! I die content and my destiny is fulfilled,' said Racine's Orestes; and there is more in his speech than the insanely bitter irony that appears on the surface. Racine, fully conscious of this tragic grandeur, permits Orestes to taste for a moment before going mad with grief the supreme joy of a hero; to assume his *exemplary* role." The heroic awareness of which André Gide speaks in his essay on Goethe was granted to Scott Fitzgerald for whatever grim joy he might find in it. It is a kind of seal set upon his heroic quality that he was able to utter his vision of his own fate publicly and aloud and in *Esquire* with no lessening of his dignity, even with an enhancement of it. The several essays in which Fitzgerald examined his life in crisis have been gathered together by Edmund Wilson—who is for many reasons the most appropriate editor possible—and published, together with Fitzgerald's notebooks and some letters, as well as certain tributes and memorabilia, in a volume called, after one of the essays, *The Crack-Up*. It is a book filled with the grief of the lost and the might-have-been, with physical illness and torture of mind. Yet the heroic quality is so much here, Fitzgerald's assumption of the "exemplary role" is so proper and right that it occurs to us to say, and not merely as a piety but as the most accurate expression of what we really do feel, that

> Nothing is here for tears, nothing to wail
> Or knock the breast, no weakness, no contempt,
> Dispraise, or blame, nothing but well and fair,
> And what may quiet us in a death so noble.

This isn't what we may fittingly say on all tragic occasions, but the original occasion for these words has a striking aptness to Fitzgerald. Like Milton's Samson, he had the consciousness of having misused the power

*Reprinted from Lionel Trilling, *The Liberal Imagination: Essays on Literature and Society* by permission of Charles Scribner's Sons. Copyright 1945, 1950 by Lionel Trilling; © renewed 1973, 1978 by Diana Trilling and James Trilling.

with which he had been endowed. "I had been only a mediocre care-taker . . . of my talent," he said. And the parallel carries further, to the sojourn among the Philistines and even to the maimed hero exhibited and mocked for the amusement of the crowd—on the afternoon of September 25, 1936, the New York *Evening Post* carried on its front page a feature story in which the triumphant reporter tells how he managed to make his way into the Southern resort hotel where the sick and distracted Fitzgerald was being cared for and there "interviewed" him, taking all due note of the contrast between the present humiliation and the past glory. It was a particularly gratuitous horror, and yet in retrospect it serves to augment the moral force of the poise and fortitude which marked Fitzgerald's mind in the few recovered years that were left to him.

The root of Fitzgerald's heroism is to be found, as it sometimes is in tragic heroes, in his power of love. Fitzgerald wrote much about love, he was preoccupied with it as between men and women, but it is not merely where he is being explicit about it that his power appears. It is to be seen where eventually all a writer's qualities have their truest existence, in his style. Even in Fitzgerald's early, cruder books, or even in his commercial stories, and even when the style is careless, there is a tone and pitch to the sentences which suggest his warmth and tenderness, and, what is rare nowadays and not likely to be admired, his gentleness without softness. In the equipment of the moralist and therefore in the equipment of the novelist, aggression plays an important part, and although it is of course sanctioned by the novelist's moral intention and by whatever truth of moral vision he may have, it is often none the less fierce and sometimes even cruel. Fitzgerald was a moralist to the core and his desire to "preach at people in some acceptable form" is the reason he gives for not going the way of Cole Porter and Rodgers and Hart —we must always remember in judging him how many real choices he was free and forced to make—and he was gifted with the satiric eye; yet we feel that in his morality he was more drawn to celebrate the good than to denounce the bad. We feel of him, as we cannot feel of all moralists, that he did not attach himself to the good because this attachment would sanction his fierceness toward the bad—his first impulse was to love the good, and we know this the more surely because we perceive that he loved the good not only with his mind but also with his quick senses and his youthful pride and desire.

He really had but little impulse to blame, which is the more remarkable because our culture peculiarly honors the act of blaming, which it takes as the sign of virtue and intellect. "Forbearance, good word," is one of the jottings in his notebook. When it came to blame, he preferred, it seems, to blame himself. He even did not much want to blame the world. Fitzgerald knew where "the world" was at fault. He knew that it was the condition, the field, of tragedy. He is conscious of "what preyed on Gatsby, what foul dust floated in the wake of his dreams." But he never made out that the world imposes tragedy, either upon the heroes of his novels, whom he called his "brothers," or upon himself. When he speaks of his own fate, he does indeed connect it with the nature of the social world in which he had his early flowering, but he never finally lays it upon that world, even though at the time when he was most aware of his destiny it was fashionable with minds more pretentious than his to lay all personal difficulty whatever at the door of the "social order." It is, he feels, *his* fate—and as much as to anything else in Fitzgerald, we respond to the delicate tension he maintained between his idea of personal free will and his idea of circumstance: we respond to that moral and intellectual energy. "The test of a first-rate intelligence," he said, "is the ability to hold two opposed ideas in the mind, at the same time, and still retain the ability to function."

The power of love in Fitzgerald, then, went hand in hand with a sense of personal responsibility and perhaps created it. But it often happens that the tragic hero can conceive and realize a love that is beyond his own prudence or beyond his powers of dominance or of self-protection, so that he is destroyed by the very thing that gives him his spiritual status and stature. From Proust we learn about a love that is destructive by a kind of corrosiveness, but from Fitzgerald's two mature novels, *The Great Gatsby* and *Tender Is the Night*, we learn about a love— perhaps it is peculiarly American—that is destructive by reason of its very tenderness. It begins in romance, sentiment, even "glamour"—no one, I think, has remarked how innocent of mere "sex," how charged with sentiment is Fitzgerald's description of love in the jazz age—and it takes upon itself reality, and permanence, and duty discharged with an almost masochistic scrupulousness of honor. In the bright dreams begins the responsibility which needs so much prudence and dominance to sustain; and Fitzgerald was anything but a prudent man and he tells us that at a certain point in his college career "some old desire for personal dominance was broken and gone." He connects that loss of desire for dominance with his ability to write; and he set down in his notebook the belief that "to record one must be unwary." Fitzgerald, we may say, seemed to feel that both love and art needed a sort of personal defenselessness.

The phrase from Yeats, the derivation of the "responsibility" from the "dreams," reminds us that we must guard against dismissing, with easy words about its immaturity, Fitzgerald's preoccupation with the bright charm of his youth. Yeats himself, a wiser man and wholly fulfilled in his art, kept to the last of his old age his connection with his youthful vanity. A writer's days must be bound each to each by his sense of his life, and Fitzgerald the undergraduate was father of the best in the man and the novelist.

His sojourn among the philistines is always much in the mind of everyone who thinks about Fitzgerald, and indeed it was always much in his own mind. Everyone knows the famous exchange between Fitzgerald and Ernest Hemingway—Hemingway refers to it in his story, "The Snows of Kilimanjaro" and Fitzgerald records it in his notebook—in which, to Fitzgerald's remark, "The very rich are different from us," Hemingway replied, "Yes, they have more money." It is usually supposed that Hemingway had the better of the encounter and quite settled the matter. But we ought not be too sure. The novelist of a certain kind, if he is to write about social life, may not brush away the reality of the differences of class, even though to do so may have the momentary appearance of a virtuous social avowal. The novel took its rise and its nature from the radical revision of the class structure in the eighteenth century, and the novelist must still live by his sense of class differences, and must be absorbed by them, as Fitzgerald was, even though he despise them, as Fitzgerald did.

No doubt there was a certain ambiguity in Fitzgerald's attitude toward the "very rich"; no doubt they were for him something more than the mere object of his social observation. They seem to have been the nearest thing to an aristocracy that America could offer him, and we cannot be too simple about what a critic has recently noted, the artist's frequent "taste for aristocracy, his need—often quite open—of a superior social class with which he can make some fraction of common cause—enough, at any rate, to account for his own distinction." Every modern reader is by definition wholly immune from all ignoble social considerations, and, no matter what his own social establishment or desire for it may be, he knows that in literature the interest in social position must never be taken seriously. But not all writers have been so simple and virtuous—what are we to make of those risen gentlemen, Shakespeare and Dickens, or those fabricators of the honorific "de," Voltaire and Balzac? Yet their snobbery—let us call it that—is of a large and generous kind and we are not entirely wrong in connecting their peculiar energies of mind with whatever it was they wanted from gentility or aristocracy. It is a common habit of writers to envision an actuality of personal life which shall have the freedom and the richness of detail and the order of form that they desire in art. Yeats, to mention him again, spoke of the falseness of the belief that the "inherited glory of the rich" really holds richness of life. This, he said, was a mere dream; and yet, he goes on, it is a necessary illusion—

> Yet Homer had not sung
> Had he not found it certain beyond dreams
> That out of life's own self delight had sprung
> The abounding glittering jet. . . .

And Henry James, at the threshold of his career, allegorized in his story "Benvolio" the interplay that is necessary for some artists between their

creative asceticism and the bright, free, gay life of worldliness, noting at
the same time the desire of worldliness to destroy the asceticism.

With a man like Goethe the balance between the world and his
asceticism is maintained, and so we forgive him his often absurd feelings—
but perhaps absurd as well as forgivable only in the light of our present
opinion of his assured genius—about aristocracy. Fitzgerald could not
always keep the balance true; he was not, as we know, a prudent man.
And no doubt he deceived himself a good deal in his youth, but certainly his self-deception was not in the interests of vulgarity, for aristocracy meant to him a kind of disciplined distinction of personal existence
which, presumably, he was so humble as not to expect from his art. What
was involved in that notion of distinction can be learned from the use
which Fitzgerald makes of the word "aristocracy" in one of those serious
moments which occur in his most frivolous *Saturday Evening Post* stories:
he says of the life of the young man of the story, who during the war was
on duty behind the lines, that "it was not so bad—except that when the
infantry came limping back from the trenches he wanted to be one of
them. The sweat and mud they wore seemed only one of those ineffable
symbols of aristocracy that were forever eluding him." Fitzgerald was
perhaps the last notable writer to affirm the Romantic fantasy, descended
from the Renaissance, of personal ambition and heroism, of life committed to, or thrown away for, some ideal of self. To us it will no doubt
come more and more to seem a merely boyish dream; the nature of our
society requires the young man to find his distinction through coopera-
tion, subordination, and an expressed piety of social usefulness, and
although a few young men have made Fitzgerald into a hero of art, it is
likely that even to these admirers the whole nature of his personal fantasy
is not comprehensible, for young men find it harder and harder to
understand the youthful heroes of Balzac and Stendhal, they increasingly
find reason to blame the boy whose generosity is bound up with his will
and finds its expression in a large, strict, personal demand upon life.

I am aware that I have involved Fitzgerald with a great many great
names and that it might be felt by some that this can do him no service,
the disproportion being so large. But the disproportion will seem large
only to those who think of Fitzgerald chiefly through his early public
legend of heedlessness. Those who have a clear recollection of the mature
work or who have read *The Crack-Up* will at least not think of the disproportion as one of kind. Fitzgerald himself did not, and it is by a
man's estimate of himself that we must begin to estimate him. For all
the engaging self-depreciation which was part of his peculiarly American
charm, he put himself, in all modesty, in the line of greatness, he judged
himself in a large way. When he writes of his depression, of his "dark
night of the soul" where "it is always three o'clock in the morning," he
not only derives the phrase from St. John of the Cross but adduces the
analogous black despairs of Wordsworth, Keats, and Shelley. A novel with

Ernest Hemingway as the model of its hero suggests to him Stendhal portraying the Byronic man, and he defends *The Great Gatsby* from some critical remark of Edmund Wilson's by comparing it with *The Brothers Karamazov*. Or again, here is the stuff of his intellectual pride at the very moment that he speaks of giving it up, as years before he had given up the undergraduate fantasies of valor: "The old dream of being an entire man in the Goethe-Byron-Shaw tradition . . . has been relegated to the junk heap of the shoulder pads worn for one day on the Princeton fresh-man football field and the overseas cap never worn overseas." And was it, that old dream, unjustified? To take but one great name, the one that on first thought seems the least relevant of all—between Goethe at twenty-four the author of *Werther*, and Fitzgerald, at twenty-four the author of *This Side of Paradise*, there is not really so entire a difference as piety and textbooks might make us think; both the young men so handsome, both winning immediate and notorious success, both rather more interested in life than in art, each the spokesman and symbol of his own restless generation.

It is hard to overestimate the benefit which came to Fitzgerald from his having consciously placed himself in the line of the great. He was a "natural," but he did not have the contemporary American novelist's belief that if he compares himself with the past masters, or if he takes thought—which, for a writer, means really knowing what his predecessors have done—he will endanger the integrity of his natural gifts. To read Fitzgerald's letters to his daughter—they are among the best and most affecting letters I know—and to catch the tone in which he speaks about the literature of the past, or to read the notebooks he faithfully kept, indexing them as Samuel Butler had done, and to perceive how con-tinuously he thought about literature, is to have some clue to the secret of the continuing power of Fitzgerald's work.

The Great Gatsby, for example, after a quarter-century is still as fresh as when it first appeared; it has even gained in weight and relevance, which can be said of very few American books of its time. This, I think, is to be attributed to the specifically intellectual courage with which it was conceived and executed, a courage which implies Fitzgerald's grasp —both in the sense of awareness and of appropriation—of the traditional resources available to him. Thus, *The Great Gatsby* has its interest as a record of contemporary manners, but this might only have served to date it, did not Fitzgerald take the given moment of history as something more than a mere circumstance, did he not, in the manner of the great French novelists of the nineteenth century, seize the given moment as a moral fact. The same boldness of intellectual grasp accounts for the suc-cess of the conception of its hero—Gatsby is said by some to be not quite credible, but the question of any literal credibility he may or may not have becomes trivial before the large significance he implies. For

Gatsby, divided between power and dream, comes inevitably to stand for America itself. Ours is the only nation that prides itself upon a dream and gives its name to one, "the American dream." We are told that "the truth was that Jay Gatsby of West Egg, Long Island, sprang from his Platonic conception of himself. He was a son of God—a phrase which, if it means anything, means just that—and he must be about His Father's business, the service of a vast, vulgar, and meretricious beauty." Clearly it is Fitzgerald's intention that our mind should turn to the thought of the nation that has sprung from its "Platonic conception" of itself. To the world it is anomalous in America, just as in the novel it is anomalous in Gatsby, that so much raw power should be haunted by envisioned romance. Yet in that anomaly lies, for good or bad, much of the truth of our national life, as, at the present moment, we think about it.

Then, if the book grows in weight of significance with the years, we can be sure that this could not have happened had its form and style not been as right as they are. Its form is ingenious—with the ingenuity, however, not of craft but of intellectual intensity. The form, that is, is not the result of careful "plotting"—the form of a good novel never is— but is rather the result of the necessities of the story's informing idea, which require the sharpness of radical foreshortening. Thus, it will be observed, the characters are not "developed": the wealthy and brutal Tom Buchanan haunted by his "scientific" vision of the doom of civiliza- tion, the vaguely guilty, vaguely homosexual Jordan Baker, the dim Wolfsheim, who fixed the World Series of 1919, are treated, we might say, as if they were ideographs, a method of economy that is reinforced by the ideographic use that is made of the Washington Heights flat, the terrible "valley of ashes" seen from the Long Island Railroad, Gatsby's incoherent parties, and the huge sordid eyes of the oculist's advertising sign. (It is a technique which gives the novel an affinity with *The Waste Land*, between whose author and Fitzgerald there existed a reciprocal admiration.) Gatsby himself, once stated, grows only in the understanding of the narrator. He is allowed to say very little in his own person. Indeed, apart from the famous "Her voice is full of money," he says only one memorable thing, but that remark is overwhelming in its intellectual audacity: when he is forced to admit that his lost Daisy did perhaps love her husband, he says, "In any case it was just personal." With that sentence he achieves an insane greatness, convincing us that he really is a Platonic conception of himself, really some sort of Son of God.

What underlies all success in poetry, what is even more important than the shape of the poem or its wit of metaphor, is the poet's voice. It either gives us confidence in what is being said or it tells us that we do not need to listen; and it carries both the modulation and the living form of what is being said. In the novel no less than in the poem, the voice of the author is the decisive factor. We are less consciously aware of it in the novel, and, in speaking of the elements of a novel's art, it cannot properly be exemplified by quotation because it is continuous and cumulative. In Fitzgerald's work the voice of his prose is of the essence of his success. We hear in it at once the tenderness toward human desire that modifies a true firmness of moral judgment. It is, I would venture to say, the normal or ideal voice of the novelist. It is characteristically modest, yet it has in it, without apology or self-consciousness, a largeness, even a stateliness, which derives from Fitzgerald's connection with tradition and with mind, from his sense of what has been done before and the demands which this past accomplishment makes. "... I became aware of the old island here that flowered once for Dutch sailors' eyes— a fresh, green breast of the new world. Its vanished trees, the trees that had made way for Gatsby's house, had once pandered in whispers to the last and greatest of all human dreams; for a transitory enchanted moment man must have held his breath in the presence of this continent, compelled into an aesthetic contemplation he neither understood nor desired, face to face for the last time in history with something commensurate to his capacity for wonder" (p. 182). Here, in the well-known passage, the voice is a little dramatic, a little *intentional*, which is not improper to a passage in climax and conclusion, but it will the better suggest in brief compass the habitual music of Fitzgerald's seriousness.

Fitzgerald lacked prudence, as his heroes did, lacked that blind instinct of self-protection which the writer needs and the American writer needs in double measure. But that is all he lacked—and it is the generous fault, even the heroic fault. He said of his Gatsby, "If personality is an unbroken series of successful gestures, then there was something gorgeous about him, some heightened sensitivity to the promises of life, as if he were related to one of those intricate machines that register earthquakes ten thousand miles away. This responsiveness had nothing to do with that flabby impressionability which is dignified under the name of the 'creative temperament'—it was an extraordinary gift for hope, a romantic readiness such as I have never found in any other person and which it is not likely I shall ever find again" (p. 2). And it is so that we are drawn to see Fitzgerald himself as he stands in his exemplary role.

Reading a Novel—
The Great Gatsby   **Norman Holmes Pearson***

Reading a novel depends a good deal on who you are—and when you read it. F. Scott Fitzgerald recognized that there were differences. "My whole theory of writing," he once said, "I can sum up in one sentence. An author ought to write for the youth of his own generation, the critics of the next, and the schoolmasters of ever afterward." Presumably, we who read *The Great Gatsby* now belong to the "ever afterward."

"The youth" of Fitzgerald's "own generation" have long since grown up. No young readers can ever again be contemporaries of the book as they were on its publication in 1925. *The Great Gatsby* is now a period piece out of the past, part of Mammon's Acre, not God's, in what was then a new regionalism of the rich. The 1920s, with its air of being a time when people were gay and there was plenty of everything, has in retrospect become little more than a version of a Currier and Ives print, with the sleighride to grandmother's farm for Thanksgiving replaced by a Stutz Bearcat on the way to a speakeasy.

But one does not really read *The Great Gatsby* as the record of a decade. It is not worth arguing with Shane Leslie as to whether or not Mgr. Fay's[1] introduction of Fitzgerald to the rich, Long Island society of the Bourke Cochrans was really responsible for his knowledge of "the grand life of multi-millionaires." I have no idea who the Bourke Cochrans are. Perhaps they really live like that either at West Egg or at East Egg. It does not even matter much that *Gatsby* as a book was based largely on Fitzgerald's experience at Great Neck. Nor that Meyer Wolfsheim, Gatsby's gangster friend who "fixed the World Series back in 1919," was based on Arnold Rothstein, even though Rothstein in fact did not fix the Series. The "rather remote model for Gatsby himself" is, Mr. Mizener also tells us, "a man named Max von Guerlach [who] is still alive to tell us about it."[2] So far, at least, Max von Guerlach hasn't told me, myself, anything. Indeed how could he tell me anything about Jay Gatsby which the novel doesn't itself relate? For the Jay Gatsby I know is the lonely visionary who moves on the pages of Scott Fitzgerald's book.

A novel creates its own world, and we can only comment on it and react to it. There have been a great many commentators on the world of *The Great Gatsby*, and they have made increasingly certain our identification of what we read. But this of course is what we mean to do on our own. The advantage of criticism is skilled companionship. No critical

*Reprinted from *Reports and Speeches of the Eighth Yale Conference on the Teaching of English* (New Haven: Yale University Office of Teacher Training, 1962), pp. 73–82.

analysis can ever take the place of the novel itself, nor can any one else be surrogate for the direct experience of a novel which reading it gives. Yet, as I say, there has indeed bountifully been this second, help-ful category which Fitzgerald established—what he spoke of as "the critics of the next [generation]." But one rule is certain. In reading a novel, we should read the novel before we read about it.

In one sense of course we do more re-reading than first reading of a novel, even from the start. The memory of the first page of its text is in our mind when the second page meets our eye. These two pages combine to repeat the experience with the next. It is the constantly re-awakened memory of what has preceded in a novel which gives us a sense of the repetitions which establish a symbol out of what was orig-inally only a citation. Whiteness reiterated in *The Great Gatsby* becomes more than color. West Egg and East Egg enlarge in their implied rela-tionship. Memory, too, establishes our awareness of the counterbalanc-ing of situations by parallelism or contrast, so that as we come to know the characters of a novel we learn of their inner natures from their differing manners and responses to mutually defining tests. This is the beginning of our sense of a novel's structure. The ordering of a novel carries with it the sense of what the novel is saying to us. The growing awareness and recognition of structure are the unfolding of the mystery; and in fact every good novel is a mystery story.

No one can read *The Great Gatsby* without being aware that one has a little jewel of a novel, beautifully shaped and polished with a sureness of craftsmanship which renders each page and each paragraph into a contribution to the whole. The style of a novel is as much a part of its structure as of its tone. Syntax is a method of formulation. Diction is a mode of meaning.

It is perhaps through the style that one first actually begins to get into a novel's meaning. An introduction of this kind is possible on almost every page of *The Great Gatsby*. One remembers, for example, Nick Carraway's first evening at a Gatsby party, at the vast mansion which the mysterious stranger had bought at West Egg, next door to Nick's own rented cottage.

> With Jordan's slender golden arm resting in mine, we descended the steps and sauntered about the garden. A tray of cocktails floated at us through the twilight, and we sat down at a table with the two girls in yellow and three men, each one introduced to us as Mr. Mumble. (p. 43)

There is a caressing elegance to the diction which chooses to cite the "slender golden arm," and there is a sense of elevated magic in the "tray of cocktails [which] floated at us through the twilight." But all of this atmosphere of romantic rhetoric is deflated by the abrupt colloquialism and precise plop of the final "Mr. Mumble." One comes to know a host through his choice of guests, but one comes to know only that this host knows no one. Jordan's arm and the dresses of the two girls are yellow, but already in the book we have had a symbolic significance established to the color, and we know we are reading more than a fashion note. We remember, among other things, the definition given by Nick's own first gesture when he had had conferred on him, in his own words, "the freedom of the neighborhood."

> And so with the sunshine and the great bursts of leaves growing on the trees, just as things grow in fast movies, I had that familiar conviction that life was beginning over again with the summer.
>   There was so much to read, for one thing, and so much fine health to be pulled down out of the young breath-giving air. I bought a dozen volumes on banking and credit and investment securities, and they stood on my shelf in red and *gold like new money from the mint*, promising to unfold the shipping secrets that only Midas and Morgan and Maecenas knew. (p. 4)[3]

This "fine health to be pulled down out of the young breath-giving air" was wealth, and what was to unfold was not a greater burst of nature's foliage but the myth of Morgan and Midas and Maecenas. It was not a casual rhetoric which compared nature to "fast movies" rather than the artificial to the natural. The passage establishes artificiality as a fundamental to a new sense of "fine health." As much has been implied as it is stated.

We are near the end of the book when Daisy's world is summed up for us, but we have been prepared for its significance from the beginning. Here is the summation:

> For Daisy was young and her artificial world was redolent of orchids and pleasant, cheerful snobbery and orchestras which set the rhythm of the year, summing up the sadness and suggestiveness of life in new tunes. All night the saxophones wailed the hopeless comment of the *Beale Street Blues* while a hundred pairs of golden and silver slippers shuffled the shining dust. At the gray tea hour there were always rooms that throbbed incessantly with this low, sweet fever, while fresh faces drifted here and there like rose petals blown by the sad horns around the floor. (p. 151)

There are some ninety words and eighteen adjectives in the passage. There is an unusual degree of richness through the preponderance of these adjectives, as though by their very lavish presence we are told how great a role the senses play in the book. We would not expect an author who chooses such words to arrive at any rational solution for the problems his novel presents. Indeed it is in terms of Gatsby's irrational dream that he attains and maintains that stature which makes it possible for Nick Carraway to say at the beginning that "Gatsby turned out all right in the end." Repeated in this summary of Daisy's world are many of the conflicts of which we have become aware. "Young" is contrasted with "artificial." "Cheerful" is set against "sadness." "Sadness" is the only "suggestiveness of life" to be found in the paradoxical promise of what is "new." Here too in the summary is the symbolic connotation of "golden and silver slippers" which shuffle in a different ballroom from the golden slippers of the Negro spiritual. This is, in fact, no heaven at all. What is "sweet" is sickened with fever. The rooms "throb" like the people in them; faces "drift," but their freshness is not that of the rose but of rose petals which have already been shed. Like petals, they are blown around by "sad horns." The stimulation of these people who dance their lives comes from outside rather than inside of themselves, as though will did not count but only the helpless stimulation of the senses as they are played upon by the winds of the band. This is not the Gay Twenties, when youth was free, but a time of illness and disease.

"A work of art," Joseph Conrad wrote in his preface to *The Nigger of the Narcissus*, "that aspires, however humbly, to the condition of art should carry its justification in every line." "All art," Conrad wrote in the same preface,

> appeals primarily to the senses, and the artistic aim when expressing itself in written words must also make its appeal through the senses, if its high desire is to reach the secret spring of responsive emotions. It must strenuously aspire to the plasticity of sculpture, to the colour of painting, and to the magic suggestiveness of music—which is the art of arts. And it is only through complete, unswerving devotion to the perfect blending of form and substance; it is only through an unremitting never-discouraged care for the shape and ring of sentences that an approach can be made to plasticity, to colour, and that the light of magic suggestiveness may be brought to play for an evanescent instant over the commonplace surface of words: or the old words, worn thin, defaced by ages of careless usage.[4]

Scott Fitzgerald tells us that he read this preface while he was working on the manuscript of *The Great Gatsby*. But we hardly need to be told by any other statement than the example of Fitzgerald's own style. The evidence is constant. When we read of the opening dinner of the novel, where Nick meets Tom and Daisy again, and meets Jordan Baker, even a single sentence like the following lets us know what kind of a restless world the novel is to picture:

> A breeze blew through the room, blew curtains in at one end and out the other like pale flags, twisting them up toward the frosted wedding-cake of the ceiling, and then rippled over the wine-colored rug making a shadow on it as wind does on the sea. (p. 8)

This is a world where, as has often been pointed out, words like "drifting" and "restless" appear and reappear as a correlative of the spirit of the characters who people it. Men and women move nervously in motor cars from one party to another.

> "What'll we do with ourselves this afternoon," cried Daisy, "and the day after that, and the next thirty years?"
> "Don't be morbid," Jordan said. "Life starts all over again when it gets crisp in the fall." (p. 118)

There are no more summers in which to begin over again, as Nick has planned when he first moved near to East Egg.

But one cannot wholly get at the meaning of a novel without being aware of still grosser elements of structure than those contained in the formulation of its style. Style is but one step in the achievement of a fictional world. The progression of scenes in a novel renders its own special contribution in terms of balance and emphasis. There are, for example, the brilliantly contrasting and mutually defining, successive descriptions of parties with which *The Great Gatsby* opens. In the first of these, at Tom Buchanan's, we are introduced to the four important persons who are present. They are paired: Tom with Daisy, and Nick with Jordan; Tom with Nick, and Jordan with Daisy. In sharp, comic, but deeply meaningful juxtaposition we are then given in Chapter II the party in Tom's New York "love-nest" with its appropriately ironic furniture, tapestried with scenes of "ladies swinging in the gardens of Versailles." Here there are new, regularly irregular pairings: Tom and Myrtle Wilson, Nick and Catherine, and a slightly wider circle of those who are little more than a shrill chorus of desires.

> "I'm going to have the McKees come up," [Myrtle] announced as we rose in the elevator. "And, of course, I got to call up my sister, too." (p. 28)

Then, suddenly, in Chapter III,

> There was music from my neighbor's house through the summer nights. In his blue gardens men and girls came and went like moths among the whisperings and the champagne and the stars. (p. 39)

It is the proper setting for the munificence of a hero, but in seeing Gatsby for the first time we only find ourselves in a variant of the parties where we have already been. People are still restlessly hungry, still involved with money and the dream of what it can bring, are simply upgraded McKees but still moths among the "champagne and the stars." We have had a series of three focuses, but they blend into a stereopticon of the illusions which give color to the world in which all of these people live, and of the reality for all which by the end of the novel has left little more than the "pyramid of pulpless halves" which were what remained on Monday of the "five crates of oranges and lemons" that arrived at Jay Gatsby's gate each Friday before.

At the center of the stereopticon is Jay Gatsby himself whom we come to know and to understand through Nick Carraway's double-visioned eyes. It was an awakened awareness of the importance of fictional structure which led Fitzgerald in the composition of *The Great Gatsby* to adopt, by the use of Carraway, a technical device which one can best describe as the use of "the intelligent but sympathetic observer." Through such an observer as Carraway, a figure like Gatsby can be described in terms of those direct impressions on a sensibility which Conrad stressed so much in his comments on fiction. It was of course Conrad, too, who by his use in *The Heart of Darkness* of Marlow as the observer of Kurtz provided Fitzgerald with the model for Carraway. Artists are linked by their common concerns.

If it were not for Carraway's response to Gatsby, Gatsby would not emerge so validly in the novel as a mythological figure. For in the truly mythological figure we see ourselves enlarged not only as individuals but as a race. Gatsby's dream becomes in a measure our own dream too, his power the power we might crave in ourselves. We share Carraway's experience of it. Gatsby's story is indeed one with which we are familiar, not uniquely as Americans by any means but certainly on terms which we have characteristically made our own during our nation's history. Our definition of Gatsby's striving comes through our ability to accept as symbolic representations the various steps he takes in the novel, and the gestures he makes. The teacher of *The Great Gatsby* will spend a good deal of his time in the cumulative analysis of the structure of the novel, pointing out the definitions of the style, images, metaphors, and symbols which the book contains. A primary focus will be on the inherent qualities of the literary work itself.

But the teacher will also understand that the fullest definition of these factors will reach outside of the novel into life. No reference to James J. Hill in *The Great Gatsby* can avoid an understanding of Hill's place in the American ambition. No hushed reference in the book to the White Sox scandal can be defined without a sense of its spiritual affront to the nation. These are the bases on which a novel which has been derived by art out of life can be returned to life again. Such a work of art must be returned, for there are only a comparatively few readers who are content only with the aesthetic *frisson* which a novel can give. The meaning of a work of fictional art cannot fully be understood without a recognition that what a novel says comes largely from the way it is said. But once we know that, we can be ready to absorb and employ our knowledge. We are involved.

Gatsby's story is familiar enough, and the biographical details with which we are finally provided only confirm what we have already sensed. He is the uncontrolled romantic, his is the American dream of success. Into his ambition, he has absorbed what a man like Benjamin Franklin, through his *Autobiography*, has come to stand for as an image: that a man can be what he makes himself to be. Money for Franklin was not an end in itself, but a means, a way by which happiness could be achieved, a dream of the achieved life of the complete man. Money was a means rather than an end for Jimmy Gatz too. He aspired towards something whose definition eluded him at first, but he caught at what symbols America offered him.

Jimmy Gatz could begin to be a new man by taking on a new name for his true identity.

> James Gatz—that was really, or at least legally his name [Carraway tells us]. He had changed it at the age of seventeen and at the specific moment that witnessed the beginning of his career—when he saw Dan Cody's yacht drop anchor over the most insidious flat on Lake Superior. It was James Gatz who had been loafing along the beach that afternoon in a torn green jersey and a pair of canvas pants, but it was already Jay Gatsby who borrowed a rowboat, pulled out to the *Tuolomee*, and informed Cody that a wind might catch him and break him up in half an hour.

> I suppose he'd had the name ready for a long time, even then. His parents were shiftless and unsuccessful farm people—his imagination had never really accepted them as his parents at all. The truth was that Jay Gatsby of West Egg, Long Island, sprang from his Platonic conception of himself. He was a son of God—a phrase which, if it means anything, means just that—and he must be about His Father's business, the service of a vast, vulgar, and meretricious beauty. So he invented just the sort of Jay Gatsby that a seventeen-year-old boy would be likely to invent, and to this conception he was faithful to the end. (pp. 98–99)

Gatsby's was the dream of all the mystery and the beauty of the world, but how are we to understand "His Father's business" as "the service of a vast, vulgar, and mereticious beauty"? The definition was Carraway's, of course, not Gatsby's. Gatsby can proceed on his grail-quest only in terms of what is given him as clues. We can remember Dreiser's *Sister Carrie*, in which Carrie's correlatives for beauty are expressed by an ascending quality of clothing, both for herself and as they are worn by the men to whom she is attached, one after the other. Dreiser used similarly material correlatives for Cowperwood, in his trilogy of the American business man, as Cowperwood's taste in women and paintings improved with each step up the ladder. Clyde Griffith in *An American Tragedy* shifted from one objective to another on his rise upward. Henry James uses similar reflectors in his novels. So do we in our lives, as we redecorate our homes or buy our cars.

Gatsby's dream required its phenomenal correlatives exactly as the theme of a novel requires its proper words. "Through all [Gatsby] said, Nick Carraway tells us at one point in the novel, "even though his appalling sentimentality, I was reminded of something—an elusive rhythm, a fragment of lost words, that I had heard somewhere a long time ago. For a moment a phrase tried to take shape in my mouth and my lips parted like a dumb man's, as though there was more struggling upon them than a wisp of startled air. But they made no sound, and what I had almost remembered was uncommunicable forever" (p. 112). *The Great Gatsby* of course does give us these "words" as well as the memory. Circumstances and society gave the correlatives to Jimmy Gatz.

To Gatz the first denotative representation of his vision came through the appearance of Dan Cody's yacht. "To young Gatz resting on his oars and looking up at the railed deck, that yacht represented all the beauty and glamour in the world" (pp. 100–1). Its next symbol came in Louisville, where he was impelled secondly in his rise by a transference from one ascending vision of beauty to another, from the yacht to Daisy and the white mansion she inhabited and the white car she drove. She seemed to be the representation of what he yearned for: the platonic essence, the noumenal as he saw it through the phenomnal metaphor. She shone before him like silver, and he rode toward her as a knight rides toward his lady. And like America itself, with its Franklinian image of a society in which there were no absolute barriers and a man could become what he wished to become, Daisy gave him the green light to move ahead. Only it took money to buy the car to join the traffic.

Everything in Gatsby's life was intended for this dream expressed always in whiteness: the perhaps white yacht; the white home and dress and car in Louisville, and the white mansion and white clothing of the Buchanans at East Egg. No wonder that Gatsby himself wore white. Even the daisy for which Daisy was named was a white flower, a Marguerite like the vision which bewitched Faust. She represented, as Helen did in other myths, the final expression, in woman, all of the mysterious beauty and the undefined satisfaction of man's longing. Gatsby had had brief tastes but no satisfaction of his longings. He had tasted her, but only briefly. He had been at Oxford, but briefly again. He had won a medal, but only a minor Montenegrin decoration. The cliches which he used to describe a past which might have been true, and was a little true, were the words that society had provided him out of its own experience of longing. The symbols shifted; only the dream persisted.

Two men had helped to make Gatsby and establish Gatsby as archetype. They represented, as the novel gives them to us, two stages in the development of America. There was Dan Cody, the old kind of economic exploiter. And there was Wolfsheim (the home of the wolf), the gangster, the completely amoral accumulator of free capital. "You're very polite," Wolfsheim tells Gatsby *and* Carraway, "but I belong to another generation." Gatsby's father speaks significantly when he describes his son to Carraway:

> "If he'd of lived, he'd of been a great man. A man like James J. Hill. He'd of helped built up the country."
> "That's true," I said, uncomfortably. (p. 169)

There were the rules for the achievement of success which Jimmy Gatz had drawn up as a boy, on the model of Franklin's own rules which he printed in his *Autobiography*. Nick Carraway was uncomfortable, because it *was* true. It was American, a dream diverted in definition though not in essence.

It was true, too, because Nick Carraway could recognize a good deal of himself in the aspiration of Jay Gatsby. He is our surrogate in the novel, our deputy or substitute. He is not blatant in his desires, but the dream is in part his when he leaves the West for New York and a Wall Street fortune, leaving his girl behind, lying a little in his letters to her, being second cousin to Daisy and a classmate of Tom's at Yale, half-loving Jordan even when he knows she is untruthful, that she is a careless driver like all the careless, restless drivers who move swiftly everywhere in the book.

> "You dream, you. You absolute little dream," [Daisy says to her daughter, when Gatsby and Nick are at the Buchanans].
> "Yes," admitted the child calmly. "Aunt Jordan's got on a white dress too." (p. 117)

The child was not shifting the subject; she was talking relevantly.

But Nick does come to understand, and to see the reality that Gatsby could never understand was impossible to balance on a moth's wing. Gatsby's belief in his dream, in the grail to which he was increasingly committed, was so great that only the dream existed for him. Daisy came to exist as a symbol, not really as a human being.

> "She's got an indiscreet voice," I remarked. "It's full of—" I hesitated.
> "Her voice is full of money," [Gatsby said suddenly.]
> That was it. I'd never understood before. It was full of money—that was the inexhaustible charm that rose and fell in it, the jingle of it, the cymbal's song of it . . . High in a white palace the king's daughter, the golden girl. . . . (p. 120)

Gatsby said it: "Her voice is full of money." But Carraway's was the understanding. He knew that these characters, the Toms and Daisies and Jordans were living people drawn by the "jingle of it," forgetting the dream. "And all the time," Carraway says of the Louisville Daisy who had been attracted by the force of Gatsby, "something within her was crying for a decision. She wanted her life shaped now, immediately—

and the decision must be made by some force—of love, of money, of unquestionable practicality . . . That force took shape in the middle of spring with the arrival of Tom Buchanan" (p. 151). But the season of *The Great Gatsby* is summer, and the only hope left for things to begin again will be in the fall. And Gatsby will be dead. Nick will have returned home, strengthened by his inheritance of a "sense of the fundamental decencies."

The story is of course as much Nick's as it is Gatsby's. One returns in retrospect to the problem of structure again. In the novel which uses the narrative device of the sympathetic observer, the reader will expect some change to have taken place in him during the progress of the fiction. Otherwise the novel is static. The observer is only a device, and not an actor in the novel. It is not simply a question of dividing the single traditional figure of the tragic hero who both suffers and understands, as King Lear does, into two: the figure of the man who suffers (in this case Gatsby) and the man who understands (as Carraway does). Although muted in his expression, Nick Carraway partakes of both emotions; and although his prologue to the story gives us an avowal of Gatsby's reason to be called "great," the final definition is not ours, or his, until the account closes. At the very end, as Nick Carraway ponders, he is able to relate the experience of the summer to his knowledge of his country, to understand that he has not been telling about Long Island or even about the East, but what has happened to make the American dream, though still beckoning, a future that recedes before us. And since the first flowering of the dream of America was in Dutch (in European) eyes, as he closes the book by saying, he is talking, at last, about mankind at large. Even within the novel he has at the end carried the theme into the life of any reader anywhere.

Nick Carraway was proceeding as F. Scott Fitzgerald had proceeded in the composition of *The Great Gatsby.* Writing an introduction to a reissue of it in 1934, Fitzgerald said:

> Now that this book is being reissued, the author would like to say that never before did one try to keep his artistic conscience as pure as during the ten months put into doing it. Reading it over one can see how it could have been improved—yet without feeling guilty of any discrepancy from the truth, as far as I saw it; truth or rather the *equivalent* of truth, the attempt at honesty of imagination. I had just re-read Conrad's preface to *The Nigger,* and I had recently been kidded half haywire by critics who felt that my material was such as to preclude all dealing with mature persons in a mature world. But, my God! It was my material, and it was all I had to deal with.[5]

No novel is alive unless it is read. *The Great Gatsby* is now our material. It is what we have to deal with "ever afterward."

Notes

1. Fitzgerald met Monsignor (then Father) Fay when he was a student at Newman school in Hackensack, NJ. Fay became a mentor to the young writer-in-the-making, attempted to guide him toward devout Catholicism, and introduced him to such of his acquaintances as Henry Adams, Shane Leslie (an Anglo-Irish writer), and—apparently—the Bourke Cochrans of Long Island.

2. The question of the prototype for Gatsby has led investigators in other directions since 1962, but Pearson's point remains unassailable.

3. The italics are Pearson's.

4. Joseph Conrad, preface, *The Nigger of the "Narcissus"* (New York: Doubleday, 1927), pp. i–xvi.

5. F. Scott Fitzgerald, introduction, *The Great Gatsby* (New York: Random, House 1934), pp. iii–xi.

Style and Shape in
The Great Gatsby   F. H. Langman*

I

From its first appearance, *The Great Gatsby* won critical applause for the excellence of its form, and it has continued to do so ever since. Critics have praised the novel for meticulous construction, rigorous selection of episodes, ingenuity in weaving past and present together, careful control of tone and point of view, and effective use of symbols. The style, too, has been often praised, although rather less pointedly, for its clarity, vitality, and flavour. Almost all discussion of the novel, however, has turned rapidly from a perfunctory, not deeply considered, tribute to the "brilliance" of Fitzgerald's style, and gone on instead to what are supposed the bigger topics raised by the novel—its legendary quality, its quintessential vision of the American dream, romantic hope and romantic disillusion. I know of only one critic (W. J. Harvey, in an essay called "Theme and Texture in *The Great Gatsby*")[1] who has looked with anything like rewarding thoroughness at the novel's prose. Yet it is surely through the special appeal of its language that *The Great Gatsby* makes its first claim on our interest: it is, in this sense, a highly poetic novel—a novel which is difficult to imagine in translation. We read and reread it for the sake of its distinctive voice, or voices, for the way in which it puts things, at least as much as for the significance of the episodes it recounts. And, of course, it is only through the persuasiveness of the prose, through its ability to convince us of the

*Reprinted from *Southern Review* (Adelaide), 6 (March 1973), 48–67, by permission of the author.

truthfulness of the account it gives and of the fairness and firmness of understanding from which it proceeds, that the story told by the novel can be brought to life. Fitzgerald himself has recorded that when writing *The Great Gatsby* he had just reread Joseph Conrad's preface to *The Nigger of the "Narcissus,"*[2] and it is fair to comment that the whole novel seems written under a powerful sense of the need, defined by Conrad in that preface, to put things vividly before the reader—to create in words a tangible, visible, world.

The evocative power of the prose in *The Great Gatsby*, the power to make us hear, to make us see, needs little illustration. Like some of the other obvious strengths of the style—its lucidity, fluency, and naturalness—it is found everywhere in the book. One might simply point to the force of individual words, to effects of novelty, precision, and suggestive power in, say, the choice of verbs. Thus, in George B. Wilson's garage "the only car visible was the dust-covered wreck of a Ford which crouched in a dim corner."[3] *Crouched* evokes the low, sagging posture of the wrecked car, brings out the frightened, fugitive quality of Wilson's hopeless endeavours, and almost subliminally, in the idea of a creature preparing to spring, reinforces the menace which cars in the novel come to signify. To take other examples almost at random, we note the evocation of force, speed, smoothness, in the way Gatsby's motor-boats "slit" the water (p. 39) or the exact rendering of sound in the description of the telephone book which "slipped from its nail and splashed to the floor" (p. 127). In that last example, the precise expression does more than create the physical reality of the instant. The scene is the stifling room of the Plaza hotel, where the main characters have foregathered, on a broiling afternoon of late summer, for their final confrontation. Gatsby has made his first challenge by asking Tom to stop criticizing Daisy. Into the moment of silence that follows, the telephone book falls, and its cool splash of pages seems to mark and measure the tension.

The Great Gatsby is the sort of novel that tempts one to make lists of felicitous expressions—it is a sort of treasure-chest of language used with originality, dexterity, sparkle—lists of adverbs and adjectives in phrases like "the young breath-giving air" (p. 4) and a "bright rosy-colored space, fragilely bound into the house by French windows" (p. 8), and "the pale gold odour of kiss-me-at-the-gate" (p. 92). Or lists of similes like the celebrated one describing Daisy and Jordan on the couch in the wind-filled room, "buoyed up as though upon an anchored balloon" (p. 8), or the one, less well known but equally astonishing and right, which describes how Myrtle Wilson dominates the party in her small living-room: "as she expanded the room grew smaller around her, until she seemed to be revolving on a noisy, creaking pivot through the smoky air" (p. 31).

To go on talking about these qualities, however, might give a false emphasis, might imply that the book is most notable for a kind of fine writing, verging at times on the precious. It isn't. In fact, to anyone who comes to it after reading Fitzgerald's earlier novels, the prose of *The Great Gatsby* is notable for its disciplined restraint, its concentration on the task in hand. Much of the time, the language is characterized not by effects of surprise or charm, but by a taut professionalism. It displays, for example, a flair for condensed, rapid narrative, which summarizes a lengthy action in a few hard, laconic phrases, yet preserves a sense of physical reality throughout and almost never lets the story lapse into mere abstraction. The single busy, agitated sentence in which Jordan Baker narrates one of the most crucial half-hours in Daisy's life well exemplifies this:

> We gave her spirits of ammonia and put ice on her forehead and hooked her back into her dress, and half an hour later, when we walked out of the room, the pearls were around her neck and the incident was over. (pp. 77–78)

It is not necessary for Jordan, or for anybody, to comment that in this half-hour Daisy's spirit of independence, her truth to her own feelings, is decisively broken: it isn't necessary to *say*, because it is so unmistakably implied by her passive subjection, in the rhythm of the sentence, to all the hasty, relentless ministrations of her well-meaning helpers. Something over a year of Gatsby's youth is given in two sentences, but given with a particularity that would make further elaboration pointless:

> For over a year he had been beating his way along the south shore of Lake Superior as a clam-digger and a salmon-fisher or in any other capacity that brought him food and bed. His brown, hardening body lived naturally through the half-fierce, half-lazy work of the bracing days. (p. 99)

It is not necessary for the narrator to comment that Gatsby acquired the toughness necessary to deal with his world by effort, in a gradual and not unenjoyable process; the sense of a process is implicit in that sequence: beating, hardening, bracing.

Related to the professional skill of such narrative passages is the economy and simplicity with which the characters are introduced, each with an individuating and identifying characteristic. It is not the sort of novel in which an interest in character predominates, or in which the complexities of inward experiences are much explored. Most of the characters, and that includes the main ones, are seen almost entirely from outside, and we are left to infer what, if anything, they feel. Tom Buchanan, we gather, seethes with strong emotions, but he is a man so habitually confused, so little able to reconcile the various sides of himself or to recognize his own feelings, that he is best understood from a detached distance. Jordan Baker is constantly on the defensive, guarding her feelings perhaps even from her own scrutiny. Gatsby for most of the novel must remain a deliberate blur, a figure of inscrutable purposes. And of Daisy, Nick says early on: "I had no sight into Daisy's heart" (p. 6). Although the later developments do offer some glimpses into Daisy's heart, this remains largely true: what Daisy feels is too well masked by her good manners, her grace and charm, and her sense of playing a role, to allow of much unauthorized revelation. What Daisy feels is also, perhaps, too little: she is not exactly *empty*, but there is nothing within her to match, to fulfil, the promise of the impression she creates. Thus the exigencies of the story itself require a rather external treatment of the characters, and the relative simplicity of character-ization in the novel marks not paucity of imagination but rather the proper subordination of interest here to the larger needs of the total design. The author is content, by and large, to create a character with a few simple strokes, and to let it stand: what comes later is usually reinforcement and repetition, rather than growth. Thus, character is largely delineated by a gesture, a phrase, a single and singular attri-bute—Tom's out-thrust, arrogant eyes; Daisy's voice; Jordan's defen-sively erect carriage and tilted chin—these, and two or three paragraphs of analysis.

To speak as I have done of professional skills, of rapid narration and simplified characterization, of a minimal interest in psychological complexities, and of people who are emotionally guarded or undeveloped, perhaps makes the novel sound hard, dry, deficient in feeling. Any-one who has read it know that this is the reverse of the truth: it is a novel radiant with feeling, various, subtle, delicate and tender. But the feelings are not, in general, expressed directly, through charac-ters in speech and action. They can't be. Instead, they are brought into the novel obliquely, through description, narrative, meditation, and symbol. To provide just such expression of feeling for characters who in the nature of the case cannot express it themselves is one of the chief functions of the narrator, Nick Carraway. This is something to which I shall turn in more detail at a later stage, but before doing so I want to show how the novel's style itself is the source of an emotional richness which seems almost the hallmark of the book.

In a sense, no doubt, the style and the narrator are indissolubly at one; in so far as it suggests a distinctive sensibility, the style is clearly Nick's own. This is established early as more than a convention: the opening pages indicate not only that the prevailing tone—that blend of moral rigour with amused, conscious tolerance—is wholly appropriate to Nick's character, but even the stylized whimsy that crops up from time to time is first heard in direct speech when he tells Daisy how she is missed in Chicago: "The whole town is desolate. All the cars have the left real wheel painted black as a mourning wreath, and there's a persistent wail all night along the north shore" (p. 10). Nevertheless, a good deal of the time, the reader need not be especially conscious that Nick is telling the story. Narrator, commentator, and participant in the action, Nick moves into the foreground from time to time, but often we do not need to think of him, his image does not intrude itself between us and the scenes he describes. There is simply a medium, a voice, a style through which events are rendered with an appropriate colouring of emotion, are registered together with a response which by its firmness, fineness, richness, can shape and direct our own.

> There was music from my neighbor's house through the summer nights. In his blue gardens men and girls came and went like moths among the whispering and the champagne and the stars. At high tide in the afternoon I watched his guests diving from the tower of his raft, or taking the sun on the hot sand of his beach while his two motor-boats slit the waters of the Sound, drawing aquaplanes over cataracts of foam. (p. 39)

Part of the feeling here, the element of wonder, delight, nostalgia, comes from the unashamed romanticism of the phrasing: music . . . through the summer nights; blue gardens; cataracts of foam. Especially striking is the word "among" in "moths among the whisperings and the champagne and the stars"—its effect is mysteriously to put all these things on a level, almost as if Gatsby dispensed the heavens as freely as the wine. Night and starlight themselves are ingredients of the party, and a couple of pages later Nick will speak of the moon as "produced like the supper, no doubt, out of a caterer's basket" (p. 43). That, however, has a conscious wit not noticeable in the longer passage. In the longer passage the romanticism goes almost unqualified, so that we can be momentarily tempted even to receive rather more than the obvious meaning from "taking the sun." Yet there is just a hint of a more critical consciousness: though the stars have been made magically accessible, "moths" hints at the transience and even the peril of the illusion. By the end of the paragraph the hint has become fully developed: the wistful opening leads to the matter-of-fact reckoning of the final sentence, which describes how on Mondays eight servants toiled all day repairing the ravages of the night before.

In an early version of the novel, Fitzgerald had adumbrated an old, broken-off love affair between Nick and Daisy.[4] Not a trace of that remains in the completed novel. In the opening chapter they are little more than strangers, so that Daisy can say "We don't know each other very well, Nick. . . . Even if we are cousins" (p. 17). Daisy does flirt humorously with Nick, but that in itself indicates how safe they feel with each other. Nevertheless, Nick's descriptions of her vibrate at times with a heightened perception of her charm. The effect is exactly in keeping with his first account of Gatsby's parties. It is not that Nick is falling in love with Daisy, but through his sympathetic responsiveness we are able to see her as she needs to be seen—seeing in such a way that we can understand how Gatsby saw her and came under her spell.

> Under the dripping bare lilac-trees a large open car was coming up the drive. It stopped. Daisy's face, tipped sideways beneath a three-cornered lavender hat, looked out at me with a bright ecstatic smile.
>
> "Is this absolutely where you live, my dearest one?"
>
> The exhilarating ripple of her voice was a wild tonic in the rain. I had to follow the sound of it for a moment, up and down, with my ear alone, before any words came through. A damp streak of hair lay like a dash of blue paint across her cheek, and her hand was wet with glistening drops as I took it to help her from the car. (p. 86)

The feeling of the passage is given as much as anything by Daisy's greeting, by its delicious, wayward, playing with romance, but the effect is strengthened by other touches: her bright ecstatic smile; the exhilarating ripple of her voice; the one word, "wild." What the passage does is to demonstrate that quality in Daisy which much earlier in the novel had been merely described: the quality of seeming to promise herself, to be wholly engaged with the one man she happens to be talking to, to offer immeasurable gaiety and excitement. The passage is also remarkably painterly. Daisy, with her face "tipped sideways beneath a three-cornered lavender hat" and "a damp streak of hair . . . like a dash of blue paint across her cheek," and the "glistening drops" of rain on her hand, has the vivid freshness of, say, a portrait by Renoir. And this, too, is typical of the novel. Highly impressionistic in its methods, it is enamoured of the visual aspect of things, of sea, sky, and city, of the interiors of rooms, and of groups of people composed as in a tableau.

All of these qualities come together in the most extraordinary passage of prose the novel contains. Gatsby has been showing Daisy all through his house. He shows her the house as at another time, or rather in another kind of tale, a monarch might have shown his beloved the realms he had conquered for her sake. The climax comes in his own apartment, when he displays trophies, or like tribute, his quantities of imported clothes.

> He took out a pile of shirts and began throwing them, one by one, before us, shirts of sheer linen and thick silk and fine flannel, which lost their folds as they fell and covered the table in many-colored disarray. While we admired he brought more and the soft rich heap mounted higher—shirts with stripes and scrolls and plaids in coral and apple-green and lavender and faint orange, with monograms of Indian blue. Suddenly, with a strained sound, Daisy bent her head into the shirts and began to cry stormily.

"They're such beautiful shirts," she sobbed, her voice muffled in the thick folds. "It makes me sad because I've never seen such—such beautiful shirts before." (pp. 93–94)

This is lyrical prose in an unusually ample sense of the term, permeated by the feeling of admiration that it names and carrying in its rhythms the impetus of Gatsby's compulsive emotion. The formal properties of language are being worked hard here, through cadence, alliteration, and rich, varied vowel-music: "shirts of sheer linen and thick silk and fine flannel, which lost their folds as they fell . . . the soft rich heap mounted higher." In this music, and in its colours, its exotic suggestions, its accumulation and abundance, the prose here has some affinity with such romantic verse as, say, "The Eve of St Agnes." Perhaps that sounds far-fetched: I'd certainly concede that the affinity, if allowed at all, has in it an element of parody, but one of my reasons for suggesting it is to intimate that the passage contains a trace of excess, of immaturity, to which we ought not, to which we are not meant, to surrender. There is something slightly absurd in the whole passage—an absurdity which supplies the real poignancy. Not only the grotesque, obsessional quality of Gatsby's emotion emerges through the passage, but also, obliquely, Daisy's discovery of the overwhelming reality, the clear, pure passion behind the clownish gestures. She weeps because she recognizes a quality of feeling, and an estimation of herself, which give a significance she has never known to her life. Yet it is a recognition she can't articulate. She says she is weeping because she has "never seen such—such beautiful shirts before."

The amalgam in this passage of lyrical tenderness and wild humour brings to a high point one of the main tendencies of the whole novel. However sombre its themes, most of the novel is conceived in a comic mode. It is, as it is surely meant to be, a very funny book. This seems an obvious comment to make, but it is worth stressing because one can read quite widely in critical discussions of the book without finding reference to the presence—let alone the preponderance—in it of comedy.

At first, certainly, the comedy is subdued. It is felt as an aspect of Nick's view of things in general, of his tolerant and sceptical attitude towards the self-absorbed intensities of men less critically mature than himself: "Frequently I have feigned sleep, preoccupation, or a hostile levity when I realized by some unmistakable sign that an intimate revelation was quivering on the horizon" (p. 1). Here, as in the description of how Nick's aunts and uncles talked over his decision to go into the bond business "as if they were choosing a prep school" (p. 3), or his account of the Finnish woman "who made my bed and cooked breakfast and muttered Finnish wisdom to herself over the electric stove" (p. 3), the facetious note seems little more than personal, the sign of a mind prone to notice, with quiet enjoyment, whatever is ridiculous in human behaviour. As the novel goes on, the comedy sharpens, it is built into scenes with a queer, desperate humour independent of Nick's commentary; but much of the cumulative effect of the novel, the general impression we take away from it, gains its strength from the steady, clear-sighted amusement we learn to expect from the commentary.

In the chief comic scenes, however, Fitzgerald generally keeps such commentary to a minimum. Tom Buchanan's ignorant fulminations about the coloured races, say, receive their perfect answer not from Nick's reflections on them but from Daisy's mocking burlesque agreement: "'We've got to beat them down,' whispered Daisy, winking ferociously towards the fervent sun" (p. 13).

In the second chapter, recounting Nick's adventures with Tom and Myrtle in New York, the main comic effects are dramatic, the products of direct presentation and still more of direct speech. No overt comment is needed to show the connection of Myrtle's unrefined avidity to her false gentility: it is sufficiently plain in the startling transition from her delicate enquiry whether the dog is "a boy or a girl" to her "violent and obscene" remark about her husband. Her confused and ignorant speech provides a series of dismaying glimpses into the dizzy shadows of her mind:

> "I had a woman up here last week to look at my feet, and when she gave me the bill you'd of thought she had my appendicitis out."
> "What was the name of the woman?" asked Mrs. McKee.
> "Mrs. Eberhardt. She goes around looking at people's feet in their own homes." (p. 31)

That "appendicitis," that "of" in "you'd of thought," are unsubtle, perhaps, but right: Myrtle can't speak correctly because she tries too hard. Exemplified here is an appreciation of language as an index to sensibility: it is not simply that Fitzgerald economically suggests the accent and idiom of different social classes, he also uses these things to bring out the differences of feeling and perception between different speakers. Nick is quick to detect the flaws of expression which betray, say, Daisy's insincerities or "the intimate revelations of young men" which "are usually plagiaristic and married by obvious suppressions." It is only with an effort that he restrains "incredulous laughter" when Gatsby too attempts to impose on him a spurious biography concocted from the threadbare phrases of magazine stories.

The scene in the New York apartment works its way ultimately to a kind of raw, sinister farce, again thoroughly dramatized. What makes it so dramatic, and gives the comedy its edge, is that it is suddenly seen not from Nick's point of view but from that of the bewildered, alcohol-stupefied Mr. McKee. Tom has ended an altercation with Myrtle by breaking her nose:

Then there were bloody towels upon the bathroom floor, and women's voices scolding, and high over the confusion a long broken wail of pain. Mr. McKee awoke from his doze and started in a daze towards the door. When he had gone halfway he turned around and stared at the scene—his wife and Catherine scolding and consoling as they stumbled here and there among the crowded furniture with articles of aid, and the despairing figure on the couch, bleeding fluently, and trying to spread a copy of *Town Tattle* over the tapestry scenes of Versailles. Then Mr. McKee turned and continued on out the door. Taking my hat from the chandelier, I followed. (pp. 37–38)

This absurd and ugly scene occurred, it's worth noting, because Tom would not allow Myrtle to mention Daisy's name: by a complex irony it reveals the attitude that will rule Tom in the sequence that this scene prefigures. Myrtle will in the end be killed because of Tom's feelings about his marriage.

Equally farcical, though farce of a different order, is the high point of the novel, Chapter 5, Fitzgerald's own favourite. This chapter presents the long-awaited reunion of Daisy and Gatsby. It would have been a scene full of peril for the writer—so easy to tip over into the merely grotesque or the merely sentimental. Fitzgerald's antidote to sentimentality is to play up the inherent absurdity of the situation while somehow preserving respect for the intensity and reality of the emotions. The effect is reminiscent, vaguely but not disadvantageously, of something in Tchekov. Gatsby, who has thought only of this meeting for almost five years, is now too worked up to endure her coming, yet desperate to retain his dignity. He attempts to go, declaring "I can't wait all day." When she does come, he bolts out the back door and appears at the front, attempting to give the impression of paying a casual call:

> ... there was a light dignified knocking at the front door. I went out and opened it. Gatsby, pale as death, with his hands plunged like weights in his coat pockets, was standing in a puddle of water glaring tragically into my eyes. (p. 86)

The entertainment-value of this should not obscure the complexity of the effect achieved. Here, as in so much else in the novel, in the accounts of Gatsby's parties for instance or in Nick's sardonic catalogue of the guests who attended them, the witty presentation seems to insist, lightly but steadily and inescapably, upon a tough underlying realism—a realism constituted not merely of common sense but even more of what Nick calls a sense of the fundamental decencies. The comedy then, is not an extraneous element of appeal added to the novel by a writer conscious, as Fitzgerald always was, of the need for popular success as well as for critical esteem. Rather, the comic mode is the novel's essential way of seeing: it is the source of the balance which can give full measure of sympathy to the characters without glossing over their folly, vanity and self-deceit. That Fitzgerald chose this mode is evidence, surprising though this may seem, of an impressive tact.

It is our recognition of this tact, I think, that makes the book seem so poised, so polished. The humour itself is sufficiently critical to keep us aware that everything is observed by an assessing, evaluating mind, without allowing the implied judgments to impair the tone. The tone for the most part remains light, detached, even when the judgments are at their most straitened. Fitzgerald does not need solemnly to lament the break-down of family life, the decline of religion, the lapse of moral standards, the universal pursuit of frivolity, when he can write a sentence like this: "On Sunday morning while church bells rang in the villages alongshore, the world and its mistress returned to Gatsby's house and twinkled hilariously on his lawn" (p. 61). Nor need he shake his head over the corruptions of capitalism when he can say instead:

> Da Fontano the promoter came there, and Ed Legros and James B. ("Rot-Gut") Ferret and the De Jongs and Ernest Lilly—they came to gamble, and when Ferret wandered into the garden it meant he was cleaned out and Associated Traction would have to fluctuate profitably next day. (p. 62)

When, indeed, the moral collapse of civilization is described in so many words, it is only through Tom Buchanan's outbursts of idiotic claptrap. The novel can amply afford the irony because, through the comic mode, it has with so much better nature and better sense defined the ethos of the society it portrays.

II

With that ethos now in the forefront of our attention, it is time to turn to the overall design of the novel. The social corruption depicted in the novel serves as more than a background or framework for Gatsby's story. Gatsby himself is at once its product and its leading spirit; and in his very weakness he represents a potential for something finer. That is why Nick can express towards him such contradictory attitudes. In the very first reference to Gatsby, Nick's ambivalance is revealed: "Only Gatsby . . . was exempt from my reaction—Gatsby, who represents everything for which I have an unaffected scorn" (p. 2). And at the end Nick measures Gatsby against their whole society and tells him "You're worth the whole damn bunch put together," yet adds "I disapproved of him from beginning to end" (p. 154).

In Gatsby himself, then, Fitzgerald's portrait of society—and, really, rather more than that—comes to a focus. I say that the novelist's concern is with more than a portrait of society because it seems to me

that too much stress has been laid by critics on the American-ness of
the book. To be sure, there is a continuous rendering of the local scene,
manners, speech; and in a host of details the novel is set firmly into its
period. Nevertheless, its essential concerns do not seem to me bound in
time or place. At least, they can be described differently; and, although
this may seem far-fetched, I have found my understanding of the novel
helped by thinking not of Hemingway or Henry James but of Blake and
Yeats. I don't mean to suggest that Fitzgerald's achievement is on the
level of theirs. It's rather that, like them, he took for theme the conflict
between the infinitude of human desire and the exigencies of the human
condition, and was not content to ignore either half of the equation.

The Great Gatsby is in a host of ways a very carefully, very tightly
constructed novel. Some of these ways are perhaps rather trivial; or at
least, they result from skills which literary critics sometimes disdain
because of a kind in which inferior writers often become expert. My
own view is that no skill can be merely contemptible. To write well in
any respect at all is something, even if it's not enough. So, in any case, I
would not think the mechanical construction of *The Great Gatsby* to be
beneath mention. But again in this novel, as with the comedy which
serves a deeper purpose as well as providing amusement, the apparently
trivial or mechanical aspect of its construction has after all an integral
function. I have in mind those features which are designed to keep up
the reader's interest during his first reading of a novel, and to urge him
towards its conclusion—the features which become the be-all and end-all
of, say, a detective-story—puzzle and suspense. It's pretty evident that
Fitzgerald has taken pains to create these qualities, partly in relation to
the outcome of the story and more largely in relation to Gatsby. He has
made a deliberate mystery of Gatsby's origins, history, purposes, and
character, and especially of his occupation, or the source of his wealth.
At the beginning of the story, when Nick goes to dinner with Tom and
Daisy, Gatsby's name crops up in tantalizing fashion. Jordan, learning
that Nick lives in West Egg, says:

> "You must know Gatsby."
> "Gatsby?" demanded Daisy. "What Gatsby?"
> Before I could reply that he was my neighbor dinner was
> announced. (p. 11)

The device here is obvious enough. It suggests something unusual about
Gatsby, of whom the reader naturally expects to learn more. It also
implants the idea of some connection between Gatsby and Daisy: his
name, evidently, has some meaning for her. Yet the scrap of conversation seems natural and casual, and it's only in retrospect that one takes
in its significance. Gatsby's name returns when Nick arrives home from
the dinner and sees his neighbour in the darkened garden behaving in
an odd way, stretching his arms towards the dark water and, Nick sees

even at that distance, trembling. Gatsby's gesture appears to betoken some strange emotion—it is full of yearning towards something unknown. The effect is piquant, raising both sympathy and curiosity. The measure of Fitzgerald's skill in this kind of thing is that he should provide this glimpse of Gatsby in an unguarded moment, bringing out his humanity and something of his real oddness, before setting out to create the whirling confusion of conjecture, fantasy, and malice that gossip weaves around Gatsby's enigmatic conduct. This gossip is reported at first straightforwardly but eventually worked up into a comical, stylized passage:

> "He's a bootlegger," said the young ladies, moving somewhere between his cocktails and his flowers. "One time he killed a man who had found out that he was nephew to Von Hindenburg and second cousin to the devil. Reach me a rose, honey, and pour me a last drop into that there crystal glass." (p. 61)

As that last sentence makes plain, this is no longer reporting actual speech. It is a distillation of the things said about Gatsby, a parody, a rhapsody, a refrain. The point it makes is that Gatsby's enigmatic behaviour is transforming him, for the people of his world, into a kind of legend. This is why I claimed that this aspect of the novel's construction serves a deeper purpose. It not only arouses curiosity, it turns Gatsby into a figure of myth. By this, I mean that he comes to represent for the people who gossip about him an incarnation of their secret imaginings about their world. He is for them a figure of potency and magical appeal, romantically linked with danger and evil. And in the imagination of that world, God having vanished behind the empty eyes of Dr. Eckleburg, the devil is not to be taken seriously. The real spell is cast by the image of the gangster, the bootlegger and the killer of men. The people who talk of Gatsby this way aren't horrified, of course, or disgusted; they are thrilled. What they attribute to him corresponds to their own inward desires and admirations: they admire, or thrill to, violence, ruthlessness, lawlessness.

Related to the creation of mystery, but not quite the same thing, is the novel's gradual revelation of the past, especially of the earlier affair between Gatsby and Daisy. This isn't a matter I want to go into in detail. I suggest merely that anyone looking over the novel again will find it rewarding to see how Fitzgerald spaces out these revelation of the past in such a way as to control the pace of the present narrative, providing lulls in the action as well as giving the explanations necessary to the following movements. At one stage in the composition of the novel, Fitzgerald had proposed to begin with a story about Gatsby's boyhood which would have established his background and his motivation.[5] Rightly, he decided against this, and the very satisfying development of the novel results from the more complex, gradually completed, understanding which emerges out of the weaving together of past and present.

III

The devices I've mentioned so far belong peculiarly to novels—to the carefully plotted prose narrative. A different element in the composition of *The Great Gatsby* is more poetic. We are likely to be more familiar with it in the structuring of a lyric—or even of an Elizabethan play. This is an element of verbal recurrence. The whole novel is strung together by repeated phrases, by motifs, ideas that appear and modulate and return. W. J. Harvey has traced some of these, especially the words "drifted" and "restless." Before the end of the novel, restlessness has been ascribed to so many of the characters, has occurred in so many situations, that it becomes a clue to a fuller understanding of all that happens: it expresses the discontent and unfulfilment, the waste and frustration of energies, the lack of satisfying ideas, beliefs, and goals, which plague almost every person in the book. Tom and Daisy drift unrestfully here and there wherever people are rich together. Jordan's movements are restless. Tom's eyes flash about restlessly. Gatsby, Nick observes,

> was continually breaking through his punctilious manner in the shape of restlessness. He was never quite still; there was always a tapping foot somewhere or the impatient opening and closing of a hand. (p. 64)

Even Nick himself is deeply involved. His very presence in the East is explained by the fact that after the war, as he puts it, "I came back restless" (p. 3). And in another passage it seems to be from his own feeling that he generalizes when he speaks of the satisfaction which the flicker of men and women and machines in New York gives to the restless eye.

Some of the reiteration in the novel works at a lower level of significance. The frequent mention of roses, for example, or of rosy light or rose-coloured rooms, functions partly as a simple unifying device, reminding us of one scene as we read another. At the same time, the motif helps to suggest the glamorous unreality of the world in which the characters think they live. Roses are particularly associated with Daisy. Nick first sees her in the novel when he comes from the vista of the Buchanan's garden, with its "half acre of deep, pungent roses" (p. 8), into the "bright rosy-colored space" of the room where she reposes on the enormous couch. It is she who calls Nick a rose, "an absolute rose" (p. 15), an appellation he rather solemnly repudiates. In the impressionistic account of Daisy's state of mind when Gatsby, after their first affair, had been sent away to the War, the crucial point is made through the imagery of the blown rose:

> All night the saxaphones wailed the hopeless comment of the *Beale Street Blues* while a hundred pairs of golden and silver slippers shuf-fled the shining dust. At the grey tea hour there were always rooms that throbbed incessantly with this low, sweet fever, while fresh faces drifted here and there like rose petals blown by the sad horns around the floor. (p. 151)

Through the nostalgic langour of this prose we feel the urgency of life's dwindling. The sadness is the sadness of youth's passing. Whether or not one recalls the traditional attitudes expressed in a tag like "Gather ye rosebuds while ye may," it's clear that Daisy's return to the life of dances and dates, a return leading to her betrayal of Gatsby and marriage to Tom, is in reaction against that malaise, that self-waste, figured by the faces like the fallen petals of a rose.

It is with all this as a background that we apprehend the climactic appearance of the rose, in Nick's imagined vision of what Gatsby saw when he woke from his dream:

> He must have looked up at an unfamiliar sky through frightening leaves and shivered as he found what a grotesque thing a rose is and how raw the sunlight was upon the scarcely created grass. (p. 162)

Here, for the first time in the novel, the rose ceases to be regarded as an emblem, a conventional image of passion, romance, glamour, and is seen as simply itself, an object, unlike any preconceived notion, and therefore grotesque. The reference moves from dream to wakefulness, from delusion to reality.

Also closely associated with Daisy, and coming in its multiple varied appearances to conjure up almost the whole gamut of her appeal, is the word "white." She is dressed in white when Nick first visits her in the house at West Egg, that cheerful red-and-white mansion with its windows "gleaming white against the fresh grass outside." She charac-terizes her very life-style as white. Nick asks whether Jordan hails from New York. Daisy replies: "From Louisville. Our white girlhood was passed together there. Our beautiful white—" (p. 20). She says this with irony, or at least with condescension, but the implication nonetheless is that she has a certain consciousness to do with the colour—it has to do with innocence, purity, youth, freshness, naivety: to do, that is, with her conception of herself before she became what she calls "sophisticated" —a sort of prelapsarian or pastoral condition like the one Nick momen-tarily imagines in Fifth Avenue in the quiet of Sunday afternoon, when he feels "I wouldn't have been surprised to see a great flock of white sheep turn the corner" (p. 28). This quality of innocence, of seeming to come from an Eden or a Heaven of ease and splendour, is part of what creates Gatsby's obsessive recollections of Daisy. When he had first met her, in Louisville, she dressed in white and drove a little white roadster. One night they had been walking and came to a place where the sidewalk was white with moonlight. As Daisy's white face came up to his own, Gatsby knew that he was about to "wed his unutterable visions to her perishable breath" (p. 112). Here, the suggestions of pastoral innocence have extended to include an element of the magical, of the transformation of the mundane world into fairy tale. When Nick first refers to the setting of Daisy's house, he says "Across the courtesy bay the white palaces of fashionable East Egg glittered along the water" (p. 5). Much later, when he knows almost the whole story of her romance with Gatsby, Nick returns to the same image, now dwelling overtly on its fairy-tale aspect. He is meditating on the potency of Daisy's voice: "the inexhaustible charm that rose and fell in it, the jingle of it, the cymbal's song of it.... High in a white palace the king's daughter, the golden girl ..." (p. 120). The king's white palace is the realm of impossible, absolute fulfilment, where the swine-herd turns into a prince and lives happily ever after. It is an image of the day-dream, the wish-begotten fantasy, by which men create for themselves pictures of an escape from the dreariness of daily reality. To the class-conscious Gatsby, with his background of the rawly commonplace, Daisy's house in Louisville was that white palace:

> he had never been in such a beautiful house before . . . There was a ripe mystery about it, a hint of bedrooms upstairs more beautiful and cool than other bedrooms, of gay and radiant activities taking place through its corridors, and of romances that were not musty and laid away already in lavender, but fresh and breathing. . . .
> (p. 148)

Clearly linked with the imagery of whiteness is a line of references to magic. Gatsby's long passion for Daisy is given a psychological groundwork in the novel, so that we can, if we choose, say that we see how he gets to be that way. We may also feel, as I'm inclined to do, that in rational terms his peculiar intensity and narrowness of devotion isn't wholly plausible; but the point is that, as the novel presents him, Gatsby does not appear as a man of ordinary disposition acting under the direction of ordinary, explicable impulses. He appears instead as one under the spell of some enchantment. The magical quality of Daisy's hold on him is brought out explicitly in a passage which speculates on the possibility of its being reversed by some new, more irresistible spell:

> Perhaps some unbelievable guest would arrive, a person infinitely rare and to be marvelled at, some authentically radiant young girl

who with one fresh glance at Gatsby, one moment of magical encounter, would blot out those five years of unwavering devotion.
(p. 110)

That Daisy herself has just such power is intimated in half a
dozen different places. She is first pictured as a witch, "just . . . blown
back in after a short flight around the house" (p. 8). She suffuses otherwise inert objects with significance for Gatsby, so that as he approaches
closer to herself, the source of the radiance, they lose something of
their reflected glow: "His count of enchanted objects had diminished
. . ." (p. 94). To Nick, too, she has this aura. He listens to her singing,
and comments: "When the melody rose her voice broke up sweetly,
following it, in a way contralto voices have, and each change tipped out
a little of her warm human magic upon the air" (p. 109). *Human* magic,
of course, isn't quite the same as the enchantment dispensed by the
king's daughter: it is a more sober, less beguiling, version, but even so
it conveys a sense of Daisy's attractiveness, the mysterious fascination
of personality.

Gatsby himself partakes in the power of magic. There is, for one
thing, his smile—that radiant and understanding smile with a quality of
eternal reassurance in it. There is his mystery—the possibility that, for
all anyone knows of him, he really is "nephew to Von Hindenburg and
second cousin to the devil." There is his role as dispenser of magnifi-
cence. Not even his turkeys are basted as ordinary turkeys are, they are
"bewitched to a dark gold" (p. 40). Even his real life has something of
this quality, rather ambiguously, but still: there is the dream-like ease
and rapidity of his rise from rags to riches, drifting "coolly out of nowhere and buy[ing] a palace on Long Island Sound" (p. 49). There is
also his war record, which he describes in a language of unbelievable
clichés but which turns out to be essentially true: "Then came the war,
old sport . . . I seemed to bear an enchanted life . . ." (p. 66).

The line of enchantment touches Nick too, in a very important
way, but as this intersects with another line of imagery I shan't deal
with it just yet. Also intertwined with the lines of whiteness and of
enchantment is a line about money. Daisy's white dresses, her white
roadster and white palace all in themselves suggest opulence. White isn't
a practical enough colour for the workaday world. But the connections
are made more explicitly than this. White is transmuted into silver. At
one point Daisy and Jordan are described as lying on the enormous
couch "like silver idols weighing down their own white dresses" (p. 115).
At another, Gatsby's discovery that he has fallen irrevocably in love
with Daisy is put like this: "Gatsby was overwhelmingly aware of the
youth and mystery that wealth imprisons and preserves, of the freshness
of many clothes, and of Daisy, gleaming like silver, safe and proud above
the hot struggles of the poor" (p. 150).

Money serves thus as the medium of the magic. It is the secret of Daisy's voice. Gatsby says, stunningly, that "her voice is full of money" (p. 120) and this is not a mystical effusion. It has, if anything, a kind of sociological exactness. Her voice has the modulations of good breeding, of confidence, of schooling, of the assurance of being always loved and provided for and free to enjoy what life offers. Money, in the imaginary world these characters seek, is all that is needed to buy happiness, beauty, time itself. Nick himself is not exempt from its spell. He is impressed by the ostentatious wealth that enables Tom to bring down a string of polo ponies from Chicago; and he is not without his own ambitions. He buys a dozen volumes on banking and credit and investment securities, and they stand on his shelf "in red and gold like new money from the mint, promising to unfold the shining secrets that only Midas and Morgan and Maecenas knew" (p. 4). That linking of Midas and Morgan, the reference to shining secrets, the notion of a promise somehow extended, all reveal in Nick some contagion from the prevailing mystique of wealth to be picked up with wondrous ease and able to turn all life into gold. The same train of ideas is hinted at in the peculiar chance that the street-vendor of dogs, obviously a charlatan in his petty way, bears an "absurd resemblance to John D. Rockfeller" (p. 27). It's almost as if they were interchangeable and only accident decreed that one should be poor and the other rich. And again, most clearly of all, this conception of money is brought out by the description of the young Englishmen at Gatsby's parties: "all well dressed, all looking a little hungry ... They were at best agonizingly aware of the easy money in the vicinity and convinced that it was theirs for a few words in the right key" (pp. 41–42).

Several other trains of connected expression or imagery run through the novel—those, for example, of flowers and freshness, of clocks and time, of riot and order, of coolness and of carelessness; and there is an important series of references to boats. The last line of the novel, "so we beat on, boats against the current," gains part of its force from the accumulation behind it of a sequence of related images. Thus, at Daisy's luncheon, where Gatsby has come to lay claim on her, the assembled company watch a boat making its way along the Sound: "Slowly the white wings of the boat moved against the blue cool limit of the sky. Ahead lay the scalloped ocean and the abounding blessed isles" (p. 118). Once again we notice how the picture hints at a transcendence, an escape from the hot reality of the day into a magical world, the beyond of the blessed isles. Later in the same scene, disguising the metaphor somewhat, we find the same words expressive of struggle that will combine with the image of the boat in the book's final phrases; Daisy's voice, we read, "struggled on through the heat, beating against it, moulding its senselessness into forms" (p. 119).

IV

No further illustration should be needed of the detailed thoroughness with which the novel has been written so as to create a unified impression. I wish now to show how the same kind of organization works through larger units, building up continuities, connections and parallels of situation and character. There are, for example, two main lines of action, two stories, in the novel. The main action traces Gatsby's endeavour to recapture the past, to win back Daisy from Tom and from time itself. The subsidiary story concerns Tom's affair with Myrtle Wilson. For almost the length of the novel, the two stories are told in separate strands, coming together only when Myrtle is killed. But a series of carefully placed passages establishes a deeper relation between the two stories. Just as Jordan Baker with her white dresses and her incurable dishonesty provides a kind of understudy for Daisy, so the story of Tom and Myrtle in its tawdry violence mirrors the romance of Daisy and Gatsby, as well as providing a contrast. The echoes, in fact, come from even wider sources. Consider this passage: the first speaker is Mrs. McKee:

> "I almost made a mistake, too," she declared vigorously. "I almost married a little kike who'd been after me for years. I knew he was below me. Everybody kept saying to me: 'Lucille, that man's 'way below you.' But if I hadn't met Chester, he'd of got me sure."
>
> "Yes, but listen," said Myrtle, nodding her head up and down, "at least you didn't marry him."
>
> "I know I didn't."
>
> "Well, I married him," said Myrtle, ambiguously. "And that's the difference between your case and mine."
>
> "Why did you, Myrtle?" demanded Catherine. "Nobody forced you to."
>
> Myrtle considered.
>
> "I married him because I thought he was a gentleman," she said finally. "I thought he knew something about breeding, but he wasn't fit to lick my shoe."
>
> "You were crazy about him for a while," said Catherine. (pp. 34–35)

The anecdote provides an obscene parody of Gatsby's quest. Like the little kike who had been after Mrs. McKee for years, Gatsby has been years in pursuit of Daisy; and like that little kike, too, he had originally lost her because he was socially below her. And Myrtle's present revulsion from her husband involves her in just the same kind of distortion of the past as Gatsby tries to extort from Daisy. Myrtle tries to deny it, but Catherine's assertion that she had been crazy about Wilson for a while seems plausible. It exactly parallels Jordan's description of Daisy after the honeymoon. "I thought I'd never seen a girl so mad about her husband" (p. 78). Tom discovers Daisy's relationship with Gatsby at the same time as Wilson discovers that Myrtle has been carrying on an affair. Fitzgerald brings the two betrayed husbands together precisely so as to underline the similarities within the differences. Wilson, Nick comments,

> had discovered that Myrtle had some sort of life apart from him in another world, and the shock had made him physically sick. I stared at him and then at Tom, who had made a parallel discovery less than an hour before. (p. 124)

It's perhaps a little too easy to miss the full significance of that parallel. Tom's responsibility for Gatsby's death is in the last analysis little less than that of Wilson. Tom knows full well what is likely to happen when he directs the grief-maddened Wilson to Gatsby's house. All through the novel, there have been indications of suppressed violence in Tom, and of violence unsuppressed when he breaks Myrtle's nose. Wilson is as he himself puts it, "one of these trusting fellas and I don't think any harm to *nobody*" (p. 159), but at the critical moment these two outraged husbands came together in incongruous but murderous complicity.

Myrtle's death is an accident. Nobody meant it to happen, nobody could have foreseen it, perhaps nobody could have averted it. This much is obvious. Yet at the same time her death has a powerful logic. It occurs at the point where several forces in the novel converge. In the world of the novel, the symbolic status of cars underlines that of women. Tom and Gatsby contend not simply for Daisy herself, but also for what possessing her will demonstrate: she is—like an expensive automobile—an emblem of the wealth and success that are necessary to anyone who would obtain a woman of her kind. It is in the general spirit of this rivalry that Tom proposes the exchange of cars which leads to the fatal accident. Myrtle's conviction that Tom will be driving the car in which she saw him earlier in the day, her mistaken belief that the girl with him was Daisy, her jealousy and self-will, together with her rebellion from her husband, combine to send her running out into the road to stop the car. Daisy's irresolution and nervous condition make the accident unavoidable. Daisy is in that car at that moment because Tom, flushed with his victory over Gatsby, has put her there. The accident happens because all the people involved are what they are and do what they do. But it is given an even stronger semblance of inevitability than this. The whole novel is structured around this incident, builds up to it through an accumulation of innuendos, images, parallels of incident. One of the guests at Gatsby's parties was "so drunk out on the gravel drive that Mrs. Ulysses Swett's automobile ran over his right hand" (p. 62). It is a society, a way of life, in which casual automobile accidents are taken for granted; but as the incidents multiply they seem more than casual—they reveal a world in which such mischances point forward to something worse. And this foreshadowing becomes very pointed indeed in two separate places. The word most emphasized in the references to Myrtle's death sickeningly rends the force of the impact upon her body. Thus we are told "The mouth was wide open and ripped at the corners" (p. 138) and, of the accident as a whole, "it ripped her open" (p. 145). The way has been carefully prepared for this effect. In an earlier escapade of Tom's, another of his girls had been more fortunate. Only her arm was broken. But, in Jordan's description of that accident, the crucial words are "Tom ran into a wagon on the Ventura road one night, and ripped a front wheel off his car" (p. 78). And the detail of the accident parallels yet another. At the end of the first party Nick attends at Gatsby's house, there occurs what he calls "a bizarre and tumultuous scene": "In the ditch beside the road, right side up, but violently shorn of one wheel, rested a new coupé . . ." (p. 54). From this car has emerged the character called Owl Eyes, very drunk and bewildered. One of the bystanders remonstrates with him:

> ". . . if you're a poor driver you oughtn't to try driving at night."
> "But I wasn't even trying," he explained indignantly, "I wasn't even trying."
> An awed hush fell upon the bystanders.
> "Do you want to commit suicide?"
> "You're lucky it was just a wheel! A bad driver and not even *trying!*"
> "You don't understand," explained the criminal, "I wasn't driving. There's another man in the car." (p. 55)

The scene is very funny, and continues to be so when the real driver of the car, after a ghastly pause, very gradually steps out and proceeds to offer imbecile solutions. But in our enjoyment of the comedy we should not overlook the extraordinary contribution this scene makes to the shaping of the book. This harmless and farcical mishap, in which the wrong person is blamed for driving, is no less than a grotesque rehearsal of the terrible events at the end.

This scene also contains an example of another major structural device of that novel. Just as the episodes I've noted echo each other, so the characters are shown again and again to resemble each other in motive and conduct. The negligence of the driver in this farcical episode parallels more than Daisy's final accident and Tom's earlier one. Reckless or lawless use of cars, indeed, becomes a sign of how almost everyone in the book lives. Nick discovers Jordan's dishonesty when she leaves a borrowed car out in the rain with the top down, and then lies about it. Another time they have a significant conversation about driving:

> It started because she passed so close to some workmen that our fender flicked a button on one man's coat.

"You're a rotten driver," I protested. "Either you ought to be more careful, or you oughtn't to drive at all."

"I am careful."

"No, you're not."

"Well, other people are," she said lightly. (p. 59)

Nick warns her that trouble is bound to come when she meets another driver as careless as herself. At the end of the novel, Jordan reverts to this discussion:

"You said a bad driver was only safe until she met another bad driver? Well, I met another bad driver, didn't I? I mean it was careless of me to make such a wrong guess. I thought you were rather an honest, straightforward person." (p. 179)

Bad, careless, drivers—Tom, Daisy, Jordan, Nick, and how many others. Fitzgerald's use of the field of ashes as a wasteland symbol has been praised often, and deservedly, but it seems to me very much slighter— less developed in the novel and expressing a less impressive insight— than his use of driving to represent a strain of irresponsibility deep in the whole society. Nick's summing up of the story goes: "It was all very careless and confused. They were careless people, Tom and Daisy— they smashed up things and creatures and then retreated back into their money or their vast carelessness" (p. 180).

Careless driving, in metaphor or in fact, provides the most schematic parallelism between characters, but there are others of significance. Tom Buchanan and Gatsby, for example, are strongly opposed characters, and yet in one way they are curiously alike. I'd go further and say that they are esesentially alike. Each of them is trapped by his own glorious past, unable to live fully for the reality of the present. Nick gathers from Gatsby that in seeking to marry Daisy, and marry her back in Louisville and be married from her house as if the past five years had never been.

. . . he wanted to recover something, some idea of himself perhaps, that had gone into loving Daisy. His life had been confused and disordered since then, but if he could once return to a certain starting place and go over it all slowly, he could find out what that thing was . . . (pp. 111–12)

What is said here of Gatsby is more elaborate and subtle than what is said of Tom, but the substance is almost exactly the same. Tom, too, is seeking for he knows not what—his restlessness is the product of a sense of loss, the loss of his own past self. For Tom, as a college footballer, had been "one of those men who reach such an acute limited excellence at twenty-one that everything afterwards savors of anti-climax" (p. 6). Now Nick conjectures, "something was making him nibble at the edge of stale ideas as if his sturdy physical egotism no longer nourished his peremptory heart" (p. 21).

There are other examples of such interlinking of character in the novel, but I must leave most of those unspecified. It's more important to come to their purpose. They serve partly to unify the novel, to give it a close-packed organization. But they also radically affect the way in which the novel is to be understood. Because of these linkages, Gatsby especially ceases to be as isolated and eccentric a figure as at first he may appear. He becomes, instead, a representative figure, one who displays most fully because at its most extreme what moves all the men around him. This is especially true and interesting in the case of Nick. That Nick is in some very important ways immensely different from Gatsby or from Tom goes without saying. As Nick expresses it, in the familiar metaphor, he is a different sort of driver: "I am slow-thinking and full of interior rules that act as brakes on my desires" (p. 59). It is this difference, of course, that makes Nick so apt a narrator. He can look on at the scene without being sucked to its centre. And yet there are moments when Nick is drawn to Gatsby by more than detached sympathy, moments when he reveals himself as far more deeply like Gatsby than unlike. There is a thematic reason for this, of course: it helps to universalize the central story. But there is also, I think, a technical reason. This is something I touched on earlier, when I said that to provide an oblique expression of feeling for characters who can't themselves express it is one of the narrator's chief functions. Again and again, Nick dips into himself to construct imaginatively out of his own experience what he supposes the others, Tom, Gatsby, even Daisy, must be undergoing. Even his affair with Jordan, such as it is, echoes their passions: "Unlike Gatsby and Tom Buchanan, I had no girl whose disembodied face floated along the dark cornices and blinding signs, and so I drew up the girl beside me" (p. 81).

Nick's role, in this respect, is to experience what Gatsby experiences— the yearning for success, for wealth, for love, for the richness and magic of life, so that he (and through him the reader) can under-stand the inward quality of Gatsby's drives. But Nick is one who can only feel these things, not translate them into action. His feelings remain diffuse, they don't attach themselves to any real object, whether it be a woman or some material prize. So Gatsby stands to him as a warning and an example, to be admired and shunned: admired for the integrity, the single-minded determination with which he pursues the dream the other men dream, shunned because he seeks to deny those conditions of mortal life that make his dream unattainable. For the theme of the novel, as I've already suggested, has just this duality. It is about the need to accept limitations, if life is to be practicable. It is, on the other hand, about the need to aspire beyond limitations, if life is to seem meaningful.

Even as narrator, simply looking on at the lives of others, Nick displays this doubleness of attitude: "I was within and without, simul-

taneously enchanted and repelled by the inexhaustible variety of life"
(p. 36). "Enchanted"—it's scarcely necessary to dwell on Nick's use of
that word. He too, as much as anyone, is under the spell of what life
seems to promise. His early enthusiasm for his new life, even his
purchase of the books on banking and his "intention of reading many
other books besides" is not all that different from Gatsby's youthful
schedule of self-improvement. But there is one particular way in which
Nick's enchantment seems most to matter. He is enchanted by New
York, by all that the city seems to represent of human possibility. The
city recurs throughout the novel as a persistent presence, full of the
enticements of a life richer, more fulfilling, than anything he has ever
known. He comes with Gatsby over the bridge,

> with the city rising up across the river in white heaps and sugar
> lumps all built with a wish out of non-olfactory money. The city
> seen from the Queensboro Bridge is always the city seen for the
> first time, in its first wild promise of all the mystery and the beauty
> in the world. (p. 69)

He feels "a haunting loneliness" at "the enchanted metropolitan twilight"
and as he walks up Fifth Avenue it pleases him to

> pick out romantic women from the crowd and imagine that in a few
> minutes I was going to enter into their lives. . . . Sometimes, in my
> mind, I followed them to their apartments on the corners of hidden
> streets, and they turned and smiled back at me before they faded
> through a door into warm darkness. (p. 51)

It's plain that Nick's hunger for the imagined intimacies, the companionship and excitement within the "warm darkness" of other peoples'
lives, makes an exact counterpart to Gatsby's dream of the beautiful
bedrooms in Daisy's house.

Notes

1. W. J. Harvey, "Theme and Texture in *The Great Gatsby*," *English Studies*, 38
(1957), 12–20. Ed. note: because of the work of the past decade, Langman's
observation is less valid now than when he made it.

2. F. Scott Fitzgerald, "Introduction to *The Great Gatsby*," *Twentieth Century
Interpretations of The Great Gatsby*, ed. Ernest Lockridge (Englewood Cliffs,
N.J.: Prentice-Hall, 1968), p. 109.

3. F. Scott Fitzgerald, *The Great Gatsby* (New York: Scribner's, 1925), p. 25.
Subsequent references are indicated parenthetically in the text.

4. See Henry Dan Piper, *F. Scott Fitzgerald: A Critical Portrait* (New York:
Holt, Rinehart and Winston, 1965), p. 108.

5. See *The Letters of F. Scott Fitzgerald*, ed. Andrew Turnbull (New York:
Scribner's, 1963), p. 164.

Something Borrowed, Something New: A Discussion of Literary Influences on *The Great Gatsby*　　Robert Roulston*

Surely few twentieth-century works have been credited with a larger and more diverse literary lineage than *The Great Gatsby*. In the three decades that F. Scott Fitzgerald has been the object of more than sporadic scholarly attention, critics have detected in his third novel influences ranging from Chaucer's to Rafael Sabatini's. A catalog of the authors whose writings have supposedly left traces on *The Great Gatsby* is as full of bizarre incongruities as Nick Carraway's list of guests at Gatsby's parties. Flaubert is there with Stephen Leacock and Dreiser with Edith Wharton. There too are Charles Dickens and Ford Madox Ford, Joseph Conrad and Anthony Hope, Coleridge and Clarence E. Mulford, Thackeray and Harold Bell Wright, T. S. Eliot and George Eliot, Petronius and Stendhal, Mark Twain and Emily Brontë, Herman Melville and Horatio Alger, Oswald Spengler and Willa Cather, John Keats and the anonymous creator of Diamond Dick, H. G. Wells and his nemesis Henry James, and poor John Lawson Stoddard, who finds himself confused with the racist Theodore Lothrop Stoddard. And not far from the center, as conspicuous as he would have wished, is the sage of Baltimore, H. L. Mencken.[1]

We have here, surely, more than the perverse fancies of desperate academics. In truth, *The Great Gatsby* invites influence studies the way William Faulkner's fiction invites myth and symbol analyses. (*The Great Gatsby* has elicited its share of the latter as well.) To begin with, Fitzgerald's own sometimes unreliable hints offer clues that scholarly sleuths evidently find irresistible. Furthermore, Fitzgerald's almost miraculous artistic maturation during the brief interval between the completion of his second novel, *The Beautiful and Damned*, and the writing of *The Great Gatsby*, cries out for an explanation. Back in the 1950s James E. Miller, Jr., offered such an explanation by attributing the superiority of *The Great Gatsby* over its predecessors to Fitzgerald's shift of allegiance from the sprawling novels of H. G. Wells, Compton Mackenzie, Theodore Dreiser, and Frank Norris to the more controlled, selectively textured fiction of subtler writers, especially Joseph Conrad.[2] Later studies have attempted to provide more evidence for the impact of the same authors or have argued for the influence of different and often quite dissimilar writers.

Obviously not all these claims are equally impressive. Some of the purported parallels seem fortuitous. And, as might be expected, critics occasionally damage valid arguments by overstating them. What is more,

*This article, written especially for this volume, appears here for the first time.

there has been some inevitable quibbling over just what Fitzgerald read, when he read it, and whether concrete evidence of his having read a work is necessary to establish an influence when the circumstantial indications that he did are compelling.

Since this paper cannot examine all the putative sources of *The Great Gatsby*, it will concentrate upon those writers whose influence on the novel either is very pronounced or has been a subject of illuminating controversy. Of the latter authors, Oswald Spengler has exemplified more than any other both the pitfalls and the possibilities for expanded insights which can confront the seeker of literary influences. Fitzgerald himself acknowledged Spengler as a major influence, avowing in a letter to Maxwell Perkins that he was under Spengler's spell during the summer of 1924 while writing *The Great Gatsby*. Nothing would seem more conclusive.[3] And so, not surprisingly, discussions of Spenglerian themes in the novel were forthcoming, most notably those of Robert W. Stallman and Richard Lehan. Then in 1967 Robert Sklar derided such enterprises by observing that Spengler's *The Decline of the West* did not appear in an English translation until a year after the publication of *The Great Gatsby*; consequently, Fitzgerald, who was ignorant of German, could not knowingly have used Spenglerian motifs in his novel.

Not so, rejoined Dalton Gross: in July 1924 a summary of Spengler's ideas appeared in *Yale Review*, the sort of magazine Fitzgerald perused "to keep abreast of current literary developments." Unchastened, Richard Lehan leapt back into the fray, first in 1970, then in 1980. In his later offering he observed that at least nine articles or review-essays on *The Decline of the West* were published in English between 1922 and 1924, including a lengthy piece in the summer of 1924 in one of Fitzgerald's favorite periodicals, the *Century*. Lehan proceeded to amplify his earlier discussion of parallels between Spengler and *The Great Gatsby*. And Lehan is right: the parallels do exist. Gatsby is a Spenglerian "Faustian" man—a product of a simpler, more dynamic milieu crushed by the post-Enlightenment, urban, moneyed Caesar—Tom Buchanan.[4] Indubitably the New York Fitzgerald depicts is analogous to Spengler's Rome, which taught "the Classical World . . . the *pre-eminence of money*" in an age when the vitality of artistic creativity had waned along with heroic values.[5] Lehan is no less correct in his contention that to insist that someone can be influenced only by the ideas of an author with whose writings he has intimate first-hand knowledge is naive and pedantic. One need not have read a page of *Das Kapital* to know something about Marx's surplus value theory or a syllable of Carl Jung to converse coherently and even accurately about archetypes and personae. It should be equally self-evident that a person need not read a novel or a poem to acquire some notion of both its contents and its technical innovations. And—especially with a mind as wide-ranging, wayward, and retentive as Fitzgerald's—influences are as likely to come from conversations, second- and third-hand published accounts, or from a derivative minor work as from direct familiarity with an apparent "source"—a fact, no doubt, vexing to poor souls who crave precision and certainty.

One writer with whom Fitzgerald was certainly familiar, however, was T. S. Eliot. "The greatest of living poets," Fitzgerald proclaimed him in an inscription in the copy of *The Great Gatsby* he sent to Eliot in 1925—an opinion he was to repeat the following year in a letter to Maxwell Perkins.[6] In the inscription he also designated himself as Eliot's "enthusiastic worshipper." We need not find as much significance in the analogues between Fitzgerald's novel and Eliot's poems as some critics have found to recognize that Fitzgerald's imagery in the "valley of ashes" episodes is reminiscent of Eliot's "The Waste Land." So also are the juxtapositions of banal details about contemporary life with objects having grand historical resonances such as those Robert Emmet Long has noted in the second chapter of *The Great Gatsby*.[7] Furthermore, many of the Spenglerian aspects of *The Great Gatsby* have counterparts in "The Waste Land," whose author, unlike Fitzgerald, read German and who was much more likely to have known Spengler's book well, and to have been familiar with an entire corpus of continental writing about the collapse of cultures in general and of modern Europe in particular.

In truth, anyone in the 1920s with a taste for apocalyptic visions did not have to reach back to Richard Wagner's *Götterdämmerung*, or out to Spengler's *Decline of the West* and Hermann Hesse's *A Glimpse into Chaos* (cited by Eliot in his notes to "The Waste Land"), or to Eliot's favorite French journalist, Charles Maurras. Such a person had merely to descend to Tom Buchanan's level and read such alarmist offerings as Madison Grant's *The Passing of a Great Race* or Theodore Lothrop Stoddard's *The Rising Tide of Color*.[8] The anti-Semitic smudges in *This Side of Paradise* and *The Beautiful and Damned*, as well as the slurs against blacks, Italians, and orientals in *Tender Is The Night*, indicate that Fitzgerald would have been less hostile to such racist fare than Nick Carraway's comments about Tom's nibbling "at the edge of stale ideas" suggest.[9] Indeed, Fitzgerald had merely to regard his own failures of will and waning energy to decay all about him, for as far back as 1921 he had written to Maxwell Perkins: "I'm sick of the flabby, semi-intellectual softness in which I flounder with my generation."[10] In short, Eliot, Spengler, and even racist pessimists like Stoddard were providing an intellectual scaffolding or useful details to support what he, Fitzgerald, perceived intuitively in himself and his contemporaries.

When in the mood for particulars about the failings of his countrymen, though, Fitzgerald had to seek no farther than the writings and conversations of his friend, mentor, and sometime publisher—that berater of the "boobus-Americanus" and the plutocracy, H. L. Mencken. As editor, first of *The Smart Set* and later of *The American Mercury*, Mencken had ushered into print such important stories by Fitzgerald as "May Day,"

"The Diamond as Big as the Ritz," and "Absolution," as well as such negligible ones as "Porcelain and Pink," "Mister Icky," and "Tarquin of Cheapside." More important, Mencken, with his formidable wit and even more formidable certitude, imposed upon Fitzgerald, as upon so many younger readers in the early 1920s, some of his own literary preferences. James R. Miller, Jr., has examined how decisively Mencken shaped Fitzgerald's artistic development by luring him away from his youthful entrancement with writers like Compton Mackenzie and Robert W. Chambers and by instilling in him an appreciation of Theodore Dreiser, Frank Norris, and Joseph Conrad.[11] Fitzgerald, moreover, was not simply flattering Mencken when he wrote to him in 1920: "I have already adopted many of your views."[12] Throughout Fitzgerald's second novel, the impact of Mencken's tastes and ideas is ubiquitous—a fact Fitzgerald himself was aware of. By spring of 1924, however, he had come to regard *The Beautiful and Damned* as "a false lead . . . a concession to Mencken."[13] All the illblended mixture in *The Beautiful and Damned* of gritty Dreiserian realism and of a whimsical cynicism redolent of *The Smart Set* reveals, as Arthur Mizener points out, that Mencken's influence was not entirely salutary and that Fitzgerald was correct in regarding certain aspects of it as qualities to be outgrown.[14] But when Mencken, after praising the writing in *The Great Gatsby*, complained that the story seemed "trivial" and hardly more than an anecdote, Fitzgerald defended its narrow focus and its omission of the kind of detail Mencken admired in *This Side of Paradise* and *The Beautiful and Damned* by evoking as a precedent Mencken's favorite living novelist, Joseph Conrad. Fitzgerald also chided Mencken's preference for sprawling fiction and added: "It is in protest against my own formless two novels, and Lewis' and Dos Passos' that this [*The Great Gatsby*] was written."[15]

Although by 1924 Fitzgerald had begun to exorcise Mencken's spell, *The Great Gatsby* nonetheless reflects Mencken's attitudes toward both the incompetent poor like George Wilson and the plutocratic rich like Tom Buchanan as well as toward the kind of plebian vulgarity embodied by Myrtle Wilson and the McKees. But the novel also expresses contrary values, as we shall see.

Deferring for awhile the more complex question of Joseph Conrad's influence upon *The Great Gatsby*, Fitzgerald's novel shows the impact of at least two other of Mencken's favorite authors, Theodore Dreiser and Willa Cather. Although Dreiser's influence upon Fitzgerald reached its apogee in *The Beautiful and Damned*, the parallels between Dreiser's "Vanity, Vanity Saith the Preacher" and *The Great Gatsby* cited by Maxwell Geismar and Eric Solomon suggest that the influence may have lingered on into the middle of the 1920s.[16] More noteworthy are the similarities between *The Great Gatsby* and the writings of Willa Cather, of whose *My Ántonia* Mencken asserted: "No romantic novel ever written in America, by man or woman, is one-half so beautiful."[17] Like *My Ántonia*, *The Great Gatsby* has a narrator who interprets—as he recounts in a series of impressionistic scenes—the fortunes and misfortunes of a protagonist at least outwardly unlike himself. Both works, too, are pervaded with a bittersweet nostalgia, and both are written in finely crafted, evocative prose which, as Mencken observed of Cather's novel, "proves . . . that careful and penetrating representation is itself the source of a rare and wonderful beauty."[18]

Although Cather's language may be less beautiful in *A Lost Lady* than in *My Ántonia*, Fitzgerald not only read the former "with great delight"; he also duplicated a passage from her book closely enough to fear she might accuse him of plagiarism. In a letter he assured her that he had written his own passage a month or two before reading hers and that, therefore, the similarity is a coincidence.[19] Matthew J. Bruccoli may be correct in concluding that, since in the same letter he claimed to have been in the middle of the first draft of *The Great Gatsby* while reading *A Lost Lady*, Fitzgerald "began work on the final plot earlier than has been supposed."[20] But, even allowing that Fitzgerald's memory about dates here was accurate, he wrote enough of his novel after his exposure to *A Lost Lady* for the latter to have had some effect upon *The Great Gatsby*. Neil Herbert's fascination with the beautiful Marian Forrester is similar enough to Jay Gatsby's obsession with Daisy Fay to justify Miller's suggestion that Cather's novel may have influenced Fitzgerald. So too are the parallels between Neil's efforts to reconcile Mrs. Forrester's resplendence with her amorality and Nick Carraway's attempts to resolve his own ambiguous feelings toward Gatsby. And if Long is correct in identifying Cather as the source of the East-West contrast which is so important to the thematic scheme of *The Great Gatsby*, then Fitzgerald's debt to her was indeed considerable.[21]

Yet Fitzgerald's antithesis between a crude but innocent West and a sophisticated, sinister East certainly has resonances of an author who rarely deigned to cast his vision beyond the western shore of the Hudson River. That writer, one of Mencken's *bête noires*, was of course Henry James. In novel after novel and story after story, from the beginning to the end of his long career, James had posed just such an antithesis—not, to be sure, between the East Coast and the Middle West as Fitzgerald does, but between complex, corrupt Europe and a simpler, more innocent America. In a sense, therefore, the geographical symbolism of *The Great Gatsby* is that of James, shifted four-thousand miles westward. There is well-nigh universal agreement that little evidence exists of Fitzgerald's having read James before writing *The Great Gatsby*. Yet the parallels Henry Dan Piper cites between Fitzgerald's novel and James's *The American* and *Daisy Miller* are pronounced enough to indicate that Fitzgerald was probably familiar with them.[22] And surely the theme and story of *Daisy Miller*, in particular, were known widely enough for anyone interested in literature to have been familiar with the work's main features. That the heroine of Fitzgerald's novel is named Daisy; that the hero of "Absolution," which was originally to have served as an introduction to *The Great Gatsby*, is named Rudolph Miller; and that Daisy Miller's brother is Randolph—all may be trivial resemblances. But trivial or not they suggest that Fitzgerald was acquainted with at least the cast of characters in James's novel.

There seems to be much less doubt that Fitzgerald has read Edith Wharton. Furthermore, his sending her an inscribed copy of *The Great Gatsby* in 1925 hardly implies that he shared the disdain toward her of his erstwhile mentor, Mencken, who tended to regard her as a Henry James in skirts. Commenting on Wharton's objections to the lack of information about Jay Gatsby, Michael Millgate has shown how she had used a similar technique herself in *The Custom of the Country*. While unwilling to assert categorically that *The Custom of the Country* directly influenced *The Great Gatsby*, Millgate agrees with Frederick J. Hoffman that Fitzgerald may have derived narrative techniques from Wharton's *Ethan Frome*—a view endorsed by Henry Dan Piper. The principal points of resemblance are, of course, the first-person narrator who, in a sequence of brief scenes, tells a story leading to a violent climax. Parallels have also been noted between *The Great Gatsby* and Wharton's *The Spark*.[23]

Nearly everyone who has addressed himself in print to this matter agrees that Joseph Conrad had some effect upon *The Great Gatsby*. Agreement vanishes, however, over how decisive that effect was and over which of Conrad's works exercised it. Although he later minimized the importance of the influence, Arthur Mizener noted its presence back in 1951. Mizener at the same time regretted what he regarded as the "not always fortunate echoes of Conrad's phrasing."[24] Apparently, though, the traces he detected there of Conrad's method of narration seemed less unfortunate to him. For Robert W. Stallman a few years later there was nothing either unfortunate or equivocal about Conrad's influence on *The Great Gatsby*.[25] Theme, characters, plot, narrative method, settings— all reflect Fitzgerald's entrancement with *Nostromo, Lord Jim*, and *Heart of Darkness*. Gatsby sometimes is Conrad's Jim in a pink suit; at other times Nostromo in a cream-colored limousine or an American Kurtz sinking into a New York no less dark at its heart than Kurtz's African counterpart. And there, reporting it all, is Fitzgerald's version of Marlow, Nick Carraway, albeit Nick's mind "lacks Marlow's range and points of curiosity," and his "provincial squeamishness" makes him a less sympathetic observer than Marlow.[26] Jerome Thale and Harold Hurwitz have found still other parallels.[27] Hurwitz makes much of apparent similarities between Marlow's conversation with Kurtz's fiancée and Nick's scene with Gatsby's father, observing that, in both instances, a narrator tries explaining a protagonist to a listener who is under an illusion about the person being discussed. The resulting irony, according to Hurwitz, is compounded in both instances by the ambivalence of the narrator's feelings about the protagonist.

For James E. Miller, Jr., Conrad gave Fitzgerald more than hints for mere themes or for the delineation of characters; Conrad provided an aesthetic theory which enabled him to transform himself in an incredibly short time from the author of sprawling cluttered novels into the creator of the brilliantly compact *The Great Gatsby*.[28] Indeed, Conrad is the true hero of Miller's book, which depicts Conrad's preface to *The Nigger of the "Narcissus"* as the guide which led Fitzgerald away from the baneful influence of the formless or cluttered writings of Wells, Dreiser, and Norris. Thanks to that preface as well as to the model provided by Conrad's own fiction, Fitzgerald could leave behind the vices of what Henry James, citing Wells as an example, had called the novel of "saturation" and could embrace the virtues of writing novels of "selection."

Although they do not go as far as Miller does, Sklar, Piper, and Perosa all regard Conrad as a major influence upon *The Great Gatsby*. Sklar maintains that Fitzgerald derived from Conrad not techniques, but an "attitude toward human hopes and human history."[29] Yet he also tries to deny the significance of some of the parallels cited by Stallman and Thale by contending that the only works of Conrad Fitzgerald had read before writing *The Great Gatsby* were *Nostromo*, *Victory*, "Youth," *The Nigger of the "Narcissus,"* and *A Mirror of the Sun*. (Sklar's assertion that Fitzgerald had not read *Lord Jim* seems to be refuted by the reference to the book in Fitzgerald's 1923 review of Sherwood Anderson's *Many Marriages*.[30])

As we have seen, however, a dearth of evidence of a first-hand knowledge by Fitzgerald of a work rarely has deterred a determined seeker of literary influences from considering it a possible source for *The Great Gatsby*. Thus Andrew Crosland, while admitting there is no proof Fitzgerald actually read Conrad's *The Secret Agent*, maintains that the similarities between it and *The Great Gatsby* are striking enough to make one "think Fitzgerald . . . had consciously echoed certain parts of it in order to generate subtle ironies and to help define character."[31] By far the most assiduous hunter of parallels between *The Great Gatsby* and works by other writers has been Robert Emmet Long. Long's most productive labors have been expended upon the Conrad-Fitzgerald connection. In addition to finding hitherto undetected resemblances between *The Great Gatsby* and *Heart of Darkness*, *Nostromo*, and *Lord Jim*, Long discusses affinities between Fitzgerald's novel and *An Outcast of the Islands*, *The Rescue*, "Youth," and, in considerable detail, *Almayer's Folly*.[32] Indeed, Conrad's tropical dreamer seems to become a veritable prototype for Jay Gatsby as Long cites similar words used by both writers to describe their protagonists. Long also finds significance in the way the illusions of both heroes are embodied in their houses and in how both houses are located near water and across from the homes of more securely established opponents. He also indicates analogues between Gatsby's and Almayer's backgrounds and believes that Dan Cody's yacht serves the same function as Captain Lingard's ship—to launch the protagonist into a splendid future that will become ultimately anything but splendid.

Where does all this leave us? Nick Carraway's function does resemble Marlow's. But it also resembles the function of narrators used by Edith Wharton, Willa Cather, and even, as I have argued elsewhere, of George Ponderevo in what was once Fitzgerald's favorite novel, H. G. Wells's *Tono-Bungay*.[33] *The Great Gatsby*, to be sure, is developed through a series of short dramatic scenes as are several of Conrad's works. But so are *My Ántonia* and *Ethan Frome*. And if analogues exist between Gatsby and Kurtz, Nostromo, Jim, and Almayer, they also exist between Gatsby and a whole range of fictional characters from Trimalchio to Horatio Alger's heroes. As for Fitzgerald's avowal that in *The Great Gatsby* he was an imitator of Conrad, he also declared that he was influenced by Thackeray. Yet the latter influence has received relatively little attention, despite resemblances between *The Great Gatsby* and *Vanity Fair* such as the parallel between Gatsby's preoccupation with Daisy and Dobbin's mooning over Amelia and the similarity between Fitzgerald's guest list and a comparably comic catalog in *Vanity Fair*.[34] And the reason for all but ignoring the Thackeray connection is obvious: whatever Fitzgerald may have appropriated from Thackeray, *The Great Gatsby* is so dissimilar to *Vanity Fair* in tone, pacing, style, and texture, that any similarity between the works seems of peripheral significance. The problem with the links between *The Great Gatsby* and the writings of Conrad is that they are numerous and important enough to tempt us to regard Fitzgerald as a disciple of Conrad who unfortunately lacks his master's profundity and deep moral seriousness.

The temptation should be resisted. Whether we accept Lawrence Thornton's suggestion that Ford Madox Ford exerted a more decisive influence on Fitzgerald than Conrad did, we must recognize the validity of Thornton's objections to regarding Conrad as the paramount model for *The Great Gatsby*. As Thornton points out, Fitzgerald's sensibility and values differed enormously from Conrad's.[35] For the brooding Pole the past is where fatal errors have been made and where evil has had its genesis. Thus it is through probing his own past or the past of some kindred soul like Jim or Kurtz that Conrad's Marlow arrives at self-knowledge and the strength to endure the tragic farce of life. Little could be more remote from what Fitzgerald informed Roger Burlingame was the unifying emotion of *The Great Gatsby*: "I was tremendously pleased that it [*The Great Gatsby*] moved you in that way 'made you want to be back somewhere so much' because that describes so much better than I could have put it myself, either in regard to the temperment [*sic*] of Gatsby himself or my own mood while writing it."[36] Now, it seems unlikely that *Lord Jim* has ever made anyone want to be aboard the sinking *Patna* or that *Heart of Darkness* has induced a desire to share the nightmarish experiences that have led the dying Kurtz to exclaim "The horror! The horror!" Yet Fitzgerald's dazzling prose and romantic vision invest Gatsby's dreams and aspirations, memories, and delusions with such a glow that for Gatsby, even more than for John Dryden's Antony or Cleopatra, the world seems "well lost." Moreover, for all their fatuous vulgarity Gatsby's parties are amusing—something that can be said for very few occurrences in Conrad.

What an undue concentration upon the influence of any single author on *The Great Gatsby* can obscure is the multi-faceted quality of Fitzgerald's novel. Just as, according to Fitzgerald, "the test of a first-rate intelligence is the ability to hold two opposed ideas at the same time, and still retain the ability to function,"[37] so the test of a perceptive critic is his ability to recognize in *The Great Gatsby* the presence not only of opposed ideas but of the influence of writers radically dissimilar from each other. It is even more important to perceive the truth of Fitzgerald's boast about *The Great Gatsby*: "It is unlike anything I have ever read before."[38] And apprehending the originality of the novel obviously entails recognizing how the novel differs from works to which it bears certain resemblances.

Just as, despite its Conradian gestures, *The Great Gatsby* is not fundamentally an exercise in Conradian moralizing, neither is it a prolonged wallow in that romantic tradition which rejects the real world as a painful sham to be shunned or transcended. To be sure, elements of that tradition are present. But whether Fitzgerald derived them from Flaubert, Stendhal, John Keats, or Ford Madox Ford[39] is less important than the way Fitzgerald combines the disillusionment of Nick Carraway with an avidity for experience so that the book as a whole justifies Nick's assertion: "I was within and without, simultaneously enchanted and repelled by the inexhaustible variety of life" (p. 36). The enchantment is no less integral to the work than the repulsion, and a failure to grasp it blinds one to at least half of the book's magic.

Gatsby's actions may be as foolish or self-destructive as Emma Bovary's. But whereas Flaubert's measured prose mocks Emma's rebellion while relentlessly exposing the coarseness of her provincial milieu, Fitzgerald's exuberant lyricism does the exact opposite. As Michael Millgate has stated: "At the end of Fitzgerald's brilliant display of advocacy we stand, despite all the evidence, with Gatsby."[40] And standing with Gatsby requires sharing at least provisionally Gatsby's awed response toward Daisy, the world of the rich, and New York.

The Great Gatsby, of course, also satirizes these things. Indeed, the most depressing aspect of some of the scholarship about the novel is how it misses not merely the satire but the humor. As Long has noted,

Meyer Wolfsheim, for all his evil, is a genuinely comic character. So are Myrtle Wilson, McKee, Klipspringer, and, as I have maintained elsewhere, Tom Buchanan.[41] Yet despite the jabs, comic or otherwise, at New York's gaudiness and seaminess, the city hardly emerges from the book as H. L. Mencken's third-rate Babylon on the Hudson.

Mencken's reservations about the worth of *The Great Gatsby*, in fact, may have resulted not merely from Fitzgerald's failure to adhere in it to Mencken's aesthetic dictates, but also from the way the novel treats respectfully things Mencken scorned—among them the American Dream. Despite his illustrious Maryland forebears, Fitzgerald was too much the parvenu to be altogether comfortable with Mencken's diagnosis that "the capital defect of culture in These States is the lack of a civilized aristocracy, secure in its position."[42]

Down the list of influences on *The Great Gatsby* we could go, observing in each instance a profound divergence for every resemblance. Thus for instance, if Fitzgerald, like Cather, could invoke the West against the corrupt East, he was no prairie primitivist, as Cather sometimes pretended to be. And whatever Fitzgerald's "valley of ashes" may owe to Eliot's "The Waste Land," Gatsby's New York is too glamorous and dynamic to be Eliot's catatonic "unreal city." Then too one can imagine the withering contempt with which Eliot would have depicted Gatsby with his flashy car and bogus Norman "Hôtel de Ville." Fitzgerald's affection for such a character would have been even more alien to Henry James and Edith Wharton. James's self-made millionaires like Christopher Newman and Adam Verver, having made their fortunes before arriving in the great centers of civilization, seem downright patrician compared to Gatsby. Edith Wharton's Ethan Frome may be a dignified yeoman, but it is hard to imagine her treating the vulgar Gatsby with less hauteur than she treats Simon Rosedale in *The House of Mirth*. As for Oswald Spengler, although Fitzgerald shared his forebodings about Western civilization, he also expressed in *The Great Gatsby* a joie de vivre absent from Spengler's somber tome.

As a book that soars and laughs no less than it laments, *The Great Gatsby* is no more a Conradian tragedy than it is a Cather-like celebration of the frontier, a Mencken-like exposé of America, a Jamesian study of fine sensibilities, a Dreiserian pageant of personal disintegration, a Flaubertian exercise in aesthetics, or a romantic flight from life. It is sui generis, not an eclectic hodgepodge or a clever reworking of one particular source—a fact not even the most convincing influence study should ever permit us to forget.

Notes

1. Nancy Y. Hoffman, "*The Great Gatsby: Troilus and Criseyde* Revisited?" *Fitzgerald/Hemingway Annual 1971*, pp. 148–58; Robert E. Morsberger, "The

Romantic Ancestry of *The Great Gatsby*," *Fitzgerald/Hemingway Annual 1972*, pp. 119–30 (Sabatini, Hope, Brontë, et al.); Leslie F. Chard, II, "Outward Forms and the Inner Life: Coleridge and *Gatsby*," *Fitzgerald/Hemingway Annual 1973*, pp. 189–94; Ralph Curry and Janet Lewis, "Stephen Leacock: An Early Influence on F. Scott Fitzgerald," *Canadian Review of American Studies*, 8 (1976), 5–14; Taylor Alderman, "*The Great Gatsby* and *Hopalong Cassidy*," *Fitzgerald/Hemingway Annual 1975*, pp. 75–87 (Mulford); Dale B. J. Randall, "The 'Seer' and 'Seen' Themes in *Gatsby* and Some of Their Parallels in Eliot and Wright," *Twentieth Century Literature*, 10 (1964), 51–63; Paul A. Makurath, Jr., "Another Source for 'Gatsby,' " *Fitzgerald/Hemingway Annual 1975*, pp. 115–16 (George Eliot); "*The Great Gatsby* and Trimalchio," *The Classical Journal*, 45 (1950), 307–14; Horst H. Kruse, " 'Gatsby' and 'Gadsby,' " *Modern American Studies*, 15 (1969–70), 539–41 (Twain); John Schroeder, "Some Unfortunate Idyllic Love Affairs: The Legends of Taji and Jay Gatsby," *Books at Brown*, 22 (1968), 143–53 (Melville); Gary Scharnhorst, "Scribbling Upward: Fitzgerald's Debt of Honor to Horatio Alger, Jr.," *Fitzgerald/Hemingway Annual 1978*, pp. 26–35; James Ellis, " 'The Stoddard Lectures' in *The Great Gatsby*," *American Literature*, 44 (1972), 470–71; Daryl E. Jones, "Fitzgerald and Pulp Fiction: From *Diamond Dick* to *Gatsby*," *Fitzgerald/Hemingway Annual 1978*, pp. 137–39. Others will be cited later.

2. James E. Miller, Jr., *The Fictional Techniques of Scott Fitzgerald* (The Hague: Martinus Nijhoff, 1957), pp. 129–33.

3. 6 June 1940, *The Letters of F. Scott Fitzgerald*, ed. Andrew Turnbull (New York: Scribner's, 1963), pp. 289–90.

4. Robert W. Stallman, "Gatsby and the Hole in Time," *Modern Fiction Studies*, 1 (1955), 2–16; Richard Lehan, *F. Scott Fitzgerald and the Craft of Fiction* (Carbondale: Southern Illinois University Press, 1966), pp. 30–36; "Focus on F. Scott Fitzgerald's *The Great Gatsby*: The Nowhere Hero," in *American Dreams, American Nightmares*, ed. David Madden (Carbondale: Southern Illinois University Press, 1970), pp. 106–14; "F. Scott Fitzgerald and Romantic Destiny," *Twentieth Century Literature*, 26 (1980), 137–56; Robert Sklar, *F. Scott Fitzgerald: The Last Laocoön* (New York: Oxford University Press, 1967), p. 24; Dalton Gross, "F. Scott Fitzgerald's *The Great Gatsby* and Oswald Spengler's *The Decline of the West*," *Notes and Queries*, 17 (1970), 476.

5. Oswald Spengler, *The Decline of the West*, trans. Charles F. Atkins, I (New York: Knopf, 1926), 36.

6. *Correspondence of F. Scott Fitzgerald*, ed. Matthew J. Bruccoli and Margaret M. Duggan (New York: Random House, 1980), p. 180.

7. Robert Emmet Long, *The Achieving of The Great Gatsby: F. Scott Fitzgerald, 1920–1925* (Lewisburg: Bucknell University Press, 1979), pp. 126, 211–12. See also Randall, pp. 51–56, and Philip Young, "Scott Fitzgerald's Waste Land," *Filologia e Letteratura*, 10 (1964), 113–20.

8. Lewis A. Turlish, "*The Rising Tide of Color*: A Note on the Historicism of *The Great Gatsby*," *American Literature*, 43 (1971), 442–44. See also Stallman, pp. 2–12.

9. *The Great Gatsby* (New York: Scribner's, 1925), p. 21. Cited hereafter in the text in parentheses.

10. 25 August 1921, *Letters*, p. 167.

11. Miller, pp. 39–43.

12. To Mencken, 20 March 1920, *Correspondence*, p. 55.

13. To Moran Tudury, 11 April 1924, *Correspondence*, p. 139.

14. *The Far Side of Paradise* (Boston: Houghton, 1951), pp. 138–39.

15. To Mencken, 4 May 1925, *Letters*, p. 480.

16. Maxwell Geismar, "Theodore Dreiser," *Rebels and Ancestors: The American Novel, 1890–1915: Frank Norris, Stephen Crane, Jack London, Ellen Glasgow, Theodore Dreiser* (Boston: Houghton Mifflin, 1953), p. 342; Eric Solomon, "A Source for Fitzgerald's *The Great Gatsby*," *Modern Language Notes*, 73 (1938), 186–88.

17. "The Novel," *Prejudices: Third Series* (New York: Knopf, 1922), pp. 210–11.

18. Ibid., p. 210.

19. Late March/Early April 1925, *Correspondence*, pp. 155–56.

20. "An Instance of Apparent Plagiarism: F. Scott Fitzgerald, Willa Cather and the First *Gatsby* Manuscript," *Princeton University Library Chronicle*, 3, (1978), 176.

21. Long, p. 181.

22. *F. Scott Fitzgerald: A Critical Portrait* (New York: Holt, 1965), pp. 128–29.

23. Frederick J. Hoffman, "Points of Moral Reference: A Comparative Study of Edith Wharton and F. Scott Fitzgerald," *English Institute Essays* (New York: Columbia University Press, 1950), pp. 147–76; Michael Millgate, *American Social Fiction: James to Cozzens* (London: Olivier & Boyd, 1964), pp. 110–11; Michael A. Peterman, "A Neglected Source for *The Great Gatsby*: The Influence of Edith Wharton's *The Spark*," *Canadian Review of American Studies*, 8 (1977), 26–35.

24. Mizener, p. 170.

25. "Conrad and *The Great Gatsby*," *Twentieth Century Fiction*, I (1955), 5–11.

26. Ibid., p. 11.

27. Jerome Thale, "The Narrator as Hero," *Twentieth Century Literature*, 3 (1955), 69–73; Harold Hurwitz, "*The Great Gatsby* and 'The Heart of Darkness,'" *Fitzgerald/Hemingway Annual 1969*, pp. 27–34.

28. Miller, pp. 67–114.

29. Sklar, p. 152. See also Piper, pp. 129–33.

30. Reprinted in *F. Scott Fitzgerald: In His Own Time: A Miscellany*, ed. Matthew J. Bruccoli and Jackson R. Bryer (New York: Popular Library, 1971), p. 138.

31. "*The Great Gatsby* and *The Secret Agent*," *Fitzgerald/Hemingway Annual 1975*, p. 75.

32. Long, pp. 88–96.

33. "Traces of *Tono-Bungay* in *The Great Gatsby*," *Journal of Narrative Technique*, 10 (1980), 68–76.

34. See Stephen Curry and Peter L. Hays, "Fitzgerald's *Vanity Fair*," *Fitzgerald/Hemingway Annual 1977*, pp. 63–75; Long, p. 214; and Fitzgerald's letter to John Jamieson, 7 April 1934, *Letters*, p. 509.

35. "Ford Madox Ford and *The Great Gatsby*," *Fitzgerald/Hemingway Annual 1975*, pp. 57–71.

36. 19 April 1925, *Correspondence*, pp. 159–60.

37. *The Crack-up*, ed. Edmund Wilson (New York: New Directions, 1945), p. 67.

38. To Maxwell Perkins, 10 September 1924, *Correspondence*, p. 146.

39. Long, p. 119, and Thornton, p. 60, suggest a possible influence of Flaubert through either Conrad or Ford. Mizener insists that similarities between Fitzgerald and Stendhal are "immeasurably more important" than any between Fitzgerald and either Eliot or Conrad; but Mizener avers that there is no evidence Fitzgerald ever read Stendhal: Preface to the Vintage Edition of *The Far Side of Paradise* (New York: Vintage, 1959), pp. vii–viii. In a letter to Holger Lundbergh in 1923, however, Fitzgerald claimed to have just finished *The Red and the Black* (*Correspondence*, p. 133). On Keats see Dan McCall, "'The Self-Same Song That Found a Path': Keats and *The Great Gatsby*," *American Literature*, 42 (1971), 521–30;

Joseph B. Wagner, "Gatsby and John Keats: Another Version," *Fitzgerald/Hemingway Annual 1979*, pp. 91–98.

40. Millgate, p. 110.

41. "Tom Buchanan: Patrician in Motley," *Arizona Quarterly*, 34 (1978), 101–11.

42. "American Culture," *A Mencken Chrestomathy*, ed. H. L. Mencken (New York: Knopf, 1949), p. 178.

The Great Gatsby and Its Sources   Richard D. Lehan[*]

In a letter to Maxwell Perkins from Rome, dated December 20, 1924, Fitzgerald discussed the creation of *The Great Gatsby*, which he was then in the process of revising. After mentioning Tom Buchanan, Gatsby, Daisy, and Myrtle, Fitzgerald says: "Jordan Baker of course was a great idea (perhaps you know it's Edith Cummings)."[1] Edith Cummings was, as I have already mentioned, a close friend of Ginevra King, both in Chicago and at Westover where they were in the class of 1917. Like Jordan Baker, in *The Great Gatsby*, she was a famous golfer—playing out of the elegant Onwentsia Club in Chicago—and once winning the national woman's golf championship. Fitzgerald met Edith Cummings a number of times—both in Lake Forest and in New York—when he was dating Ginevra King.

Fitzgerald met Ginevra when she was invited to St. Paul by Marie Hersey, and he described their first meeting—on January 4, 1915 at a dinner dance at the Town and Country Club—in "Babes in the Woods," published in the *Nassau Literary Magazine* in May of 1917 and later included in *This Side of Paradise*. He later described the unhappy end of his love in "The Debutante," *Nassau Literary Magazine*, January, 1917. Ginevra encouraged Fitzgerald for a while, along with many other boys. In June of 1915, they met in New York and went to *Nobody Home* and the Midnight Frolic. In March of 1916, Ginevra was expelled from Westover by Miss Hillard, the headmistress. Fourteen years later, in September of 1930, Fitzgerald was still interested enough in Ginevra to write a short story about her expulsion, entitled "A Woman with a Past," for the *Saturday Evening Post*. This later became one of the Josephine stories and was included in *Taps at Reveille*.

In the story, Josephine is put on probation by a Miss Kwain who maintained that Josephine was flirting with boys calling to her from under her dormitory window. Soon after, while walking with Ernest Waterbury near the campus chapel, Josephine "slipped" into his "unwilling arms, where she lay helpless, convulsed with irresistible laughter.

[*]Reprinted from Richard D. Lehan, *F. Scott Fitzgerald and the Craft of Fiction* (Carbondale: Southern Illinois University Press, 1966), pp. 91–102, 122–23, by permission of the author.

It was in this position that Miss Brereton and the visiting trustee had found them."[2] Miss Brereton expelled Josephine and then retracted, just as Miss Hillard had expelled Ginevra and then retracted. Neither Ginevra nor Josephine, however, would return to the school.

In August of 1916, Fitzgerald visited Ginevra in Lake Forest. Peg Cary, Edith Cummings, Courtney Letts—the old Westover crowd—were all there, and, according to Fitzgerald's Ledger, there was a "petting party" and many gay evenings. The Kings made it clear that they disapproved of Fitzgerald. In his Ledger, Fitzgerald wrote that someone at this time told him, "Poor boys shouldn't think of marrying rich girls."[3] If Mr. King would not put it this crudely, these were his sentiments.[4]

The next time that Fitzgerald saw Ginevra King was with Peg Cary at the Yale game in November of 1916. Ginevra met Fitzgerald once again in January of 1917, at which time she broke with him for good.

The conclusion of "A Woman with a Past" is thus pure daydream. When Josephine leaves school, she goes to Hot Springs where she meets a young man who "had flunked out of Princeton in February" (p. 195). (Fitzgerald had not exactly "flunked out" of Princeton, but the reference is obvious.) Josephine learns at Hot Springs something that Nick Carraway learns in *The Great Gatsby*—that playing with other's affections has moral consequences: "One mustn't run through people . . . for the sake of a romantic half-hour" (p. 199). The moment she realizes this she sees Mr. Gordon Tinsley, from Yale, "the current catch of Chicago, reputedly the richest young man in the Middle West. He had never paid any attention to young Josephine until tonight. Ten minutes ago he had asked her to go driving with him." She rejects him because "the Princeton man was still at her ear, still imploring her to walk out with him into the night" (pp. 199–200).

It did not happen this way in life. In June of 1917, Fitzgerald suspected that Ginevra was engaged; in September of 1917, he wrote in his Ledger, "Oh Ginevra"; by June of 1918, while he was stationed at Camp Sheridan near Montgomery, Alabama, he found out that Ginevra King was to be married in September. She was marrying William Mitchell who, like Gordon Tinsley in the story, was "the current catch of Chicago." Mitchell was from an extremely wealthy family, long associated with Chicago banking—especially with the Continental Illinois Bank. After he married Ginevra, Mitchell became a director in the family firm of Mitchell, Hutchins & Co., and served on the boards of Balaban and Katz, Inland Glass, and Elgin Clock.

Ginevra King's father, like Josephine's father, went to Yale (class of 1894), and Charles King and William Mitchell both owned a string of polo ponies, Mr. King bringing his East to Long Island where he often rode with Louis E. Stoddard who was on the American team that played England in the twenties. The principal characters in *The Great Gatsby* thus begin to emerge: a great deal of Ginevra King went into Fitz-gerald's conception of Daisy Fay; Tom Buchanan—who came from a wealthy Chicago family, went to Yale, owned a string of polo ponies on Long Island—is the fusion of Mr. King and William Mitchell; Jordan Baker is Edith Cummings, a friend of Ginevra, just as Jordan is a friend of Daisy.

Fitzgerald came away from Ginevra with a sense of social inade-quacy, a deep hurt, and longing for the girl beyond attainment. He expressed these sentiments first, not in *The Great Gatsby*, but in "Winter Dreams," published in December of 1922 in *Metropolitan Magazine*. In this story, the two lovers are separated by money—Dexter Green is the son of a grocer, just as Fitzgerald's maternal grandfather was in the grocery business—and Judy Jones's father is as wealthy as his Pierce-Arrow automobile indicates. When he is twenty-three, Dexter falls in love with Judy, who encourages and then drops him. At twenty-five Dexter is engaged to another girl, but he breaks his engagement when Judy once again shows interest in him. When Judy has proved to herself her complete power over Dexter, she dismisses him once and for all from her life. At thirty-two, Dexter is a Jay Gatsby, preserving his "old" image of Judy, his "winter" dreams: Dexter learns at this time that Judy, who has since married, is having marital troubles and that she has "faded" and is considered "too old" for her husband. The news shocks him because suddenly he realizes that his youth is gone—and with it an ideal conception of perfect beauty that had kept the world resplendent and alive:

> He had thought that having nothing else to lose he was invulnerable at last—but he knew that he had just lost something more, as surely as if he had married Judy Jones and seen her fade away before his eyes.
>
> The dream was gone. Something had been taken from him. . . . For he had gone away and he could never go back any more. . . . Even the grief he could have borne was left behind in the country of illusion, of youth . . . where his winter dreams had flourished.
>
> "Long ago," he said, "long ago, there was something in me, but now that thing is gone. . . . I cannot cry. I cannot care. That thing will come back no more."5

As in "Winter Dreams," Fitzgerald gets his feelings of lost youth and beauty into *The Great Gatsby*. He also gets into the novel his sense of social inadequacy and his emotion of hurt when the dream is betrayed by lack of money. "'The whole idea of Gatsby,'" Fitzgerald said, "'is the unfairness of a poor young man not being able to marry a girl with money. This theme comes up again and again because I lived it.'"6

Fitzgerald had almost lost Zelda also because of his lack of money;

but he finally won her. It was the wound over Ginevra that never healed (Fitzgerald described it "as the skin wound on a haemophile"). Fitzgerald kept all of Ginevra's letters to the end of his life. He even had them typed up and bound in a volume that runs 227 pages.

The "dreams" in "Winter Dreams" are an eternal yearning for the promise of summer and the fulfillment of romance. When Fitzgerald lost Ginevra, he came to believe that such yearning was an end in itself; he believed in the need to preserve a romantic state of mind where the imagination and the will are arrested—in a state of suspension—by an idealized concept of beauty and love. The loss creates an eternal striving, and keeps the world beautifully alive.

When Gatsby kisses Daisy his mind "would never romp again," his conception of beauty was fixed, and his will yearned eternally for that beauty. "It is sadder to find the past again," Fitzgerald once wrote, "and find it inadequate to the present than it is to have it elude you and remain forever a harmonious conception of memory."[7]

As long as one cares, the loss can keep the world alive with expectation. Nick Carraway expresses Gatsby's loss of expectation when he surmises that perhaps Gatsby "no longer cared" and if so, then his sky must have suddenly become "unfamiliar," the leaves "frightening," and a rose "grotesque." As Daisy was the source of Gatsby's ideal beauty, Ginevra King was the source of Fitzgerald's. In October of 1937, when he was writing for Hollywood, Fitzgerald went up to Santa Barbara to see Ginevra who was there on a visit. He was overcome with fear because "She was the first girl I ever loved and I have faithfully avoided seeing her up to this moment to keep that illusion perfect."[8]

Fitzgerald saw the need for a "perfect illusion" as part of the creative impulse. In "The Pierian Spring and the Last Straw," an early (1917) short story, the author gets his girl and then no longer feels the need to write. Not only did Ginevra King go into *The Great Gatsby*; she was in many ways part of Fitzgerald's motive for writing the novel in the first place. Is it any wonder that at one point in *The Great Gatsby* Daisy Fay is described as "the king's daughter"?

In the same passage in which Fitzgerald tells us that Jordan Baker is modelled on Edith Cummings, he also tells us that "after careful searching of the files (of a man's mind here) for the Fuller Magee [sic] case and after having Zelda draw pictures until her fingers ache I know Gatsby better than I know my own child."[9] Fitzgerald met Fuller when both were living in Great Neck on Long Island during 1922 and 1923.

The Fuller-McGee case began quietly enough. Tucked away in the November 14 (Tuesday) 1922 issue of the *New York Times* between an item about the annual report of Crucible Steel Company of America and foreign securities was a nine-line item about Edward M. Fuller and William Frank McGee:

> The examination of witnesses at the trial of Edward M. Fuller of the
> bankrupt firm of E. M. Fuller and Co. will begin today in General
> Sessions. William F. McGee, a co-defendant with Fuller, on an indict-
> ment charging bucketing of orders, will have a separate trial. The jury
> in Fuller's case was completed yesterday.[10]

The case came about when Franklin B. Link of Westmoreland, Tennessee charged Fuller and McGee of bucketing his order for $1,500 worth of
Middle States Oil stock. At this point, Fuller and McGee declared bank-
ruptcy. After an examination of the firm's books, the liabilities of Fuller
and McGee were first set at five million dollars and later at slightly less
than two million ($1,888,812).

The Fuller-McGee scheme seems to have worked this way: A. J.
Harold Braid, of the brokerage firm of Braid and Vogel on the New
York Exchange, allowed his name to be used in making stock transactions for which he received two dollars per share of business. An Albert
Biehman, a clerk for Fuller and McGee, would take the prices of stock
from the ticker tape, quote the prices to the customers, take the customers' orders, but never make the transactions to a broker, "bucketing"
the money for Fuller and McGee.

This practice was not new. Since 1917 scores of brokerage firms
had gone bankrupt in New York with liabilities of more than 150 million
dollars. These companies would sell stock on worthless businesses—
especially mineral mines. As long as such "mines" existed and people
were willing to buy their stock, this was not illegal. These same brokerage firms, however, often accepted money on legitimate stock and then
"bucketed"—that is, pocketed—the money and never completed the cus-
tomer's order. This was extremely profitably—and extremely illegal.

The four trials of Fuller and McGee were a series of farces. The
first trial resulted in a hung jury. The second was declared a mistrial
because J. Harold Braid, the state's principal witness, disappeared. The
third trial—in which four witnesses and important documents disappeared
—also resulted in a hung verdict, the grand jury later investigating attempts to bribe one of the jurors. The fourth trial, which resulted in the
conviction of Fuller and McGee, also brought Arnold Rothstein on the
stage when it was learned that Rothstein had "borrowed" $187,000 from
Edward Fuller. Later investigation showed that Rothstein was the man
behind Fuller and McGee from the very beginning.

When the warrants were first issued, and Fuller and McGee were
charged with "bucketing," they could not be found. Arthur Garfield
Hays, in his *City Lawyer*, describes how he was summoned to assist
Fuller and McGee:

> After the bankruptcy of E. M. Fuller and Company, the assets,
> Fuller, and McGee all vanished. A few weeks later a telephone call
> summoned me to a brownstone house of the upper West Side I asked

who lived there. "Arnold Rothstein." . . . . Fuller and McGee were comfortably living in Rothstein's home, waiting for the storm to subside. They were expecting Bill Fallon [another attorney] that afternoon.[11]

Arnold Rothstein, of course, is the model for Meyer Wolfsheim in *The Great Gatsby*. Rothstein had moved from small time gambler to become king of the New York bookmakers, the proprietor of a big gambling hotel, and the owner of a profitable racing stable. He was also the man behind New York bootlegging and behind the bucket shops. He was, furthermore, as Nick Carraway learns about Meyer Wolfsheim, the man who fixed the World Series in 1919. As Nick Carraway had met Meyer Wolfsheim, Fitzgerald had met Rothstein—and the meeting left an indelible impression on his imagination. Fitzgerald recalled in July of 1937:

> In *Gatsby* I selected the stuff to fit a given mood or "hauntedness" or whatever you might call it, rejecting in advance in *Gatsby*, for instance, all of the ordinary material for Long Island, big crooks, adultery theme and always starting from the *small* focal point that impressed me—my own meeting with Arnold Rothstein for instance.[12]

Fitzgerald knew both Rothstein and Fuller, and there is in *The Great Gatsby* the same relationship between Meyer Wolfsheim and his lieutenant, Jay Gatsby, as there was in real life between Rothstein and his lieutenant, Edward Fuller. When Fitzgerald said that Gatsby "started as one man I knew and then changed into myself,"[13] that man was Edward Fuller, Fitzgerald's Great Neck neighbor (just as Nick is Gatsby's West Egg neighbor).

Fitzgerald could depict Gatsby (Fuller) as a bootlegger, since Rothstein (Wolfsheim) controlled New York bootlegging. But Gatsby is more than a bootlegger—and Fitzgerald makes it clear that Gatsby, like Edward Fuller, was in the bond business, a point that most of the critics have never noticed. When Gatsby asks Nick to arrange the meeting with Daisy, he suggests that he can help Nick who is also selling bonds:

> "I carry on a little business on the side, a sort of side line, you understand. And I thought that if you don't make very much—You're selling bonds, aren't you, old sport?"
> "Tryng to."
> "Well, this would interest you. It wouldn't take up much of your time and you might pick up a nice bit of money. It happens to be a rather confidential sort of thing."[14]

When Tom confronts Gatsby at the Plaza hotel, he insinuates that Gatsby's business is more than just bootlegging. "That drug-store business was just small change, continued Tom slowly, 'but you've got something on now that Walter's afraid to tell me about'" (p. 135). And when Nick answers the phone, after Gatsby's death, the unsuspecting caller tells him:

"Young Parke's in trouble," he said rapidly. "They picked him up when he handed the bonds over the counter. They got a circular from New York giving 'em the numbers just five minutes before. What d'you know about that, hey? You never can tell in these hick towns—" (p. 167).

Why Fitzgerald chose to model Gatsby on a crooked stock broker is an interesting question. One answer is that perhaps this was Fitzgerald's private joke—a subtle way of getting back at Charles King and William Mitchell, both of whom were in the bond business. By modelling Gatsby on Edward Fuller, and then by allowing Gatsby to embody many of his own feelings, Fitzgerald was ironically depicting the gap between himself and the Kings-Mitchells. In this way, Jay Gatsby of West Egg becomes comically related to Tom Buchanan of East Egg; one is the ersatz parallel of the other.

In an apprentice story, "The Pierian Springs and the Last Straw" (*Nassau Literary Magazine*, October, 1917), George Rombert has many of the qualities of *both* Jay Gatsby and Tom Buchanan. Like Gatsby, he loses the love of his life when he is betrayed by his "emotional imagination"; and when he loses his girl, time stops: "'When I crossed the threshold,'" he says, "'it was sixteen minutes after ten. At that minute I stopped living.'"[15] Like Buchanan, George Rombert is an overbearing bully. In *The Great Gatsby* Daisy accuses Tom of bruising her finger, and in this early story George Rombert breaks Myra's finger. The narrator of the story, another parallel to *The Great Gatsby*, has the same reservations about George Rombert that Nick Carraway has about Tom Buchanan, and he is not afraid to pass moral judgment: "My Uncle's [George Rombert's] personality had dropped off him like a cloak. He was not the romantic figure of the grill, but a less sure, less attractive and somewhat contemptible individual." Myra's husband, we are told, is a broker—a "crooked broker," according to George Rombert, a "'damn thief that robbed me of everything in this hellish world.'" In "The Pierian Springs and the Last Straw" we have the germ of Jay Gatsby and Tom Buchanan—and the theme of the "crooked broker." Fitzgerald later gave Tom and Gatsby separate qualities—modelling Gatsby on Edward Fuller, and Tom on William Mitchell-Charles King. His models, however, were all brokers; and in *The Great Gatsby* there is an amusing although slightly hidden, relationship between Gatsby and Tom Buchanan—both were at least in conception, "crooked brokers." The broker will steal the object of love in Fitzgerald's late as well as early fiction. Tommy Barban, who takes Nicole Warren away from Dick Diver in *Tender Is the Night*, is among other things, a broker.

Fitzgerald also saw that Edward Fuller's social position was a kind of grotesque embodiment of his own. He was rejected by Ginevra for being socially inferior. Fitzgerald extended the difference between himself and Ginevra by making Gatsby into the essence of the social impostor. At one point in *The Great Gatsby*, when Daisy seems about ready to leave Tom for Gatsby, they hear—ironically enough—the chords of Mendelssohn's Wedding March from the ballroom of the Plaza hotel. Daisy suddenly remembers a man named Biloxi who fainted at their wedding, and they discover that each thought that the other knew him. Biloxi, in fact, told Daisy that he was president of Tom's class at Yale. Biloxi, the impostor, embodies the very spirit of Gatsby in the world of Tom Buchanan. Tom, in fact, asks Gatsby if he went to Oxford "about the time Biloxi went to New Haven" (p. 129). Biloxi, like Gatsby, is an exaggerated expression of Fitzgerald's own feelings with the high rich of Lake Forest and elsewhere.

Fitzgerald was doing something in *The Great Gatsby* that he had not done before. He was pushing his sense of experience away from the middle ground of verisimilitude toward extremes—toward two kinds of distortions. The dreamer distorted becomes Gatsby—a man whose hopelessly vulgar taste allows an eternal yearning for a meretricious beauty. The rich man distorted becomes Tom Buchanan—a man whose ruthlessness preserves his worldly comfort, and whose shoddy ideas keep intact his sense of superiority. Both Gatsby and Tom Buchanan are men without conscience. Gatsby is just as intent on taking Daisy from Tom as Tom is on keeping Daisy from Gatsby. Both caricature Fitzgerald's own experience—his own sense of combat: the dreamer in conflict with a rigid reality; the promises of youth in conflict with the ravages of time; and the man of suspect means in conflict with the established rich.

Fitzgerald wrote out of his own sense of experience as openly in *The Great Gatsby* as he did in his earlier novels; but never before was he able to transmogrify that experience into forms that carried it beyond its own literal meaning—and never before was Fitzgerald able to use irony and descriptive detail to plumb the complexity of this life and to control his tendency to sentimentalize. *The Great Gatsby* is the most pure product of Fitzgerald's imagination that we have, a novel in which experience is metamorphosized—heightened and extended—and at the same time brilliantly under control.

Notes

1. *The Letters of F. Scott Fitzgerald*, ed. Andrew Turnbull (New York: Scribner's, 1963), p. 173.

2. "A Woman with a Past," *Saturday Evening Post*, September 6, 1930; reprinted in *Taps at Reveille* (New York: Scribner's, 1935), p. 193. All further quotations from this story will be cited to this edition, page reference indicated in brackets after the quote.

3. Fitzgerald's Ledger, p. 70. The total context of these quotes as they appear in the Ledger are as follows: "Aug 1916—Lake Forest. Peg Carry. Petting Party.

Ginevra Party. The bad day at the McCormicks. The dinner at Pegs. Disapoint-ment. Mary Birlard Pierce. Little Marjorie King [Ginevra's sister] & her smile. Beautiful Billy Mitchell [whom Ginevra eventually married]. Peg Carry stands straight. "'Poor boys shouldn't think of marrying rich girls."

4. Mrs. Marjorie King Belden, Ginevra's sister, told me (February 21, 1965) that there were abrasive feelings between Fitzgerald and Charles King.

5. "Winter Dreams," *Metropolitan Magazine*, December, 1922; reprinted in *All the Sad Young Men* (New York: Scribner's, 1926), p. 90. All further quotations from this story will be cited to this edition, page reference indicated in brackets after the quote.

6. Andrew Turnbull, *Scott Fitzgerald* (New York: Scribner's 1962), p. 150.

7. "Show Mr. and Mrs. F. to Number—," *Esquire*, May–June, 1934; reprinted in *The Crack-Up*, p. 50.

8. *Letters*, p. 19. This experience later became the basis for the story "Three Hours Between Planes," published in *Esquire*, July of 1941, and reprinted in *The Stories of F. Scott Fitzgerald*, pp. 464–69.

9. *Letters*, p. 173. For another possible source, see Matthew J. Bruccoli, "'How Are You and the Family Old Sport?'—Gerlach and Gatsby," *Fitzgerald/Hemingway Annual 1975* (Englewood, Colorado: Microcard Editions, 1975), pp. 33–36.

10. *New York Times*, November 14, 1922, p. 31:2.

11. Arthur Garfield Hays, *City Lawyer* (New York: Simon and Schuster, 1942).

12. *Letters*, p. 551.

13. *Ibid.*, p. 358.

14. F. Scott Fitzgerald, *The Great Gatsby* (New York: Charles Scribner's Sons, 1953), p. 83. All further quotations are from this edition, page reference indicated in brackets after the quote.

15. *The Apprentice Fiction of F. Scott Fitzgerald 1909–1917*, ed. John Kuehl (New Brunswick: Rutgers University Press, 1965), p. 170. All further quotations from this story will be cited to this edition, page reference indicated in brackets after the quote. John Kuehl has discussed the theme of unrequited love in this story and *The Great Gatsby* and compared George Rombert to Tom Buchanan. Cf. "A Note on the Begetting of Gatsby," *University: A Princeton Magazine*, No. 21 (Summer, 1964), pp. 26–32.

The Artist at Work

Theme and Texture in
The Great Gatsby

W. J. Harvey*

Criticism of *The Great Gatsby*, when it has not been sidetracked
into biography or reminiscence of the Jazz Age, has tended to concentrate on two issues. The first of these has been concerned with the
moral seriousness of the book, with what answer, if any, can be given
to the hostile critic of whom John Farelly, writing in *Scrutiny*, is a
good example:

> I want to suggest that there is an emptiness in his ·work that makes
> "convincing analysis" honestly difficult, but leaves a hollow space
> where critics can create their own substitute Fitzgerald. And I should
> probe for that hollow space in what we call the *centre* of a writer's
> work—that around which and with reference to which he organizes
> his experiences; in short, his values.[1]

Closely related to this is the problem of what status we should allow
Gatsby himself; in particular, we may note the attempt to see him as
a mythic character and the novel as the expression of some deep-rooted
and recurrent "American Dream."[2]

The first of these questions has been exhaustively debated and if
neither side has much shaken the other's conviction, the issues are at
least clearly defined; while anyone who is not an American will feel a
natural diffidence about expressing any opinion on the second topic.
In fact, what immediately impresses itself upon most readers—espec-
cially if they have come to *The Great Gatsby* after reading Fitzgerald's
earlier novels—is not moral theme or national archetype but something
much simpler, something so obvious, perhaps, that it has received
remarkably little close critical attention. I mean the astonishing accession of technical power and skill. Less pretentious than his earlier work,

*Reprinted from *English Studies*, 38 (February 1957), 12–20, by permission of
Swets Publishing Service.

The Great Gatsby achieves much more; in it Fitzgerald discovers not only his true subject but a completely adequate form. To say this, no doubt, is to say also that he has attained a maturity that transcends the merely aesthetic, that reveals itself also in the moral implications of the fable.

Nearly every critic of *The Great Gatsby* has stressed the tremendous structural importance of the narrator, Nick Carraway, the character through whom Fitzgerald is able to achieve that aesthetic distance from his own experience necessary for firmness of control and clarity of perception, through whom he he can express that delicately poised ambiguity of moral vision, the sense of being "within and without, simultaneously enchanted and repelled by the inexhaustible variety of life" out of which insight into the truth of things must grow. William Troy has summed it up neatly and concisely:

> In the earlier books author and hero tended to melt into one another because there was no internal principle of differentiation by which they might be separated; they respired in the same climate, emotional and moral; they were tarred with the same brush. But in *Gatsby* is achieved a dissociation, by which Fitzgerald was able to isolate one part of himself, the spectatorial or esthetic, and also the more intelligent and responsible, in the person of the ordinary but quite sensible narrator, from another part of himself, the dream-ridden romantic adolescent from St. Paul and Princeton, in the person of the legendary Jay Gatsby.[3]

Again, most critics of the novel have amply demonstrated its economy, the clarity of its narrative outline and the forceful, unbroken drive of it forward from the first page to the last, an impetus which incorporates, and even gains momentum from, the cunningly interpolated flashbacks. Many critics have expanded and expounded the significance of the major symbolic structures of the book; indeed, to insist upon its legendary nature is to insist upon these. What more, then, can be said about the mastery of Fitzgerald's technique; what aspect of it has received less than its fair share of attention?

I should like, quite simply, to discuss the language of the book. Here we find, co-existing with economy, clarity and force, an extreme density of texture. It is this which ultimately gives richness and depth to the novel, this without which the larger symbols would lose their power of reverberating in the reader's mind and the major themes of the book would seem intellectual or emotional gestures, without the pressure of felt and imaginatively experienced life behind them.

We may best begin with a fairly detailed analysis of one passage; my aim here will be to show that textural detail is not merely local in its point and effect but relates to the central themes and dominant moral attitudes expressed in the book. Analysis of prose is always liable to be

cumbrous and clumsy but this very clumsiness is an oblique tribute to
the dexterity and economy with which Fitzgerald achieves his effects.
I take as my example a passage dealing with the end of the first of
Gatsby's parties to be described in the book. The glamour and enchantment of the party, so brilliantly evoked by Fitzgerald, has here
dissolved; the intoxication of night and music, champagne and youth,
has vanished and the scene is closed by a dismal return to the world of
sober reality, or more precisely, to the disenchanted world of the
hangover. The party is over; it is time to go home. Here is the passage:

> I looked around. *Most of the remaining women were now having
> fights with men said to be their husbands.* (1) Even Jordan's party,
> the quartet from East Egg, were rent asunder by dissension. *One of
> the men was talking with curious intensity to a young actress,* (2)
> and his wife, after attempting to laugh at the situation in a dignified
> and indifferent way, broke down entirely and resorted to flank at-
> tacks—at interval she appeared suddenly at his side like an angry
> diamond, and hissed "You promised!" into his ear.
>
> The reluctance to go home was not confined to wayward men. *The
> hall was at present occupied by two deplorably sober men and their
> highly indignant wives.* (3) The wives were sympathizing with each
> other in slightly raised voices.
>
> "Whenever he sees I'm having a good time he wants to go home."
> "Never heard anything so selfish in my life."
> "We're always the first ones to leave."
> "So are we."
> "Well, we're almost the last tonight," said one of the men sheepishly.
> "The orchestra left half an hour ago."
>
> *In spite of the wives' agreement that such malevolence was beyond
> credibility, the dispute ended in a short struggle, and both wives were
> lifted, kicking, into the night.* (4) (p. 52)

At first we might seem to be concerned with a piece of merely slick,
glossy writing; the simile, *like an angry diamond*, is perhaps a little too
smart, a little too consciously clever and contrived; it trembles on the
verge of preciosity. But leaving this aside, we may see how most of the
main themes are touched on tangentially in what appear to be superficial and cynical comments. I wish to concentrate on the four short
passages I have, for convenient reference, italicized and numbered.

(1) This sentence apart from the obvious implication about the
sexual morality of such a society, relates as well to the rootlessness and
transience of these people, the lack of any stable relationship—a point
I shall discuss later. It is also one strand in the complex network of
gossip, rumour and innuendo which fills the whole book.

(2) Here, the intensity is in one sense anything but curious; the relationship implied is obvious; but in another sense the intensity *is*
curious in that this is a society which is flippant and cynical, gay and

hedonistic, but definitely not intense in its feeling for anyone or anything; as such, it contrasts with the real intensity of the outsider who is its host, with the passion of Gatsby's dream of Daisy.

(3) Here Fitzgerald is employing a common satirical device; he is enforcing his morality by pretending to accept its opposite as the norm—sobriety becomes deplorable. Further, however, the syntactical balance of the sentence leads us to infer a casual relationship between the balanced parts—the wives are indignant because the men are sober Fitzgerald often uses, namely, his method of making his point by simple juxtaposition without any comment. It is a method akin to Pope's in, for example, the often-quoted line:

> Puffs, powders, patches, Bibles, billets-doux.

In a catalogue like this each object assumes an equal status, and the fact that a bible may be seen as sharing the importance or triviality of its context is comment enough on the society in which such an equivalence can be contemplated. So in Fitzgerald. For example, we are told that Tom and Daisy drifted around "wherever people played polo and were rich together." There, the juxtaposition of playing a game and being wealthy indicates the superficiality and frivolity of the rich. One finds a rather different effect achieved when Fitzgerald describes Gatsby's party: "In his blue gardens men and girls came and went like moths among the whisperings and the champagne *and the stars*," where the phrase I have italicized illuminates by contrast the transience and evanescence of the whisperings, champagne and the moth-like men and girls.

(4) Here Fitzgerald achieves yet another effect, this time by a contrast of diction. The first half of the sentence, with its polysyllabic abstraction, approaches the inflation of mock-heroic; it is promptly deflated by the abrupt, racy description of action in the second half of the sentence.

Such analysis may seem to be breaking a butterfly upon a wheel, but the fact that it is so laboured is merely the result of trying to bring to a conscious formulation something that we respond to immediately and unconsciously in our casual reading of the novel. But it will have served its purpose if it helps to show that beneath the gaiety and wit of his prose Fitzgerald is maintaining a light but insistent moral pressure and is guiding and preparing our attitudes and responses so that we shall make a correct evaluation when the need arises. All this is done through his manipulation of the point of view afforded us by the narrator, Nick Carraway, who acts as the moral seismograph of the novel's uneasiness, premonitory quakings and final eruption into catastrophe.

We may extend this analysis by noticing how key phrases are repeated subtly but insistently and how the work is so admirably organized, so intact as well as compact, that any one of these phrases inevitably leads to another and then to another, so that wherever the reader enters the book—whatever aspect of it he chooses to emphasize—his attention is engaged in a series of ever-widening perspectives until the whole of the novel is encompassed. Let us take, quite arbitrarily, the word *restless*; if we follow up this tiny and apparently insignificant verbal clue we shall find that it leads us swiftly and decisively to the heart of the book. Any one of a dozen other starting-points would do the same. Consider these examples:

(a) Of Nick: "A little later I participated in that delayed Teutonic migration known as the Great War. I enjoyed the counter-raid so thoroughly that I came back restless." (p. 3)

(b) Of Tom, surveying his Long Island estate: " 'I've got a nice place here,' he said, his eyes flashing about restlessly." Later he is seen "hovering restlessly about the room." (pp. 7, 10)

(c) Of Jordan Baker: "Her body asserted itself with a restless movement of her knee, and she stood up." (p. 18)

These instances of our chosen key-word, all occurring within the first twenty pages of the novel, are complicated and supplemented by other phrases suggesting sudden movement, either jerky and impulsive, as of Tom:

Wedging his tense arm imperatively under mine, Tom Buchanan compelled me from the room as though he were moving a checker to another square. (pp. 11–12)

or by contrast, of Jordan:

She yawned and with a series of rapid, deft movements stood up into the room. (p. 11)

We may notice again how Fitzgerald often obtains his local effects; how in the second example the unusual preposition *into* gives a peculiar force to the sentence, how, in the description of Tom, the word *imperatively* interacts with the word *compelled* so that the latter also contains the sense of *impels* and how the simile of checkers gives one the sense of manipulation, a sense which expands into the whole complex of human relationships, plots, intrigues and dreams that fills the novel.

In this context, repose is seen as a strained effort, the result of which is precarious; thus Jordan

was extended full length at her end of the divan, completely motionless, and with her chin raised a little, as if she were balancing something on it which was quite likely to fall. (p. 8)

Even the house seems unable to stay still:

A breeze blew through the room, blew curtains in at one end and out the other like pale flags, twisting them up toward the frosted wedding-

cake of the ceiling, and then *rippled over the wine-coloured rug,
making a shadow on it as wind does on the sea.* (p. 8)

The only completely stationary object in the room was an enormous
couch on which two young women *were buoyed up,* as though upon
an *anchored* balloon. They were both in white, and their dresses were
rippling and fluttering as though they had just been blown back in
after a short flight around the house. I must have stood for a few
minutes listening to the whip and snap of the curtains and the
groan of a picture on the wall. (p. 8)

In this passage one verbal trail intersects another and it is by this
continual criss-cross of phrases and images that Fitzgerald achieves the
effect I have already mentioned of a widening perspective. The image
here, submerged beneath the surface elaboration of the prose and
coming out in the phrases I have italicized is not, as one might expect,
of flight but rather one of ships and the sea; a complicated image, a
double exposure, so to speak, in which the whole house is seen as a
ship groaning in the wind, with its flags flying, and at the same time
in which the divan is a kind of ship within ships, upon the wine-coloured
sea of the rug. The connecting link between the two aspects of the
image is, of course, the activity and effect of the wind; both curtains
and dresses ripple. There is a great deal that could be said about this
kind of submerged activity in the novel to which we respond unconsciously in a casual nonanalytical reading of it; for the moment, however, I am concerned only to note how the idea of restlessness is linked
with the idea of the sea. We will return to this connection shortly: we
may first notice how this restlessness expands and fills the opening of
the book, especially the scene of the first dinner party at the Buchanans.

The dinner begins quietly enough "with a bantering inconsequence
that was never quite chatter" but the inconsequence is soon out of control; people are continually interrupting each other, changing the subject,
Tom becomes vehement. Daisy is possessed by "turbulent emotions,"
the air is full of whispers, implications, innuendos, people are always
shifting around, the "shrill metallic urgency" of the telephone is never
absent for long. The following passage is a good example of the general
atmosphere:

Miss Baker and I exchanged a short glance consciously devoid of
meaning. I was about to speak when she sat up alertly and said
"Sh!" in a warning voice. A subdued impassioned murmur was
audible in the room beyond, and Miss Baker leaned forward unashamed, trying to hear. The murmur trembled on the verge of coherence, sank down, mounted excitedly and then ceased altogether.
(p. 15)

This atmosphere is most completely expressed in Nick's feeling about
Daisy:

as though the whole evening had been a trick of some sort to exact a contributory emotion from me. I waited, and sure enough, in a moment she looked at me with an absolute smirk on her lovely face, as if she had asserted her membership in a rather distinguished secret society to which she and Tom belonged. (p. 18)

Just as this passage anticipates the moment after the catastrophe when Daisy and Tom look as though they are conspiring together, so the whole scene prepares us for the picture of Tom's affair with Mrs. Wilson which by its squalor, its triviality, its commonplaceness is a preparatory contrast with the naive grandeur of Gatsby's schemes to meet Daisy once again. The atmosphere of the dinner, as I have tried to describe it, is thus established as part of the emotional and moral climate of the whole book. But it is much more than mere scene-setting; let us follow out a little further some of the implications of the restlessness motif. Ultimately this derives from the rootlessness of those people; they are strangers not only to their own country but also to their past. They live in houses that may be palaces but are certainly not homes; their intellectual ideas are shoddy and their moral attitudes to life are at best the detritus of a collapsed social framework, second-hand and conventionally assumed, so that Nick is tempted to laugh at Tom's abrupt "transition from libertine to prig" while the most he can find to admire is the "hardy scepticism" of Jordan Baker.

All the implications of this rootlessness radiate from another key-word, *drifting*, and we may notice how Fitzgerald, early in the book, links this idea with the idea of restlessness, when he writes of Daisy and Tom:

Why they came East I don't know. They had spent a year in France for no particular reason, and then drifted here and there unrestfully wherever people played polo and were rich together. (p. 6)

Each example of this kind of thing, when taken in isolation, may seem neutral, empty of metaphorical richness, but the interaction of these two ideas is so insistent that each tiny accretion of phrase and image builds up a powerful cumulative charge. We have already seen the image of the sea at work beneath a passage of descriptive prose, but it extends with a deceptive casualness throughout the whole book; at Gatsby's parties Nick notes "the sea-change of faces and voices and color" and is "rather ill at ease among swirls and eddies of people"; at these parties Tom says one meets "all kinds of crazy fish" and later protests that people will "throw everything overboard." Examples could be multiplied but we need only notice the recurrence of the metaphors of sea, drifting and voyaging in two crucial passages. The first is towards the end of Nick's prefatory comments:

No—Gatsby turned out all right at the end; it is what preyed on Gatsby, what foul dust floated in the wake of his dreams that temporarily closed out my interest in the aborted sorrows and short-winded elations of men. (p. 2)

and in the very last words of the book: "So we beat on, boats against the current, borne back ceaselessly into the past."

I would like to suggest that far below the surface of *The Great Gatsby*—below the particular interest of the narrative, below Fitzgerald's analysis of society, below even the allegedly "mythic" qualities of the book—is a potent cliché, a commonplace of universal human experience to which we all respond. To say one of the bases of the novel is a cliché is not to dispraise Fitzgerald—most great art is built upon similar platitudes and it is probably why the novel is alive for another age than Fitzgerald's and for non-Americans—what we should admire is the way in which he has refreshed the cliché, given it a new accession of life in his story. The cliché I refer to is easily summed up; in the words of a popular hymn it is this:

> Time, like an ever-rolling stream,
> Bears all its sons away;
> They fly forgotten, as a dream
> Dies at the opening day.

The simple truth of this fact of life is everywhere implicit in the texture of the novel, and sometimes it is more than implicit. The appropriateness of the way in which Nick records the names of all those people who went to Gatsby's house that summer has often been remarked:

> Once I wrote down on the empty spaces of a time-table the names
> of those who came to Gatsby's house that summer. It is an old
> time-table now, disintegrating at its folds, and headed "This schedule
> in effect July 5th, 1922." (p. 61)

There could be no more decorous memorial to those "men and girls" who "came and went like moths among the whisperings and the champagne and the stars."

It is essential to Gatsby's tragic illusion, his belief in "the unreality of reality; a promise that the rock of the world was founded securely on a fairy's wing," that he should deny this fact of life and try to make the ever rolling stream flow back up-hill.

> "I wouldn't ask too much of her," I ventured. "You can't repeat
> the past."
> "Can't repeat the past?" he cried incredulously. "Why of course
> you can!" (p. 111)

It is not insignificant that Nick should be so acutely aware of the passing of time, while in this context Gatsby's apology, "I'm sorry about the clock" acquires a new level of unconscious ironic meaning. This has been stressed often enough before; the point I wish to make is that the theme, basic to *The Great Gatsby*, is not merely adumbrated, is not merely translated into terms of narrative and character, but is also expressed in the very texture of the prose, in the phrases and images, for example, which centre on words like *restless* and *drifting*. Thus the moral attitude of Nick is conveyed in precisely these terms. We may note in passing that Nick is not the fixed, static point of view some critics have supposed him; he is not the detached observer but is deeply implicated in the story he is telling and his attitude evolves and changes as the story progresses; in a sense what *The Great Gatsby* is about is what happens to Nick. At the outset he "began to like New York, the racy adventurous feel of it at night, and the satisfaction that the constant flicker of men and women and machines gives to the restless eye." The attractiveness and glamour of Gatsby's parties needs no stressing but Nick begins to feel oppressed and uneasy at the "many-coloured, many-keyed commotion." And his reaction after the catastrophe is naturally expressed in an antithesis to the terms already established: "When I came back from the East last autumn I felt that I wanted the world to be in uniform and at a sort of moral attention forever" (p. 2).

Similarly, the ambiguity of Gatsby himself comes over to us in these terms. He is not the simple antithesis of Tom and Daisy; he is implicated in their kind of corruption too, and his dream is proved hollow not only by the inadequacy of the actual correlative—that is, Daisy— to the hunger of his aspiring imagination, but also by the means he uses to build up the gaudy fabric of his vision. He, too, shares in the restlessness of the actual world which will defeat his ideal Platonic conceptions:

> This quality was continually breaking through his punctilious manner in the shape of restlessness. He was never quite still; there was always a tapping foot somewhere or the impatient opening and closing of a hand. (p. 64)

and a little later he tells Nick:

> "You see, I usually find myself among strangers because I drift here and there trying to forget the sad thing that happened to me." (p. 64)

This note of drifting is frequently reiterated in connection with Gatsby but it does not, as in the case of Daisy and Tom, remain unqualified; Gatsby comes out all right at the end. What we remember about him is not the restlessness or the drifting but "an unbroken series of successful gestures," Gatsby standing in the moonlight outside the Buchanans' house, rapt in "the sacredness of the vigil"; Gatsby in his own temple-cum-roadhouse between "the great doors, endowing with complete isolation the figure of the host, who stood on the porch, his hand up in a formal gesture of farewell," or above all, Gatsby stretching out his arms towards the green light that is the vain promise of his future. We remember these formal poses as something theatrical or religious, but they *are* poses, moments of suspended time, something static and as such are the stylistic equivalents of Gatsby's attempt to impose his dream upon reality, his effort to make the ever-rolling stream stand still. We remember Gatsby not as drifting but as voyaging to some end and it is this sense, hinted at all the way through the book, which gives impetus to that imaginative leap whereby we encompass the ironic contrast between Gatsby and Columbus or those Dutch sailors in that moment when "man must have held his breath in the presence of this continent, compelled into aesthetic contemplation he neither understood nor desired, face to face for the last time in history with something commensurate to his capacity for wonder" (p. 182).

Thus, starting with the idea of restlessness and going by way of its enlargement into the idea of drifting we are brought to face the largest issues that the novel propounds. This is, of course, not the only—or even the most important—strand in the textural pattern of the whole; any one of a dozen other starting points might have been taken—the contrast between East and West, for example, the subtle choreography of the terms *reality* and *unreality*, the functional role of the machine which enlarges to provide metaphors, for the emotional and moral life, the religious overtones that some critics have noted, or the ideas of money and value. All of these combine and interact to give *The Great Gatsby* its satisfying depth and richness of suggestion without which the themes so often abstracted for discussion would lack both definition and reverberant power and the novel would fail to achieve that quality which Mark Schorer has described as "language as used to create a certain texture and tone which in themselves state and define themes and meanings; or language, the counters of our ordinary speech, as forced, through conscious manipulation, into all those larger meanings which our ordinary speech almost never intends."[4]

Notes

1. John Farelly, "Scott Fitzgerald: Another View," *Scrutiny*, 18 (1952), 266–72.
2. For example, Edwin S. Fussell, "Fitzgerald's Brave New World," *English Literary History*, 19 (1952), 291–306.
3. William Troy, "Scott Fitzgerald—The Authority of Failure," *Accent*, 6 (1945), 56–60.
4. Mark Schorer, "Technique as Discovery," *Hudson Review*, 1 (1948), 67–87.

The Craft of Revision:
The Great Gatsby
Kenneth E. Eble*

"With the aid you've given me," Fitzgerald wrote Maxwell Perkins in December, 1924, "I can make *Gatsby* perfect."[1] Fitzgerald had sent the manuscript of the novel to Scribner's in late October, but the novel achieved its final form only after extensive revisions Fitzgerald made in the next four months. The pencil draft and the much revised galley proofs now in the Fitzgerald collection at Princeton library show how thoroughly and expertly Fitzgerald practiced the craft of revision.[2]

I

The pencil draft both reveals and masks Fitzgerald's struggles. The manuscript affords a complete first version, but the pages are not numbered serially from beginning to end, nor are the chapters and sections of chapters all tied together. There are three segments (one a copy of a previous draft) designated "Chapter II," two marked "Chapter VI." The amount of revising varies widely from page to page and chapter to chapter; the beginning and end are comparatively clean, the middle most cluttered. Fitzgerald's clear, regular hand, however, imposes its own sense of order throughout the text. For all the revisions, the script goes about its business with a straightness of line, a regularity of letter that approaches formal elegance. When he is striking out for the first time, the writing tends to be large, seldom exceeding eight words per line or twenty-five lines per page. When he is copying or reworking from a previous draft, the writing becomes compressed—but never crabbed—and gets half again as much on a page.

An admirer of Fitzgerald—of good writing, for that matter—reads the draft with a constant sense of personal involvement, a sensation of small satisfied longings as the right word gets fixed in place, a feeling of strain when the draft version hasn't yet found its perfection of phrase, and a nagging sense throughout of how precariously the writer dangles between the almost and the attained. "All good writing," Fitzgerald wrote his daughter, "is *swimming under water* and holding your breath."[3]

At the beginning of the draft, there appears to have been little gasping for air. There at the outset, virtually as published, is that fine set piece which establishes the tone of the novel with the creation of Nick Carraway and his heightened sense of the fundamental decencies. As one reads the first chapter, however, the satisfaction of seeing the right beginning firmly established soon changes to surprise. The last page of the novel—"gradually I became aware of the old island here that flowered

*Reprinted from *American Literature*, 36 (November 1964), 315–26, by permission of the publisher. © 1964, Duke University Press, Durham, N.C.).

once for Dutch sailors' eyes—a fresh, green breast of the new world."[4] was originally written as the conclusion of Chapter I. Some time before the draft went into the submission copy, Fitzgerald recognized that the passage was too good for a mere chapter ending, too definitive of the larger purposes of the book, to remain there. By the time the pencil draft was finished, that memorable paragraph had been put into its permanent place, had fixed the image of man holding his breath in the presence of the continent, "face to face for the last time in history with something commensurate to his capacity for wonder."

The three paragraphs which come immediately after, the last paragraphs of the novel, grew out of one long fluid sentence which was originally the final sentence of Chapter I in the draft: "And as I sat there brooding on the old unknown world I too held my breath and waited, until I could feel the motion of America as it turned through the hours—my own blue lawn and the tall incandescent city on the water and beyond that, the dark fields of the republic rolling on under the night." Fitzgerald expanded this suggestion into a full paragraph, crossed out the first attempt, and then rewrote it into three paragraphs on the final page of the draft. There, almost as it appears in the novel, is the green light on Daisy's dock ("green glimmer" in the draft), the orgiastic future (written "orgastic"),[5] and that ultimate sentence, "So we beat on, a boat [changed to "boats"] against the current, borne back ceaselessly into the past." So the draft ends, the last lines written in a "bold, swooping hand," as Fitzgerald described Gatsby's signature, a kind of autograph for the completed work.

The green light (there were originally two) came into the novel at the time of Daisy's meeting with Gatsby. "If it wasn't for the mist," he tells her, "we could see your house across the bay. You always have two green lights that burn all night at the end of your dock." Fitzgerald not only made the green light a central image of the final paragraph, but he went back to the end of the first chapter and added it there: "Involuntarily I glanced seaward—and distinguished nothing except a single green light, minute and far away, that might have been the end of a dock" (pp. 21–22).

II

Throughout the pencil draft, Fitzgerald made numerous revisions which bring out his chief traits as a reviser: he seldom threw anything good away, and he fussed endlessly at getting right things in the right places. The two parties at Gatsby's house, interesting as illustrations of Fitzgerald's mastery of the "scenic method," are equally interesting as examples of how he worked.

The purpose of the first party as it appears in the draft (Chapter

III in the book) was chiefly that of creating the proper atmosphere. Though Gatsby makes his first appearance in this section, it is Gatsby's world that most glitters before our eyes. The eight servants (there were only seven in the draft), the five crates (only three in the draft) of oranges and lemons, the caterers spreading the canvas, the musicians gathering, the Rolls-Royce carrying party-goers from the city, are the kind of atmospherics Fitzgerald could always do well. The party itself as it unfolds in the draft reveals a number of intentions that Fitzgerald abandoned as he saw the possibilities of making the party vital to the grander design of the novel.

Originally, whether from strong feelings or in response to his readers' expectations, he took pains to bring out the wild and shocking lives being lived by many of Gatsby's guests. Drug addiction was apparently commonplace, and even more sinister vices were hinted at. A good deal of undergraduate party chatter was also cut from the draft. What a reader of the novel now remembers is what Fitzgerald brought into sharp relief by cutting out the distracting embellishments. "The Jazz History of the World" by Vladimir Tostoff (it was "Leo Epstien" [sic] originally; Fitzgerald deleted a number of "Jewish" remarks from the draft) was described in full. When Fitzgerald saw the galleys he called the whole episode "rotten" and reduced the page-and-a-half description to a single clause: "The nature of Mr. Tostoff's composition eluded me. . . . (p. 50). By the time the party scene had been cut and reworked, almost all that remained was the introduction of Gatsby's physical presence into the novel and the splendid scene of Owl-Eyes in Gatsby's high Gothic library.

Among the many excisions in this party scene, one seemed far too good to throw away. In the draft, it began when Jordan Baker exchanges a barbed remark with another girl.

> "You've dyed your hair since then," remarked Miss Baker and I started but the girls had moved casually on and were talking to an elaborate orchid of a woman who sat in state under a white plum tree.
>
> "Do you see who that is?" demanded Jordan Baker interestly. [I use Fitzgerald's spelling here and elsewhere in quoting from the draft.]
>
> Suddenly I did see, with the peculiar unreal feeling which accompanies the recognition of a hitherto ghostly celebrity of the movies.
>
> "The man with her is her director," she continued. "He's just been married."
>
> "To her?"
>
> "No."
>
> She laughed. The director was bending over his pupil so eagerly that his chin and her mettalic black hair were almost in juxtaposition.
>
> "I hope he doesn't slip," she added. "And spoil her hair."

> It was still twilight but there was already a moon, produced no doubt like the turkey and the salad out of a caterer's basket. With her hard, slender golden arm drawn through mine we decended the steps. . . .

It is a fine scene, and the girl with the dyed hair, the moon, and the caterer's basket can be found on page 43 of the novel, so smoothly joined together that no one could suspect, much less mourn, the disappearance of that "elaborate orchid" of a woman. But, of course, she did not disappear. The scene was merely transported to the second party where the actress defined the second party as Owl-Eyes defined the first:

> "Perhaps you know that lady," Gatsby indicated a gorgeous, scarcely human orchid of a woman who sat in state under a white-plum tree. Tom and Daisy stared, with that peculiarly unreal feeling that accompanies the recognition of a hitherto ghostly celebrity of the movies.
> "She's lovely," said Daisy.
> "The man bending over her is her director." (p. 106)

Two pages later, at the end of the second party, we see her again:

> It was like that. Almost the last thing I remember was standing with Daisy and watching the moving-picture director and his Star. They were still under the white-plum tree and their faces were touching except for a pale, thin ray of moonlight between. It occurred to me that he had been very slowly bending toward her all evening to attain this proximity, and even while I watched I saw him stoop one ultimate degree and kiss at her cheek.
> "I like her," said Daisy, "I think she's lovely."
> But the rest offended her. . . . (p. 108)

One can almost see the writer's mind in action here. The scene was first created, almost certainly, from the rightness of having a "ghostly celebrity of the movies" at the party. It first served merely as scenery and as a way of hinting at the moral laxity of Gatsby's guests. The need to compress and focus probably brought Fitzgerald to consider cutting it out entirely though it was obviously too good to throw away. By that time, perhaps, the second party scene had been written, another possibility had been opened up. Maybe at once, maybe slowly, Fitzgerald recognized that the scene could be used to capture Daisy's essential aloofness which was to defy even Gatsby's ardor. It may well be that this developed and practiced ability to use everything for its maximum effect, to strike no note, so to speak, without anticipating all its vibrations, is what separates Fitzgerald's work in *The Great Gatsby* from his earlier writing, what makes it seem such a leap from his first novels.

Among the many lessons Fitzgerald applied between the rough draft and the finished novel was that of cutting and setting his diamonds so that they caught up and cast back a multitude of lights. In so doing, he found it unnecessary to have an authorial voice gloss a scene. The brilliance floods in upon the reader; there is no necessity for Nick Carraway to say, as he did at one point in the pencil draft: "I told myself that I was studying it all like a philosopher, a sociologist, that there was a unity here that I could grasp after or would be able to grasp in a minute, a new facet, elemental and profound." The distance Fitzgerald traveled from *This Side of Paradise* and *The Beautiful and Damned* to *The Great Gatsby* is in the rewriting of the novel. There the sociologist and philosopher were at last controlled and the writer assumed full command.

III

Rewriting was important to Fitzgerald because, like many other good writers, he had to see his material assume its form—not in the *idea* of a character or a situation—but in the way character and situation and all the rest got down on paper. Once set down, they began to shape everything else in the novel, began to raise the endless questions of emphasis, balance, direction, unity, impact.

The whole of Chaper II in the finished novel (Chapter III in the draft) is an illustration of how the material took on its final form. That chapter begins with Dr. T. J. Eckleburg's eyes brooding over the ash heaps and culminates in the quarrel in Myrtle's apartment where "making a short deft movement, Tom Buchanan broke her nose with his open hand." Arthur Mizener first pointed out that the powerful symbol introduced in the chapter—Dr. Eckleburg's eyes—was the result of Fitzgerald's seeing a dust jacket portraying Daisy's eyes brooding over an amusement park world. "For Christ's sake," he wrote to Perkins, "don't give anyone that jacket you're saving for me. I've written it into the book."[6] The pencil draft indicates that the chapter—marked Chapter III in the manuscript—was written at a different period of time from that of the earlier chapters. The consecutive numbering of the first sixty-two pages of the novel (the first two chapters) shows that for a long time Fitzgerald intended Chapter II as it now stands in the novel to be the third chapter.

In substance, the chapter remained much the same in the finished novel as it was in the draft. But, in addition to moving the chapter forward, Fitzgerald transposed to the next chapter a four-page section at the end describing Nick's activities later in the summer. Summing up Nick's character at the end of the third chapter gave more point to his concluding remark: "I am one of the few honest ["decent" in the draft] people that I have ever known" (p. 60). Bringing the Eckleburg chapter forward meant that the reader could never travel to or from Gatsby's house without traversing the valley of ashes. And ending the second chapter where it now ends meant that the reader could never get to Gatsby's blue gardens where "men and girls came and went like moths among the whisperings and the champagne and the stars" without waking up waiting for a four o'clock train in Penn Station.

But putting a brilliant chapter in place was only part of the task Fitzgerald could see needed to be done once the material was down on paper. Within that chapter, Fitzgerald's pencil was busily doing its vital work. The substance was all there: Tom and Myrtle and Nick going up to New York, the buying of the dog, the drinking in the apartment, the vapid conversations between the McKees and sister Catherine and Myrtle, the final violence. But some little things were not. The gray old man with the basket of dogs did not look like John D. Rockefeller until Fitzgerald penciled it in between lines; the mongrel "undoubtedly had Airedale blood" until Fitzgerald made it "an Airedale concerned in it somewhere"; and finally, the pastoral image of Fifth Avenue on a summer Sunday—"I wouldn't have been surprised to see a great flock of white sheep turn the corner"—this didn't arrive until the galleys.

IV

The appearances of Gatsby, as might be expected, are among the most worked-over sections in the draft. Even when the manuscript was submitted, the characterization was not quite satisfactory, either to Fitzgerald or to Maxwell Perkins. The "old sport" phrase which fixes Gatsby as precisely as his gorgeous pink rag of a suit is to be found in only one section of the pencil draft, though it must have been incorporated fully into his speech before Fitzgerald sent off the manuscript. "Couldn't you add one or two characteristics like the use of that phrase 'old sport'—not verbal, but physical ones, perhaps," Perkins suggested.[7] Fitzgerald chose the most elusive of physical characteristics—Gatsby's smile. How he worked it up into a powerfully suggestive bit of characterization can be seen by comparing the pencil draft and the final copy. Gatsby is telling Nick about his experiences during the war:

Rough Draft	Final Version
"I was promoted to be a major/ and every Allied government gave me a decoration—/ even ~~Bul~~ Montenegro little Montenegro down on the Adriatic/ Sea!"	"I was promoted to be a major, and every Allied government gave me a decoration—even Montenegro, little Montenegro down on the Adriatic Sea!"
~~He lifted up the w~~ Little Montenegro! He lifted up the ⟨them⟩ words/ and nodded at ~~it~~ with a faint smile. My incredulity had/ had turned to facination now; ~~Gatsby was no longer a~~ it was/ ~~person he was a magazine I had~~	Little Montenegro! He lifted up the words and nodded at them—with his smile. The smile comprehended Montenegro's troubled history and sympathized with the brave struggles of the Montenegrin people. It appreciated fully the chain of national circumstances which had elicited this

~~picked up on the casually train~~
like
~~and I was~~ reading the climaxes of
only
all the stories/~~it contained~~ in a
magazine.

tribute from Montenegro's warm little heart. My incredulity was submerged in fascination now; it was like skimming hastily through a dozen magazines. (pp. 66–67)

The smile is described in even fuller detail in a substantial addition to galley 15 (page 48 of the novel). One can virtually see Fitzgerald striking upon the smile as a characteristic which could give Gatsby substance without destroying his necessary insubstantiality.

Gatsby is revised, not so much into a real person as into a mythical one; what he *is* is not allowed to distract the reader from what he stands for. Without emphasizing the particulars of Gatsby's past, Fitzgerald wanted to place him more squarely before the reader.[8] Many of the further changes made in the galley proofs were directed toward that end. In the first five chapters of the galleys, the changes are the expected ones: routine corrections, happy changes in wording or phrasing, a few deletions, some additions. But at Chapter VI the galley proofs become fat with whole paragraphs and pages pasted in. Whole galleys are crossed out as the easiest way to make the extensive changes Fitzgerald felt were necessary. Throughout this section, he cut passages, tightened dialogue, reduced explicit statements in order to heighten the evocative power of his prose.

The major structural change brought the true story of Gatsby's past out of Chapter VIII and placed it at the beginning of Chapter VI. Chapter V, the meeting between Gatsby and Daisy, was already at the precise center of the novel.[9] That scene is the most static in the book. For a moment, after the confusion of the meeting, the rain and his own doubts, Gatsby holds past and present together. The revision of Chapter VI, as if to prolong this scene in the reader's mind, leaves the narrative, shifts the scene to the reporter inquiring about Gatsby, and fills in Gatsby's real past. "I take advantage of this short halt," Nick Carraway says, "while Gatsby, so to speak, caught his breath" (p. 102). The deliberate pause illustrates the care with which the novel is constructed. The Gatsby of his self-created present is contrasted with the Gatsby of his real past, and the moment prolonged before the narrative moves on. The rest of Chapter VI focuses on the first moment of disillusion, Gatsby's peculiar establishment seen through Daisy's eyes.

The rewriting so extensive in this chapter is as important as the shifting of material. The draft at this point has five different sets of numbers, and these pieces are fitted only loosely together. The Gatsby who finally emerges from the rewritten galleys answers the criticisms made by Maxwell Perkins and, more important, satisfies Fitzgerald's own critical sense. "ACTION IS CHARACTER," Fitzgerald wrote in his notes for *The Last Tycoon*. His revisions of dialogue, through which the novel often makes its vital disclosures and confrontations, shows his adherence to that precept. The truth of Gatsby's connection with Oxford was originally revealed to Nick Carraway in a somewhat flat, overly detailed conversation in which Gatsby tries to define his feeling for Daisy. Most of that conversation was cut out and the Oxford material worked into the taut dialogue between Tom Buchanan and Gatsby in the Plaza Hotel which prefaces the sweep of the story to its final action.[10]

In the draft, Gatsby reveals his sentimentality directly; he even sings a poor song he had composed as a boy. In the novel, a long passage of this sort is swept away, a good deal of the dialogue is put into exposition, and the effect is preserved by Nick's comment at the end: "Through all he said, even through his appalling sentimentality. . . ." (p. 112). In the draft, Gatsby carefully explains to Nick why he cannot run away. "'I've got to,' he announced with conviction, 'that's what I've got to do—live the past over again.'" Substance and dialogue are cleared away here, but the key idea is kept, held for a better place, and then shaped supremely right, as a climactic statement in a later talk with Nick: "'Can't repeat the past?' he cried incredulously. 'Why of course you can!'" (p. 111). In the draft, much of Gatsby's story is told in dialogue as he talks to Nick. It permits him to talk too much, to say, for example: "'Jay Gatsby!' he cried suddenly in a ringing voice. 'There goes the great Jay Gatsby! That's what people are going to say—wait and see.'" In the novel even the allusion to the title is excised. Gatsby's past is compressed into three pages of swift exposition punctuated by the images of his Platonic self, of his serving "a vast, vulgar, and meretricious beauty," and of Dan Cody and "the savage violence of the frontier brothel and saloon" from which he had come. Finally, in the draft, the undercurrent of passion and heat and boredom which sweeps all of them to the showdown in the Plaza is almost lost. Instead of going directly to the Plaza that fierce afternoon, they all went out to the Polo Grounds and sat through a ball game.

Of the changes in substance in this section—and in the novel—the most interesting is the dropping of a passage in which Gatsby reveals to Nick that Daisy wants them to run away. Daisy, elsewhere in the draft, reveals the same intentions. Perhaps Fitzgerald felt this shifted too much responsibility upon Daisy and made Gatsby more passive than he already was. Or perhaps his cutting here was part of a general intention of making Daisy less guilty of any chargeable wrong. Earlier in the draft, Fitzgerald removed a number of references to a previous romance between Daisy and Nick, and at other points he excised uncomplimentary remarks. The result may be contrary to expectation—that a writer ordinarily reworks to more sharply delineate a character—but it was not contrary to Fitzgerald's extraordinary intention. Daisy moves away from actuality into an idea existing in Gatsby's mind and ultimately to a kind of abstract beauty corrupted and corrupting in taking on material form.

V

After Chapter VI and the first part of Chapter VII, to judge both from the draft and the galleys, the writing seemed to go easier. The description of the accident with its tense climax—"her left breast was swinging loose like a flap"—is in the novel almost exactly as in the pencil draft. "I *want* Myrtle Wilson's breast ripped off"—he wrote to Perkins, "it's exactly the thing, I think, and I don't want to chop up the good scenes by too much tinkering."[11] Wilson and his vengeance needed little reworking, and though the funeral scene is improved in small ways, as is the conversation with Gatsby's father, no great changes occur here. The last ten pages, the epilogue in which Nick decides to go back West, are much the same, too.

In these last pages, as in the rest of the manuscript, one can only guess at how much writing preceded the version Fitzgerald kept as the pencil draft. "What I cut out of it both physically and emotionally," he wrote later, "would make another novel!"[12] The differences in hand, in numbering of pages, in the paper and pencils used, suggest that much had preceded that draft. Few of the pages have the look of Fitzgerald's hand putting first thoughts to paper, and fewer still—except those obviously recopied—are free of the revision in word and line which shows the craftsman at work.

These marks of Fitzgerald at work, the revelation they give of his ear and his eye and his mind forcing language to do more than it will willingly do, run all through the manuscript.

The best way of summarizing what Fitzgerald did in shaping *The Great Gatsby* from pencil draft to galley to book is to take him at his word in the introduction he wrote in 1934 for the Modern Library edition of the novel. "I had just re-read Conrad's preface to *The Nigger*, and I had recently been kidded half haywire by critics who felt that my material was such as to preclude all dealing with mature persons in a mature world. But, my God! it was my material, and it was all I had to deal with." What he did with it was what Conrad called for in his Preface, fashioned a work which carried "its justification in every line," and which "through an unremitting, never-discouraged care for the shape and ring of sentences" aspired to "the magic suggestiveness of music."

Notes

1. *The Letters of F. Scott Fitzgerald*, ed. Andrew Turnbull (New York: Scribner's, 1963), p. 172.

2. This study is based on an examination of the original pencil draft and the galley proofs in the Fitzgerald collection in the Princeton Library and subsequent work with a microfilm copy of this material. I am indebted to the University of Utah Research Fund for a grant which enabled me to study the materials at Prince-

ton, to Alexander P. Clark, curator of manuscripts, for his indispensable help in making this material available, and to Ivan Von Auw and the Fitzgerald estate for permission to use this material.

3. F. Scott Fitzgerald, *The Crack-Up*, ed. Edmund Wilson (New York: New Directions, 1945), p. 304.

4. All citations hereafter are from the Scribner Library edition of *The Great Gatsby*.

5. Arthur Mizener points out that Fitzgerald corrected the spelling from "orgastic" to "orgiastic" in his own copy of the book (*The Far Side of Paradise* [Boston: Houghton Mifflin, 1951], p. 336, n. 22). Yet Fitzgerald's letter to Maxwell Perkins of 24 January 1925 defends the original term: "'Orgastic' is the adjective for 'orgasm' and it expresses exactly the intended ecstasy. It's not a bit dirty" (*Letters*, p. 175). The word appears as "orgiastic" in most editions of the novel, including the current Scribner's printings.

6. *The Far Side of Paradise*, p. 170. The entire letter is in *Letters*, pp. 165–67.

7. *Editor to Author: The Letters of Maxwell E. Perkins*, ed. John Hall Wheelock (New York: Scribner's, 1950), p. 39.

8. Fitzgerald wrote in response to Perkins's criticism: "His [Gatsby's] vagueness I can repair by *making more pointed*—this doesn't sound good but wait and see. It'll make him clear." In a subsequent letter, he wrote: ". . . Gatsby sticks in my heart. I had him for awhile, then lost him, and now I know I have him again" (*Letters*, pp. 170, 173).

9. Fitzgerald called this chapter his "favorite of all" ("To Maxwell Perkins," circa 1 December 1924, *Letters*, p. 170).

10. Mizener points out that Fitzgerald was revising almost up to the day of publication. The revision of this section came some time around 18 February 1925, when Fitzgerald cabled Maxwell Perkins: "Hold Up Galley Forty for Big Change" (*The Far Side of Paradise*, p. 164; p. 335, n. 63). Fitzgerald returned the proofs about February 18th. In a letter to Perkins, he listed what he had done: "1) I've brought Gatsby to life. 2) I've accounted for his money. 3) I've fixed up the two weak chapters (VI and VII). 4) I've improved his first party. 5) I've broken up his long narrative in Chapter VIII" (Letters, p. 177).

11. *Letters*, p. 175.

12. Introduction to the Modern Library edition of *The Great Gatsby* (New York: Random House, 1934), p. x.

Patterns in *The Great Gatsby*   Victor A. Doyno*

When Fitzgerald was revising a scene at the end of the second chapter of *The Great Gatsby*, he added some phrases which have no apparent relevance to the novel. The scene involves a photographer showing an album to the narrator, Nick Carraway. Fitzgerald inserted four picture titles: "Beauty and the Beast . . . Loneliness . . . Old

*Reprinted from *Modern Fiction Studies*, 12 (Autumn 1966), 415–26, by permission of the publisher. *Modern Fiction Studies*, © 1967 by Purdue Research Foundation, West Lafayette, Indiana 47907.

Grocery Horse . . . Brook'n Bridge. . . ." Why did he, when preparing the novel for the printer, wish to insert these titles? What function does this seemingly irrelevant list have? A clue to the answer lies, I think in two letters from Fitzgerald to his editor, Maxwell Perkins. In 1922, after he began planning his third novel, Fitzgerald wrote that he wanted "to write something *new*—something extraordinary and beautiful and simple & intricately patterned." And in 1924, speaking about his difficulties in composition, Fitzgerald said:

> So in my new novel I'm thrown directly on purely creative work—not trashy imaginings as in my stories but the sustained imagination of a sincere yet radiant world. So I tread slowly and carefully & at times in considerable distress. This book will be a consciously artistic achievement & must depend on that as the 1st books did not.[1]

These statements suggest that a careful study of the text might reveal *The Great Gatsby* to be indeed "a consciously artistic achievement" that is "intricately patterned."

Fortunately, this close study of the patterning can draw upon a wealth of material: the holograph pencil version, the galley proofs, and the extensive galley revisions. Portions of the holograph text include several stages of composition: some parts of this version, usually those written in a large hand, are extensively revised early drafts; those parts written in a small, precise hand with fewer revisions seem to be transcriptions of earlier drafts. The holograph text was revised, presumably in a lost typescript; the revised readings can be found in the galley proofs. This material, with the galley revisions, allows us to see the patterns which appear in the final text are often the result of laborious revisions.[2]

Several patterns in the novel are obvious. The first three chapters present the different settings and social groupings of three evenings: dinner and strained conversation at Tom Buchanan's house, drinks and a violent argument at Myrtle's apartment, a party and loutish behavior at Gatsby's mansion. Fitzgerald calls attention to this pattern when he has Nick say, "Reading over what I have written so far, I see I have given the impression that the events of three nights several weeks apart were all that absorbed me" (p. 56). Similarly, through Nick, Fitzgerald emphasizes the patterning of situation which presents two very different characters, George Wilson and Tom Buchanan, as cuckolded husbands: "I stared at him and then at Tom, who had made a parallel discovery less than an hour before" (p. 124). Clearly Fitzgerald is aware of these patterns and wishes the reader to share this awareness.

There are, moreover, numerous less obvious patterns in the novel which have the important functions of deepening characterization, shaping the reader's attitudes toward events and major themes, and creating and controlling unity and emphasis. These patternings which affect characterization include the repetition of dialogue, gesture, and detail. For example, Daisy's speech is used to characterize her in two comparable scenes which are far apart. Fitzgerald indicates the relation between the scenes by presenting the same tableau as Nick enters: Daisy and Jordan Baker, both in white, wind-blown dresses, lounge on a couch on a wine or crimson rug. The first scene (in Chapter I) occurs as Nick renews his acquaintance with Daisy; the second (in Chapter VII) when Gatsby intends to reclaim Daisy. In the latter scene Jordan and Daisy say together, "We can't move," and the speech is perfectly appropriate to the hot weather. In the first scene Daisy says, as her first direct statement in the novel, "I'm p-paralyzed with happiness." This statement, however, was inserted after the second scene was written, since it first occurs in the galley proof. This inserted statement, besides presenting an apt characterization of Daisy, likens her feelings at the beginning to those which she has shortly before the argument about leaving Tom. Through this repetition Fitzgerald emphasizes Daisy's lack of growth within the novel.

Fitzgerald also deepens characterization by the repetition of gesture. Nick says that when he first saw Gatsby, "he gave a sudden intimation that he was content to be alone—he stretched out his arms toward the dark water in a curious way, and, far as I was from him, I could have sworn he was trembling" (p. 21). This picture of Gatsby in the coda of Chapter I presents him with an air of mystery, and in the reader's memory he stands etched reaching for the green light. Gatsby's mysteriousness is transformed later in the novel when he tells Nick that as he was leaving Louisville he went to the open vestibule of the coach and "stretched out his hand desperately as if to snatch only a wisp of air, to save a fragment of the spot that she had made lovely for him" (p. 153). This repetition of the reaching gesture explains the first picture of Gatsby, establishes the durability of his devotion, and thereby evokes sympathy for one who loves so fervently.

The characterization of Gatsby's rival, Tom Buchanan, is influenced by the repetition of details. Arthur Mizener has noted that Fitzgerald can "sum up all he wants to say about Tom" in his last meeting with Nick.[3] An examination of the composition of the passage leads to a fuller explanation of Mizener's insight and an increased respect for Fitzgerald's craftsmanship. The manuscript version reads: "Then he went into the jewellry store *for a* to buy a *pair of c* pearl necklace *and* or pair of cuff buttons," (MS. VIII, 42).[4] The evidence indicates that Fitzgerald probably planned for a moment simply to mention the cuff links, then decided to begin with the necklace. What is gained by the inclusion of a pearl necklace? Tom's wife, Daisy, already has the pearl necklace which was her wedding gift; the necklace is probably not for Daisy; perhaps Tom has found a replacement for his dead mistress. This meeting, which also associates Tom with cuff buttons, occurs directly after Nick's condemnation of the Buchanans for their callous inhumanity: "they smashed up things and creatures and then retreated back into their money or their vast carelessness . . ." (p. 180). Fitzgerald may have realized that the inhumanity of their attitude could be subtly reinforced by an unfavorable association with the cuff buttons. At any rate he decided to introduce an anterior reference to cuff buttons. Accordingly the galley proofs contain a passage not in the manuscript version in which Meyer Wolfsheim mentions his cuff buttons and calls them "Finest specimens of human molars." The attitude of gross inhumanity latent in this remark carries over to Tom. With the insertion of this unfavorable association for cuff buttons, Fitzgerald decided to alter the syntax of the later reference. The galley proof version is: "Then he went into the jewelry store to buy a pearl necklace, or perhaps only a pair of cuff buttons,". This version, which created a deceptively casual tone while subordinating the cuff links, was modified when Fitzgerald, in revising the galleys, changed the commas to dashes and raised the importance of the alternative (Galley sheet 57). The final elaborated version conveys, in a devastatingly casual tone, oblique references of approximately equal emphasis to Tom's lust and to his inhumanity.

And this passage is not the only implicit character assassination of Tom brought about by a patterning of details. While leaving Gatsby's first party, Nick observes the aftermath of a car accident in which the vehicle is "violently shorn of one wheel." The confusion and discordant noise of the scene create an unfavorable impression which is intensified when Nick tells of the driver's stupid, irresponsible drunkenness. With this scene in mind we can easily visualize an accident which Jordan Baker describes only briefly in the next chapter:

> A week after I left Santa Barbara Tom ran into a wagon on the Ventura road one night, and ripped a front wheel off his car. The girl who was with him got into the papers, too, because her arm was broken—she was one of the chambermaids in the Santa Barbara Hotel. (P. 78)

The accident is primarily another indictment of Tom's lust, but the repetition of detail—the loss of a wheel in a night accident—associates Tom with the irresponsible drunken driver.

Besides adding depth to characterization, patterning also shapes the reader's attitudes toward events and themes in the novel. As it happens, this kind of repetition also includes a case of poor driving. Surprisingly few commentators have criticized Fitzgerald for the highly improbable plot manipulation whereby Daisy runs down her husband's mistress. The reader's uncritical acceptance of the accident is influenced, I suggest, by something Nick says in the coda of Chapter III about his relationship with Jordan Baker: "It was on that same house party that we had a curious conversation about driving a car. It started because she passed so close to some workmen that our fender flicked a button on one man's coat" (p. 59). This near-accident subliminally prepares the reader to think of Daisy's hitting Myrtle not as an unbelievable wrenching of probability but as a possible event. After all Jordan nearly did a similar thing. Nick's ensuing conversation with Jordan reveals his attitude toward carelessness. This dialogue seems to be relevant only to Nick and Jordan's friendship, but the casual banter presents the same diction and attitude found in Nick's final condemnation of Daisy and Tom for their carelessness. In this case patterning leads the reader to accept both an improbable event and the narrator's final judgment of it.

The reader's attitude is more frequently shaped by an ironic juxtaposition of such themes as romantic idealization and realistic disillusionment.[5] For example, Nick learns from Myrtle of her first meeting with Tom Buchanan on the train to New York, and as she relates the story her limited word choice, additive syntax, and rushing narration establish both her character and her attitude toward the pickup:

> "It was on the two little seats facing each other that are always the last ones left on the train. I was going up to New York to see my sister and spend the night. He had on a dress suit and patent leather shoes, and I couldn't keep my eyes off him, but every time he looked at me I had to pretend to be looking at the advertisement over his head. When we came into the station he was next to me, and his white shirt-front pressed against my arm, and so I told him I'd have to call a policeman, but he knew I lied. I was so excited that when I got into a taxi with him I didn't hardly know I wasn't getting into a subway train. All I kept thinking about, over and over, was 'You can't live forever; you can't live forever.'" (p. 36)

The style and growing desperation of tone suggest that Myrtle is a socially and morally limited character who acted in an understandable way because of her romantic expectation. But her romantic opinion of her meeting with Tom contrasts with another version of the same situation which is told in a realistic style from a masculine and definitely unromantic point of view when Nick tells this tale of the commuter train:

> The next day was broiling, almost the last, certainly the warmest, of the summer. As my train emerged from the tunnel into sunlight, only the hot whistles of the National Biscuit Company broke the simmering hush at noon. The straw seats of the car hovered on the edge of combustion; the woman next to me perspired delicately for a while into her white shirtwaist, and then, as her newspaper dampened under her fingers, lapsed despairingly into deep heat with a desolate cry. Her pocket-book slapped to the floor.
>
> "Oh, my!" she gasped.
>
> I picked it up with a weary bend and handed it back to her, holding it at arm's length and by the extreme tip of the corners to indicate

that I had no designs upon it—but every one near by, including the woman, suspected me just the same.

"Hot!" said the conductor to familiar faces. "Some weather! . . . Hot! . . . Hot! . . . Hot! . . . Is is hot enough for you? Is is hot? Is it . . .?"

My commutation ticket came back to me with a dark stain from his hand. That any one should care in this heat whose flushed lips he kissed, whose head made damp the pajama pocket over his heart! (pp. 114–15)

Nick's scornful attitude toward romance refers, in context, primarily to the love of Gatsby for Daisy, but the situation parallels Myrtle's first meeting with Tom and reflects a disillusioned view of such an event. Fitzgerald has controlled his material to make each of the attitudes— Myrtle's desperate romanticism and Nick's uncomfortable realism—valid in its own moment of presentation; but in the context of the novel each thematic attitude toward love is juxtaposed to and qualifies the other.

A similar attempt to influence the reader's attitudes occurs with the use of analogous scenes in the codas of Chapters V and VII. And, as shall later become clear, the positioning of the scenes lends them importance. In each case Nick sees a tableau of Daisy sitting and talking with a man who is holding her hand. In Chapter V, of course, the man is Gatsby, who has just re-won Daisy and is experiencing sublime happiness. Nick says:

As I watched him he adjusted himself a little, visibly. His hand took hold of hers, and as she said something low in his ear he turned toward her with a rush of emotion. I think that voice held him most, with its fluctuating, feverish warmth, because it couldn's be over-dreamed—that voice was a deathless song.

They had forgotten me, but Daisy glanced up and held out her hand; Gatsby didn't know me now at all. I looked once more at them and they looked back at me, remotely possessed by intense life. Then I went out of the room and down the marble steps into the rain, leaving them there together. (p. 97)

However, Fitzgerald balances this moment of romantic bliss with a parallel but decidedly realistic description of Daisy after the auto accident:

Daisy and Tom were sitting opposite each other at the kitchen table, with a plate of cold fried chicken between them, and two bottles of ale. He was talking intently across the table at her, and in his earnestness his hand had fallen upon and covered her own. Once in a while she looked up at him and nodded in agreement.

They weren't happy, and neither of them had touched the chicken or the ale—and yet they weren't unhappy either. There was an unmistakable air of natural intimacy about the picture, and anybody would have said that they were conspiring together. (p. 146)

This second scene signals, of course, Gatsby's loss of Daisy. In addition, the repetition destroys the uniqueness of Gatsby's moment of happiness and thereby makes the reader question the validity of his romantic idealization.

The reader's attitude toward romantic idealization and realistic disillusionment is also shaped by the elaborate patterning of a natural enough event—a man and woman kissing. In Chapter VI Nick tells of the movie director bending over his star, who had been described as "a scarcely human orchid of a woman": "They were still under the white-plum tree and their faces were touching except for a pale, thin ray of moonlight between. It occurred to me that he had been very slowly bending toward her all evening to attain this proximity, and even while I watched I saw him stoop one ultimate degree and kiss at her cheek" (p. 108). Although the setting is described romantically, the event itself is narrated with touches of sarcasm in the involved syntax, elevated diction ("attain this proximity"), and precision of word choice ("kiss *at* her cheek"). The presentation of this kiss, which does not involve any of the major characters, prepares the reader to adopt a complex attitude toward the other kisses. In the coda of the same chapter, Nick relates Gatsby's description of kissing Daisy. Once more Nick's incongruous word choice, e.g., "romp," helps give the passage a peculiar texture.[6] The dominant tone of the passage is, however, certainly one of romantic idealization, culminating in the flower simile:

> His heart beat faster and faster as Daisy's white face came up to his own. He knew that when he kissed this girl, and forever wed his unutterable visions to her perishable breath, his mind would never romp again like the mind of God. So he waited, listening for a moment longer to the tuning-fork that had been struck upon a star. Then he kissed her. At his lips' touch she blossomed for him like a flower and the incarnation was complete. (p. 112)

The idealization of Gatsby's description is touching, but Nick's sarcastic insertions are not the only means of qualifying the romantic point of view. The reader's attitude toward the kiss has already been influenced by the movie star's kiss and, more importantly, by a similar incident described from a less romantic point of view. In the coda of Chapter IV Nick says:

> We passed a barrier of dark trees, and then the façade of Fifty-ninth Street, a block of delicate pale light, beamed down into the park. Unlike Gatsby and Tom Buchanan, I had no girl whose disembodied face floated along the dark cornices and blinding signs, and so I drew up the girl beside me, tightening my arms. Her wan, scornful mouth smiled, and so I drew her up again closer, this time to my face. (p. 81)

Throughout this sardonic description Nick has certainly reserved his emotional commitment; neither his motivation nor his choice of words like "scornful" conveys idealistic enthusiasm. As in the other passages the setting is described, and Nick even calls attention to the relation between the kisses by saying "Unlike Gatsby. . . ." Furthermore, the relationship between the kisses in the codas of Chapter IV and VI is subtly emphasized early in Chapter VII, when Tom goes out to make drinks and leaves Daisy alone with Gatsby in front of Nick and Jordan:

> . . . she got up and went over to Gatsby and pulled his face down, kissing him on the mouth.
> "You know I love you," she murmured.
> "You forget there's a lady present," said Jordan.
> Daisy looked around doubtfully.
> "You kiss Nick too."
> "What a low, vulgar girl!" (p. 11)

In this patterning Fitzgerald has presented in order Nick's disenchanted personal account, his sarcastic third-person narration, and Gatsby's romantic, personal version of a kiss; in addition, Fitzgerald includes a scene which draws a parallel between the kisses involving major characters. The sheer idealization of Gatsby's love is qualified by this elaborate repetition, and the reader develops a complex attitude toward a major theme.

With all this evidence of patterning in mind, we may establish still a third function by returning to our original question. Beyond combining the romantic and the mundane, what possible relevance have the picture titles, "Beauty and the Beast . . . Loneliness . . . Old Grocery Horse . . . Brook'n Bridge . . ."? The first title, of course refers to the well-known fairy tale or folk tale in which a lowly creature regains his former princely condition by the transforming power of a beautiful girl's kiss.[7] Gatsby's background is analogous to this tale, since he was "a son of God" (p. 99) whose imagination had never accepted his mother and father as his real parents. The transformation of James Gatz to Jay Gatsby was, of course, gradual, but when Gatsby kissed Daisy "the incarnation was complete" (p. 112): she embodied his dreams, and his princely status was confirmed by the love of "the king's daughter" (p. 120). And Gatsby's casual remark that in Europe he "lived like a young rajah" (p. 66) seems quite appropriate to the prince motif.

The next title, "Loneliness," calls to mind Nick's first sight of Gatsby, when "he gave a sudden intimation that he was content to be alone." Several references to Gatsby's loneliness follow: he is "standing alone on the marble steps" (p. 50) during his party, and Nick mentions the "complete isolation" of the host (p. 56). The scenes of Gatsby's vigil outside the Buchanans' and of his body's floating in the pool also reinforce the motif of loneliness. Gatsby, when alive, seems quite content with his isolation, but Nick, in a contrapuntal fashion, frequently refers to his own loneliness in terms of discomfort or unhappiness. Nick's dissatisfaction with loneliness makes Gatsby's satisfaction in isolation more striking, more mystic.

Since these motifs sufficiently account for the insertion, admittedly very tenuous suggestions about the last two titles may be offered. The word *grocery* occurs twice in connection with financial necessity. Nick, when he is preparing to leave for the Midwest, sells his car to the grocer. And Tom Buchanan scoffs at Gatsby's financial and social inferiority when he first knew Daisy by saying, "and I'll be damned if I see how you got within a mile of her unless you brought the groceries to the back door" (p. 132). The other two words of the title also possess some relevance to Gatsby's inferiority. Tom's wealth, of course, is old and established, while Gatsby's richness is quite *nouveau*. Tom's wealth and aristocratic background are indicated by his transportation of his string of polo ponies, and Gatsby's social ineptitude appears in Chapter VI when Tom and the haughty Mr. Sloane dispose of a dinner invitation Gatsby should have refused by riding away without him. There is, then, some evidence that the third title may be a complex and subtle reference to the financial and social differences between Tom and Gatsby.

The last of the titles, "Brook'n Bridge," is even less obvious and has no relevance—unless we consider Fitzgerald's aural imagination and the context of the title within the novel. The brilliance of the catalogue of guests' names at the beginning of Chapter IV is a critical commonplace, but the person who reads these names silently misses a good bit. One must read aloud to appreciate names such as "the Dancies," "Gus Waize," "young Brewer," "Miss Haag," and "Miss Claudia Hipp." That Fitzgerald's imagination upon occasion worked aurally is beyond question. The title "Brook'n Bridge" occurs just after Tom has broken Myrtle's nose and may be a punning reference to this incident and thus to the leitmotif of violence in the novel. Each chapter from the first, with Daisy's bruised finger, to the last, with Tom's story of Wilson's forced entry, includes some sort of violence. The only exception to this, of course, is the more or less idyllic Chapter V, in which Daisy and Gatsby are reunited.

Fitzgerald's decision to insert these picture titles in the version used for type setting is quite significant. The titles serve as an index of leitmotifs within the novel. By picking these motifs from the many others in the book, Fitzgerald has singled them out for emphasis, and the presentation in one group subtly helps create unity in the novel.

In addition, the placing of this index in the coda of Chapter II contributes to the structural patterning for unity and emphasis. The conclusion of Chapter III, we remember, is also of particular importance, since by presenting Jordan's near-accident with the discussion of carelessness it prepares for what is to follow. Fitzgerald consciously uses this emphatic position at each chapter's end to call attention to major elements of the novel and frequently creates relations between the structural units.

For example, the codas of Chapters IV and VI present Nick's and Gatsby's versions of a kiss. Fitzgerald's awareness of this patterning is implied in the extensive revisions which brought Gatsby's story to its present parallel position. The story appears in manuscript in the beginning of an early version of Chapter VI and in galley proof at the beginning of Chapter VII (MS VI. 3; Galley 35). In the galley version Fitzgerald has added a paragraph about a forgotten phrase in Nick's mind. This paragraph dealing with the forgotten phrase was originally written to follow Gatsby's singing of a song he composed in his youth, and Fitzgerald shifted the paragraph, with only a minor change, to its present position after Gatsby's kiss. This shift serves two purposes: it comments upon Gatsby's story, and it creates another analogy to Nick's narration of a kiss, because Nick also had a phrase in mind when he kissed Jordan. The similarities of the events and the phrases were then put into an unmistakable relationship when, in revising the galleys, Fitzgerald shifted Gatsby's narration and the paragraph about the forgotten phrase to a position parallel to Nick's. Thus the codas of IV and VI help unify the book by treating two similar events, and control thematic emphasis by presenting contrasting points of view toward romance. And, of course, the codas of V and VII, which picture first Gatsby and then Tom holding Daisy's hand, also function in this way.

The patterning of alternate codas is tightened to one of direct connection in the last three chapters. In VII and VIII, Gatsby is pictured as alone, first on his vigil and then in his pool. In the one chapter Gatsby is the faithful, devoted, vigilant protector of his lady. In the next he is dead. This contrast, a commentary on romantic idealization, works within the leitmotif of "Loneliness." A similar commentary also links the eighth with the ninth and final coda. At the novel's conclusion Nick likens the human struggle to "boats against the current." And the previous coda presents the image of Gatsby, his struggle over, on a boat going against the current, as the faint wind and a cluster of leaves disturb the course of his mattress in the current of the pool.

The last coda must be discussed in conjunction with the first, since their composition is related. The conclusion of the first chapter was once very different. For example, the manuscript version does not mention that Gatsby was "content to be alone," nor does it include the symbolic green light. Both these insertions were made, however, by the time the novel was ready for typesetting. The insertion of the green light picks up other uses of green as a symbol of romance which occur later in the novel, such as the "green card" which Daisy jokes about as entitling Nick to a kiss, the "long green tickets" which carried young Nick to Midwestern parties, and the "fresh, green breast of the new world" of the conclusion. The description of Gatsby reaching out was not, however, the original end of the chapter. The manuscript first chapter ends with a passage we now find at the novel's conclusion. Only by cutting away this material did Fitzgerald raise the importance of the picture of Gatsby on his lawn, reaching toward Daisy.

It is crucial to a complete understanding of the novel that we realize that this portion of the conclusion was composed early in the writing process:

> And as the moon rose higher the inessential houses began to melt away until gradually I became aware of the old island here that flowered once for Dutch sailors' eyes—a fresh, green breast of the new world. Its vanished trees, the trees that had made way for Gatsby's house, had once pandered in whispers to the last and greatest of all human dreams; for a transitory enchanted moment man must have held his breath in the presence of this continent, compelled into an aesthetic contemplation he neither understood nor desired, face to face for the last time in history with something commensurate to his capacity for wonder. (p. 182)

The references to the past in this section and in the remainder of the conclusion raise the thematic importance of Gatsby's "Can't repeat the past? . . . Why of course you can!" (p. 111) and of Tom's conversion of a garage into a stable. Both Gatsby and Tom are, each in his own way, borne back into the past. From the early composition of this section we can also surmise that several of the leitmotifs mentioned in the conclusion, such as the notion of pandering and the Edenic conception of America, may have been in Fitzgerald's mind from the beginning.

Similarly, the "new world" seen by the Dutch sailors was already in Fitzgerald's mind when he wrote of the "new world" which Gatsby had seen shortly before being killed by Wilson in the coda of Chapter VIII:

> He must have looked up at an unfamiliar sky through frightening leaves and shivered as he found what a grotesque thing a rose is and how raw the sunlight was upon the scarcely created grass. A new world, material without being real, where poor ghosts, breathing dreams like air, drifted fortuitously about . . . like that ashen fantastic figure gliding toward them through the amorphous trees. (p. 162)

Fitzgerald's decision to present these radically different "new worlds"—Nick's imputation of Gatsby's realistic disillusionment and the Dutch sailors' romantic idealization—in the codas to the last two chapters reveals once more his consummate use of patterning.

It is clear, I think, that Fitzgerald fulfilled his intention to write a "consciously artistic achievement." And a knowledge of the ways in which the novel is "intricately patterned," from minor details up to large structural units, partially explains how Fitzgerald created a novel that is "something extraordinary and beautiful and simple."

Notes

1. Both letters are quoted by Andrew Turnbull, *Scott Fitzgerald* (New York: Scribner's, 1962), pp. 146–47.

2. I am very grateful to the Firestone Library of Princeton University and to Mr. Alexander P. Clark, curator of manuscripts, for aiding my study, and to Mrs. Samuel J. Lanahan and Mr. Ivan Von Auw, her agent, for permitting manuscript and galley proof quotation. Similarly, I am indebted to Charles Scribner's Sons, publishers of *The Great Gatsby*, for permission to quote the text of the novel.

3. *The Far Side of Paradise* (Boston: Houghton Mifflin, 1951), p. 174.

4. The cancelled *c* is followed by what appears to be the first vertical curve of a *u*.

5. For a discussion of the importance of these themes throughout Fitzgerald's career see John R. Kuehl, "Scott Fitzgerald: Romantic and Realist," *Texas Studies in Literature and Language*, 1 (1959), 412–26.

6. The complete passage, which begins with the setting and is too long to quote, has several complicating aspects: it also includes allusions to such religious matters as Jacob's ladder and the incarnation.

7. For another example of the use of folklore in the novel see Tristram P. Coffin, "Gatsby's Fairy Lover," *Midwest Folklore*, 10 (1960), 79–85.

The Great Gatsby—
The Intricate Art   **Robert Emmet Long***

After finishing *The Beautiful and Damned*, Fitzgerald wrote to Maxwell Perkins: "I want to write something *new*—something extraordinary and beautiful and simple and intricately patterned." He did not then have his conception for *The Great Gatsby*, but it was at its completion everything Fitzgerald had written he hoped to achieve in his next novel. *The Great Gatsby* has an apparently simple, pellucid surface, but its patterning is intricate, so much so that the novel comes to seem, on examination, like a large structure of interwoven detail and nuance in the tradition of Flaubert. It makes extensive use of iterative imagery, leitmotivs, character doubles, parallel and symbolic scenes, and has been given an intense visual focus that contributes to the novel's scenic and dramatic form.

The Great Gatsby develops in a series of sharply focused scenes, like Edith Wharton's *Ethan Frome*, but Fitzgerald's scenes are more intricately modeled than Mrs. Wharton's. Beneath the enamel of their realistic surfaces there is an elaborate play of implication and suggestion. The first three of Fitzgerald's "scenic" chapters work together, particularly, as a novelistic unit. All of the principals appear in these chap-

*Reprinted from *The Achieving of "The Great Gatsby": F. Scott Fitzgerald, 1920–1925* (Lewisburg, Pa.: Bucknell University Press, 1979), pp. 119–29, by permission of Associated University Presses.

ters, and the reader is introduced to their backgrounds and situations as they are defined by the three distinctly separate social spheres to which they belong—East Egg, with its affluence and prerogatives; the valley of ashes, where the lower middle class has a hazy existence; and West Egg, an upper middle class suburb inhabited, in part, by the newly rich. By the end of these opening chapters, the several social worlds to be explored have been presented to the reader distinctly, and it remains, suspensefully, to be seen how they will interact.

These three opening chapters also reveal a common pattern, since a party or social gathering takes place in each. In the first chapter it is a social call by invitation; the occasion is exclusive and limited to a single individual who qualifies. Carraway is not a member of the Buchanans' set, having nothing like their wealth, but his background makes him acceptable. He is a second cousin, once removed, of Daisy, and was a classmate of Tom's at Yale and a member of the same senior society. The time is established by Daisy's remarking that "in two weeks it'll be the longest day of the year" (p. 12), so that it must be nearly the middle of June, the time of the year when, as it will come out later, Daisy married Tom Buchanan. As Carraway arrives, the sense of place is established immediately. He finds a red and white Georgian Colonial mansion, which Tom has acquired from the oil man, Demaine; its architecture suggests an early America, but the ownership of the estate passing to Demaine ("of main force") to Buchanan intimates the big money it now represents. The substantial nature of Buchanan's wealth is indicated in the opening pages in Carraway's remark that Buchanan casually brought with him to East Egg a string of polo ponies from Lake Forest. "It was hard to realize," he adds, "that a man in my own generation was wealthy enough to do that" (p. 6). When Carraway reaches their estate, he is greeted by Buchanan, shown in a proprietary posture as he stands, in the swank of a riding outfit, "with his legs apart on the front porch" (p. 7).

Inside there is an atmosphere that is both gracious and disturbing. Upon his arrival in their living room, under "the frosted wedding cake of the ceiling" (p. 8), Carraway finds Daisy and Jordan Baker seated on a sofa, both wearing white dresses that stir in a breeze moving through the room, creating an idyllic impression. As soon as Tom appears, however, shutting the windows with a bang, the vision is immediately deflated, and the young women appear to balloon down from their cloud-like couch. This opening impression—the sense of a beguiling vision and its deflation—is in small what the chapter will be in large. Impressions of Daisy and Jordan that follow are conveyed through "gestures" almost entirely, as, for example, in Daisy's enchantment-promising voice and in Jordan's elaborate attitude of self-sufficiency, her appearance of balancing an invisible object on her chin. "At any rate," Carraway remarks facetiously of their introduction, "Miss Baker's lips fluttered, she nodded at me almost imperceptibly, and then quickly tipped her head back again—the object she was balancing had obviously tottered a little and given her something of a fright" (p. 9). Both Daisy and Jordan have about them an aura of private understandings, inaccessible to an outsider, which underscores the special world of wealth to which they belong. At one point Daisy tells a story about her butler, who had previously cleaned a wealthy family's silver until at last the silver cleaning affected his nose, and he was forced to leave their employment. There is an implication in this brief account of something malodorous about the rich—something relevant to the world of the Buchanans, which is not without charm but is also disquieting.

For the "superior" world in which they live is filled with tensions, communicated by gestures that do not belong to real emotions and by innuendoes of a vaguely disturbing kind. At one point, Tom says: "Oh, I'll stay in the East, don't you worry," and then glances at Daisy, and back at Carraway, "as if he were alert for something more" (p. 10). An impression is given (and later confirmed) that the Buchanans left Chicago over some unpleasantness involving Tom's infidelity. His infidelity comes out later that afternoon with a "shrill metallic" (p. 16) ring of the telephone, and at this point Carraway learns that Tom keeps a mistress. In one passage it is implied, comically, that Tom, a horseman, has this woman "in his stable." As he refers to his stable, the telephone rings again, and the group is frozen in a tense silence. The earlier gracious appearances dissolve into discord and are replaced by a sense of a deep unease, as Carraway leaves with a feeling of disgust and "confusion." He returns to his cottage, from the lawn of which he detects the figure of the man he will later know as Gatsby, his arms outstretched worshipfully toward a point somewhere across the darkness and the bay. He is as yet a shadowy figure, but Fitzgerald has already hinted at some depth of emotion in him that is antithetical to the group Carraway has left at East Egg, particularly that figure of chronic unfaithfulness, Tom Buchanan.

The first chapter leads into the second by the telephone call from Myrtle, but otherwise the transition is a study in contrasts, from great wealth to bare subsistence—to a land of ashes and powdery shapes, which may be buildings or men, but are all equally indistinct. It is an area in which "the only building in sight [is] a small block of yellow brick sitting on the edge of the waste land, a sort of compact Main Street ministering to it" (p. 24), a description linking the valley of ashes, and its spiritual condition, to the middle-class world pictured by Sinclair Lewis and T. S. Eliot. Presiding over this exhausted acreage is George Wilson, who runs a garage—filling station and is called colorless, spiritless, and anemic. When his wife, Myrtle, appears, she seems to walk "through her husband as if he were a ghost" (p. 25), and when Wilson enters the garage, he mingles "immediately with the cement color of the walls" (p. 26). This valley of ashes is a dumping ground where "ashes grow like wheat" (p. 23), but ashes are not fertile like wheat, and the phrase merely reinforces the implication of infertile life. Ironically, it is close to Independence Day when Carraway enters this forsaken area, as his own words make clear: "It was a few days before the Fourth of July, and a gray, scrawny Italian child was setting torpedoes in a row along the railroad track" (p. 26). The valley of ashes, at the approach of the Fourth of July, is the novel's second comment on the new republic and the society it has fostered.

Myrtle's name has a number of associations that confirm her role as a character double of several others in the work. With her green name, she is a double of Gatsby, and her aspiration is played off, in a horrible way, with his, heightening Gatsby's stature by contrast. At the same time, she is a double of Daisy, for she, too, has a floral name. But if the daisy is a flower with a bright, petite, and particular distinctness, myrtle is an ivy, growing close to the earth, with no individual distinctness at all. There is, furthermore, nothing of the "fay" or elfin quality in Myrtle—nothing of the slight, beguiling, and graceful. She is captured with comic effect in her first appearance: "In a moment the thickish figure of a woman blocked out the light from the office door" (p. 25). It is noted that she has "rather wide hips" (p. 26), and in a sense, she is the heavy-hipped Venus of the valley of ashes. "Her face . . . contained no facet or gleam of beauty, but there was an immediate perceptible vitality about her as if the nerves of her body were continually smouldering" (p. 25). She boards the train at the same time as Tom and Carraway, joining them when they arrive at the station in New York, and there, before leaving for the Washington Heights apartment, she buys a puppy "of an indeterminate breed" (p. 27), an incident that suggests the idea of Tom's "buying" the mongrel Myrtle for his amusement.

The Washington Heights apartment has an atmosphere that is quite strange. "The living-room," Carraway comments, "was crowded to the doors with a set of tapestried furniture entirely too large for it, so that to move about was to stumble continually over scenes of ladies swinging in the gardens of Versailles" (p. 29). These Watteauesque tapestried scenes set the tone of the "love nest," of Myrtle's movie-magazine notion of romance. The strangeness of the apartment, however, is also reflected in the characters encountered in the scene. Myrtle's sister, Catherine, for example, has a "solid, sticky bob of red hair, and a complexion powdered milky white" (p. 30), and has thus something of a clown's appearance (part of the motif of mockery that runs through the scene). There are, too, many oddly blurring impressions, which are part of the concern in the chapter with seeing, or with being unable to see, with vision and sightlessness. Figuring appropriately in the scene is Chester McKee, a photographer who tells Carraway that he is in "the artistic game" (p. 30). If the role of the artist is to achieve a vision underlying the inchoate material of reality, McKee is an artist *manqué*, who records only surfaces. Of his wife, called "shrill, languid, handsome, and horrible" (p. 30), he has taken one hundred twenty-seven photographs, a figure that, in its exactness, emphasizes the hopeless literalness of his mind.

Myrtle's personality, as it is brought out by Fitzgerald, has special interest in respect to the scene. What she is like has been suggested on her first appearance, in the fact that she wears "a spotted dress of dark blue crepe-de-chine" (p. 25) at the Wilson garage. A woman might wear a sheer crepe de chine dress at an early evening cocktail party, or at formal occasions, but she would not normally wear crepe de chine in the afternoon, or at a garage. Her wearing the crepe de chine dress at the garage suggests that she pretends to, or has some vulgar notion of, social distinction. At the station in New York, she lets four cabs pass before selecting one that is painted lavender, and when they reach the apartment building in Washington Heights, Fitzgerald remarks that she "went haughtily in" (p. 28). "The intense vitality that had been so remarkable in the garage," he comments, "was converted into an impressive hauteur" (pp. 30–31). Myrtle is reminiscent, indeed, at this point, of the young woman with violets on her hat, in the "brummagem cabaret" scene in *The Beautiful and Damned*, who pretends to belong to a higher social class than she does, a figure who suddenly expands into a whole roomful of people who are pretending in the same way. An impression is given, through her, and again through Myrtle, that the middle-class imagination can aspire toward the ideal no further than, say, the possession of a showier dress or house. In the course of this brief chapter, in fact, Myrtle wears three different dresses, and speaks of going out the next day to buy another. "Her laughter, her gestures, her assertions became more violently affected moment by moment," until she seems to be "revolving on a noisy, creaking pivot" (p. 31)— an image that suggests something on public show, something wooden and overburdened. "The room rang full of her artificial laughter" (p. 37).

Myrtle's pretensions, however, are shared by the other women at the apartment. Fitzgerald remarks that Myrtle's elaborate chiffon dress "gave out a continual rustle as she swept about the room" (p. 30); but the sense of a too obtrusive showiness is also conveyed in Fitzgerald's description of Myrtle's sister, Catherine, of whom he says that when she moved about "there was an incessant clicking as innumerable pottery bracelets jingled up and down upon her arms" (p. 30). And like Myrtle, Mrs. McKee has social pretensions, the baselessness of which her own words betray. " 'I almost made a mistake, too' [Mrs. McKee] declared vigorously. 'I almost married a little kike who'd been after me for years. I knew he was below me. Everybody kept saying to me: "Lucille, that man's 'way below you!" But if I hadn't met Chester, he'd of got me sure' " (pp. 34–35).

Myrtle, however, remains the presiding figure, and she queens it over Mrs. McKee as she announces that she is going to give her the dress she is wearing—when she is ready to discard it. There is an extremely comic moment when, in referring to menials, Myrtle remarks that "all they think of is money" (p. 31). It is particularly comic because at that moment Myrtle is imagining herself as an aristocrat, a big consumer whose day is taken up with purchases at various shops. "I'm going to make a list," she says, "of all the things I've got to get. A massage and a wave, and a collar for the dog, and one of those cute little ash-trays where you touch a spring and a wreath with a black silk bow for mother's grave that'll last all summer. I got to write down a list so I won't forget all the things I got to do" (p. 37). (At the height of her pretending to largeness, the shopping list also comments tersely on her narrow scope—the ash tray, her valley of ashes background; the dog collar, her relationship with Tom Buchanan; the cemetery wreath, her fate.)

Myrtle's pretensions collapse suddenly when, with "a short deft movement" (p. 37), Tom breaks her nose. The scene had been building steadily toward this climax, the room growing dimmer with a heavy haze of cigarette smoke, insinuating again the "fatal" region of the valley of ashes. People now stumble confusedly about through the cigarette haze while there is heard "high over the confusion a long broken wail of pain" (p. 38). Myrtle is seen lying on a couch, bleeding profusely, while the others attempt to spread copies of "Town Tattle" over the tapestry scenes of Versailles. In this telescoped detail, a contrast is implied between the court of Versailles, with its formal elegance and aristocratic associations, as well as its court romance and love intrigues, and the "love intrigue" that has just been witnessed. This kind of detail, emphasizing through historical contrast the banality of the present moment, is reminiscent of *The Waste Land,* and may have been inspired by it; but not even in Eliot is the detail worked in more tellingly.

The apartment sequence "freezes" a moment of time, and its implications. Its implications are several, for Tom's affair with a married woman will be played off against Gatsby's with Daisy. But it is already apparent that Tom's affair has a purely physical nature, is imaginatively vacant, while Gatsby's affair with Daisy is of quite another kind. The whole scene at the apartment evokes the idea of vacancy, as well as failure and casualty, not the least of these casualties being Chester McKee, the wife-dominated photographer hinted to be more homosexual than heterosexual. As he first appears, an impression is given that he has just been shaving, for he has a "white spot of lather on his cheekbone" (p. 30), a detail that makes Chester seem like an ineffectual little man. Ironically, he is shown again near the end of the scene "asleep on a chair with his fists clenched in his lap, like the photograph of a man in action" (p. 37). Carraway sees him to his apartment and practically tucks him into bed. Sitting up in bed, rather like a child, McKee shows Carraway samples of his photographs, with titles like *Loneliness* and *Brook'n Bridge*, which suggests his own painful failure. Failed as artist and as man, McKee is a small figure in relief, set against the figure of Gatsby, who is to dominate the following chapter.

The dinner party at East Egg was exclusive and limited to a few, but Gatsby's party at West Egg has a vast scale and is open to "the world and its mistress" (p. 61). Gatsby's house, a "factual imitation of some Hôtel de Ville in Normandy" (p. 5) also indicates Gatsby's nature; as a Hotel de Ville, it is a town or city hall, and implies Gatsby's inclusiveness rather than exclusions. (His inclusiveness is also underlined quietly in the volumes of *Stoddard's Lectures*, the travel books taking in the entire world, which are found on Gatsby's book shelves.) Although the interior of the house is shown, the scene is set for the most part at night in Gatsby's "blue gardens [where] men and girls came and went like moths among the whisperings and the champagne and the stars" (p. 39). Gatsby and his moonlit world of festival are at the very furthest remove from the valley of ashes, noted immediately before, in the previous chapter.

Gatsby's "enormous garden" is strung with colored lights and is the scene of a "spectroscopic gayety," a night world where magic and reality mingle. People come uninvited from everywhere, crowding onto his lawn, enjoying his apparently endless supply of champagne, his buffets of pastry, pigs and turkeys bewitched to a dark gold, and dinners served at different times of the night, while a large orchestra plays the "Jazz History of the World." To Carraway, the party has an incredible gaudiness; yet he remarks: "I had taken two fingerbowls of champagne, and the scene had changed before my eyes into something significant, elemental, and profound" (p. 47). *It is exactly at this moment* that he meets Gatsby, the creator of this raw splendor. Gatsby is "placed" here as having creative energy; he has the power to make others share in his own vision, to make them participate in something outside of and larger than themselves. From the raw material of reality, he produces wonder, but his wonder-making imagination, in which discrimination is in abeyance, is also his tragic flaw. For this reason, it is reasonable that Owl Eyes should be found in Gatsby's library, expressing amazement at Gatsby's world and its doubtful relation to reality. Owl Eyes inspects the library shelves, surprised to find that the books are authentic, and then compares Gatsby with Belasco, who used real props to heighten stage illusion. Gatsby's implications, his inner self, are evoked through setting and scene in a way that is similar to Fitzgerald's presentation of his characters in the preceding chapters.

But these first three chapters do more than introduce Fitzgerald's characters and their social settings; they also intimate what is to follow. The Buchanans are shown first at their great shorefront estate, which, partly by its appearance at the opening, has primacy as solid fact. The time of the scene is also important, since it initiates a time sequence in the first three chapters. In the opening scene at the Buchanans' home, sunset is approaching, but the late afternoon sunlight is still strong. The New York apartment scene begins in the afternoon and fades into evening. It is late at night, however, past midnight, when Gatsby is shown and his party observed. There is thus a continuance in time, although the parties occur on different days, from afternoon to midnight, that binds the opening chapters together and adumbrates the novel's movement from day into night, from light into darkness.

The chapters are given internal unity, also, by the motif of confusion that runs through them. Its source originates, significantly, with the Buchanans, who establish the theme of money at the outset. In the opening section, the telephone call shatters brittle appearances, and the scene ends with a feeling of confusion and disgust on the part of Carraway, which will later be enacted on a larger scale. In the apartment scene, a sordid confusion follows the love tryst that leaves Myrtle broken and bleeding, prefiguring her role in the novel as victim, her life to be violently extinguished by Daisy, as Gatsby's is to be, through Wilson, by Tom. The third version of confusion appears again in the chapter devoted to Gatsby, in the procession of stalled cars and the honking of their horns, on Gatsby's drive; but from this scene, Gatsby himself is aloof, as he stands under the moon in an imposing isolation, gesturing farewell, that is like a signaling of the role he is to play in the novel. The theme of a deepening confusion is insinuated in the first three chapters, even before the novel has well begun.

The Great Gatsby: The Final Vision

Christiane Johnson*

The last page of F. Scott Fitzgerald's The Great Gatsby is a vision. In this passage, the novel is given a dimension that has been latent all along. Here, from the temporal and the inessential, we pass on to the timeless and the essential, in a typically Fitzgeraldian manner: nothing is fixed, everything is fluid, moving, changing. And imperceptibly we are carried from the palaces of Long Island into the eternal flow of time.

In his original manuscript, Fitzgerald had put the first long paragraph of his last page at the end of the first chapter of his novel: it accompanied the gesture that Gatsby made toward Daisy's dock lit by

*Reprinted from Fitzgerald/Hemingway Annual 1976 (Englewood, Colo.: Information Handling Services, 1978), pp. 109–15, by permission of the publisher.

its green light. But the novelist soon realized that, at that place and moment of the narrative, the evocation of the past, of the primitive island, betrayed both too much and too little: it lost its power of evocation and became forgotten in the course of the novel. On the contrary, as a conclusion, it gives the novel a mythical dimension, often pointed out by critics, which is so characteristic of American literature: Gatsby is much more than a Midwesterner come East; the story of his dream together with his "heightened sensitivity to the promises of life" are those of America itself, and his tremendous and misled hope becomes that of mankind. Fitzgerald has prepared us for that dimension all through the novel, particularly in the passages of an elegiac nature in which Nick, the narrator, meditated on Gatsby, and which because of their very tone, were meant to receive our spontaneous and irrational response. This page is the outcome of those passages.

The vision starts from reality: the narrator, ready to leave for the Middle West, his home, throws a last glance on Long Island where he has spent a momentous summer. Gatsby's house, which he has just called "that huge incoherent failure of a house" (p. 181) is closed, like all the other palaces, because it is autumn. All lights are out, even though, not so long ago, the fantastic lighting of Gatsby's house made it look like "the World's Fair" (p. 82). The only feature alive is the ferryboat crossing Long Island Sound, that ferryboat which, for Fitzgerald in "My Lost City," represented the triumphal entrance into New York, since it allowed him to apprehend the city in all its glory, New York, for him the city of all mysteries and of all promises; but here the ferryboat is only a "shadowy moving glow," already losing itself in the vision. Replacing the artificial lighting, is the light of the moon, primitive and elementary, which seems to have nothing in common with that moon that shone over Gatsby's parties, "produced like a supper, no doubt, out of a caterer's basket" (p. 43). Nick, who earlier compared himself with Kant (p. 89), is capable of seeing beyond reality, of grasping the essence beyond existence. This is why the houses, with all the pretension and ostentation they imply, now become "inessential," and give way to the vision. The fluidity of the successive transformations is expressed through the terms: "began to melt away," "gradually I became aware"; for the full extent of the vision does not come at once.

The vision begins with a return to the origins of the American nation, to a primitive past, imagined as pastoral and idyllic, for which Americans have nostalgically been yearning since the remote beginning. Long Island becomes "the old island . . . that flowered, and it is called "a fresh, green breast," and these few words are sufficient to suggest the essence of that pastoral past; but the maternal image, "breast," betrays an even deeper longing in man, the desire to be united again to nature as mother (the buried cause of America's attraction to its pastoral past). Nick, who is from the rural Middle West, is liable to be particularly aware of that nostalgia (and he gives hints of his insight when he remarks on the pastoral character of Fifth Avenue in summer).

Then follows a vast period which takes us beyond reality, beyond space, beyond time. Reality is there only in the negative: "vanished trees," implying, although in a very minor key, the ruthless destruction of those primitive trees, so much more essential than the present houses. And now the sentence erases limitations: it deals at once with a certain man, with man, with the continent, with "the greatest of human dreams." Dreams, the enchanted moment, aesthetic contemplation, wonder: all this belongs to the field of the irrational, for the sentence does not express a rational, intellectual reaction, but a purely emotional and instinctive response to a moment of perfect harmony between aspiration and reality, in which man was "compelled into an aesthetic contemplation he neither understood nor desired." The reader is compelled, too, through the power of words, of sounds, of repetitions, but mainly of the epic rhythm: he is made to share that moment. But at the same time, the ephemeral quality of the scene gives it its poignancy: the adjective "last" is repeated twice: "man must have held his breath" contrasts, with its connotations of short duration, of precarious balance, with the solidity of "this continent." Regret and nostalgia are evoked at the very climax of the vision, the phrases "transitory enchanted moment" and "for the last time in history" suggesting that, in its very perfection, the vision carries its unavoidable destruction. The only thing left at the end is the unsubstantial "capacity for wonder."

We are now, so it seems, far from Gatsby and his story. But all along, we are constantly, even if imperceptibly and almost unconsciously, brought back to his particular case by verbal suggestions, associations and echoes. Speaking of the old island, the narrator says that it *"flowered once for Dutch sailors' eyes"*; thus Daisy, when Gatsby kissed her for the first time, "blossomed for him like a flower" (p. 112). The maternal image of the "green breast" recalls another maternal image, just before Gatsby incarnates his dream in Daisy: "he could suck on the pap of life, gulp down the incomparable milk of wonder" (p. 112), in which love for a woman, motherly love and love for nature as mother become one. And of course the 'green breast" is also evocative of Daisy's "green light." The word "pandered," with its connotations of illicit love, while it announces how the first settlers would exploit the virgin land that was revealed to them, also ties the dream to the deceitful attraction of the girl who is both too fragile and too corrupt to carry it. In the next paragraph, more explicitly, "the greatest of all human dreams" becomes "his dream," and "Gatsby's wonder" echoes man's "capacity for wonder." "This blue lawn" calls back the "blue gardens" of the third chapter, in which the famous parties took place. And "he could hardly fail to grasp it" takes us back to the end of the first chapter, when Gatsby, stretching out his arms towards Daisy's dock, had so intrigued Nick. Thus the whole novel—and more than the novel—is present in this last page, through suggestions and allusions; but everything is transformed, transposed. At the same time, the choice of words entertains a confusion which is intended to enlarge Gatsby's dream and to merge it with the dream of a whole nation. Through a very Fitzgeraldian dialectic, the very mention of Gatsby, the man, suggests the deceiving, adulterated quality of his dream and of the broader dream as well; just as the verb "pandered," in the context of the "fresh, green breast of the new world," is bound to evoke the Fall from the Garden of Eden. But all this is allusive to the extreme, a minimum of words carrying a maximum of meaning.

The deliberate confusion is carried further through the constant passing from present to past, then to future, and later the expression of all three at the same time. The "new world," which, for the first settlers, the Dutch sailors, represented the future, is now for Nick "the old, unknown world." The present, pregnant with the future, has become itself the past. It has been necessary for the narrator to be of the present in order to know and express what the Dutch sailors could not know: that their dream vision was the greatest one in the history of mankind, but also the last one, that the enchanted moment was only passing, transitory. What was for them a marvellous future is for us only a past, just as Gatsby's dream "was already behind him" when he thought he had attained it with Daisy. And Gatsby and the Dutch sailors became identified with the same words, "dream" and "wonder," applying to both. The very parallelism of grammatical constructions underlines this identification: "man *must have held* his breath," and "his [Gatsby's] dream *must have seemed* so close"; in those constructions, the present is relived in its compulsiveness at the same time as it is experienced as past. In a subtler manner, the sentence "he could hardly fail to grasp it," if it recalls, as we said, Gatsby's gesture at the end of the first chapter, also announces "stretch out our arms further," expressed in the future in the next paragraph. Therefore this page is more than timeless: it partakes of past, present and future at once, and shows how it is their interplay that causes timelessness.

If Gatsby's dream is "already behind him," it is because it is connected with past hope, the past hope of a whole nation, as is once more, suggested by "the dark fields of the republic." The word "republic," with its implications of aspirations and ideals, prolongs the fresco which started with the Dutch sailors and the discovery of the continent, and contributes further to place the novel in a historical context much wider than the 1920's. Those fields which "rolled on" are the Middle West and the West, the Frontier, still unknown to the first settlers, but which was to feed the dream here first revealed to them and which would continue to exist long after them. "Fields" and "republic" also evoke Jefferson's democratic ideal and dream of keeping the country rural. Furthermore, the word "fields" recalls battlefields, the battlefields of the Civil War and of the American Revolution, fields on which the *Republic* fought for its very survival.

In Fitzgerald's first draft, this passage was very personalized: it was Nick who "could feel . . . beyond that [the city] the dark fields of the republic rolling on under the night." But here, the novelist moved the emphasis from the narrator's personal immediate experience to a contemplation in which the persons of Nick and of Gatsby himself have become accessory. The comforting Eden-like and maternal vision of the beginning is gone, leaving only obscurity; even the elementary light of the moon has disappeared. And the paragraph ends on that notion of darkness on which the novelist insists: "vast obscurity," "dark fields," "under the night." The scene takes us "back in that vast obscurity," which suggests confrontation with the primeval darkness that is not without anguish: the anguish of primitive man cut off from maternal earth, the anguish at the thought of the future, the metaphysical anguish of man faced with the darkness of destiny.

At this point, Gatsby's dream becomes completely transcended: from "I" and "he," the narrator passes on to "we," through a process of assimilation: "*Gatsby* believed in the green light, the orgastic future that year by year recedes before us." We have now become Gatsby, but at the same time Gatsby is us, Gatsby is every man. And the green light is much more than the light "at the end of Daisy's dock;" it is now called "the orgastic future." We know Fitzgerald meant "orgastic," which, he said, "is the adjective for 'orgasm' and it expresses exactly the intended ecstasy. It is not a bit dirty." The fact that the one term is most likely to suggest the other underlines the ambivalence of Gatsby's dream which partakes both of the kind of ecstasy Fitzgerald had in mind and of the orgies into which Gatsby's parties degenerated. And what is implied here is that no dream is exempt from this ambivalence.

In the first paragraph, the dream was associated with the "fresh, green breast of the new world"; in the preceding sentence, it was "already behind him," lost in "the dark fields of the republic"; and now it becomes the ungraspable future that "recedes before us." It is at the same time behind and before, the very contradiction is expressed by the terms "future" and "recedes," the first leading forward, and the second expressing a movement backward. The fusion of past, present and future is complete, and the three grammatical tenses are used, strikingly, in the same sentence: "It eluded us then, but that's no matter— tomorrow we will run faster . . .," after the back and forth movement that continually led from the one to the other (the present here being a timeless present).

Let us notice the choice of physical gestures in the whole passage: trying to grasp, running forward, stretching out arms; they are all gestures of a quest, an unceasing quest toward a goal that is never reached. The human condition is to aspire, and the quest counts more than the goal which remains unattainable. With Gatsby, the reason is clear: the future to which he is aspiring is a false future, it is a future that attempts to repeat the past, it is both before and behind.

But the movement of the third and fourth paragraphs, by carrying us toward the last sentence and the final image, seems to suggest that all men are likewise endlessly aspiring toward the past. The movement of that ending is swifter, the sentences are shorter, more syncopated, as if to render those constant and vain attempts at reaching a receding goal. The numerous nouns and adjectives of the beginning, which contributed to evoke the vision, are now being replaced by a great number of verbs, in order to express movement. And the reader is led irresistibly to the final image of the current, the flow of life on which men are only frail boats. The alliterative b's give that last sentence a decisive and final quality. All limitations, in time as well as in space, have disappeared. Just as Gatsby's hope was both before and behind him, we don't know whether the current is carrying us forward or backward. Man is at the same time acting and acted upon: "we beat on," but we are "borne back." And the last word is "past." Man is endlessly aspiring toward the past, toward a lost paradise. His continual quest for the future can only lead him into the past. But there is grandeur in his constant quest in spite of his helplessness.

In this whole passage, Fitzgerald carries his reader, not through any logical reasoning, since he is in a field where logic simply does not apply, but through the power of words and the primordial and mythical images they suggest. He succeeds, in an extremely poetical page, where serenity prevails, in evoking the whole human condition. And this seems to us its greatest value: the breadth of its vision lending it an archetypal quality.

Style as Meaning in
The Great Gatsby:
Notes Toward a New Approach   Jackson R. Bryer*

In the nearly six decades since its publication, *The Great Gatsby* has probably elicited more scholarly, critical, and popular attention than any other modern American novel. On three separate occasions, in 1926, 1949, and 1974, it has served as the basis of a major Hollywood movie; the 1974 version received extensive media coverage, including *Time* and *Newsweek* cover stories. In 1926, it was adapted into a successful Broadway play by Owen Davis.

*This article, written especially for this volume, appears here for the first time.

Its fate among journalists and academic critics has been even more spectacular. The book, which reviewer H. L. Mencken described as "no more than a glorified anecdote" and whose characters outside of Gatsby himself he called "mere marionettes,"[1] has been explicated, analyzed, explained, criticized, puzzled over, and praised at an alarming rate, especially since Fitzgerald's death. By actual count, since 1940 there have been well over three hundred books, book chapters, essays, articles, and notes solely devoted to *Gatsby*. These include John S. Whitley's *F. Scott Fitzgerald: "The Great Gatsby"* (London: Edward Arnold, 1976), a 64-page pamphlet in the prestigious *Studies in English Literature* series edited by David Daiches (of 61 titles in print in 1976, *Gatsby* was only the third in the series on a work by an American author and the first on a modern American writer), and Robert Emmet Long's excellent book, *The Achieving of "The Great Gatsby"—F. Scott Fitzgerald, 1920–1925* (Lewisburg, Pa.; Bucknell University Press, 1979). In devoting individual chapters to showing how Fitzgerald's earlier stories and novels were an important apprenticeship for *Gatsby*, to demonstrating how "Conrad's early fiction was influential on Fitzgerald's conception of *The Great Gatsby*," to examining "the art of *The Great Gatsby* and the aesthetic strategies it involves," and to placing it "in the context of the American literary milieu of the early twenties, out of which it evolves and which it also expresses," Long efficiently and effectively approaches the novel from each of the major perspectives which have concerned its critics over the past four decades.

Scholarly study of *Gatsby* began in the 1940s and 1950s and the earliest focus was on it as a criticism of the American experience and as a work with universal themes and appeal. Two important expressions of this viewpoint are Lionel Trilling's "Introduction" to the 1945 New Directions edition and Marius Bewley's "Scott Fitzgerald's Criticism of America" (*Sewanee Review*, Spring 1954), Robert Ornstein's "Scott Fitzgerald's Fable of East and West" (*College English*, December 1956); John Henry Raleigh's "Fitzgerald's *The Great Gatsby*" and "F. Scott Fitzgerald's *The Great Gatsby*—Legendary Bases and Allegorical Significances" (*University of Kansas City Review*, June 1957 and October 1957); and Richard Chase's section on *Gatsby* in his *The American Novel and Its Tradition* (Garden City, N. Y.: Doubleday, 1957) are other worthy early examples of this approach. In the 1960s and 1970s, notable criticism came from Charles Thomas Samuels' "The Greatness of 'Gatsby'" (*Massachusetts Review*, Autumn 1966); David F. Trask's "A Note on Fitzgerald's 'The Great Gatsby'" (*University Review*, March 1967); Kermit W. Moyer's "*The Great Gatsby*: Fitzgerald's Meditation on American History" (*Fitzgerald/Hemingway Annual*, 1972); and Brian M. Barbour's "*The Great Gatsby* and the American Past" (*Southern Review*, Spring 1973).

Another approach that has been extremely popular in *Gatsby* criticism is to compare the novel with other great works of literature, often with a suggestion of influence. The most consistently argued candidates for this sort of study have been Eliot's *The Waste Land*, Conrad's fiction, James's novels, especially *The American*, Keats's poetry, and various Christian and pagan myths. Long has done the best work on the Conrad connections, in his book and in his *"The Great Gatsby* and the Tradition of Joseph Conrad" (*Texas Studies in Literature and Language*, Summer 1966 and Fall 1966). Don McCall's "'The Self-Same Song That Found a Path': Keats and *The Great Gatsby"* (*American Literature*, January 1971) is the most persuasive essay on the Keatsian influences. Good studies of the Jamesian echoes are Kermit Vanderbilt's "James, Fitzgerald, and the American Self-Image" (*Massachusetts Review*, Winter-Spring 1965), Cleanth Brooks's "The American 'Innocence': In James, Fitzgerald, and Faulkner" (*Shenandoah*, Autumn 1964), which convincingly links Gatsby with Thomas Sutpen and Christopher Newman, and David L. Minter's "Extension of the Form: Henry James, and Fitzgerald's *The Great Gatsby*," in his *The Interpreted Design as a Structural Principle in American Prose* (New Haven, Ct.: Yale University Press, 1969).

The best early essay on *Gatsby* and *The Waste Land* is John W. Bicknell's "The Waste Land of F. Scott Fitzgerald" (*Virginia Quarterly Review*, Autumn 1954); while Robert Shulman's "Myth, Mr. Eliot, and the Comic Novel" (*Modern Fiction Studies*, Winter 1966–67) and Letha Audhuy's "*The Waste Land*: Myth and Symbolism in *The Great Gatsby*" (*Études Anglaises*, January-March 1980) are good later ones. Douglas Taylor, in "*The Great Gatsby*: Style and Myth" (*University of Kansas City Review*, Autumn 1953), did pioneering work on the mythic elements, as did Wilfred Louis Guerin, in "Christian Myth and Naturalistic Deity: *The Great Gatsby*" (*Renascence*, Winter 1962). But the definitive exploration of this area is Robert J. Emmitt's "Love, Death and Resurrection in *The Great Gatsby*," in Donna G. Fricke and Douglas C. Fricke, eds. *Aeolian Harps* (Bowling Green, Ohio: Bowling Green University Press, 1976), which examines in great detail Fitzgerald's uses of the Grail legend, the Waste Land myth, and the "ancient Semitic and Egyptian resurrection myths."

In the late 1960s, 1970s, and early 1980s, these comparative and influence studies proliferated greatly and *Gatsby* was linked with Coleridge's "Dejection Ode," Milton's *Paradise Lost*, Melville's *Mardi*, Chaucer's *Troilus and Criseyde*, Twain's *Huckleberry Finn*, Norris' *Vandover and the Brute*, Pope's *Moral Epistles*, Brontë's *Wuthering Heights*, Wells's *Tono-Bungay*, Wharton's *The Spark*, Dreiser's *An American Tragedy*, Orwell's *1984*, Steinbeck's *Cup of Gold*, and Raymond Chandler's *The Long Goodbye*.[2] The most rewarding of the comparative pieces, however, are Norman Friedman's "Versions of Form in Fiction—'Great Expectations' and 'The Great Gatsby'" (*Accent*, Autumn 1954), Steven Curry and Peter L. Hays's study of the possible influence of *Vanity Fair* on *Gatsby* (*Fitzgerald/Hemingway Annual*, 1977), and Lawrence Thornton's "Ford Madox Ford and *The Great Gatsby*" (*Fitzgerald/Hemingway Annual*, 1975), which suggests parallels with *The Good Soldier*. James E. Miller, Jr.'s, "Fitzgerald's *Gatsby*: The World as Ash Heap," in Warren French, ed. *The Twenties* (Deland, Fla.: Everett/Edwards, 1975), explores both the *Waste Land* and Jamesian elements of the novel, as well as a variety of other aspects, in what is the best essay on *Gatsby* published in the 1970s.

Not surprisingly, despite Mencken's description of them as "mere marionettes," most of the major characters in *Gatsby* have been examined in individual essays. Early attention focused on Nick and he is still the most popular subject for this type of article. Thomas A. Hanzo's "The Theme and the Narrator of 'The Great Gatsby'" (*Modern Fiction Studies*, Winter 1956–57), E. Fred Carlisle's "The Triple Vision of Nick Carraway" (*Modern Fiction Studies*, Winter 1965–66), and Peter Lisca's "Nick Carraway and the Imagery of Disorder" (*Twentieth Century Literature*, April 1967) are good early articles. Debate regarding Nick's reliability as a narrator was spurred by Gary J. Scrimgeour's "Against 'The Great Gatsby'" (*Criticism*, Winter 1966). It was further fueled by Oliver H. Evans's "'A Sort of Moral Attention': The Narrator of *The Great Gatsby*" (*Fitzgerald/Hemingway Annual*, 1971), which questioned Nick's credibility, and Albert E. Elmore's "Nick Carraway's Self-Introduction" (*Fitzgerald/Hemingway Annual*, 1971), which defended it. In the 1980s it has continued in Colin S. Cass's "'Pandered in Whispers': Narrative Reliability in *The Great Gatsby*" (*College Literature*, Spring 1980) and Susan Resneck Parr's "Individual Responsibility in *The Great Gatsby*" (*Virginia Quarterly Review*, Autumn 1981).

In the late 1960s and in the 1970s, just as the comparative studies of *Gatsby* began to look further afield, so did the essays on individual characters. There are now worthwhile pieces on Daisy by Joan Korenman (*American Literature*, January 1975) and Leland S. Person, Jr. (*American Literature*, May 1978); on Myrtle by Barry E. Gross (*Tennessee Studies in Literature*, 1963) and E. C. Bufkin (*Modern Fiction Studies*, Winter 1969–70); on Tom by Christian Messenger (*Journal of Popular Culture*, Fall 1974) and Robert Roulston (*Arizona Quarterly*, Summer 1978); on Meyer Wolfsheim by Josephine Z. Kopf (*Tradition*, Spring 1969); and on George Wilson by G. I. Hughes (*English Studies in Africa*, September 1972).

Still another group of essays through the years has concentrated on symbol patterns in *Gatsby*. The most frequently investigated of these have been Dr. T. J. Eckleburg's eyes, colors, Gatsby's guest list, and automobiles. Some of the earliest scholarly articles on *Gatsby* dealt with Dr. Eckleburg's eyes, among them Tom Burnam's "The Eyes of Dr. Eckleburg: A Re-examination" (*College English*, October 1952); Milton Hindus' "The Mysterious Eyes of Doctor T. J. Eckleburg" (*Boston Uni-*

versity Studies in English, Spring 1957); and Robert F. McDonnell's "Eyes and Eggs in *The Great Gatsby*" (*Modern Fiction Studies*, Spring 1961). But the seemingly already exhausted subject has more recently interested Sanford Pinsker (*College Literature*, Winter 1975) and Marie J. Kilker (*Publications of the Missouri Philological Association*, 1980).

Daniel J. Schneider's "Color-Symbolism in *The Great Gatsby*" (*University Review*, October 1964) is the earliest and remains one of the best discussions of that topic, along with A. E. Elmore's "Color and Cosmos in *The Great Gatsby*" (*Sewanee Review*, Summer 1970). Rita Gollin's "The Automobiles of *The Great Gatsby*" (*Studies in the Twentieth Century*, Fall 1970); John J. McNally's "Boats and Automobiles in *The Great Gatsby*" (*Husson Review*, No. 1, 1971); Laurence E. MacPhee's "*The Great Gatsby's* 'Romance of Motoring': Nick Carraway and Jordan Baker" (*Modern Fiction Studies*, Summer 1972); Kenneth S. Knodt's "The Gathering Darkness: A Study of the Effects of Technology in *The Great Gatsby*" (*Fitzgerald/Hemingway Annual*, 1976); and Irving S. Saposnik's "The Passion and the Life: Technology as Pattern in *The Great Gatsby*" (*Fitzgerald/Hemingway Annual*, 1979) have more than fully discussed the topic of car, boat, and train imagery. Similarly, Gatsby's guest list and its symbolic implications have been amply perused by Lottie R. Crim and Neal B. Houston (*Research Studies*, June 1968) and by Ruth Prigozy (*Fitzgerald/Hemingway Annual*, 1972). Other symbols that have been traced through the novel include telephones, noses, houses, water, light, and music.[3]

Many of the best of the essays in each of the categories discussed above, especially those written in the 1950s and 1960s, have been reprinted in one or more of the three collections of *Gatsby* criticism in print—Frederick J. Hoffman's "*The Great Gatsby*": *A Study* (New York: Charles Scribner's, 1962); Ernest H. Lockridge's *Twentieth Century Interpretations of "The Great Gatsby"—A Collection of Critical Essays* (Englewood Cliffs, N.J.: Prentice-Hall, 1968); and Henry Dan Piper's *Fitzgerald's "The Great Gatsby": The Novel, The Critics, The Background* (New York: Charles Scribner's, 1970). And, of course, some of the best commentary on *Gatsby* can be found in individual chapters of such full-length studies as Arthur Mizener's *The Far Side of Paradise* (rev. ed.; Boston: Houghton Mifflin, 1965); Kenneth Eble's *F. Scott Fitzgerald* (rev. ed.; Boston: Twayne, 1977); James E. Miller, Jr.'s, *F. Scott Fitzgerald—His Art and His Technique* (New York: New York University Press, 1964); Sergio Perosa's *The Art of F. Scott Fitzgerald* (Ann Arbor: University of Michigan Press, 1965); Richard D. Lehan's *F. Scott Fitzgerald and the Craft of Fiction* (Carbondale: Southern Illinois University Press, 1966); Robert Sklar's *F. Scott Fitzgerald—The Last Laocoön* (New York: Oxford University Press, 1967); Milton Hindus' *F. Scott Fitzgerald—An Introduction* (New York: Holt, Rinehart and Winston, 1968); Milton R. Stern's *The Golden Moment—The Novels of F. Scott Fitzgerald* (Urbana: University of Illinois Press, 1970); John E. Callahan's *The Illusions of a Nation—Myth and History in the Novels of F. Scott Fitzgerald* (Urbana: University of Illinois Press, 1972); and Brian Way's *F. Scott Fitzgerald and the Art of Social Fiction* (London: Edward Arnold, 1980; New York: St. Martin's Press, 1980). Some of these chapters—but, again, only those published in the 1950s and 1960s—have also been reprinted in one or more of the three earlier *Gatsby* collections. There is obviously a need for this collection which includes examples of the best *Gatsby* studies done in the 1970s and early 1980s.

These studies, as previously noted, have in many instances reiterated or broadened approaches introduced in the 1950s and 1960s. In two significant areas, however, research on *Gatsby* in the 1970s has explored new and fertile territory. The first of these is what might be broadly described as bibliographical and textual study. Matthew J. Bruccoli's edition of *"The Great Gatsby"—A Facsimile of the Manuscript* (Washington, D.C.: Microcard Editions, 1973) provides, in its introduction and in the facsimile of Fitzgerald's final holograph draft, the fullest evidence we have of his meticulous work on the novel. This subject had been surveyed briefly by Kenneth Eble in "The Craft of Revision: *The Great Gatsby*" (*American Literature*, November 1964). Similarly, the highly corrupt text of the most frequently used editions of *Gatsby* had been first pointed out by Bruce Harkness (*Studies in Bibliography*, 1958). But Bruccoli's *Apparatus for F. Scott Fitzgerald's "The Great Gatsby"* [*Under the Red, White, and Blue*] (Columbia: University of South Carolina Press, 1974), in supplying "a do-it-yourself kit for converting the best available edition [the 1925 first printing] . . . into a definitive edition," goes well beyond Harkness and such other more recent essays and notes on the text of *Gatsby* as those by Bruccoli himself, in Francess G. Halpenny, ed. *Editing Twentieth Century Texts* (Toronto: University of Toronto Press, 1972); Jennifer E. Atkinson (*Fitzgerald/Hemingway Annual*, 1970); and Margaret M. Duggan (*Fitzgerald/Hemingway Annual*, 1976). Andrew Crosland's *A Concordance to F. Scott Fitzgerald's "The Great Gatsby"* (Detroit: Gale/Bruccoli Clark, 1975), the first concordance of an American novel, is enormously helpful in tracing Fitzgerald's use of specific recurrent words and phrases.

These various bibliographical and textual aids have undoubtedly been instrumental in giving impetus to the second approach to *Gatsby* which has blossomed in the 1970s, that of careful attention to the novel's style and language. Until quite recently, the only pieces that had dealt with this topic were W. J. Harvey's "Theme and Texture in *The Great Gatsby*" (*English Studies*, February, 1957) and Guy Owen's "Imagery and Meaning in 'The Great Gatsby,' " in Richard E. Langford, ed. *Essays in Modern American Literature* (Deland, Fla.: Stetson University Press, 1963). In the past fifteen years, valuable and much needed close readings have appeared with regularity. These include Victor Doyno's "Patterns in *The Great Gatsby*" (*Modern Fiction Studies*, Winter 1966–67); F. H. Langman's "Style and Shape in *The Great Gatsby*" (*Southern Review* [University of Adelaide, Australia], March 1973); Bruce R. Stark's "The Intricate Pattern in *The Great Gatsby*" (*Fitzgerald/Hemingway Annual*, 1974); Robert Emmet Long's "The Opening Three Chapters of 'The Great Gatsby'" (*English Record*, Fall 1975 and incorporated into his book); Joan S. Korenman's "A View From the (Queensboro) Bridge" (*Fitzgerald/Hemingway Annual*, 1975); Barbara Gerber Sanders' "Structural Imagery in *The Great Gatsby*: Metaphor and Matrix" (*Linguistics in Literature*, Fall 1975); Christiane Johnson's "*The Great Gatsby*: The Final Vision" (*Fitzgerald/Hemingway Annual*, 1976; Takashi Tasaka's "The Meaning of Oxymoron in *The Great Gatsby*" (*Yasuda Joshi Daigaku Kiyō*, November 1977); and Leonard A. Podis' " 'The Unreality of Reality': Metaphor in *The Great Gatsby*" (*Style*, Winter 1977).

In this necessarily limited survey, I have tried to outline the major trends in *Gatsby* scholarship and to highlight the most worthwhile pieces. I have also attempted to indicate how redundant much of the scholarship has been. With well over three-hundred essays in print, a very high proportion of these have clustered around such oft-debated topics as the novel's affinity with Eliot's *Waste Land*, Nick's reliability as a narrator, the symbolism of Dr. Eckleburg's eyes, *Gatsby* as a criticism of the American experience, and its universality. To be sure, there have been good articles on these subjects, as I have suggested; but there has also been too narrow a focus. Within the past decade, however, focus has begun to widen. As the generally accepted picture of Fitzgerald as the Bard of the Jazz Age and the consummate and emblematic depicter of and participant in the excesses of the Roaring Twenties has, with the recent availability of textual and bibliographical aids, gradually given way to a view of him as a careful, conscious, and extremely skillful fictional craftsman whose novels and stories were the result of painstaking effort, study of *Gatsby* has increasingly concerned itself with style and language. This is a particularly felicitous shift, because surely one of the major reasons for its success and for its advance over Fitzgerald's previous works is its style.

With the exception of the Langman and Tasaka essays, none of the recent studies of style deal in any detail with the way in which the smallest units in the language of the novel function as indicators of its meaning as a whole. That this pattern represents deliberate intention on Fitzgerald's part is suggested most clearly in a letter which he wrote to his daughter in October 1936, just after Scottie had entered the Ethel Walker School in Connecticut and when her father was apparently feeling the need to act as her unofficial writing instructor:

If you have anything to say, anything you feel nobody has ever said before, you have got to feel it so desperately that you will find some way to say it that nobody has ever found before, so that the thing you have to say and the way of saying it blend as one matter— as indissolubly as if they were conceived together.

Let me preach again for a moment: I mean that what you have felt and thought will by itself invent a new style, so that when people talk about style they are always a little astonished at the newness of it, because they think that it is only *style* that they are talking about, when what they are talking about is the attempt to express a new idea with such force that it will have the originality of the thought.[4]

When Fitzgerald speaks of finding "some way to say it that nobody has ever found before" and explains that, in doing so, "the thing you have to say and the way of saying it blend as one matter—as indissolubly as if they were conceived together," he is obviously speaking from his own experience. He is also providing us with an excellent description of the way style functions in *The Great Gatsby*. A focus on the smallest elements of language in that novel, his choices of individual words and phrases, shows recurrent patterns that achieve three simultaneous and deliberate objectives: 1.) they are marvelously descriptive and evocative; 2.) they are often so original and witty that they surprise and capture the reader's attention; in Fitzgerald's own words, they astonish by their "newness"; and 3.) they metaphorically encapsulate or suggest in microcosmic form the meanings of the novel as a whole, thus achieving the blend of "the thing you have to say and the way of saying it" to which Fitzgerald refers. And, of course, this blend represents at this level exactly the sort of concision and economy which critics have pointed out at larger structural levels in many of the stylistic and image pattern studies mentioned previously. A brief and preliminary survey of what some of these small elements of style are and how they operate will, I hope, stimulate others to look at this aspect of Fitzgerald's style more closely, in *Gatsby* as well as in his other fiction.

If one examines the use of adjectives and adjective phrases in *Gatsby*, one finds a pattern of linked ambivalence or oxymorons ("contradictory expressions having 'semantic incompatibility'"[5]) which implies the thematic ambivalences and contradictions of the novel. These are most overtly expressed in Nick's remark, "I was within and without, simultaneously enchanted and repelled by the inexhaustible variety of life."[6] But they are also suggested throughout the novel in a recurrent pattern of descriptive phrases which are evocative and apt as well as original and metaphorically meaningful. Jordan Baker has a "charming, discontented face" (p. 11), with a "pleasing, contemptuous expression" (p. 19) and a "cool, insolent smile" (p. 59) which satisfies the demands of her "hard, jaunty body" (p. 59). Elsewhere, she is described as a "clean, hard, limited person" (p. 81) with a "wan, scornful mouth" (p. 81).

Daisy laughs "an absurd, charming little laugh" (p. 9). Mrs. McKee is "shrill, languid, handsome, and horrible" (p. 30); Gatsby's parties are characterized by "happy, vacuous bursts of laughter" (p. 47), by the presence of a "gorgeous, scarcely human orchid of a woman" (p. 106), and by "confused and intriguing sounds" (p. 51). Nick's final vision of West Egg is of a "night scene by El Greco: . . . at once conventional and grotesque" (p. 178). Here, as in all these phrases, there is an element of wit and "newness"—words not normally paired in description are linked—along with an aptness which denotes as well the jarring ambivalences and contradictions in the novel.

Another recurrent pattern in *Gatsby* is the linking of nouns with unusual descriptive adjectives. We read of Meyer Wolfsheim's "tragic nose" (p. 73), of the "triumphant hat-boxes" (p. 64) which adorn Gatsby's car, and of New York's "throbbing taxicabs" (p. 57). Daisy speaks with "tense gayety" (p. 16) and laughs "with thrilling scorn" (p. 18); while Jordan looks with "contemptuous interest" (p. 42) at the revellers at Gatsby's party. Owl-Eyes stares "with unsteady concentration" (p. 45) at the books in Gatsby's library; and Wolfsheim eats "with ferocious delicacy" (p. 71). Tom Buchanan insists "with magnanimous scorn" (p. 136) and speaks with "soothing gruffness" (p. 141). Gatsby is an "elegant young roughneck" (p. 48). There are two sub-categories in this pattern. One is, strictly speaking, not a noun modified by an unusual adjective, but the achieved effect is very similar. This is the repetition in Gatsby's guest list of names which combine an aristocratic or pretentious first name or names with an ordinary—or obviously ethnically inappropriate—surname: the Stonewall Jackson Abrams, the O. R. P. Schraeders, S. B. Whitebait, G. Earl Muldoon, S. W. Belcher. Here the intention is plainly satiric but the effect is also to create the same sort of arresting linkage present in the noun-adjective pairings. Similarly, while studies of color symbolism in *Gatsby* are numerous, few have noted how strikingly unusual and jarring these colors seem when paired with the objects they describe. Again, the effect is a mixture of surprise and a realization of appropriateness as we visualize Gatsby's "blue gardens" (p. 39), his "blue lawn" (p. 182), his pink suit, his yellow car, his silver shirt, and his golden-colored tie; or hear the yellow cocktail music (p. 40) at his parties. On a literal level, the garishness of Gatsby's car and wardrobe speak eloquently of his lack of style and foreshadow the inevitability of his defeat by the Buchanans, whose world is described in more muted colors. Daisy, as has often been pointed out, is associated throughout the novel, ironically, with the color white. But when these unusual color-noun sets are seen as part of a larger pattern of arresting adjective-noun linkages, they, like the linked adjectives, certainly mirror and suggest the ambivalent, contradictory, and jarring world of this novel.

In another letter to his daughter, Fitzgerald instructs her to "read carefully" Keats's "Ode to a Nightingale," where she will find "a phrase which will immediately remind you of my work." The phrase, of course, is "tender is the night"; but Fitzgerald goes on to ask Scottie to find in the same stanza of the poem "another phrase which I rather guiltily adapted to prose, in the 2nd paragraph on p. 115 of *The Great Gatsby*." Keats's phrase is, "But here there is no light, / Save what from heaven is with the breezes blown / Through verdurous glooms and winding mossy ways." Fitzgerald's adaptation reads, "He lit Daisy's cigarette from a trembling match, and sat down with her on a couch far across the room, where there was no light save what the gleaming floor bounced in from the hall" (p. 96). Fitzgerald ends his letter with a question— "When you have found what I refer to have you learned anything about the power of the verb in description?"[7] Again, Fitzgerald is speaking from his own experience here, because "the power of the verb in description" describes another recurrent pattern in *Gatsby* which "indissolubly" weds style to meaning. F. H. Langman has pointed out several examples of what he calls the "effects of novelty, precision, and suggestive power" in Fitzgerald's "choice of verbs." In George Wilson's garage, "the only car visible was the dust-covered wreck of a Ford which crouched in a dim corner" (p. 25). *Crouched* catches our attention, just as the other patterns we have examined do, because it is an unusual word choice, a verb not normally associated with a parked car. But, as Langman observes, it "brings out the frightened, fugitive quality of Wilson's hopeless endeavours, and, almost subliminally, in the idea of a creature preparing to spring, reinforces the menace that cars in the novel come to signify." To which one can add only that it surely also foreshadows Wilson's crouching and lurking in the bushes around Gatsby's pool as he prepares to commit the double murder which completes what Nick calls the novel's "holocaust."

Langman also discusses the phrase in the climactic scene in the stiflingly hot Plaza Hotel parlor when the telephone book "slipped from its nail and splashed to the floor" (p. 127), noting that "the precise expression does more than create the physical reality of the instant. . . . Gatsby has made his first challenge by asking Tom to stop criticizing Daisy. Into the moment of silence that follows, the telephone book falls, and its cool splash of pages seems to mark and measure the tension." The same combination of newness, aptness, and metaphorical suggestiveness can be found in other verbs used descriptively in the novel. Gatsby's motor-boats "slit" the waters of Long Island Sound (p. 39), evoking, in Langman's words, "force, speed, smoothness,"[8] all words that can just as easily be applied, but not without some irony, to Gatsby himself. On his buffet tables, "spiced baked hams crowded against salads of harlequin designs" (pp. 39–40); his car is "terraced with a labyrinth of windshields" (p. 64); as his party begins, the "earth lurches away from the sun" (p. 40).

In focusing on these small units of style, I have not meant to imply that *The Great Gatsby* depends on a self-conscious pretentious writing style. On the contrary, I have tried to reinforce the sense of its concision, of how a very few words are used to describe, arrest attention, entertain, and suggest all at once. Brief phrases characterize more fully and effectively than whole paragraphs of analysis, and this is often achieved through use of a simile or metaphor. Tom "compelled" Nick from the room "as though he were moving a checker to another square" (p. 12), a phrase which implies Tom's physical strength and also how he plays with the lives of those around him as if they were pawns in a game, thus foreshadowing the casual manner in which he betrays Gatsby to Wilson at the end of the novel. Jordan sits with her shoulders back "like a young cadet" (p. 11) and moves "as if she had first learned to walk upon golf courses on clear, crisp mornings" (p. 51). The guests at Gatsby's parties come and go "like moths among the whisperings" (p. 39); his station wagon "scampers like a brisk yellow bug" (p. 39) to meet trains. When Nick first meets them, Daisy and Jordan are seated on a couch in a wind-filled room, "buoyed up as though upon an anchored balloon" (p. 8).

These descriptive phrases and similes manifest all of the characteristics of the other small units of style; and they also exemplify another quality, a quality often present in the stylistic features I've examined earlier, that of wit and humor. This is suggested by the contrast between Keats's use of the "verb in description" and Fitzgerald's. Keats's highly romantic verb "blown" becomes, in Fitzgerald's adaptation, the playful, amusing verb "bounced." As Langman has quite accurately noted, *The Great Gatsby* is surely meant to be "a very funny book"; and yet "one can read quite widely in critical discussions without finding reference to the presence—let alone the preponderance—in it of comedy." Langman offers a number of specific examples of how humor functions in the novel and quotes several passages, including the scene at Tom and Myrtle's apartment in chapter 2 and Daisy and Gatsby's reunion in chapter 5. He asserts that the comic mode is "the novel's essential way of seeing: it is the source of the balance which can give full measure of sympathy to the characters without glossing over their folly, vanity and self-deceit."9 In other words, humor contributes in a major way to the presence in *Gatsby* of what Malcolm Cowley has called Fitzgerald's "double vision."10 And it is humor often built on the ironic, witty, and unexpected juxtapositions, pairings, and verbs which I have examined. Gatsby's guest list is the best instance of this, combining witty satire with bitter commentary on the world it portrays. But it is also present in such noun-adjective linkings as "tragic nose" and "ferocious delicacy," in adjective phrases like "shrill, languid, handsome, and horrible," and in descriptive verbs like "splashed." The humor of these small units, then, is yet another instance of how style and meaning blend seamlessly in *Gatsby*.

By focusing on small units of style in *The Great Gatsby*, I have tried to show how Fitzgerald achieves at that level the kind of blending of what he has to say and his way of saying it that he refers to in his 1936 letter to Scottie. In turn, I feel that this exercise has provided new and fruitful evidence of the linguistic concision which is at the heart of the achievement of the novel. As numerous critics have suggested, *Gatsby* can, and in many ways should, be studied like a poem, for the "sake of its distinctive voice, or voices, for the way in which it puts things, at least as much as for the significance of the episodes it recounts."[11] Until the 1970s, much of the *Gatsby* criticism was concerned with "the significance of the episodes it recounts"; within the past decade, attention has begun to be paid to "the way in which it puts things." In this preliminary study, I have tried to make a further contribution to this effort—an examination of how several kinds of small verbal units in the novel combine evocative and witty description with microcosmic suggestions of the macrocosm of this remarkable work. For Fitzgerald, style was meaning; and we need to examine that style in greater detail for the truest evidence of his achievement as a writer.

Notes

1. H. L. Mencken, "As H.L.M. Sees It," *Baltimore Evening Sun*, May 2, 1925, p. 9.
2. Cf. Leslie F. Chard, II, "Outward Forms and the Inner Life," *Fitzgerald/Hemingway Annual*, 5 (1973), 189–94; William H. Scheuerle, "'The Valley of Ashes': Fitzgerald's Lost Paradise," *Iowa English Yearbook*, 11 (1966), 55–58; John Shroeder, "'Some Unfortunate Idyllic Love Affair': The Legends of Taji and Jay Gatsby," *Books at Brown*, 22 (1968), 143–53; Nancy H. Hoffman, "*The Great Gatsby*: Troilus and Criseyde Revisited?" *Fitzgerald/Hemingway Annual*, 3 (1971), 148–58; Joseph Brogunier, "An Incident in *The Great Gatsby* and *Huckleberry Finn*," *Mark Twain Journal*, 16 (Summer 1972), 1–3; D. B. Graham, "Fitzgerald's Valley of Ashes and Frank Norris' 'Sordid and Grimy Wilderness,'" *Fitzgerald/Hemingway Annual*, 4 (1972), 303–06; Harry Williams, "An Epistle to Gatsby: On the Use of Riches," *Fitzgerald/Hemingway Annual*, 4 (1972), 61–65; Robert E. Morsberger, "The Romantic Ancestry of *The Great Gatsby*," *Fitzgerald/Hemingway Annual*, 5 (1973), 119–30; Robert Roulston, "Traces of *Tono-Bungay* in *The Great Gatsby*," *Journal of Narrative Technique*, 10 (Winter 1980), 68–76; Michael A. Peterman, "A Neglected Source for *The Great Gatsby*: The Influence of Edith Wharton's *The Spark*," *Canadian Review of American Studies*, 8 (Spring 1977), 26–35; Terence Doody, "Clyde and Jephson, Gatsby and Nick," in *Confession and Community in the Novel* (Baton Rouge: Louisiana State University Press, 1980), pp. 101–32; Norman Friedman, *Form and Meaning in Fiction* (Athens: University of Georgia Press, 1975), pp. 106–11; Kiyohiko Tsuboi, "Steinbeck's *Cup of Gold* and Fitzgerald's *The Great Gatsby*," in Tetsumaro Hayashi, Yasao Hashiguchi, and Richard F. Peterson, eds. *John Steinbeck: East and West* (Muncie,

Ind.: Steinbeck Society of America, Ball State University, 1978), pp. 40–47; and Leon Howard, "Raymond Chandler's Not-So-Great Gatsby," *Mystery & Detection Annual*, 2 (1973), 1–15. [Editor's note: see Robert Roulston's essay for a comprehensive discussion of "influence" studies.]

3. Cf. B. Bernard Cohen, "Telephone Symbolism in *The Great Gatsby*," *Folio* (Indiana University), 20 (Winter 1954), 19–23; John C. Weston, Jr., "From Romance to Ritual," *Fitzgerald Newsletter*, No. 4 (Winter 1959), 2; Barry E. Gross, "A Note on F's Use of the House," *Fitzgerald Newsletter*, No. 23 (Fall 1963), 2–4; Richard Cohen, "The Inessential Houses of The Great Gatsby," *Husson Review*, 2 (November 1968), 48–57; W. T. Lhamon, Jr., "The Essential Houses of *The Great Gatsby*," *Markham Review*, 6 (Spring 1977), 56–60; James F. Slevin, "Water Images in GG," *Fitzgerald Newsletter*, No. 39 (Fall 1967), 12–13; J. S. Lawry, "Green Light or Square of Light in *The Great Gatsby*," *Dalhousie Review*, 55 (Spring 1975), 114–32; and Bruce Bawer, " 'I Could Still Hear the Music': Jay Gatsby and the Musical Metaphor," *Notes on Modern American Literature*, 5 (Fall 1981), Item 25.

4. Andrew Turnbull, ed. *The Letters of F. Scott Fitzgerald* (New York: Charles Scribner's, 1963), p. 11.

5. Takashi Tasaka, "The Meaning of Oxymoron in *The Great Gatsby*," *Yasuda Joshi Daigaku Kiyō*, 6 (November 1977), 31.

6. F. Scott Fitzgerald, *The Great Gatsby* (New York: Charles Scribner's, 1953), p. 36. Future references to the novel are to this Scribner Library edition and will be cited in the text.

7. Matthew J. Bruccoli, Margaret M. Duggan, eds., with the assistance of Susan Walker, *Correspondence of F. Scott Fitzgerald* (New York: Random House, 1980), p. 522.

8. F. H. Langman, "Style and Shape in *The Great Gatsby*," *Southern Review* (University of Adelaide, Australia), 6 (March 1973), 48–49.

9. Langman, pp. 53–56.

10. Malcolm Cowley, "Fitzgerald: The Double Man," *Saturday Review of Literature*, 34 (February 24, 1951), 42–44.

11. Langman, p. 48.

Fresh Approaches

The Trouble with Nick
Scott Donaldson*

Nick Carraway is a snob. He dislikes people in general and denigrates them in particular. He dodges emotional commitments. Neither his ethical code nor his behavior is exemplary: propriety rather than morality guides him. He is not entirely honest about himself and frequently misunderstands others. Do these shortcomings mean that Nick is an unreliable narrator? At times and in part, yes. But they also mean that he is the perfect narrator for *The Great Gatsby*, and hence it is true that Fitzgerald's greatest technical achievement in the novel was to invent this narrative voice at once "within and without" the action.[1]

The first clue to Nick's makeup comes on the first page of the book, where he totally misunderstands his father's advice. "Whenever you feel like criticizing any one," his father had told him in his "younger and more vulnerable years," he was to remember that not everyone had enjoyed "the advantages" he has had. Clearly Nick's father is advising tolerance here, and it seems likely that he had detected in his son a propensity to find fault. Nick, however, interprets the remark as a judgment on others, who—lacking what he calls that "sense of the fundamental decencies . . . unequally parcelled out at birth"—consequently misbehave. This interpretation, Nick acknowledges, is an extraordinarily snobbish one, the interpretation of a snob who admits to the charge as if to say that there are far worse things than snobbery in the world: bad manners, for example. Nick's undoubted "advantages," which include good schools, social position, family background, and even an exclusive senior society at Yale, may eventuate in an awareness of the "fundamental decencies" if one construes the phrase narrowly as conforming to conventional standards of propriety, but they hardly guarantee any moral acumen. So it is with Nick Carraway. Most of all he disapproves of those who do *not know how to act*. That is why it takes him so long to ascertain that Jay Gatsby, a walking compendium of social gaucheries, is nonetheless worth any number of Buchanans.

*This article, written especially for this volume, appears here for the first time.

Nick's misunderstanding of his father should also put us on guard against his claim that he's "inclined to reserve all judgments," especially when in the next breath he speaks of the "veteran bores" and "wild, unknown men" who have made him privy to "intimate revelations . . . usually plagiaristic and marred by obvious suppressions." Had they suppressed less, Nick might have been more interested. "Reserving judgments is a matter of infinite hope," he observes, and he is not the character in the novel possessed by infinite hope. He listens to confessions since he is "a little afraid of missing something" (p. 1) otherwise: a vicarious sense of having drunk his cup to the lees.[2] But he does not suspend judgment. In fact, he judges, and condemns, practically everyone he meets in the course of the novel.

Collectively he speaks of closing off his interest in the "abortive sorrows and short-winded elations of men" (p. 2). Introducing individual specimens of this sorry genus, he delineates more specific physical deficiencies. Tom Buchanan has straw hair, a hard mouth, a supercilious manner, and a cruel body with which he pushes people around. There had been men at Yale who hated his guts, and if Nick is not among them, it's not because he can't see why (p. 7). His wife Daisy, Nick's second cousin once removed, speaks in a thrilling voice, but she murmurs so low that people must bend toward her to hear. Her insincere remark about having "been everywhere and seen everything and done everything" strikes Nick as "a trick of some sort" to exact an emotional commitment from him (pp. 9, 18).

With the lower orders Nick is still less charitable. Myrtle Wilson, smoldering with vitality, carries her "excess flesh sensuously" (p. 25) and comically takes on airs in the West 158th St. apartment Tom has secured for their rendezvous. Meyer Wolfsheim is presented as a small Jew with tiny eyes, a flat nose (in whose nostrils "fine growths of hair" luxuriate), and cuff buttons made of "finest specimens of human molars" (pp. 69–72). Sentence is passed rapidly on minor characters. Myrtle's sister Catherine—"a slender, worldly girl of thirty" with a sticky bob of red hair, rakishly painted eyebrows, and eternally jangling bracelets—is disposed of in a paragraph (p. 30). And in the catalog of those who attend Gatsby's parties, people are labeled and found wanting by name alone. "The Dancies came, too, and S. B. Whitebait, who was well over sixty, and Maurice A. Flink, and the Hammerheads, and Beluga the tobacco importer, and Beluga's girls": something is fishy here (p. 62).

Nick's basic contempt for mankind emerges in what he says and thinks as well as in descriptions of others. His particular way of telling the story—his voice—has been variously characterized in the critical literature on *Gatsby*, but surely a dominant characteristic of that voice is its irony.[3] This sometimes leads to light-hearted bantering in conversation, as with Daisy. Is she missed in Chicago, she asks? "All the cars have the left hear wheel painted black as a mourning wreath," he answers, "and there's a persistent wail all night along the north shore" (p. 10).[4] Would Nick like to hear about the butler's nose, she inquires? "That's why I came over to-night," he responds (p. 14). His unspoken thoughts, however, tend toward a more "hostile levity" (p. 1): toward sarcasm, in fact.

In his mind Nick constantly puts others down. After listening to Tom Buchanan maunder on about impending racial struggles and the increasing (or is it declining?) heat of the sun, he devastates the man he has helped cuckold when, with his eyes finally opened to the affair between Daisy and Gatsby, Tom begins to expound on the scientific proof for his "second sight" and then stops, the "immediate contingency" having "pulled him back from the edge of the theoretical abyss." Soon after, Nick characterizes Tom's hypocritical defense of family solidarity as "impassioned gibberish" (pp. 122, 130). Buchanan probably deserves such treatment, but what of poor Henry Gatz who proudly shows Nick his dead son's schedule for self-improvement, written on the fly-leaf of his copy of *Hopalong Cassidy?* "He was reluctant to close the book, reading each item aloud and then looking eagerly at me. I think he rather expected me to copy down the list for my own use," Nick sniffily observes (pp. 175–76). Then there is the "persistent undergraduate" who brings Jordan Baker to one of Gatsby's parties under the impression that sooner or later she will "yield him up her person." When that prospect seems unlikely to develop, the undergraduate becomes engaged in an obstetrical conversation with two chorus girls" and "implore[s]" Nick to join him. As Wolfsheim remarks in another sense, he has "a wrong man" (p. 71). Nick is not interested in making improper connections. He's not interested in making any *lasting* connections at all.

Nick carefully avoids emotional entanglements. He writes letters signed "Love, Nick" to a girl back home, but one reason he's come to New York is to avoid "being rumored into marriage" with her. Unable to stop thinking how "a faint mustache of perspiration" develops on her upper lip when she plays tennis (pp. 20, 59–60), he severs the relationship. In the East he has "a short affair with a girl who live[s] in Jersey City and work[s] in the accounting department," but lets it "blow quietly away" when her brother begins "throwing mean looks" in his direction (p. 57).[5] Jordan, his social peer, poses a more serious threat to his bachelor status. He is attracted to her hard, jaunty body and superior chin-in-air attitude, even though he knows she will lie to avoid responsibility and cheat to win at golf. But in the end she seems too much of a piece with Tom and Daisy, so he breaks off with her, too, before returning to the Middle West. It is not surprising that Nick has reached thirty without being married or engaged: he does not reserve judgment, he reserves himself.[6] Prufrock-like, he contemplates his future: "a decade of loneliness, a thinning list of single men to know, a thinning briefcase of enthusiasm, thinning hair" (p. 136).

In the light of this pattern of evasion, one regards with suspicion Nick's claim that releasing himself from a "vague understanding" with the girl back home before pursuing another with Jordan makes him "one of the few honest people" he's ever known (p. 60).[7] In fact he regards telling the truth as less important than avoiding the unseemly. A case in point is his remark that Catherine had shown "a surprising amount of character" at Myrtle's inquest by falsely swearing that her sister "had been into no mischief whatever" (p. 164), thus averting a public scandal. Decorum ranks extremely high on his scale of values—certainly higher than honesty.

He demonstrates a similar pattern on the question of sexual morality. References to adultery abound in *The Great Gatsby*. It is rather the expected thing among the idle rich—as Jordan says, Daisy "ought to have something in her life" (p. 81)—and among the "guests" at Gatsby's parties, though only those who contract liaisons with lovers of higher social standing (Myrtle and Gatsby) are punished for their sin or for their presumptuousness. What is Nick's attitude about this extramarital coupling? It depends: what concerns him most is how people *act*, not what they *do*. Daisy, he thinks, should "rush out of the house, child in arms" upon discovering Tom's infidelity. At the same time Nick is not particularly shocked to discover that Tom has "some woman in New York" (pp. 20–21). What he cannot approve of, however, is the way Tom conducts the affair. He takes his mistress to popular restarants to show her off, for example, and then leaves her to chat with acquaintances. He also concocts the lie that Daisy is Catholic to explain why he cannot be divorced. As voyeur, Nick is curious to see Tom's girl; as snob he has no desire to meet her. When they do meet, she proves a veritable model of social pretentiousness. In clothes, in gestures, in conversation, she is, simply, ridiculous; not until Tom breaks her nose does she merit any sympathy whatever (pp. 29–37).

Nick himself seems almost ridiculous when, in his obsession with propriety, he twice insists on having actually been invited to Gatsby's first party, unlike most of the gate crashers. Moreover, although all around him people are conducting themselves "according to the rules of behavior associated with amusement parks" (p. 41), he repeatedly tries to meet and thank his host, as at a formal gathering. This proves difficult, and meanwhile Jordan turns up, relieving him of the danger of addressing "cordial remarks to passers-by" (p. 42). When he finally does encounter Gatsby later in the evening, Nick is caught off guard: he'd been expecting "a florid and corpulent person in his middle years" (pp. 48–49). For a long time Gatsby continues to confound Nick's expectations. Unlike almost everyone else in his world, Gatsby resists classification.

It's not merely that he's curious about Gatsby: *everyone's* curious about Gatsby, this young man who "drift[ed] coolly out of nowhere and [bought] a palace on Long Island Sound" (p. 49). But while others merely speculate about his relationship with von Hindenburg or his career as killer, Nick is exposed through two rather remarkable coincidences—moving in next door and knowing Daisy—to more intimate revelations from the figure of mystery himself. Gatsby's first preposterous account (wealthy parents from the middle west city of San Francisco, war hero educated at Oxford who subsequently "lived like a young rajah in all the capitals of Europe . . . collecting jewels, chiefly rubies, hunting big game, painting a little . . . and trying to forget something very sad. . . .") tends to confirm Nick in his view of his neighbor as pretentious arriviste, inventing a background to replace the one he lacks. Though Gatsby produces the medal from Montenegro and the cricket photograph, Nick is not persuaded. "Then it was all true," he proclaims in humorous overstatement. "I saw the skins of tigers flaming in his palace on the Grand Canal; I saw him opening a chest of rubies to ease, with their crimson-lighted depths, the gnawings of his broken heart" (pp. 66–67). Nick's cynicism on this score is underlined in two subsequent incidents. Stopped for speeding, Gatsby flashes the policeman a white card which purchases instant immunity. "What was that?" Nick asks. "The picture of Oxford?" (p. 68). Later, during the tour of the mansion (and after the lavish display of shirts), Nick has a characteristically sardonic thought: "I was going to ask to see the rubies when the phone rang . . ." (p. 95).

Under the circumstances Nick hardly expects *any* section of Gatsby's fabulous story to be true, and when Gatsby modifies his tale to explain why and for how long he'd actually gone to Oxford, Nick is willing to put all the young rajah balderdash out of mind: "I had one of those renewals of complete faith in him that I'd experienced before" (p. 130). Clearly, one part of Nick wants to believe in Gatsby, just as another part holds him up for ridicule.

The snob in Nick Carraway finds Gatsby contemptible. He makes the point both on page two of the novel ("Gatsby . . . represented everything for which I have an unaffected scorn") and on page one hundred fifty-four (". . . I disapproved of him from beginning to end"). Significantly, this second statement immediately follows Nick's "You're worth the whole damn bunch put together" speech. He can simultaneously praise Gatsby, in other words, and still disapprove of the "gorgeous pink rag of a suit" he's wearing, scorn his "old sport" affectation, disapprove of his ostentatious Hotel de Ville and extravagant parties, scorn his shady business "gonnegtions"—above all, disapprove of Gatsby's social incompetence.

Gatsby obviously lacks that "sense of the fundamental decencies" that comes with the right background. He seems to think that his awful parties are socially respectable gatherings. He does not take in the situation when Tom Buchanan, Mr. Sloane, and "the lady" with Mr.

Sloane stop by and the lady invites him and Nick to dinner. As Nick sees at once, no matter what the lady said "Mr. Sloane had determined" that Gatsby shouldn't come along. By declining the invitation himself, Nick provides his neighbor with a model to emulate. But Gatsby ignores the clue, and so is humiliated when, as he changes clothes to accompany the others, they ride off without him (pp. 103–5). The following Saturday night, at Gatsby's next party, Nick is startled to witness his socially inept host dancing a "graceful, conservative fox-trot" (p. 106). Yet this is the man whose affair with Daisy he facilitates by inviting the two of them for tea ("Don't bring Tom," he warns her) and whose continuing relationship he encourages by "remaining watchfully in the garden" while they talk on the steps of his house for half an hour (pp. 80, 84, 107). The question is why. For one thing, Jordan asked him to arrange the tea; for another, Nick dislikes Tom and knows of his unfaithfulness and brutality. Yet he would not have so willingly played the role of go-between had he not felt a curious kinship with the "elegant young roughneck" (p. 48) in the mansion next door.

The fact is that both Nick and Gatsby have romantic inclinations. The difference is that Gatsby guides his life by his dream, while Nick carefully separates romance from reality. What he most admires in Gatsby is the "extraordinary gift for hope," the "romantic readiness" he has found in no one else (p. 3).

Nick's first glimpse of his neighbor comes after the dinner party at the Buchanans, when he returns home to catch sight of someone on the lawn next door. He is about to call out (having concluded, in his obsessive concern with etiquette, that Jordan's mentioning Gatsby "would do for an introduction") when the solitary figure stretches "out his arms across the water" as if to reach the green light at the end of Daisy's dock. Far away though Nick is, he could swear that the man is trembling (pp. 21–22).[8] This is a gesture he can understand and identify with. It appeals to the side of his nature that conjures up "sumptuous and romantic apartments" concealed above Wilson's garage (!) in the valley of ashes (p. 25), the side that imagines entering the lives of "romantic women" on Fifth Avenue, "and no one would ever know or disapprove" (p. 57). But as that last thought suggests, Nick is too proper, and too emotionally cautious, to bring his fantasies about strangers to life: who would introduce them? He contents himself with vicarious experience instead. Walking alone through the theater district, Nick watches and dreams:

> Forms leaned together in the taxis as they waited, and voices sang, and there was laughter from unheard jokes, and lighted cigarettes outlined unintelligible gestures inside. Imagining that I, too, was hurrying toward gayety and sharing their intimate excitement, I wished them well. (p. 58)

In something of that same spirit, he wishes Gatsby and Daisy well, too.

Nick imagines glamorous encounters, but reads about banking after dinner in the Yale Club. Gatsby makes his fortune, and sets out to capture the rest of his dream. Because of his remarkable commitment to that dream—exactly the sort of commitment Nick declines to make—Nick can almost forgive Gatsby his presumption in courting Daisy under cover of a uniform that let "her believe he was a person from much the same stratum as herself . . ." Because of it he can very nearly pardon Gatsby's taking Daisy "one still October night," taking her "because he had no real right to touch her hand" (p. 149). Because of it, too, he can temporarily efface from memory Gatsby's tactless offer of a chance to "pick up a nice bit of money" in return for arranging the meeting with Daisy (pp. 83–84). On the evidence it's clear that Gatsby as parvenu will manage to do or say the wrong thing if given an opportunity to do so. Yet Nick finally puts aside his offended sense of propriety and decides to stick it out with Gatsby. After his death, in fact, "it grew upon me [Nick] that I was responsible, because no one else was interested— interested, I mean, with that intense personal interest to which every one has some vague right at the end" (p. 165). In the end, and for the only time in his life, Nick makes a commitment himself. And it is because this decision is so difficult for him, a judgmental snob who invariably keeps his emotional distance, that it seems inevitable for the rest of us. That is why he is the right narrator for *The Great Gatsby*.

Fitzgerald enhances his accomplishment in point of view by not letting the change in Nick go beyond the bounds of credibility. Thus even while taking his "intense personal interest" in Gatsby, he behaves very much like the old Nick, trying above all to arrange a proper funeral with a respectable company of mourners and without sight-seers (pp. 165–66, 170). Moreover, he goes through the ritual of shaking hands with Tom *despite* finding out that Tom had directed the murderous Wilson to Gatsby's house. "I shook hands with him; it seemed silly not to, for I felt suddenly as though I were talking to a child" (p. 181). But Tom and Daisy are not children who damage toys that can be re- placed or scrawl dirty words Nick himself can erase. The Buchanans destroy *people*: Myrtle Wilson, George Wilson, and Jay Gatsby are dead because of them, and they do not even feel remorse. Even at the end, then, Nick lets social form obscure his moral judgment.

Nor is practical, realistic Nick converted into a practicing romantic by Gatsby's example. The logic of Fitzgerald's technique demands that only the narrator go inside Gatsby's head. When Nick does so in a series of reflections on Gatsby's ecstatic commitment to Daisy, he re- peatedly imposes his own reserve on Gatsby's thoughts. On the day of the tea, for example, Nick notes an expression of bewilderment on Gatsby's face and decides that there "must have been moments even that afternoon when Daisy tumbled short of his dreams—not through her own fault, but because of the colossal vitality of his illusion" (p. 97). Similarly, on the day of Gatsby's death, Nick has an idea that Gatsby didn't believe Daisy would telephone "and perhaps he no longer cared. If that was true he must have felt that he had lost the old warm world, paid a high price for living too long with a single dream" (p. 162). Nothing that Gatsby says or does warrants either of these conclusions. It is just that Nick is unable to conceive of the depth and vigor of Gatsby's dream.

Throughout the novel Gatsby is associated with the night, and more particularly with the moon. In four of the nine chapters the action ends with Gatsby alone in the night, and twice—near the end of chapter three, when a "wafer of a moon" shines over Gatsby's house as he gestures farewell to his guests (p. 56) and again at the very end of chapter seven, where Nick leaves Gatsby "standing there in the moonlight—watching over nothing" (p. 146)—the moon seems to symbolize Gatsby's capacity for reverie.[9] Hence it is surely significant that on the last pages of the novel Nick Carraway—alone in the night—wanders over to Gatsby's house in the moonlight, sprawls on the sand, and thinks of Gatsby's wonder when he picked out the green light at the end of Daisy's dock (pp. 181–82). For a moment, perhaps, Nick felt a sense of identity with the moon-person who had lived and died next door. But only for a moment, and then the rational Nick takes over to provide the novel with its coda about the Dutch sailors and the corruption of the American dream.

Nick Carraway and Jimmy Gatz came from the same part of the country, but they belong to vastly different worlds. At the Buchanans, Nick plays the naif by asking Daisy, "Can't you talk about crops or something?" But this is obvious irony coming from a man who is simultaneously evaluating the wine as "corky but rather impressive claret" (p. 13). Nick is no farmer from the country. He graduated from Yale, and so did his father. He knows about El Greco and Kant and Petronius. He has a sense of history. At college he wrote editorials for the *News*, which hardly makes him "literary" (as he claims) but does suggest a breadth of knowledge and a judgmental nature. Moreover, unlike Gatsby, Nick has a place where he's known and accepted to go back to in St. Paul. As he acknowledges, he's "a little complacent from growing up in the Carraway house in a city where dwellings are still called through decades by a family's name" (p. 177).[10] He has learned a good deal during the summer of 1922, especially about the very rich. Yet, aside from a diminished curiosity that desires "no more riotous excursions with privileged glimpses into the human heart" (p. 2), Nick's basic way of life seems unlikely to change. What has happened to Gatsby can hardly cure his misanthropy or open the floodgates of his emotional reserve. But if Nick is not changed, many others have been. *The Great Gatsby* is a novel that has made a difference in the lives of many who have or will read it. One does not have to like Nick Carraway to discover something about oneself in the tale he tells.

Notes

1. The subject of Nick's character and competence as narrator has been examined at length in many critical articles. Among the most important are Thomas A. Hanzo, "The Theme and the Narrator of *The Great Gatsby*," *Modern Fiction Studies*, 2 (1956–1957), 183–90; Jerome Thale, "The Narrator as Hero," *Twentieth Century Literature*, 3 (1957), 69–73; R. W. Stallman, "Gatsby and the Hole in Time," *The House that James Built and Other Literary Studies* (East Lansing: Michigan State University Press, 1961), pp. 131–50; Gary J. Scrimgeour, "Against *The Great Gatsby*," *Criticism*, 8 (1966), 75–86; Charles Thomas Samuels, "The Greatness of 'Gatsby,'" *Massachusetts Review*, 7 (1966), 783–94; and Richard Foster, "The Way to Read *Gatsby*," *Sense and Sensibility in Twentieth Century Writing: A Gathering in Memory of William Van O'Connor*, ed. Brom Weber (Carbondale: Southern Illinois University Press, 1970), pp. 94–108.

2. The page reference, like the others to follow, is to the Scribner Library edition of *The Great Gatsby*.

3. Among those who have called attention to Nick's irony and to his comic sense are Foster and E. Fred Carlisle, "The Triple Vision of Nick Carraway," *Modern Fiction Studies*, 11 (1965–1966), 351–60. On the subject of Nick's multiple voices, see Carlisle; Tom Burnam, "The Eyes of Dr. Eckleburg: A Re-examination of *The Great Gatsby*," *College English*, 14 (1952), 7–12; A. E. Elmore, "Nick Carraway's Self-Introduction," *Fitzgerald/Hemingway Annual 1971*, ed. Matthew J. Bruccoli and C. E. Frazer Clark (Washington, D.C.: Microcard Editions, 1971), pp. 130–47; and Oliver H. Evans, "'A Sort of Moral Attention': The Narrator of *The Great Gatsby*," *Fitzgerald/Hemingway Annual 1971*, pp. 117–29.

4. But notice how this casual remark gains resonance from subsequent events related to the motif of careless driving.

5. The word "affair" probably did not carry the specific meaning of sexual liaison in 1925. One of Fitzgerald's friends and contemporaries from St. Paul, Xandra Kalman, uses the word in a far more general sense.

6. Samuels, p. 791, makes the same point.

7. Susan Resneck Parr, "Individual Responsibility in *The Great Gatsby*," *Virginia Quarterly Review* 57 (1981), 662–80, points out that Fitzgerald changed "one of the few decent people" to "one of the few honest people" in revision. Other revisions "added material which stressed Nick's belief in his own honesty and deleted passages which might undercut Nick's integrity," such as his offering the keys of his house to Gatsby and Daisy. In the earliest surviving manuscript, apparently, Fitzgerald had made Nick too obviously untrustworthy a narrator.

8. Gatsby trembles elsewhere (p. 96) and so do Tom, Daisy, and Mr. Gatz (pp. 119, 133, 168). Nick does not, himself, tremble.

9. For an analysis of this pattern see Barbara Gerber Sanders, "Structural Imagery in *The Great Gatsby*: Metaphor and Matrix," *Linguistics in Literature*, 1 (1975), 53–75.

10. The city is certainly St. Paul, where the Ordways and Herseys and Schultzes (real names on p. 176 of the novel) did indeed have Christmas parties during Fitzgerald's youth. Unlike Nick, however, Fitzgerald felt insecure in St. Paul: he did not grow up in a family house, but in three different cities and in a series of houses and apartments.

Another Reading of
The Great Gatsby   Keath Fraser*

I

Begin with an individual, and before you know it you find that you have created a type; begin with a type, and you find that you have created—nothing. That is because we are all queer fish, queerer behind our faces and voices than we want any one to know or than we know ourselves. When I hear a man proclaiming himself an "average, honest, open fellow," I feel pretty sure that he has some definite and perhaps terrible abnormality which he has agreed to conceal—and his protestation of being average and honest and open is his way of reminding himself of his misprision.

Narrator in "The Rich Boy"[1]

Every one suspects himself of at least one of the cardinal virtues, and this is mine: I am one of the few honest people that I have ever known.

Narrator in The Great Gatsby[2]

"Gonnegtions" are of course important in *The Great Gatsby*, for without them Gatsby's rumoured association with crime, and its particular dialect, would not ring as true. The presence of Wolfsheim serves to connect Gatsby with the underworld from which his riches are hatched and his plans to marry Daisy made possible. "Gonnegtions" are Gatsby's dream and also Nick's. What Gatsby of West Egg is seeking, by means of the lucrative business afforded by the underworld portrayed in Wolfsheim, is a con*egg*tion with Daisy Fay of East Egg. In this light, Gatsby's "Platonic conception of himself" is enriched by what I take to be Fitzgerald's allusion to Plato's parable in *The Symposium* about the origin of love. In *The Symposium* Aristophanes is made to tell how Zeus, angered at the behaviour of the three circular shapes constituting the original sexes, decides to cut each in half: like eggs, says Plato, sliced in half by a hair. Yearning ever since to be reunited with himself, man has sought to couple with his other half. According to Plato, the resultant halves of the original hermaphrodite became heterosexual men and women; halves of the original female, lesbian, woman; while fragments of the first male turned into men who have devoted their lives (honourably in Plato's eyes) to the intimacy of boys and other men ("it requires," says Plato, "the compulsion of convention to overcome their natural disinclination to marriage and procreation").[3] If *The Great Gatsby* is a love story, and it is, it is one aware of this complex sexuality of antiquity. As we shall see, it is not only to *The Symposium* that we must

*Reprinted from *English Studies in Canada*, 5 (Autumn 1979), 330–43, by permission of the publisher.

turn for confirmation of the novel's peculiar and hitherto unnoticed sexuality—the theme of what follows—but also to *The Satyricon* of Petronius.

II

Here and there in Fitzgerald's novel inklings of depravity turn reader
into voyeur. One never quite knows, for example, how to read the last
page of Chapter 2, a scene which follows the dissolute party in Myrtle
Wilson's apartment, when Nick Carraway follows Mr. McKee out to the
elevator. Descending, McKee suggests Nick have lunch with him some
day—anywhere—and the elevator boy snaps: "Keep your hands off the
lever" (p. 38). Apologetic, McKee says he was unaware he was touching
it. The narrator says he would be glad to go. Where they go is to McKee's
bedroom: "... It was standing beside his bed and he was sitting up
between the sheets, clad in his underwear, with a great portfolio in his
hands." Then some more of the narrator's ellipses between what we pre
sume are titles of photographs taken by McKee are followed by Nick's
abrupt removal to "the cold lower level" of Pennsylvania Station where
he lies waiting for the morning train. It is an odd scene because Nick
never goes to lunch with McKee and McKee never reappears. Odder still
is the fact that Nick joins McKee in his apartment when no invitation,
apart from the one to lunch, is spoken, and no rapport between the two
men at Myrtle's party is established—except for Nick's having wiped a
spot of dried lather from McKee's cheekbone when McKee has dozed
off in a chair.

What I am about to suggest is that the quality of concealment in
The Great Gatsby is adroit enough to have caused us to read over scenes
we are intended to read through. Is there in the novel a cultivated ambiguity, such as that of the McKee episode, which flirts with, but never
answers the question of Nick Carraway's sexuality, because Nick refuses
to tell us the whole truth about himself? What is recoverable of Fitzgerald's earliest intentions, in Bruccoli's edition of *The Great Gatsby: A
Facsimile of the Manuscript* (1973),[4] may help to cloud the issue more
than clear it up. Deleted from the novel we now have are words, phrases,
and sentences of a section which, in the manuscript, follows directly from
what now is the conclusion of Chapter 2—that is, the scene in McKee's
bedroom. (In the final version of the novel this section, which concludes
with the second epigraph quoted above, is removed to become the conclusion to Chapter 3, the account of Gatsby's first party.) More willing
in the *Facsimile*, it would seem, to acknowledge the ambiguous nature
of the bedroom scene, Fitzgerald pauses to compound the mystery by
conceding that "a false impression" (*F*, 120) has been given by virtue of
the fact that the few events discussed thus far in the story appear to
have occupied all of Nick's time. Fitzgerald's original intention, if it can
be rescued from pencilled-out lines in the manuscript, was to suggest
that these events, in Nick's words, "were merely incidents sandwiched in

between other incidents that interested me or fascinated just as much—in fact the man I balled around with most all summer doesn't appear in this story at all" (*F*, 120). This revelation is cancelled out in favour of the more concealed phrase, "my own affairs"—which became the phrase we now have, "my personal affairs" (p. 56). It may be merely coincidental that McKee, who never reappears, and the man Nick says he "balled around with most"—but who is hushed up—appear at the same stage of the original novel, when Fitzgerald is in the process of establishing the character of his narrator. Yet sexual implications, even in the muted final version, are not lost on us, and in the manuscript do serve to challenge our accepted reading of Nick's sexuality.

In this section of the *Facsimile* Nick goes on to mention a brief affair with a girl from the accounting department of the Probity Trust company he works for in New York. The reason for his letting "the affair blow quietly away," in the manuscript, is the same offered in the final version—because, according to Nick, the girl's brother "began throwing mean looks in my direction" (p. 57). What is perhaps revealing are Nick's original words, the words Fitzgerald began to use, then scratched out and buried beneath the curious reason Nick offers for his escape from this girl. The words he starts to use, to explain the breakup, are "but her brother began *favoring me with* . . ." (my emphasis, *F*, 120). With what? It seems a peculiar phrase to start explaining the reason for leaving this brother's sister. Does the rewritten version lead us away from a more honest confession? Probity Trust—Nick's company—tends to affirm those qualities which Nick would have us believe are his—honesty, conscientiousness, uprightness—and yet one is left wondering whether Nick is telling us the whole truth about abandoning the girl, indeed the whole truth for abandoning any girl, especially the one out West. As for his dropping Jordan Baker, we have tended to believe him when he calls Jordan "incurably dishonest" (p. 58), and because of this seldom have we believed Jordan when she, in turn, claims Nick to have been less than honest and straightforward in his relationship with her.

In view of what has been presented so far it may not be too soon to suggest that what Nick might in part be concealing, even escaping from, is what the narrator of "The Rich Boy" (agreed to be among Fitzgerald's finest short stories, and written immediately after *The Great Gatsby*) calls "abnormality." Perhaps we have taken Nick too much at his word—without trying to read through such a scene as the one in McKee's bedroom with the whole of Nick's character in view. Conceivably, his penetrating self-analysis on the opening page of the novel has lulled us into accepting his own protestation of being "normal."

He appears to begin his story in a way calculated to disarm his reader, encouraging him "to reserve all judgments" (p. 1). By suggesting that he himself has refrained from criticizing others—by following his father's advice—Nick may be pleading his own case with us. "The abnormal mind," he observes, "is quick to detect and attach itself to this quality when it appears in a normal person, and so it came about that in college I was unjustly accused of being a politician, because I was privy to the secret griefs of wild, unknown men." Such men, alongside Nick, are categorized by him as "abnormal" because they are attracted to him. And so when "an intimate revelation was quivering on the horizon" he has tried to appear tolerant, yet disinterested: "for the intimate revelations of young men, or at least the terms in which they express them, are usually plagiaristic and marred by obvious suppressions." The choice of words and phrases is peculiar. Why, for example, are such intimate revelations—flawed as they are by plagiarism and suppression—"abnormal"? Presumably, because such revelations are offered by "unknown" men, and are therefore gauche and indiscreet.[5] But rather than perceiving these as a "normal" hazard for a man as attractive to other men as Nick boasts he is, he condemns them as belonging to those who were born with rather less than their share of "the fundamental decencies" (p. 1). Mainly because of his disarming admission of snobbery, we have always been convinced of Nick's own fundamental decencies—indeed doubtful if there is another narrator in modern literature more trustworthy than he. Yet in *The Satyricon* there is a narrator who is almost certainly as much a model for Fitzgerald's character as Conrad's trusty and frequently mentioned Marlow, and to that narrator's indecencies we will return.

For the moment it is worth going back to the second chapter in order to make sure the sexual nuances I have touched upon are clear enough to support the implications already made about McKee, and to anticipate some observations about others, including Nick, which remain to be made. McKee is introduced by the narrator as "a pale, feminine man from the flat below" (p. 30). He is, he tells Nick, in the "artistic game." His wife (who does not, incidentally, leave the party with her husband) tells Nick that her husband has photographed her a hundred and twenty-seven times since they were married. Nick calls her "handsome, and horrible." A bit later Tom Buchanan is amused at McKee's interest in getting more work on Long Island, if he can "get the entry" (p. 33), and suggests with a laugh that McKee "do some studies" of Myrtle's husband Wilson. Later still Wilson and McKee are discussed by their respective wives, and while Mrs. McKee is relieved to have escaped marrying a "kike," Myrtle claims to have in fact married one: "I thought he knew something about breeding, but he wasn't fit to lick my shoe" (p. 35). The allusion to breeding appears to be about class, but the drift beneath seems sexual. The highly-sexed Myrtle is childless; and her husband's impotence, if that is the reason for her constant desire to escape him, seems suitably complemented by the wasteland of ashes in which he dwells. Also childless, so far as we know, is Mrs. McKee, whose husband's assiduous use of his camera lens since their wedding appears to suggest a clear substitute for sex with his wife. Just as cars are what stimulate Wilson, as we shall see, so photographs can be seen to preoccupy McKee—particularly in the bedroom, where he shows his "great" portfolio to Nick, with the same hands which apologetically grasped the elevator lever moments earlier. This last glimpse of McKee between the sheets, while not the end of phallic imagery, illustrates what is typical of Fitzgerald's treatment of sex in the novel, that is, ambiguity. It remains to be explored just how far, and for what reason, this ambiguity is deliberately cultivated by the narrator himself.

III

Still of little interest to scholars is the way Fitzgerald handles sexuality in his writings. The truly great artists, according to Virginia Woolf, are androgynous in mind, and Leslie Fiedler, in passing, has noted this interesting quality in Fitzgerald (it is a quality Fiedler is reluctant to admire): "In Fitzgerald's world, the distinction between sexes is fluid and shifting, precisely because he has transposed the mythic roles and values of male and female, remaking Clarissa in Lovelace's image, Lovelace in Clarissa's. With no difficulty at all and only a minimum of rewriting, the boy Francis, who was to be a center of vision in *The World's Fair*, becomes the girl Rosemary as that proposed novel turned into *Tender is the Night*. Thematically, archetypally even such chief male protagonists as Gatsby and Dick Diver are females."[6] Fitzgerald himself, of course, acknowledged that "I am half feminine—at least my mind is. . . . Even my feminine characters are feminine Scott Fitzgeralds."[7] This last sentence could be put another way: his masculine characters are masculine Scott Fitzgeralds, which is to say they are no less feminine than his own "half feminine" mind. At the party in Myrtle Wilson's flat, for example, Nick, looking out the window, makes an admission which is generally read as a comment on the tension created by the technique which critics have admired in the novel: Fitzgerald's ability to observe as well as to participate. "I was within and without, simultaneously enchanted and repelled by the inexhaustible variety of life" (p. 36).[8] It has never been read as a suggestion of the narrator's epicene nature.

Writing to Maxwell Perkins before the publication of his novel, Fitzgerald confessed that "it may hurt the book's popularity that it's a *man's book*."[9] By this he meant that his best characters were men and that his women faded out of the novel.[10] In the same letter Fitzgerald had to agree with his editor that until now he had not revealed enough about Gatsby—which would allow Gatsby, and not Tom Buchanan, to dominate his story. Throughout the novel Nick holds the masculine forms of Gatsby and Tom in sharp contrast. For him, Gatsby's form seems preferable to Tom's, yet it is Tom's masculinity which captures Nick's attention in so convincing a manner that critics of the novel, in identifying the grander theme of the American dream, have perceived in Tom the cruel and palpable foil to Gatsby's idealism and illusion. For Nick the "gorgeous" Gatsby fails to come "alive" until Jordan Baker explains to him that Gatsby's house was deliberately chosen by its owner to be across the bay from Daisy's own house in East Egg. Then, says Nick, "He came alive to me, delivered suddenly from the womb of his purposeless splendor" (p. 79). In contrast to the insuperably *physical* purpose in the novel of Tom Buchanan, Gatsby and his purpose seem clearly metaphysical, springing agilely from that "Platonic conception of himself" (p. 99). Imagery associated with Gatsby suggests solipsism, sexlessness. It is otherwise with Tom: "Not even the effeminate swank of his riding clothes," Nick observes, "could hide the enormous power of that body—he seemed to fill those glistening boots until he strained the top lacing, and you could see a great pack of muscle shifting when his shoulder moved under his thin coat. It was a body capable of enormous leverage—a cruel body" (p. 7).

Here is a body of rather more interest to Nick than the one he courts in Jordan Baker. In fact, it fascinates him. As the novel progresses Tom's body comes to represent, far more than Gatsby's corruption and criminal associates do, the threat and evil force of the book. "Making a short deft movement, Tom Buchanan broke her nose with his open hand" (p. 37). The nose, of course, is Myrtle's. Myrtle's husband, on the other hand, suffers Tom's cruelty in a more subtle and central way, reaching its culmination on the fatal day Nick lunches with the Buchanans. The day is blisteringly hot. On his way to lunch Nick comments to himself, "That any one should care in this heat whose flushed lips he kissed, whose head made damp the pajama pocket over his heart!" Upon entering Tom's house he records what he overhears: " 'The master's body!' roared the butler into the mouthpiece. 'I'm sorry, madame, but we can't furnish it—it's far too hot to touch this noon!' " (p. 115). Nick then adds: "What he really said was: 'Yes . . . Yes . . . I'll see' " (p. 115). In fact the caller is Myrtle's husband, hard up for cash, hoping Tom will sell him the car on which Wilson hopes to make enough profit to take his wife away. What Nick purports to hear first is an illusion, yet it is an illusion artistically contrived to make the scene which follows between Tom and Wilson at the garage all the more adroit with respect to the underlying competition between the two rivals for Myrle Wilson's favours. More particularly, it causes us to examine Nick's own narration of the scene.

"Let's have some gas!" cried Tom roughly. "What do you think we stopped for—to admire the view?"

"I'm sick," said Wilson without moving. "Been sick all day."

"What's the matter?"

"I'm all run down."

"Well, shall I help myself?" Tom demanded. "You sounded well enough on the phone."

> With an effort Wilson left the shade and support of the doorway and, breathing hard, unscrewed the cap of the tank. In the sunlight his face was green.
>
> "I didn't mean to interrupt your lunch," he said. "But I need money pretty bad, and I was wondering what you were going to do with your old car."
>
> "How do you like this one?" inquired Tom. "I bought it last week."
>
> "It's a nice yellow one," said Wilson, as he strained at the handle.
>
> "Like to buy it?"
>
> "Big chance," Wilson smiled faintly. "No, but I could make some money on the other."
>
> "What do you want money for, all of a sudden?"
>
> "I've been here too long. I want to get away. My wife and I want to go West." (p. 123).

I want to suggest that this scene, like the McKee scene, is easily passed over, and that the sexual undertow adrift in the particular images which link Wilson and Tom has been carefully set up by Fitzgerald to contrast the two male rivals. We recall that three chapters earlier Nick had admired the incomparable form of Gatsby's car—the one Tom now is driving—"swollen here and there," observes Nick, "in its monstrous length" (p. 64). In *The Great Gatsby* it is worth remembering that the car is a symbol of masculinity, and the women (Jordan and Daisy) who drive cars do so badly, upsetting, even killing people. In the same chapter that Nick draws our attention to Gatsby's proud possession, he also glimpses "Mrs. Wilson straining at the garage pump with panting vitality as we went by" (p. 68). The scene above, with Tom and Wilson, seems therefore suggestive in the images it chooses to repeat. There is the elongated car driven by the potent Tom; and in the pump yet another phallic image, at which Wilson strains with rather less vitality than his wife, who has thrown him over for Tom.

At this point the afternoon sun continues to play chimerically with Nick's perception—this time of Wilson: "The relentless beating heat was beginning to confuse me and I had a bad moment there before I realized that so far his suspicions hadn't alighted on Tom" (p. 124). What follows is a curious generalization by Nick "that there was no difference between men, in intelligence or race, so profound as the difference between the sick and the well." It is precisely this difference one feels tempted to rephrase (without necessarily replacing one chimera with another), in order to suggest that in sexual terms what Fitzgerald is implying is that there is no difference so great as the difference between the normal and the abnormal. For Nick goes on to equate Wilson's sickness with guilt—and the simile he uses to illustrate this guilt is, it will have to be agreed, ambivalent: "Wilson was so sick that he looked guilty, unforgivably guilty—as if he just got some poor girl with child" (p. 124).

For Wilson (about whom we recall his wife having earlier said he knows nothing about "breeding"), such a potent act might indeed be upsetting, indeed abnormal. (Our sense of Wilson's guilt is made the more ambivalent perhaps by our recollection of Tom's earlier joke that Wilson would make quite a suitable study for the effeminate photographer McKee—"*George B. Wilson at the Gasoline Pump*" [p. 33].) Naturally what Wilson looks guilty about is having had to lock up his wife— upstairs in the garage. This act is the reality Nick cannot foresee in Chapter 2, when he and Tom first visit the garage, and Nick observes only half correctly, "It had occurred to me that this shadow of a garage must be a blind, and that sumptuous and romantic apartments were concealed overhead" (p. 25). There Nick's perception is illusory, but such perception has continued to bear upon what is normal and abnormal. On the day Myrtle is to die, Nick has overheard Tom telling Gatsby, "I've heard of making a garage out of a stable . . . but I'm the first man who ever made a stable out of a garage" (p. 119). As a stud, Tom clearly has what Wilson does not, though he, as much as Wilson, has made a mess of his relationship with Myrtle. The curious conjunction of these two men is the inevitable result of Nick's apparently random association of garages, cars, pumps, and cameras; for in spite of the romantic ideals normally associated with Nick, the reality of sex through his eyes is both a shifty and a mechanical proposition.

After Myrtle's death it is the "enormous leverage" of Tom's body (earlier observed by Nick in the same, apparently irrelevant way as the "lever" in the elevator with McKee) which seems to pry its way into the garage where Wilson has begun to come apart, gripping the doorposts of his office. "His eyes would drop slowly from the swinging light to the laden table by the wall, and then jerk back to the light again, and he gave out incessantly his high, horrible call: 'Oh, my Ga-od! Oh, my Ga-od!'" (140). This orgastic call emitted in mechanical jerks, seems complemented in the next sentence by Tom when he lifts his head with a "jerk" (the word repeated). Tom proceeds to extricate himself from the death for which he is, in effect, responsible (though of course, ironically, it is his wife who has driven over Myrtle, in Gatsby's car), by seizing Wilson "firmly by the upper arms" (p. 141), telling him "with soothing gruffness" to pull himself together. The narrator tells us Tom keeps "his hands firm on Wilson's body," insisting to the investigating policeman that Wilson is a friend of his, and claiming that the car which "did it" was yellow; the colour of his car, he says, is blue. Then he picks up Wilson "like a doll" (p. 142), deposits him in a chair, and escapes with Nick in tow. Worth noting, I think, is that Tom has no more perceived his cruelty to Wilson than he has his cruelty to Daisy, when much earlier she accuses him of injuring her little finger: "You did it, Tom . . . I know you didn't mean to, but you *did* do it. That's what I get for marrying a brute of a man, a great, big, hulking physical specimen of a—" (p. 12). If it is the lover which intrigues Nick in Gatsby, it is the *man* which intrigues him in Tom; our failure to notice the delicate way in which Fitzgerald allows Nick to perceive Tom's relationship with Wilson has limited our response to the full play of sexuality in the story. Fitzgerald, by letting Nick have the kind of reverberating observations he does—observations increasingly integral to the way his narrator comes to look at the world—creates a kind of sexual anarchy in *The Great Gatsby*. It is a narrative of potency and impotency, of jealous sex and Platonic love, of sexuality, in fact, owing more to the simultaneity of withinness and withoutness than the narrator appears to be aware of confessing.

IV

So far only Fiedler has cared, if in a dismissive way, to suggest that Fitzgerald's fiction is sexually ambiguous. What he notices about *Tender is the Night*, it should be noted, is perhaps ultimately more pertinent to *The Great Gatsby*:

> Indeed, the book is shot through with a thematic playing with the ambiguity of sex: Dick Diver makes his first entrance in a pair of black lace panties, and homosexuals, male and female, haunt the climaxes of the novel. "Economically," Rosemary's mother tells her at one point, "you're a boy, not a girl." Economically! One recalls the portrait of Fitzgerald as the most beautiful showgirl in the Triangle Show.[11]

The last reference, incidentally, is inaccurate, for it was not a single photograph taken of Fitzgerald as a showgirl, but a series of them in 1915 to publicize a Princeton musical staged by the Triangle Club, of which he was a member. Fitzgerald fell sick and couldn't make the show—even though his scholastic ineligibility would have assured his absence. According to his biographer Arthur Mizener, however, he did reappear in drag: "In February he put on his Show Girl make-up and went to a Psi U dance at the University of Minnesota with his old friend Gus Schurmeier as escort. He spent the evening casually asking for cigarettes in the middle of the dance floor and absent-mindedly drawing a small vanity case from the top of a blue stocking. This practical joke made all the papers, but it was an inadequate substitute for the flowers he had looked forward to as the Most Beautiful 'Show Girl' in the Triangle Club.' "[12]

Of course biography is slippery ground upon which to parade an argument about sex in a writer's art, and quoting from his notebook—with a view to the same argument—may be just as elusive. Yet in view of what remains to be said of Nick's peculiar relationship with girls, the entry in Fitzgerald's posthumously published notebook, in the section called "Karacters," may encourage us to appraise further our reservations about his narrator's sometimes ambiguous account. "He," writes Fitzgerald of a "Karacter," "had once been a pederast and he had perfected a trick of writing about all his affairs as if his boy friends had been girls, thus achieving feminine types of a certain spurious originality."[13] At this point the opening sentence of "The Rich Boy," quoted at the outset, should be recalled in order to compare Nick's narrative approach with the one in the short story: "begin with a type, and you find that you have created—nothing." These words of the narrator in "The Rich Boy" may help to explain why Fitzgerald told Perkins he felt *The Great Gatsby* was "a *man's book*"; why, in other words, he felt that his women faded out of the novel.

But if Jordan Baker, for example, is a "type" she is one whose "typical" qualities are significant in our appreciation of why Nick Carraway is attracted to them. As a champion athlete she, like Tom, is at home in the world of men. In addition, according to Nick, she has a "hard, jaunty body" (p. 59), a body "like a young cadet" (p. 11). She is, moreover, androgynously named; and her name—for someone as impressed by the shapes of cars as Nick—"combines two automobile makes" (according to one scholar), "the sporty Jordan and the conservative Baker electric."[14] The car metaphor is dually important in the novel, for not only does it connect Tom and Wilson—a connection leading to Myrtle's death as well as Gatsby's—but it also connects Nick and Jordan soon after they meet, and here, when they part:

> We shook hands.
> "Oh, and do you remember"—she added—"a conversation we had once about driving a car?"
> "Why—not exactly."
> "You said a bad driver was only safe until she met another bad driver? Well, I met another bad driver, didn't I? I mean it was careless of me to make such a wrong guess. I thought you were rather an honest, straightforward person. I thought it was your secret pride."
> "I'm thirty," I said, "I'm five years too old to lie to myself and call it honor."
> She didn't answer. Angry, and half in love with her, and tremendously sorry, I turned away (p. 179).

Just why they part is not clear, though to Jordan it is evident that their incompatibility derives from duplicity on Nick's part. Nick, it seems, always has been "half" attracted to women ("I wasn't actually in love, but I felt a sort of tender curiosity" (p. 58); and in the passage above he confirms Jordan's final realization that he is less honest and straightforward than he first comes on, even though critics have usually agreed that Nick's other words, quoted as an epigraph to this paper, convey Fitzgerald's exact estimation of his narrator. Interestingly, in the manuscript version of an earlier encounter between Nick and Jordan, at Gatsby's first party, Nick half objects to what he knows is untrue (this version was later removed):

"You appeal to me," she said suddenly as we strolled away, "You're sort of slow and steady and all that sort of thing, aren't you. I mean you've got everything adjusted just right."

"On the contrary—"

"That's true though," she went on, " I used to know lots of people like you three or four years ago. But they either just stayed boys and didn't develop, or else they changed altogether" (*F*, 48).

The fact that Nick has *not* got everything adjusted just right is borne out by the observation he permits himself on the climactic evening of his thirtieth birthday: "Thirty—the promise of a decade of loneliness, a thinning list of single men to know, a thinning briefcase of enthusiasm, thinning hair" (p. 136). For a few last minutes—before the imminent discovery of Myrtle's mutilated body, and Tom's subsequent attempt to console Wilson—Jordan's presence seems to reassure Nick. Then the effort of living distortedly (cf. the nightmarish world of the East, pp. 177–78) leads him back to where he comes from.

Clearly it is not back to the girl out West, from whom he has escaped to come to New York. "The fact that gossip had published the banns," Nick comments early on, "was one of the reasons I had come East" (p. 20). Of the girl he says little, except to tell us "how, when that certain girl played tennis, a faint mustache of perspiration appeared on her upper lip" (pp. 59–60). Rather secretive, the relationship is dismissed by Nick as perfunctory—and is over by Chapter 4. By the end of the last chapter it seems evident that the loneliness which he prophesies on his thirtieth birthday is all Nick has to anticipate—that, and the task of recording, in his own account of the summer, a justification of his part in the events which have transpired. But does he, we come down to asking, justify everything? His activities referred to at the outset as "my personal affairs" (p. 56) are never really accounted for, nor is his relationship with women quite understood: unless it is accounted for in a more *subtle* way than we have hitherto suspected.

V

The critical problem is thus simple: is the novel plainly weak in those parts, for example Nick's relationship with McKee, his affair with Jordan, which remain shady and ambiguous; or do we give Fitzgerald the benefit of the doubt and look for other, perhaps deeper reasons to explain his apparent shortcomings in the novel? What *The Great Gatsby* seems about in part, and where it derives its suggestiveness and energy, lies in what is not accounted for, what is undisclosed. The whole of Gatsby's affair with the underworld is the obvious example of this theme and its expression. But an important statement of the theme is also, one feels, Nick's "protestation of being average and honest and open"—to put into his mouth the narrator's words in "The Rich Boy." It is not unreasonable to suppose that Nick's readiness to declare his cardinal virtue to be honesty, is deliberately intended to mislead us. This declaration tempts us into accepting everything he tells us as the whole truth, though my evidence so far is intended to suggest that the oblique or metaphoric power of the novel prevents a simple reading of the way Nick looks at the world and at himself. In any effort to understand Gatsby, there are connections ("gonnegtions") that need to be made about the story-teller himself, but which we have traditionally ignored because we have always trusted Nick as average, honest, and above board.

What, then, is he hiding? An uncertain sexuality becomes an unavoidable conclusion. He is no longer simultaneously enchanted and repelled by the double vision from the window in Myrtle Wilson's New York apartment, nor is he, upon his return to the West, that "well-rounded man" he had hoped to become when "life is much more successfully looked at from a single window" (p. 4). His return to the West is not a solution, but a desire to escape the indecent ambiguities of conduct, "founded" on either "hard rock" or else "wet marshes" (p. 2). No longer tolerant of the excesses of others, Nick reaffirms his own Puritanical heritage with an extreme desire to see "the world . . . in uniform and at a sort of moral attention forever" (p. 2). His return is not to the girl he left behind, for he does not seem naturally inclined, in Plato's words, to marriage and procreation, and only in an oblique way is he prepared to acknowledge his own ambivalent sexuality by the association Fitzgerald allows him through the important classical echo of Petronius. (Nick, we remember, confesses his having been "rather literary" at college, and his allusion to "the shining secrets that only Midas and Morgan and Maecenas knew" (p. 4) is his way of introducing himself and us to the "bond business.")

Persuasive evidence of the theme of impotence and bisexuality in *The Great Gatsby* is discoverable in *The Satyricon* of Petronius, to which Fitzgerald was so sufficiently drawn that at different times he wished to call his novel after one of its characters. *Trimalchio* and *Trimalchio in West Egg* were the working titles which strongly guided Fitzgerald's composition of *The Great Gatsby* (a title which never satisfied him). Trimalchio, of course, is the name of the wealthy and vulgar host who throws the garish party in the chapter of *The Satyricon* called the "Cene Trimalchionis." What is crucial to my own discussions is not so much Trimalchio, which is what Nick calls Gatsby in the novel, as the narrator of *The Satyricon*, who attends Trimalchio's party, and whose name is Encolpios. Encolpios, who has in some way offended the fertility god, Priapus, provides what plot survives in *The Satyricon* by journeying, so scholars believe, from Marseilles east to Italy, and quite likely to the centre of the empire, Rome. Encolpios—and his name may well derive from the Greek word, *kolpos*, which, among several definitions, means vagina and womb—is a sort of Odysseus in quest of love: he is certainly a conscious parody of Odysseus, but an Odysseus both impotent and bisexual.[15]

Now Nick (or Dud, as Fitzgerald conceived him) fails with women as Encolpios does, though not for lack of trying. Mistaken by Wolfsheim for another man who is looking for a "gonnegtion," Nick, like Gatsby, is nevertheless seeking a connection with women. Interestingly, the "gon" of "gonnegtion" is the Greek root for seed (*goné*), and one wonders, in light of Fitzgerald's subtle and conscious use of names, whether Carraway, which after all is a seed, isn't seeking "egg" in the same sense that he is portrayed as a "bond" salesman looking for business connections—from which he also flees, incidentally, rather than become tainted with the seediness (the pun seems suitable) of easy money proffered by the likes of Gatsby (pp. 83–84) and Wolfsheim. There is nothing as blatantly ambivalent about Nick Carraway's sexuality as there is about that of Encolpios. Yet Fitzgerald's narrator, not unlike Petronius's, does describe in his own odyssey a parody, a parody of the American dream which rises to the poetic height we have come in *The Great Gatsby* to accept as its most indigenous quality. In Fiedler's words, "Fitzgerald's young men go east . . . in quest . . . of . . . an absolute America; a happy ending complete with new car, big house, money, and the girl."[16] That Gatsby and Nick *both* fail to win the girl is an interesting comment upon the subtlety of the novel. For if we begin to read through the novel with the problem of sexuality in mind, then the normal critical interpretations which focus mainly on Gatsby are seen to be too straightforward. These interpretations fail to recognize that the corruption of the novel originates not merely in Gatsby's shady business connections, but also in Nick Carraway's disingenuous sexuality. This sexuality, when peered at beside the bright and ethereal sexuality of Gatsby, or the dark and cruel sexuality of Tom, may well shed more light on why, in the novel's concluding words, "the orgiastic[17] future . . . year by year recedes before us" (p. 182), and why the dud-like and impotent pursuit of that future diminishes the American dream of attaining what Anson Hunter in "The Rich Boy" tries over and over to get—the girl.

Notes

1. The opening short story in Fitzgerald's *All the Sad Young Men* (New York: Scribner's, 1926), p. 1.

2. *The Great Gatsby* (New York: Scribner's, 1925). Subsequent references will be indicated parenthetically in the text.

3. *The Symposium*, trans. Walter Hamilton (Harmondsworth: Penguin, 1951), p. 63.

4. Matthew J. Bruccoli, ed. (Washington: NCR Microcard Editions, 1973). Further references to this facsimile will be indicated F in the text.

5. For even if there is a sexual suggestiveness implicit in Nick's choice of words and phrases, surely Fitzgerald would have agreed that men "normally," if not

often, confide in one another, as he apparently did to Hemingway in a discussion on the size of his penis. See Ernest Hemingway, *A Moveable Feast* (New York: Scribner's, 1965), pp. 187–89.

6. Leslie Fiedler, *Love and Death in the American Novel* (New York: Dell, 1960), p. 312.

7. Quoted by Jackson R. Bryer and John Kuehl, eds., *The Basil and Josephine Stories* (Princeton University Press, 1973), p. xxi.

8. In "Some Notes on F. Scott Fitzgerald," *F. Scott Fitzgerald: A Collection of Critical Essays*, ed. Arthur Mizener (Englewood Cliffs, N.J.: Prentice Hall, 1963), p. 74, Fiedler comments "that at the end of [Fitzgerald's] writing career the outsider had become defined as the Young Girl, a kind of anima figure, desiring hopelessly the older man who is *also* Fitzgerald, himself double: in the eyes of the girl all power and glamour, in his own view aging and corrupt or at the point of death."

9. *The Letters of F. Scott Fitzgerald*, ed. Andrew Turnbull (New York: Scribner's, 1963), p. 173.

10. As he summed up his novel to H. L. Mencken, "the influence on it has been the masculine one of *The Brothers Karamazov*, a thing of incomparable form, rather than the feminine one of *The Portrait of the Lady*." *Letters*, p. 480.

11. *Collection*, p. 74.

12. *The Far Side of Paradise* (Boston: Houghton Mifflin, 1951), p. 57.

13. *The Crack-Up*, ed. Edmund Wilson (New York: New Directions, 1945), p. 166.

14. Matthew J. Bruccoli, *Apparatus for F. Scott Fitzgerald's "The Great Gatsby"* (Columbia: University of South Carolina Press, 1974), p. 122.

15. He is enamoured, for example, of his young travelling companion, Giton, and when he attempts to oblige a certain seductive Circe, he is unable to rise to the occasion because—according to Circe—of his attraction to the boy.

16. *Love and Death*, p. 313.

17. The sexual connotations of this famous line are less than clear until we read Bruccoli on the subject of "orgiastic": "Fitzgerald clearly intended *orgastic*—not *orgiastic*—and explained to Perkins that 'it expresses exactly the intended ecstasy' (January 24, 1925)." *Apparatus*, p. 50.

Beneath the Mask:
The Plight of Daisy Buchanan   Sarah Beebe Fryer[*]

With two noteworthy exceptions,[1] *Gatsby* critics have generally been content to dismiss Daisy Buchanan as the "shallow," "foolish," "unworthy" woman who happens to embody Jay Gatsby's dream. Guided only by Nick's very limited view of Daisy, readers often judge Daisy solely on the basis of her superficial qualities, with no apparent awareness that her silly manner conceals a woman of feeling or that her final "irresponsibility" towards Gatsby stems from an acute sense of responsibility

[*]Adapted from Conference Proceedings, University of Minnesota Conference on "F. Scott Fitzgerald, St. Paul's Native Son and Distinguished Writer," October 1982. Printed by permission of the author.

towards herself. Certainly it is easy to join Nick in lumping Daisy and Tom together at the end of the novel and condemning them both for being "careless." But such a narrow estimation of Daisy's character is far too simplistic, for, although Nick conscientiously relates what Daisy does, he clearly does not understand what motivates her. In fact, Daisy baffles Nick from the opening chapter, when he observes her unhappy situation with Tom and wonders why she doesn't leave him:

> . . . I was confused and a little disgusted as I drove away. It seemed to me that the thing for Daisy to do was to rush out of the house, child in arms—but apparently there were no such intentions in her head.[2]

Just as Nick fails to comprehend Daisy's reluctance to leave Tom at the beginning of the novel, he continues to be confused by her in the last chapter. In his final reference to Daisy, Nick once more acknowledges his uncertainty about what keeps Tom and Daisy together:

> They were careless people, Tom and Daisy—they smashed up things and creatures and then retreated back into their money or their vast carelessness, or whatever it was that kept them together. . . . (pp. 180–81)

Nick's prolonged confusion about Daisy's continued association with Tom reflects a weakness in her characterization. Since he is the narrator of the story, his failure to perceive the things that make Daisy do the things she does makes it easy for readers to jump to the conclusion that she is "shallow"—that she behaves as she does for no good reason at all, either because she is incapable of genuine feeling or because she just doesn't care. But the very fact that Nick is perplexed about Daisy suggests that she ought not to be dismissed as the "beautiful little fool" she says she wants her daughter to be. Despite his inability to understand Daisy, Nick's keen observations of her behavior demonstrate not that she is unable to feel and express strong emotions, but that she deliberately avoids them, because she recognizes the pain they can entail. Daisy clings—unsuccessfully—to a gay, superficial, "careless" world in an effort to protect herself from what are for her the terrifying dangers inherent in caring.

Without a doubt, Nick's confusion about what motivates Daisy is rooted in Fitzgerald's own uncertainty about his development of her character. Even before *The Great Gatsby*'s 1925 publication, Fitzgerald revealed his dissatisfaction with Daisy in a letter to Maxwell Perkins:

> . . . Chapter 7 (the hotel scene) will never quite be up to the mark— I've worried about it too long and I can't quite place Daisy's reaction. . . . I'm sorry Myrtle is better than Daisy. . . . It's Chapter VII that's the trouble with Daisy and it may hurt the book's popularity that it's *a man's book*.[3]

Evidently, Fitzgerald—like Nick—did not quite know what to make of Daisy. Shortly after the book came out, he referred again to the problem of Daisy in letters to both Edmund Wilson and H. L. Mencken. A harsh critic of his own work, he wrote to Edmund Wilson that

> The worst fault in it, I think is a BIG FAULT: I gave no account (and had no feeling about or knowledge of) the emotional relations between Gatsby and Daisy from the time of their reunion to the catastrophe.[4]

In his letter to H. L. Mencken, he pinpointed the problem more precisely:

> There is a tremendous fault in the book—the lack of an emotional presentment of Daisy's attitude toward Gatsby after their reunion (and the subsequent lack of logic or importance in her throwing him over).[5]

Fitzgerald was a remarkably perceptive judge of his own work, and it is worth noting that his acute, valid sense of Daisy's inadequate development concerned only the second half of the novel. Apparently he was satisfied with Daisy's coexistence with Tom, his "best character," up to and including the scene of her reunion with Gatsby. And with good reason—for Nick's painstaking portrayals of Daisy when he visits her and Tom at their home in Chapter I and again when she comes to his home for the surprise reunion with Gatsby in Chapter V clearly reveal much more about her character than his depiction of her subsequent sudden, unexplained renunciation of Gatsby does. In fact, even though Fitzgerald himself may not have consciously been able to "place Daisy's reaction," his description of her up to the hotel scene indicates that he was at least intuitively aware of some "logic or importance" in her behavior during the confrontation between Tom and Gatsby.

Most studies of *The Great Gatsby* eventually focus at least briefly on Nick Carraway, and this one is no exception. We see Daisy, as we see Gatsby, only through Nick's eyes. But, although Nick thoroughly assesses and obviously admires Gatsby's character and behavior, his perception of Daisy is far more limited. Perhaps this is what Fitzgerald was thinking of when he called *Gatsby* "a man's book," for, despite Daisy's important role in the story, the male narrator focuses almost exclusively on two men: Gatsby and Tom. Except for his account of one brief, private conversation with Daisy in the opening chapter, Nick's revelations about Daisy are restricted to her observable behavior among people and to other people's remarks about her. Nick describes Daisy in terms of gaiety, restlessness, fear, artificiality—but while he recognizes that she is affected, he fails to comprehend what lies beneath her affectation. And since he is *Gatsby*'s narrator, his ignorance of—and apparent lack of curiosity about—what Daisy's affectation conceals inevitably influences our opinion of her.

But Nick's impressions of Jordan Baker, who grew up with Daisy in Louisville and who also reflects Fitzgerald's view of Southern womanhood, can shed some light on Daisy's character. Nick establishes his "tender curiosity" toward Jordan, then reveals an insight:

> The bored haughty face that she turned to the world concealed something—most affectations conceal something eventually, even though they don't in the beginning—(p. 58)

In Jordan's case, Nick develops his casual observation about affectations by saying that she is "incurably dishonest" and therefore feels safest "on a plane where any divergence from a code would be thought impossible." Later he engages in a playful spat with her about her careless driving, and she reveals her assumption that other people are cautious: she evidently expects to be protected from her own vulnerability by the precautions other people take.

Like Jordan, Daisy is affected. Nick demonstrates his awareness of her affectation throughout the novel by commenting on her insincerity, as he does in Chapter I, following her private disclosures to him about her unhappy marriage.

> "You see I think everything's terrible anyhow," she went on in a convinced way. "Everybody thinks so—the most advanced people. And I *know*. I've been everywhere and seen everything and done everything." Her eyes flashed around her in a defiant way, rather like Tom's, and she laughed with thrilling scorn. "Sophisticated— God, I'm sophisticated!"
>
> The instant her voice broke off, ceasing to compel my attention, my belief, I felt the basic insincerity of what she had said. (p. 18)

Daisy may indeed have "been everywhere and seen everything and done everything," but her pretensions of "sophistication"—her insistence that "everything's terrible"—aren't convincing to Nick, perhaps because they aren't convincing to her. She's playing a part, saying what she considers appropriate, but not what she really feels. She goes on "in a convinced way" instead of actually being convinced. Earlier in the same scene, when Daisy complains about her bruised finger, Nick observes that she wears an "awed expression," suggesting that she is not in fact "awed." And later in the novel Nick pointedly reaffirms his sense of Daisy's affectation when she is reunited with Gatsby: Nick overhears her initiating a conversation—apparently with difficulty—"on a clear artificial note" (p. 87).

Jordan and Daisy are not the first Southern women Fitzgerald portrays in terms of affectations. Sally Carrol Happer, the young protagonist in "The Ice Palace," first published in 1920, is similarly wealthy, popular, and affected. Caught between her fear of stultification in the dying South and her craving for the security of marriage, she agrees to go North to marry Harry Bellamy. She explains to a Southern friend, Clark Darrow:

". . . tied down here I'd get restless. I'd feel I was—wastin' myself. There's two sides of me, you see. There's the sleepy old side you love; an' there's a sort of energy—the feelin' that makes me do wild things."[6]

Though her Southern friends warn her against marrying a Yankee, Sally Carrol goes North to visit Harry and his family. There she begins to miss the security of an established code of behavior, much as Jordan and Daisy later do in *The Great Gatsby*. Confused, she fervently seeks Harry's advice about Northern etiquette, and he responds with a demand that she tell him how glad she is to be there.

> "Glad—just awful glad!" she whispered, insinuating herself into his arms in her own peculiar way. "Where you are is home for me, Harry."
> And as she said this she had the feeling for almost the first time in her life that she was acting a part. (p. 11)

Sally Carrol chooses to act a part in an effort to resolve her conflicting needs for adventure (flight to the North) and security (suitable marriage). But soon after she recognizes that she is "acting a part," she argues with Harry over his unkind remarks about Southerners. "A Southerner wouldn't talk the way you're talking now" (p. 18), she insists, demonstrating still further that she misses the comfort of courtesy and manners. It is no surprise, then, that, after getting lost for a brief but horrifying time in the ice palace at the winter carnival, she chooses to go back home.

Sally Carrol Happer is an important forerunner of Daisy Buchanan, for they suffer the same kinds of conflicts and attempt similar solutions. Fitzgerald got the idea for "The Ice Palace" from Zelda, and her sympathetic view of the conflicting needs and desires of Southern women enabled him to portray Sally Carrol with generosity. He seems to admire the character, as he admired Zelda, for "her courage, her sincerity, and her flaming self-respect."[7] He describes Sally Carrol's affectation as something she recognizes and finds intolerable in herself. Moreover, he leaves the reader with a strong sense of her integrity, which she exhibits both as she openly tells Roger Patton her reasons for marrying and as she courageously leaves the cold North to go back home, where she feels she belongs.

Five years elapsed between the publication of "The Ice Palace" and *The Great Gatsby*, and during that time the erosion of Fitzgerald's marriage to Zelda may have decreased his sympathy for feminine characters. Furthermore, Daisy Buchanan, unlike Sally Carrol in "The Ice Palace," is not the protagonist of the novel, and Fitzgerald is less thorough in his characterization of her. Although Nick is intuitively aware of Daisy's affectations, he utterly fails to explore its origins. Nevertheless, we can begin to understand Daisy better by closely examining Nick's observations of her behavior. In three key scenes—Nick's first visit to the Buchanans, Gatsby's reunion with Daisy, and the hot afternoon at the Plaza—Nick's simple descriptions of Daisy reveal her genuine love for Gatsby, her intense fear of emotions in general, and her craving for stability. The juxtaposition of these forces suggests the severity of Daisy's conflict: her longing for personal freedom is expressed by her deep-rooted love of Gatsby, but her fear of emotions and her need for stability make her cling to her unsatisfactory marriage to Tom.

Nick's first description of Daisy's face when he visits the Buchanans for dinner at their home suggests that she is burdened with a serious internal conflict: "Her face was sad and lovely with bright things in it, bright eyes and a bright passionate mouth. . . ." (p. 9). Though her overall countenance is of sorrow, her face is somehow fragmented—turned into a set of beautiful objects, much as Tom and Gatsby turn her into an object to suit their needs. And in her face, as in her life, vitality coexists with suffering.

In the opening chapter, Fitzgerald clearly indicates that Daisy embodies a war between hope and despair. At dinner, Daisy eagerly asks:

"Do you always watch for the longest day of the year and then miss it? I always watch for the longest day in the year and then miss it." (p. 12)

Bored, Jordan suggests that they ought to "plan something."

"All right," said Daisy. "What'll we plan?" She turned . . . helplessly: "What do people plan?" (p. 12)

Daisy's childlike anticipation of the longest day of the year and her gay eagerness to "plan something" demonstrate the optimistic aspect of her character. But her hopeful nature is thwarted by experience and her attitude grows cynical. First she recognizes that looking forward to something doesn't always pay off, and then she realizes that she doesn't know how to exert any control over the situation: she'll miss the day she looks forward to, and she doesn't know what to plan anyway. As Barry Gross observes in "Back West: Time and Place in *The Great Gatsby*," ". . . the future for Daisy is not that orgastic consummation devoutly to be wished."[8] Yet Daisy can't help looking forward to the future, despite her acute sense of futility.

From the opening of the novel, Fitzgerald demonstrates that Daisy, like Gatsby, is at least in part a romantic.[9] The first clue that Daisy remembers Gatsby with more than just a passing interest appears during Nick's first visit to the Buchanans' home. Jordan tells Nick that she knows a man named Gatsby in West Egg, and Daisy, alert to an old lover's name despite five years of separation, her marriage to another man, and the birth of a daughter, suddenly interrupts: " 'Gatsby?' demanded Daisy. 'What Gatsby?' " (p. 11) Because dinner is announced, Daisy doesn't get an immediate answer, and her question may seem insignificant by itself. But later in the novel, we learn that Daisy cared enough about hearing Gatsby's name that evening to wake Jordan up—after she had retired early to rest before a tournament—to get news of him. This incident hardly proves that Daisy's love for Gatsby approaches his for her, but, coupled with the events that follow, it certainly suggests that she, like Gatsby, cultivates fond memories of their previous relationship.

Severe tension pervades the Buchanan home as Nick dines with Jordan, Tom, and Daisy. Even before Nick learns that "Tom's got some woman in New York" (p. 15), his observations of the interplay between Daisy and Tom reflect the animosity between them. Their exchanges seem playful at first. Daisy accuses Tom of hurting her finger, then childishly calls him "hulking" repeatedly, since she knows it upsets him. But gradually their feud escalates. The telephone reminders of Tom's sexual infidelity contribute to Daisy's flirtatious behavior towards Nick at the dinner table. When Tom is first called away to the telephone, Daisy affects indifference by "enthusiastically" recounting a funny story to Nick. And when the phone calls Tom away again only a few moments later, Nick observes: "As if his absence quickened something within her, Daisy leaned forward again, her voice glowing and singing" (p. 15).

Certainly Nick perceives that Daisy is reacting to an emotional situation, but her response is not immediately directed towards the source of her tension. Daisy responds to tension with energy, but, instead of openly confronting Tom with her anger, she enthusiastically engages herself with Nick and needles Tom through ironic remarks. Characteristically, she subjugates her desire to assert herself to her need for security. But the simple fact that she is anxious in the face of evidence of Tom's infidelity suggests that she has an emotional investment in her relationship with him. A woman who felt less would react less.

Daisy displays her intelligence, sensitivity, and suffering as she attempts to square accounts with Tom. When Tom criticizes Jordan's family for letting her "run around the country," Daisy says, "She's going to spend lots of week-ends out here this summer. I think the home influence will be very good for her" (p. 19). Tom, recognizing sarcasm, stares at her in silence. And Daisy continues to annoy him by making a joke about his concern with racial purity.

> "Did you give Nick a little heart-to-heart talk on the veranda?" demanded Tom suddenly.
> "Did I? . . . I can't seem to remember, but think we talked about the Nordic race. Yes, I'm sure we did. It sort of crept up on us and first thing you know—" (p. 20)

At this stage Tom interrupts Daisy and addresses Nick, thus demonstrating that he's aware of Daisy's covert hostility and determined to disregard it.

By this point, of course, Daisy *has* had a little "heart-to-heart talk" with Nick, and in it she has disclosed that she is vulnerable to emotions, and that she has been deeply—perhaps irreparably—hurt. When Nick, having recognized "that turbulent emotions possessed her," asks Daisy about her daughter, she exposes her feelings in her account of the child's birth:

> "Well, she was less than an hour old and Tom was God knows where. I woke up out of the ether with an utterly abandoned feeling, and asked the nurse right away if it was a boy or a girl. She told me it was a girl, and so I turned my head away and wept. 'All right,' I said, 'I'm glad it's a girl. And I hope she'll be a fool—that's the best thing a girl can be in this world, a beautiful little fool.' " (p. 17)

Here Daisy reveals her own unhappiness. She would choose to be a fool—to be incapable of and invulnerable to ideas and emotions—*if* she could. She does feel, she has suffered, and her desire that her daughter be a "fool" is actually a desire to shelter her from experiencing the pain that Daisy herself has known. Her remarks about the child's birth may be pitiful, but they are rooted in the authority of bitter experience, and they are not shallow.

Daisy's capacity for feeling also emerges in Jordan's story about her romance with Gatsby in Louisville. As Jordan indicates, Daisy was very wealthy and very popular. Moreover, she was apparently already cultivating a certain mystique: she customarily "dressed all in white" and drove "a little white roadster." Jordan remembers one morning when Daisy and a young officer, Gatsby, "were so engrossed in each other that [Daisy] didn't see [her]" (p. 76). The affection that flowed between Daisy and Gatsby at that time was unquestionably reciprocal. And Jordan strengthens the suggestion that Daisy was in love with Gatsby by her references to Daisy's behavior after Gatsby went to war:

> ". . . I didn't see Daisy very often. She went with a slightly older crowd—when she went with anyone at all. Wild rumors were circulating about her—how her mother had found her packing her bag one winter night to go to New York and say good-by to a soldier who was going overseas. She was effectually prevented, but she wasn't on speaking terms with her family for several weeks. After that she didn't play around with the soldiers any more, but only with a few flat-footed, short-sighted young men in town, who couldn't get into the army at all." (p. 76)

Jordan's history shows that Daisy was strongly attached to Gatsby—so fond of him, in fact, that she was willing to risk the wrath of her parents by running off to see him without permission. But she wasn't free. She was a young Southern belle, dependent on her "good" family and consequently protected and restricted by its established code of behavior. She was angry when they interfered with her plans, but her anger was ineffectual since she lacked the courage and conviction to break away from them in pursuit of her happiness. But the unhappy end of her affair with Gatsby did have a profound impact on her: for a year she withdrew from her customary social engagements and rejected dates with attractive, eligible men. The girl who had been so sought after began to associate only with men who could not possibly compete with Gatsby. Daisy had, in effect, retreated from the risk of falling in love again.

As Jordan continues her monologue, she remarks that Daisy returned to her previous gay social circle a little over a year later. She was still affected—but now her affectation concealed her fear of love:

> By the next autumn she was gay again, gay as ever. She had a debut after the Armistice, and in February she was presumably engaged to a man from New Orleans. In June she married Tom Buchanan of Chicago . . . (pp. 76–77)

Daisy's new gaiety was a false gaiety. After a year of avoiding any involvement with potentially serious suitors, Daisy's sudden engagements first to one man and then to another reflect emotional commitment less than a sense of urgency to get on with her life. Her increasingly desperate letters underlined the point:

> . . . there was a quality of nervous despair in Daisy's letters. She didn't see why he couldn't come. She was feeling the pressure of the world outside, and she wanted to see him and feel his presence beside her and be reassured that she was doing the right thing after all. (p. 151)

Daisy has sustained her love for Gatsby through correspondence for more than a year. But she was a victim of her need for stability, and, despite their mutual love, Gatsby was unable to meet that need:

> She wanted her life shaped now, immediately—and the decision must be made by some force—of love, of money, of unquestionable practicality—that was close at hand. (p. 151)

Daisy couldn't wait forever. Her need for stability was immediate, and she attempted to satisfy that need through something tangible, something close at hand. It is significant that she planned to marry one man and wound up marrying another, for her need was not for any particular person (unless it was for Gatsby, who didn't come to her), but simply for an attainable partner who could provide—through marriage—the sense of security she so desperately craved.

Judging from these accounts, Daisy was so in love with Gatsby—and so hurt by his failure to come to her when she needed him—that she virtually married Tom on the rebound. The vivid scene of Daisy's drunkenness when she's "change' her mine" after receiving a letter from Gatsby clearly indicates her devotion. Significantly, she asks that someone return the wedding pearls to "whoever they belong to": her future husband has no particular identity for her. She clings pathetically to Gatsby's letter, symbol of the man she really loves, because he himself is not available to her.

Nevertheless, Jordan tells Nick that Daisy married Tom "without so much as a shiver" (p. 78). And, having made a formal commitment to her choice of Tom Buchanan for a husband, Daisy apparently allowed herself to fall in love with him. Jordan describes Daisy's devotion to Tom shortly after they returned from their honeymoon:

> . . . I thought I'd never seen a girl so mad about her husband. If he left the room for a minute she'd look around uneasily, and say: "Where's Tom gone?" and wear the most abstracted expression until she saw him coming in the door. She used to sit on the sand with his head in her lap by the hour, rubbing her fingers over his eyes and looking at him with unfathomable delight. It was touching to see them together—it made you laugh in a hushed fascinated way. (p. 78)

Such devotion, even between honeymooners, may seem excessive. But Daisy, profoundly disappointed by her first lover, struggled valiantly to grasp and maintain her husband's love. If, as Jordan suggests, Daisy was genuinely in love with Tom following their wedding, that love was short-lived. Daisy's affection for Tom—like her earlier love for Gatsby—was soon shattered by his breach of trust. When Tom's illicit liaison with at chambermaid in their Santa Barbara hotel became public knowledge, Daisy retreated once more from the risks of love. Although she remained married to him (she was already pregnant with their daughter) their relationship clearly deteriorated. Probably Tom did not suspect how much he'd forfeited through his philandering until he discovers that Daisy loves Gatsby and he sees her "as someone he knew a long time ago" (p. 119).

The history of Daisy's severe disappointments in love is important preparation for the reunion scene with Gatsby, which Fitzgerald once called his "favorite" of the novel.[10] Through Tom as well as through Gatsby, Daisy has discovered that romantic love leads to emotional anguish. Thus, it is not surprising that Daisy's overwhelming emotion when she first sees Gatsby at Nick's house is fear. She is deeply shaken by seeing him again, and it takes her considerable effort just to remain calm. Nick describes the couple's appearance as he enters the room immediately after they've seen each other:

> Gatsby, his hands still in his pockets, was reclining against the mantelpiece in a strained counterfeit of perfect ease, even of boredom. His head leaned back so far that it rested against the face of a defunct mantelpiece clock, and from this position his distraught eyes stared down at Daisy, who was sitting, frightened but graceful, on the edge of a stiff chair. (p. 87)

Here Nick's description of the characters captures the tension in the air, just as his earlier description of the Buchanans' dinner does. Matters are so tense, in fact, that serving tea provides them all with a "welcome confusion."

Daisy is stunned by the reappearance of Gatsby in her life. Her usual carefree manner is swept aside by the renewal of contact with the first man she ever loved in a romantic sense. She is drawn to him, but she is afraid of him: after all, she had trusted him—needed him—in the past, and he had failed her. She's been hurt, and her intense anxiety at the sight of Gatsby reflects that she's suffering from conflicting impulses. She still needs his love, yet she also needs the stability that Tom provided for her when Gatsby couldn't.

Nick doesn't assess Daisy's reaction to Gatsby much further during tea, but when he returns from his brief stay under the tree in the rain, he observes: "Her throat, full of aching, grieving beauty, told only of her unexpected joy" (p. 90). He also reveals that Daisy has been crying —letting down her defenses—but that she dabs her tears away and goes to wash her face when Nick comes in. Evidently, Daisy is a different person when she is alone with Gatsby.

Throughout their late afternoon visit to Gatsby's mansion, Daisy exhibits her need for tangible connections with Gatsby. As they visit his room, she touches his brush "with delight" and later buries her head in his shirts, sobbing. These things are important to her not because they are beautiful in and of themselves, but because they are Gatsby's. She is reestablishing contact with him through gradual, gentle contact with his things. That she shows her affection through touching his things instead of more direct expressions suggests the severity of her fear of emotional relationships. Eventually, though, she dares to put her arm through his, and Nick recognizes the importance of their reunion—to both of them— as he leaves:

> They had forgotten me, but Daisy glanced up and held out her hand; Gatsby didn't know me now at all. I looked once more at them and they looked back at me, remotely, possessed by intense life. (p. 97)

Daisy's renewed connection with Gatsby has brought her back from the world of the emotionally dead. As she accepts and reciprocates Gatsby's love, she is "possessed by intense life."

Shortly after this reunion Daisy and Tom attended one of the lavish parties at Gatsby's mansion. There she once more responds to an emotional situation with anxiety. As soon as they arrive, she begins nervously flirting with Nick:

> "These things excite me *so*," she whispered. "If you want to kiss me any time during the evening, Nick, just let me know and I'll be glad to arrange it for you. Just mention my name. Or present a green card. I'm giving out green—" (p. 105)

Of course, Nick is not the genuine object of her affection, but only a convenient distraction. Her real anxiety stems from the emotional ordeal of attending Gatsby's party with Tom. Soon Tom's undisguised interest in another woman stirs up old injuries, and Daisy reacts with her customary irony, ". . . if you want to take down any addresses here's my little gold pencil" (p. 107).

Daisy is uncomfortable with the party and the feelings it arouses in her. But before she leaves she appears fascinated by the image presented by an actress, "a gorgeous, scarcely human orchid of a woman" (p. 106). After Daisy expresses her approval of the actress by calling her "lovely," Nick reports that the rest of the party "offended her—and inarguably, because it wasn't a gesture but an emotion" (p. 108). But the actress appeals to Daisy, not because she is too shallow to appreciate emotion, but because the actress appears to have achieved the emotional invulnerability that Daisy herself has come to desire.

As Fitzgerald lamented in his personal correspondence, he fails to develop the emotional attachment between Daisy and Gatsby between the reunion and the catastrophe. He merely hints at an affair by Gatsby's remark to Nick that "Daisy comes over quite often—in the afternoons" (p. 114). But when Nick sees them together again, he recognizes—as even Tom Buchanan is forced to recognize—that Daisy loves Gatsby. She reveals herself inadvertently through the way she looks at Gatsby, the way she admires him verbally, and especially the way she can't keep her hands off him. She needs his love, but she needs it to be tangible.

During the critical scene at the Plaza, Daisy's conflicting needs for love and for safety from emotions take on new dimensions. As is her custom, her impulse is to run away as soon as she senses a messy emotional situation on the horizon. Before they even leave for the city, she tells Tom, "Oh, let's have fun . . . it's too hot to fuss". (p. 120). And then at the hotel, she warns him, ". . . If you're going to make personal remarks I won't stay here a minute" (p. 127). But her pleading is to no avail. Tom precipitates a confrontation with Gatsby, and Daisy's fear mounts.

> "Please don't!" she interrupted helplessly. "Please let's all go home. Why don't we all go home?" (p. 131)

But Daisy cannot stop the building tension as Tom, the embodiment of her need for stability, and Gatsby, the embodiment of her need for love, battle over her. "I won't stand this—" she cries. "Oh, please let's get out" (p. 134). Still, her desperation goes unappeased, and she cannot avoid the anguish of being asked to choose between the two men. Backed up against the wall, she ultimately chooses Tom, though she knows that neither can meet her needs by himself. Tom cannot satisfy her expectations of romantic devotion, and Gatsby, who made his fortune illegally, cannot meet her need for stability and social respectability.

When Gatsby wants Daisy to tell Tom she never loved him, she refuses:

> "Oh, you want too much!" she cried to Gatsby. "I love you now—isn't that enough? I can't help what's past." She began to sob helplessly. "I did love him once—but I loved you too." (p. 133)

Daisy's insistence that she loved them both is honest—she loved Gatsby in a romantic way, and she loved Tom in a more practical way. They each met some of her needs, and so she loved them both. Her simple statement that she loved both marks a brief emergence from behind her affectations. But, as Nick has observed frequently throughout the novel, Daisy is "helpless." Gatsby cannot tolerate her honest expression of her feelings. He wants to see her alone, perhaps to see if she'll change her story. But Daisy refuses, displaying her fundamental but, so far, well-hidden, integrity:

> "Even alone I can't say I never loved Tom," she admitted in a pitiful voice. "It wouldn't be true." (p. 133)

Daisy's sudden, simple respect for the truth is startling to *The Great Gatsby*'s readers, because Nick's perceptions of her throughout the novel are limited to her superficial manner. Her stubborn honesty under duress is a logical outgrowth of her inner struggle to resolve conflicting needs. She has made a futile attempt to declare emotional independence, but still needs the security of an established code of behavior and finds it easier to leave her lover than her husband.

Just as Fitzgerald fails to explore fully the nature of Daisy's affair with Gatsby, he fails to account clearly for her behavior following the scene at the Plaza. After the accident that kills Myrtle, Nick observes Daisy and Tom for the last time through their kitchen window:

> They weren't happy, and neither of them had touched the chicken or the ale—and yet they weren't unhappy either. There was an unmistakable air of natural intimacy about the picture, and anybody would have said that they were conspiring together. (p. 146)

Perhaps Daisy believed Tom's statement, that afternoon, that his extramarital affairs were over. Perhaps she simply needed him so badly after learning the truth about Gatsby that she didn't care about his shortcomings any more. In any case, Nick clearly perceives a renewal of communication between Daisy and her husband. Sadly, but predictably, Daisy rapidly retreats into her unhappy life with Tom—abandoning her dream of a romantic lover to cling desperately to the unsatisfactory stability her husband represents. She is a victim of a complex network of needs and desires; she deserves more pity than blame.

Notes

1. Joan S. Korenman examines Fitzgerald's contradictory descriptions of Daisy's coloring in terms of her "embodiment of traits associated with the fair and the dark women of romantic literature" in "Only Her Hairdresser . . .': Another Look at Daisy Buchanan" in *American Literature*, 46 (Jan. 1975), 574–78; and Leland S. Person, Jr., considers Daisy "more victim than victimizer" in " 'Herstory' and Daisy Buchanan" in *American Literature*, 50 (May 1978), 250–57.

2. F. Scott Fitzgerald, *The Great Gatsby* (New York: Scribner's, 1925), pp. 20–21. Subsequent references will be to this edition.

3. Andrew Turnbull, ed., *The Letters of F. Scott Fitzgerald* (New York: Scribner's, 1963), pp. 172–73.

4. *Letters*, p. 341.

5. *Letters*, p. 480.

6. F. Scott Fitzgerald, *Babylon Revisited and Other Stories* (New York: Scribner's, 1960), p. 4. Subsequent references will be to this edition.

7. In a 1920 letter to Isabelle Amorous, Fitzgerald wrote about Zelda: ". . . I fell in love with her courage, her sincerity and her flaming self-respect. . . ." The letter appears in Sheilah Graham's *The Real F. Scott Fitzgerald* (New York: Grosset and Dunlap, 1976), p. 58.

8. Barry Gross, "Back West: Time and Place in *The Great Gatsby*," *Western American Literature*, 8, Nos. 1 & 2 (1973), p. 7.

9. For fuller discussions of the romantic aspects of Daisy's character, see both the Korenman and the Person articles cited previously.

10. *Letters*, p. 170.

The Essential Houses of *The Great Gatsby*   W. T. Lhamon, Jr.*

Although Nick Carraway tells the entire story of his experiences on Long Island in 1922, there is much information which he reports but does not assimilate. This information consistently undercuts Nick's interpreted version of events and quietly asserts Fitzgerald's assumptions about America. In short, *The Great Gatsby* has an authorial structure independent of Nick's. Fitzgerald's undercutting of his narrator is neither extreme nor should it be surprising, for Nick is not so much morally deficient as morally normal. He is an experienced man caught in a world more corrupt and resistant to will than his upbringing has led him to expect. Nick is not as perceptive about or as honest with himself as one might hope; but the same is also true of Tom and Gatsby. Who or what, then, may guide the novel's readers? However consciously, Fitz-

*Reprinted from *Markham Review*, 6 (Spring 1977), 56–60, by permission of the publisher.

gerald has written a consistent "sociology" into the novel—a sociology larger than any of the characters: the intricate and ineluctable structure of America.

Nick's rhetoric is footloose and magic, but it is also tirelessly expansive. When Gatsby tells him that Daisy's "voice is full of money," Nick extends that banality into: "that was the inexhaustible charm that rose and fell in it, the jingle of it, the cymbals' song of it. . . . High in a white palace, the king's daughter, the golden girl" (p. 120), his voice trailing not off but up. On Fifth Avenue Nick expects to "see a great flock of white sheep turn the corner" (p. 28). Even though his next paragraph has a dead man passing in a hearse, Nick thinks the view of New York City from the Queensboro Bridge has "wild promise of all the mystery and the beauty in the world" (p. 69). Nick and Jordan ultimately believe their actions replay the edenic pastoral when she alludes to the "overripe" and "funny fruits" about to fall in their hands and he thinks of a "damp snake" crawling around his legs (pp. 125–26). These are hyperbolic romantic images prompted by Nick's provincial past and his need to understand America as a place of opportunity. But Fitzgerald has designed Nick's experience to show the closing off of that opportunity, those romantic hopes.

Nowhere is Nick's hyperbole more pronounced than on the last page, where he looks at the looming houses of Long Island Sound. These are the buildings which have housed the novel, structured Nick's experience, and shaped his narrative. Yet Nick pronounces them "inessential." They are not at all inessential, however, as Gatsby knew when Daisy turned him down five years before and he turned all his energy to amassing a house commensurate to her sense of security. Those houses are the essential rock on which Fitzgerald founded his story. Separate from Nick and more detailed than any of the characters, the houses are a major part of the intricate pattern to which Fitzgerald aspired as he wrote. The houses are so complexly patterned within themselves that they countermand the intricacy with which Nick laces the story. And much of the resonant depth the novel still has derives from this crucial standoff between Nick's complex romanticism and Fitzgerald's edifice complex.

In succession at the outset, Nick visits first the Buchanan home, then Myrtle's Manhattan apartment, then Gatsby's "amusement park." These are strategic moves in a pattern which attempts to penetrate the surface of money to the skeleton of power. Indeed, the focus in *Gatsby* is on power, on the ability to control reality for one's purposes. Therefore, Fitzgerald demonstrates social position most notably by his characters' ability to order environmental elements: material space, time, and people. And the opening presentation of their three houses carefully places the novel's classes: Buchanan's power to control his world is greatest; Myrtle's power, like her husband's is least (even though she is financed by

Tom); and Gatsby's power falls between the two. The unobtrusive thoroughness of this theme—which is the more nuanced for its quietness—is truly remarkable.

The arrangement of space at the Buchanan house is flowing and smooth:

> Their house was even more elaborate than [Nick] expected, a cheerful red-and-white Georgian Colonial mansion, overlooking the bay. The lawn started at the beach and ran toward the front door for a quarter of a mile, jumping over sun-dials and brick walks and burning gardens—finally when it reached the house drifting up the side in bright vines as though from the momentum of its run. The front was broken by a line of French windows . . . (pp. 6–7).

The run of the lawn overcomes the obstacles (sun-dials, brick walks, burning gardens) in its way, and also overcomes Nick's first observation that the house "was even more elaborate" than he expected. The term "elaborate" means here that the Buchanans (and, before them, "Demaine, the oil man" [p. 8]) have paid painstaking attention to the thousand details necessary to create the artificial "momentum" of this lawn. For it is only momentum that can smoothly integrate such a vast spatial area, which is in fact interrupted during its quarter of a mile by a number of stationary objects and finally stopped—"broken"—by the French windows. The Buchanans have achieved an impression of organicism that is much more than "elaborate," although Nick correctly establishes its artificial roots with his phrase. Surely it is an elaborately acquired social momentum that carries the Buchanans themselves. A sort of momentum lends the only coherence there is to their lives. They are like their lawn. But, like the stationary objects of the lawn, the Buchanans are also swept along in the integrated momentum of their social position. It is part of Fitzgerald's genius to show how even the Buchanans would like to escape their station—he via Myrtle, she via Gatsby—but in the end they cannot. The house, the lawn, and the elaborate life claim them. We shall return to this idea.

When Nick and the narration go inside, he reveals that the lawn also continues into the house, seemingly unbroken by the windows as it was not stopped by sun-dials, walks, or gardens before—the interior is only a different ripple in the "sea" that was the grass:

> We walked through a high hallway into a bright rosy-colored space, fragilely bound into the house by French windows at either end. The windows were ajar and gleaming white against the fresh grass outside that seemed to grow a little way into the house. A breeze blew through the room, blew curtains in at one end and out the other like pale flags, twisting them up toward the frosted wedding-cake of the ceiling, and then rippled over the wine-colored rug, making a shadow on it as wind does on the sea (p. 8).

There are spatial divisions here—rosy-colored space, white windows, grass outside—just as there were divisions outside ("the front vista [included] in its sweep a sunken Italian garden, a half acre of deep, pungent roses, and a snub-nosed motor-boat that bumped the tide offshore"). But the Buchanans and Demaine before them, thus their social class, are able to elaborate a smoothness that exorcises the layered reality outside and in. Outside, the momentum of the lawn runs all together— inside, the curtains blow back and forth, "in at one end and out the other," the "fresh grass outside . . . seemed to grow a little way into the house," and that wine-colored rug is as thick as the manicured grass trying to come through the windows.

The Buchanans' power is finely studied in these passages, but not primarily as an index of sensibility, for it is distinctly in contrast to the ability of Myrtle Wilson and Gatsby to achieve the same conquest of chaos. Fitzgerald was interested in showing through close nuance the uncontained power people like the Buchanans gather, not in a vacuum, but in relation to other things, and to other people in their society.

From the top, Nick next goes to the bottom, to 158th Street, where he finds material space much more assertively random, much less con-quered, and Myrtle's attempts to arrange it pathetic:

> The apartment was on the top floor—a small living-room, a small dining-room, a small bedroom, and a bath. The living-room was crowded to the doors with a set of tapestried furniture entirely too large for it, so that to move about was to stumble continually over scenes of ladies swinging in the gardens of Versailles (p. 29).

Of course, the swinging ladies of Versailles and many of the other choices characters make in the ensuing afternoon reflect simply banal taste. Catherine, Myrtle's sister, for instance, has a "solid, sticky bob of red hair, and a complexion powdered milky white. . . . When she moved about there was an incessant clicking as innumerable pottery brackets jingled up and down upon her arms" (p. 30). Some conversation con-cerns the getting of liquor, ice, and mineral water; some of the rest is of the problems with feet, appendicitis, borrowed suits, and kikes. Still, this is more than an exploration of taste and sensibility—it indicates the inability of Myrtle and her friends to maintain any order.

She is just an object of chance. Although Tom desires Myrtle for her "intense vitality" (p. 30), there is little specific reason for his particular choice of Myrtle beyond their random meeting on the commuter train one day. Because her friends are as windblown as she is, Myrtle is no aberration. Chance governs their lives. If man's lowest, most-stripped station is to be an "accidental burden" on an "accidental course," as is the case with Gatsby at his death (p. 162), then Myrtle's coterie flirts with that station continuously. The slipcovers with scenes of Versailles on them are pitifully continuous with the landscaped lawn used by the

Buchanans—both lawn and covers attempt to lend a theme to random matter, in both cases a garden theme—but Myrtle's effort is clumsy, stumbling. More importantly, it lacks scope, she hasn't the capacity to shape things that the Buchanans can assume. She and her group, more blatantly even than Gatsby, are caught between the accidental state of a dead Gatsby and the hypothetical ability to elaborate one's purposes in the world.

These are Myrtle's long-range plans:

> "I'm going to give you this dress as soon as I'm through with it. I've got to get another one tomorrow. I'm going to make a list of all the things I've got to get. A message and a wave, and a collar for the dog, and one of those cute little ash-trays where you touch a spring, and a wreath with a black silk bow for mother's grave that'll last all summer. I got to write down a list so I won't forget all the things I got to do." (p. 37)

All her days, the parts of her life will remain discrete *things*, no purpose animating them. Like the crowded furniture in the room, like the topics of conversation, like the puppy on the table, "with blind eyes . . . groaning faintly," the parts of her life are merely piled one on the other. And when Tom Buchanan breaks Myrtle's nose with a "short, deft movement," Fitzgerald reveals the inherent slackness of this pile-up: "[Mrs. McKee] and Catherine scolding and consoling as they stumbled here and there among the crowded furniture with articles of aid, and [Myrtle] despairing . . . on the couch, bleeding fluently, . . . trying to spread a copy of *Town Tattle* over the tapestry scenes of Versailles" (p. 38). Here is a kind of thrice unsuccessful layering of poses—the Versailles tapestries cover conventionally ugly furniture and are in turn futilely covered by *Town Tattle* magazines to protect them from blood no one is able to avenge. This scene anticipates the sudden one of her death, itself a violent accident inexplicable within the terms available to her class, and as equally unavenged—despite George's murdering Gatsby—as her fractured nose. Because Myrtle manages only a broken series of unsuccessful gestures, she is directly opposed to Nick's characterization of Gatsby's achievement as an "unbroken series of successful gestures" (p. 2). Whether Gatsby lives up to Nick's claim is important to test.

Nick first visits Gatsby's house when the host gives one of his famous, superbly chaotic parties, at which guests conduct themselves "according to the rules of behavior associated with an amusement park" (p. 41). This is the night the orchestra appropriately played the *Jazz History of the World* while guests broke into "fraternal hilarity," "went off into a deep vinous sleep," or tried to leave in a car missing one of its wheels (pp. 50, 51, 54). Befitting an amusement park, the groupings of people are almost random. There were no reasons for their congregation: "People were not invited—they went there. They got into automobiles which bore them out to Long Island, and somehow they ended up at Gatsby's door" (p. 41).

All this herding together of people is however more planned than Nick first understands. Gatsby, it turns out, provides pasture and grazing because he hopes Daisy will someday mosey in like the others. Yet Daisy does not mosey—a fact which places her code of behavior in a closed circle and shows Gatsby's misestimation of his social milieu. Instead, Gatsby must entice Daisy through a contrived invitation via Nick before he can take her on a guided tour of his house.

They enter by the "big postern" at the road, admire the "feudal silhouettes," pass various flowers and fruit trees in gardens, cross marble steps to the door. Inside, on the first floor, there are "Marie Antoinette music-rooms" (shades of Versailles tapestries), "Restoration salons," and, of course, the library, where the books are real, but the pages uncut. Then they go "upstairs, through period bedrooms swathed in rose and lavender silk and vivid with new flowers, through dressing-rooms and poolrooms, and bathrooms, with sunken baths. . . . Finally we came [Nick reports] to Gatsby's own apartment, a bedroom and a bath, and an Adam study, where we sat down and drank a glass of some Chartreuse he took from a cupboard in the wall" (pp. 91, 92). These indeed constitute an unbroken series of gestures, but whether they are successful, as Nick would have it, is doubtful; in fact, they aren't even persuasive to Daisy. In his bedroom, "the simplest room of all," where the dresser was, unsimply, "garnished with a toilet set of pure dull gold," the series of gestures reaches a climax:

> He took out a pile of shirts and began throwing them, one by one, before us, shirts of sheer linen and thick silk and fine flannel, which lost their folds as they fell and covered the table in many-colored disarray. While we admired he brought out more and the soft heap mounted higher—shirts with stripes and scrolls and plaids in coral and apple-green and lavender and faint orange, with monograms of Indian blue. Suddenly, with a strained sound, Daisy bent her head into the shirts and began to cry stormily.
> "They're such beautiful shirts," she sobbed, her voice muffled in the thick folds. "It makes me sad because I've never seen such—such beautiful shirts before." (pp. 93–94)

Past the last door to the last room and Gatsby's facade is still up; he is still marshalling, even in his bedroom, "many-colored disarray," literally piling it up: there is no end to his "soft rich heap." He will, in the words of the epigraph, wear the gold hat and bounce high too, will yoke together Marie Antoinette and the Restoration, poolrooms and Indian blue monograms, an Adam study and "his shirts, piled like bricks in stacks of a dozen high" (p. 93). But, despite all the wealth they embody, they remain piles of things.

Gatsby's heaped belongings are fundamentally similar to Myrtle's. He speaks more smoothly than she, and his house is grander, but their fates are the same. They both die trying to imitate the Buchanans; the Buchanans, if indirectly, kill them both. Or, more precisely, they die because of their essential powerlessness which their houses represent. When Gatsby attempts to emulate with his hotel the series of gestures that elaborate the Buchanans, the result is a heap of shirts, of rooms, of guests—expensive disarray. It is disarray for Gatsby, but it is mess for Myrtle.

Landscaped lawns, crowded furniture, piles of shirts, "short deft movement[s]," car "accidents," and mistaken murders are finally not accidents, as the reductive "simplest form" of the story adhered to in the official inquest suggest (pp. 164–65). Nor are they due to a "vast carelessness" attributable to a "child," as Nick claims at the end (pp. 180–81). Children are careless, yes, but not as vastly careless as Tom and Daisy. Children, that is, do not have the power available to the Buchanans. Children do not own Georgian Colonial mansions. A child's mess can be cleaned up. So, although Nick says the Buchanans "let other people clean up the mess they had made" (p. 181), there is still no bringing Jay Gatsby back, nor Jimmy Gatz, nor George Wilson, nor Myrtle Wilson.

This is not spilt milk. Children are not careless on such a scale: only power gone amuck is, and then it is not a mess, but social disorder. Society is fate here; the Buchanans control that society; luck in this novel is social in origin. Daisy has told Nick in the beginning, in one of those anticipatory jokes which come true: " 'Come over often . . . and I'll sort of—oh—fling you together [with Jordan]. You know—lock you up accidentally in linen closets and push you out to sea in a boat, and all that sort of thing——' " (p. 19). At a verbal level it is all chuckles, as a child's mess is cute, but when her pushes, flings, and conspiracies are actual they are deadly. For the joke is real at the end when Nick describes the way Tom dismisses Daisy and Gatsby: "They were gone, without a word, snapped out, *made accidental,* isolated like ghosts, even from our pity" (p. 136; my emphasis). This language is critical because it is illustrative of the way "accidents" happen in this novel: Tom has snapped them out like ghosts, and it is Tom who sends Wilson as a "ghost" (p. 162) to murder Gatsby later. There aren't really ghosts, nor accidents, just a society with people in it who have too much power. "Accidents" are made.

For Fitzgerald, there are real groups in the society with real differences between them holding them apart. Gatsby and Myrtle are unlike Tom, in that they cannot scape land, people, or things as well as he can, and Myrtle can less than Gatsby. Nevertheless, they are all caught in a single tissue of values extant in American life. There are real differences separating, by turns, Buchanan's Georgian Colonial mansion from Gatsby's Hotel de Ville and Myrtle's apartment. Yet each house exhibits the same themes and goals—goals which only the Buchanan mansion successfully approximates. And, of course, in personal terms, Tom Buchanan represents the values these buildings are meant to house. The houses of *The Great Gatsby* manifest at a subtle, structural level the seeming variety but underlying unidimensionality that the novel postulates. There is only one chain of values in the worlds of *The Great Gatsby*, only one ladder, and everyone in the novel is on it, not just with one foot, but totally. Much more than just for Daisy, the competition between Tom and Gatsby pervades the novel.

Gatsby's claim that he can "repeat the past" is doubtlessly brash, but is it a key to his failure? Does it differentiate him from others in the novel? Rather than separating Gatsby from his reputedly more realistic countrymen, the statement unites him with them. Tom Buchanan set precedents for Gatsby; could Gatsby but duplicate Buchanan's career, the upstart's brashness would be commonplace. Tom can casually say, and never be challenged, " 'I've heard of making a garage out of a stable . . . but I'm the first man who ever made a stable out of a garage' " (p. 119). Although Gatsby cannot, Tom does indeed repeat the past; he marshals the power to relive a more privileged era. He does it not only with physical matter such as garages, but also in his marriage with his wife; he did so after the affair with the chambermaid in Santa Barbara, presumably did so in Chicago (p. 132), and does so again after Myrtle.

Tom beats Gatsby in the repetition of time, in the organization of space, and finally also in the control of people. Tom habitually uses people, both casually and designedly—as with George Wilson throughout—but the best example of how he beats Gatsby in the use of men comes to focus in Nick, whom they compete to control. For Tom, Nick is explicitly a "checker" to be moved from square to square (p. 12); for Gatsby, he is a part of the apparatus built to snare Daisy. But when he keeps quiet at the inquest Nick is the ultimate piece in Tom's checker game because his silence protects the Buchanans and validates Gatsby's official guilt. (It is, indeed, perhaps to lessen some unconscious sense of his functional alliance with Tom that Nick has felt compelled to write his narrative of Gatsby.)

Moreover, while Nick describes Gatsby's parties as unique in their extraordinarily gaudy largesse, they are actually imitative failures compared to Tom's wedding party. For that party, Tom traveled with "a hundred people in four private cars" from Chicago to Louisville, "hired a whole floor of the Muhlbach Hotel, and . . . gave [Daisy] a string of pearls valued at three hundred and fifty thousand dollars" (p. 77). More important than its extravagance is that Tom's party won the girl. His party also included at least one uninvited guest—"Blocks" Biloxi, a precise prototype for Ewing Klipspringer, the boarder at Gatsby's hotel. Tom naturally chooses to forget all his *infra dig* social past and calls Gatsby's party life a "pigsty" (p. 131), but his extreme attack only betrays his sensitivity to Gatsby's extreme emulation. Myrtle Wilson's parties are also similar in kind. Complete with their uninvited guests, like Nick who wanders in and out, Myrtle's parties are just a cheaper version of Gatsby's "pigsty" and Buchanan's wedding train.

Everyone in the novel, Westerners all, or would-be Westerners (in the case of the Wilsons), is bent on finding a frontier in New York City, bent on beginning anew. They all fail. Only Tom is still left: he has what the others cannot have no matter how much they desire it. Tom does all the things that Gatsby and Myrtle and Jordan and Nick and George would like to do. Therefore, while it has often been said that Gatsby fails because he overdreams his possibilities, that's not so. Gatsby's dreams are not fantastic; all he wants is what Tom has. All he lacks, all that ruins him, is Tom's power.

Is Tom special? Is he safe from the penalties of this social structure? If Fitzgerald has written a novel about the way a single set of values has, just like Daisy's joke, flung everyone together "accidentally," it ought to be expected that Tom too is bound up, some way, in this web. He is. Daisy killed Myrtle Wilson: wife murdered mistress. She neither decapitated Myrtle nor left her internally hemorrhaging, and there was no self-induced heart-attack from, perhaps, overexcitement. It was her breast torn off. Breasts are as important to this novel as they are to America. Daisy's breast, for example, at which Gatsby dreamed he could "suck on the pap of life, gulp down the incomparable milk of wonder" (p. 112); and Myrtle's breast; "when they had torn open her shirtwaist, still damp with perspiration, they saw that her left breast was swinging loose like a flap, and there was no need to listen for the heart beneath" (p. 138). Daisy ran Gatsby's fancy car into Myrtle's breast, and thus into Tom's hopes, into the hopes that made Tom like everyone else in the novel. No one can have the "green breast of the new world," to which Nick refers on the last page. Although all his characters desire ineffable escape; for Fitzgerald there are no longer new worlds.

This socially unified need placed against the inability to have is what the novel so drastically asserts. Class from class, the society is divided. Yet nearly everyone in the society subscribes to the single set of values represented rhetorically in Gatsby's image of the ladder—through his Daisy, to "a secret place above the trees" (p. 112)—and represented structurally in the continuity of the novel's houses. Gatsby is not to have Daisy, nor the secret place, nor even any good way to spend his money. Tom is not to have satisfaction in his wandering empty life; certainly Tom is not to have Myrtle, nor she him. Jordan is not to have Nick nor anything but another tournament in which she will cheat, and thus cheat herself of any possible satisfaction. Nick is left without a stake in the bond business, without a girl, without order in the world, without conviction of Gatsby's worth (for he has to convince himself during the writing of the novel), and perhaps even without belief in the real worth of the romanticism with which the novel ends. He is left thirty years old and very lonely.

Despite Nick, Fitzgerald wrote a novel clearly establishing profoundly different groups of people in American society, characterized by their relative access to a broad notion of power (meaning the ability to "elaborate"). His groups should therefore show quite different needs. But his society nevertheless has as its mucilage an established set of values epitomized by those who are most powerful, subscribed to by everyone else, and represented in the novel by its structure which centers on the three houses of its three classes. These values are mostly in the interest of the powerful, and tender only misery and "hot struggles" to the poor. But the critique goes further to say that the values are destructive also for the rich. Their social position, their fulfillment and protection of the roles they inherit, prompt the Buchanans to their violence, paranoia, restlessness, and brutality. And no character in the novel, certainly not Nick, sees this covert sociology entirely clearly. That is perhaps Fitzgerald's most important point throughout and the last bleakness of the novel: the sham consciousness of America has seemed impenetrable and thus insoluble. This last is important. Although the essential houses provide an underlying structure to *The Great Gatsby* —a structure which is independent of Nick or any other character—it is available only in hindsight to readers who participate only emotionally. Structure is as covert in the novel as it is in the society. Fitzgerald's genius, conscious or not, is that his truest novel is as secretly shaped as is the society it describes.

Photography and *The Great Gatsby*

Lawrence Jay Dessner*

The Great Gatsby repeatedly investigates how photography expresses and affects the ways its characters think. Fitzgerald's novel surveys and evaluates many uses of photography and borrows cinematic techniques for Nick Carraway's narration. In that it is a mode of perception, photography carries implicit philosophic assumptions. Fitzgerald shows us that photography is not merely a means of entertainment, professional or domestic, and a method of documentation, but a way people who are not self-conscious philosophers reinforce their assumptions about the nature of reality and time.

In its largest perspective, *The Great Gatsby* is a philosophic novel in which philosophic questions underlie social, political, and psychological

*Reprinted from *Essays in Literature*, 6 (Spring 1979), 79–89, by permission of the publisher.

concerns. The novel has to do with the disparity between aspiration and achievement, between the "Dutch sailor's" vision of a "fresh, green . . . new world" (p. 182) and Nick Carraway's stunned observations of contemporary American life. The *"Great"*-ness of Gatsby is his remarkable and, in his context inspiring, innocence. He has drunk deep at the springs of American popular ideology, got, directly or through modulating transmissions, some of the assumptions that made potent the legends of Hopalong Cassidy, Buffalo Bill Cody, Horatio Alger, and the Benjamin Franklin of the *Autobiography*. He has become the quintessential American, the New World's version of the landed aristocrat—and all through his adherence to the creed of the self-made man. "The truth," Nick tells us, "was that Jay Gatsby . . . sprang from his Platonic conception of himself. He was a son of God . . ." (p. 99). The past, in the Utopian and absolute democracy of Gatsby's vision, does not matter. History is to him what it was to Henry Ford (himself an historical version of Fitzgerald's novel): "Bunk."

Photography, in its ability to freeze time—or to run it backwards—may be a symbolic denial of history, a metaphor of transcendence. So thoroughly has Gatsby absorbed the idea of freedom from the constraints of history, so vital and earnest is his hold on the paradox of the unmoved mover, that he transforms it from a motto into a myth of eternal return to a timeless Eden. Like Bounderby in Dickens's *Hard Times*, Gatsby comes to believe that the past which does not matter did not exist. The pasts he invents for himself are those which claim his purest allegiance, Daisy's past, her years with Buchanan and the three-year-old toddling and unblinkable evidence and result of history's irreversible flow, are, miraculously, blinked. It is not enough for Daisy to renounce Tom, to wipe the slate clean; she must avow that the slate has never been sullied. Gatsby tells Tom that Daisy " 'doesn't love you' " and later even claims that " 'she's never loved you.' " Daisy can accept this obliteration of history through a rhetorical ploy: " 'Why—how could I love him—possibly?' " But Gatsby wants more than rhetoric, he wants "the truth"; " 'It doesn't matter any more. Just tell him the truth—that you never loved him—and it's all wiped out forever.' " Here The Power of Positive Thinking is exalted into something more than a psychological method. Daisy knows that her suitor " 'want[s] too much,' " that one " 'can't help what's past,' " and when Buchanan comes to her aid with hints of particular events of their marital past, "the words seemed to bite physically into Gatsby" (pp. 132, 133). Nick had warned his neighbor of that painful possibility: " 'I wouldn't ask too much of her. . . . You can't repeat the past.' " To which Gatsby replies, "incredulously," "Why of course you can!' " (p. 111). In Gatsby's world, things can always be as good as new again—and again. It is nostalgia propelled into a metaphysical principle. It becomes a version of the grand American joke of the used-car driven only by a little old lady, on Sundays, to the nearby church; and even what wear she does inflict on the mechanism is discounted, not believed in. This mechanical immortality has an analogue in the imagined life made so convincingly real by the marvels of photography. Ageless, forever new, the photographic image incessantly implies that the life it captures is itself subject only to the desires and manipulations of the photographer. And with any "son of God," what the photographer sees is what is. The images he presents reinforce our desires to believe in the ultimate reality of what our needs prompt our imaginations to envisage. The characters in *The Great Gatsby* live in a world of photographic images, and have developed habits of mind, tacit philosophies of ideal existence. The novel itself is a treatment of the concept of time,[1] for it is time's incessant flow that forever separates dream from deed, aspiration from achievement.[2]

The years immediately following World War I were important ones for American photography. New technologies in photography could be turned to civilian use. The Kodak line of inexpensive roll-film cameras, introduced in 1890, improved by advances in chemistry and mechanics, became increasingly simple and sure. By 1920, several manufacturers were offering 16mm motion picture cameras for home use. The first Leica, introduced in 1924, boosted the new vogue for smaller and more versatile cameras which used the 35mm film designed for professional motion pictures. Practitioners and theorists of photographic art—among them Edward Steichen, Alfred Stieglitz, and Edward Weston—made what are now seen as crucial strides in the development of a fine art of photography.[3] The editor of *The American Annual of Photography* had good reason to preface his volume for 1924 with this boast: "Photography has at last reached a position where we can truthfully say it has a place in all our lives, whether we are actively engaged in it or not."[4] The omnipresence of photography in America is accurately portrayed in *The Great Gatsby* and is related to ways in which its characters react to their experience and think about their histories. Nick Carraway, too self-conscious and detached an intelligence to be caught up utterly in Gatsby's dream world, becomes a critic of his defiantly non-historic solipsism and of the habitual faith in the illusions of photography.

For all his protestations to the contrary, Gatsby is a true son of his father, the dismal Gatz from the dismal swamps of Minnesota. The father displays, in his grief, a mixture of awe and "pride," and as that pride increases, and as grief gives place to excitement, "with trembling fingers" he shows Nick a photograph of Gatsby's house, the very house in which they are both standing. Nick had known from the first that Gatsby's imitation "Hôtel de Ville" lacked the patina and authenticity of age: it is "spanking new under a thin beard of raw ivy" (p. 5). That early assessment is hardly profound, but by the end of the novel, Nick, having fallen under the spell of Gatsby's dream, having found himself Gatsby's survivor and mourner, comes to see that the house, like all the houses that line the Sound, are "inessential" and "melt away gradually" (p. 182).

Not the houses but the energies that imagined them are of the essence. The thinness and rawness of Gatsby's ivy is insignificant when one considers the grandeur of his belief, however grotesquely vulgarized, in the power of human aspiration and endeavor. West Egg is a grotesque version, but a version nonetheless of Tennyson's Camelot and of its mythical forebears: "[a] city . . . built / To music, therefore never built at all, / And therefore built for ever."[5] Mr. Gatz senses some of this. The photograph he proffers, showing the signs of much handling and folding, incorporates the essence of his son's dream; the house itself does not: "He pointed out every detail to me eagerly. 'Look there!' [he repeated], and then sought admiration from my eyes." Nick draws the point for us, and not without the sympathy which comes with understanding: "He had shown it so often that I think it was more real to him now than the house itself." Nick noticed that Gatz "seemed reluctant to put away the picture, held it for another minute, lingeringly, before my eyes." The mundane photograph of the great mansion, "cracked in the corners and dirty with many hands" (pp. 173, 174), is Gatz's Platonic idea of a house. It is, for him, the timeless, unchanging promise, a well-wrought urn on which the ideal life, stopped and frozen, is eternally lived. It is his version of eternity, of the immortality which is ours through our imaginative victories over time. Photography lends substance to that vision.

There is something ludicrous in the great philosophic weight which Gatz, and Fitzgerald, and now the present writer, assign to this snapshot. But then there is much ludicrous in Nick's admiration for Gatsby— perhaps "love" would not be too strong a word for it—and in Fitzgerald's single direct valuation of the man: "*Great.*" The snapshot may bear its moral and philosophic weight more gracefully when we notice that the novel has prepared us to see its significance. Just as there are a number of minor automobile accidents before the climactic one which kills Myrtle, the last accident making explicit the meaning of the others, so are there many seemingly trivial references to photographs before this last one of which so much is being made and which is indeed the culmination and explication of the series.

Before turning to the specific references to photography in *The Great Gatsby*, it may be be useful to glance at *The Romantic Egoists*,[6] a collection of Fitzgerald memorabilia. The oversize volume is largely an album of domestic photographs, some of them taken, mounted, labeled, and even listed by Scott and Zelda. They are, of course, black-and-white still photographs, utterly unpretentious, poorly lit and compased, and now, redolent of nostalgia. We see Scott at age four in as technically and aesthetically amateurish a photograph as one could imagine. If Henry C. Gatz had snapped his young James, it might have looked like this: a picture that only a parent could be expected to love. Later we have what appears to be Scott and his daughter,[7] both faces obscured in the shadows of their hat brims, posed before the large white columns of a large house. And before that same house we have the "Last photo of father," so the picture is captioned, by hand, in its lower border. Here father and son have removed their hats; "father" holds his towards the lens in what might be taken as a gesture of farewell. *The Romantic Egoists* conveniently and repeatedly demonstrates the large part snap-shots played in making and preserving the Fitzgerald family record, their personal pasts. One is tempted to insist that before the days of the Polaroid camera, of high-quality color and high-speed films, before the phenomenon of professional photographic equipment in millions of middle-class households and the explosion of interest in photography as Art, before our days of excellent photographs, in magazines, or television, on color slides, the homely snapshot of Fitzgerald's day, which is Gatsby's day too, mattered a good deal more than we are likely to immediately remember or imagine.

The technological photographic advance whose great impact on the American of the 1920's is well-remembered was the commercial motion picture. As a new business it made new money and new delegates to Gatsby's conventions of the *nouveaux riches*. Nick Carraway—while not the reader of motion-picture magazines that Myrtle Wilson is (p. 27), nor even sympathetic to Jordan Baker's resort to "the movies" in times of great heat and ominous ennui (p. 125)—after properly introducing himself with the sunshine and the great bursts of leaves growing on the trees, and his situation to his reader, begins his narrative with this: "And so with the sunshine and the great bursts of leaves growing on the trees, just as things grow in fast movies, I had that familiar conviction that life was beginning over again with the summer" (p. 4). "Fast movies" are, no doubt, sequences of time-lapse photography, from rose bud to full flowering, from eggshell to hatched chick, in thirty seconds. The photographic *tour de force* conspires with that of the bursting leaves to press the wistful dream which, in a radically different key, is Gatsby's dream of "beginning over again." A variant on this photographic link with the novel's theme, and further evidence of Nick's familiarity with the techniques of photography and their philosophic tendencies, occurs in his description of Myrtle Wilson as she peers out over her garage apartment: "So engrossed was she that she had no consciousness of being observed, and one emotion after another crept into her face like objects into a slowly developing picture" (p. 125).[8] Photography by its distortion of time is a begetter and sustainer of illusion, but it is also a potential aid to truer seeing, to revelation.

This motif of photography's dual and contradictory possibilities is fleetingly suggested when Nick recalls that he "had seen her [Jordan Baker], or a picture of her somewhere before" (p. 11). Discovering and coming to grips with the moral identity of Jordan Baker, her true "picture," illusion or revelation, will be part of Nick and the novel's business from now on. But it is with our introduction to Mr. Chester McKee, photographer *extraordinaire*, that the photographic motif comes front and center. Too ignorant to be a scoundrel, too absurdly ineffectual to be taken seriously, we remember him as does Nick as less a photographer than a photograph: "asleep on a chair with his fists clenched in his lap, like a photograph of a man of action" (p. 37). His devotion to the "artistic game" (p. 30), as he calls it, is less disturbing to Nick than the "spot of dried lather" (p. 37) which he wipes from the cheek of the sleeping figure. McKee is so fatuous, Nick's shocked response to him so comic, that we may fail to notice how tenuous is his relationship to the novel's tightly structured plot. McKee leaves the story at the end of Chapter Two and neither returns nor affects the unfolding of the story.

Unlike the generalized guests at Gatsby's parties, McKee is particularized a character rather than a caricatured name or a briefly embodied joke. He is Myrtle's guest and thus a structural equivalent of Gatsby's party guests, but more important is McKee's function in establishing the photographic theme. The paradoxical nature of photography is noted in the double paradox of the sleeping man who looks like "a photograph of a man of action." Gatsby's dream of recapturing his past relationship with Daisy is prefigured and parodied by McKee's repeated attempts, since his marriage, to capture the ideal essence of his wife on photographic film: he "had photographed her a hundred and twenty-seven times since they had been married" (p. 30). Bungling artist that he is, harridan that *she* is, surely these explain his continued because presumably unsuccessful attempts. McKee's "over-enlarged" photograph of Mrs. Wilson's mother "hovered like an ectoplasm on the wall" and appeared to be "a hen sitting on a blurred rock," although "looked at from a distance . . . the hen resolved itself into a bonnet, and the countenance of a stout old lady beamed down into the room" (p. 29). McKee has evidently overreached himself, sought to make more of his negative, and more of his neighbor's mother, than either could justify. His attempts at self-improvement and timeless idealization of the female through the camera's distorting potential wholly fail. Even without the benefit of McKee's artistry, Myrtle's sister Catherine, in her attempts to improve the countenance Nature gave her, has produced "a *blurred* air to her face" (p. 30, my emphasis). She too, having plucked and redrawn her eyebrows, finds only confusion in her distortion for aesthetic effect. As Myrtle's company, they are both under the influence of Doctor T. J. Eckleburg, that gigantic but sham purveyor of optical improvements.

The novel's social and historical context, the pathos of Gatsby's "factual imitation of some Hôtel de Ville in Normandy" (p. 5), is picked up by the ersatz French old-world elegance of Myrtle's furniture above which, in sole possession of her walls, Mrs. Wilson's mother broods: "The living-room was crowded to the doors with a set of tapestried furniture entirely too large for it, so that to move about was to stumble

continually over scenes of ladies swinging in the gardens of Versailles"
(p. 29). "Bleeding fluently" from the nose Tom Buchanan has just
broken, Myrtle seeks to limit the damage to her pretensions by protecting
the tapestried Versailles with, of all things, her copy of *Town Tattle*
(p. 38).

Despite his ghastly surroundings, McKee the photographer is a
Gatsby who has not "made it," although Buchanan's malicious suggestion that he produce a photograph formally titled *"George B. Wilson at
the Gasoline Pump"* (p. 33) sounds a good deal like the sort of aesthetic
realism on which successful photographic careers have in fact long
been based. McKee has Gatsby's old faith in his chances—in the chances,
in this America, for effort to be rewarded. All he needs is a chance:
" 'If Chester could only get you in that pose,' " Mrs. McKee whines. Her
husband takes up her plaintive conditional mode: " 'I'd like to. . . .' "
" 'All I ask is that they should give me a start' " (pp. 31, 33). If only I
could, if only he would, if only. This is a parodic version of Gatsby's
old yearnings, of those dreams which, in their energetic innocence, in the
"colossal vitality of his illusion" (p. 97), earned Carraway's fascinated
admiration. McKee's aspirations, like his photographs, hardly seem promising, but who is to say that he will not meet his appropriate Dan Cody,
his saving "gonnegtion" (p. 71).

Echoing over Chester McKee's self-pitying tale of his as yet un-
satisfied dreams is Myrtle Wilson's blunt and bald statement of the spur
to such aspirations: " 'All I kept thinking about, over and over, was
"You can't live forever; you can't live forever" ' " (p. 36). Against time's
inexorable flow, McKee props not only his mundane ambitions but his
aesthetic achievement, his "great portfolio": "Beauty and the Beast . . .
Loneliness . . . Old Grocery Horse . . . Brook'n Bridge' " (p. 38). His
"portfolio" is not made up of illicit bonds or of drugstores selling grain
alcohol, but it is in its own way, as is Gatsby in his, "great." (Fitzgerald's
detailed portrait of McKee tempts us to wonder if he was based on an
historic original. Both the titles of McKee's photographs and their extremely soft focus are reminiscent of much of the aesthetic photography
of the 1920's.[9] A common criticism from those, like Nick, who disparaged
the new "Artistic Photography," was that its results were no more than
"fuzzy, blurred pictures.")[10]

McKee's photographs are still pictures of aesthetic provenance and
so he is not, quite yet anyway, among those makers and sellers of commercial motion pictures who fill Gatsby's gardens. Not yet a fit companion
for "Newton Orchid, who controlled Films Par Excellence [yet another
Francophile], and Eckhaust and Clyde Cohen and Don S. Schwartze
(the son) and Arthur McCarty, all connected with the movies in one way
or another" (p. 62). We are to assume, although Nick does not say so,
that these movie people owe their status and celebrity to their successful
exploitation of the mass instincts for beauty, romance, escape, for a vision

—however vulgarized—of perfection and permanence. It is ironic that the pictures that move may capture, hold clear and out of the flow of time, the infinite moments. And ironic also is that this paradox is presented not through any scene from a particular film, but in a prose description of a "moving-picture director and his Star": "They were still under the white-plum tree and their faces were touching except for a pale, thin ray of moonlight between. It occurred to me that he had been very slowly bending toward her all evening to attain this proximity, and even while I watched I saw him stoop one ultimate degree and kiss at her cheek" (p. 108). Nick has applied to these movie people the photographic conceit of the "fast movies" and the "slowly developing picture." The lovers are "still" but so posed and so seen that they suggest an almost infinite suspension of time, a supernally patient and gradual movement.

The Keatsian impulse runs deep in Carraway, and he is moved when he recognizes its manifestations. The imperceptible movement, the change that stands still is a staple of motion pictures technique, accomplished by simple technical means: freeze-frame, slow motion, dissolve, fade, etc. Nick has an eye for these. He notes "the eyes of Doctor T. J. Eckleburg, which had just emerged, pale and enormous, from the dissolving night" (p. 160). He thinks of West Egg's "quality of distortion" as if it were "a night scene by El Greco" (p. 178), and, returning to the more modern distortions of photography, has the "inessential houses . . . melt away . . . gradually" (p. 182).

If time can be slowed, distorted, if even the illusion of that possibility can be glimpsed, then Gatsby's absurd insistence that you can "repeat the past" is less utterly absurd. Nick transfers the imagery of the "moving-picture director and his Star" to Gatsby's five-year movement from and then again toward Daisy's lips. He imagines Gatsby thinking that "if he could once return to a certain starting place and go over it all slowly," he could transcend his present confusion. Nick ghostwrites for Gatsby a wildly surrealistic version of his embrace with Daisy, in the old moonlight of Louisville. "His heart beat faster and faster as Daisy's white face came up to his own. He knew that when he kissed this girl . . . his mind would never romp again like the mind of God. So he waited, listening for a moment longer to the tuning-fork that had been struck upon a star. Then he kissed her. At his lips' touch she blossomed for him like a flower and the incarnation was complete" (p. 112). Despite what he calls the "appalling sentimentality" of this telling of Gatsby's story, it reminds Nick "of something—an elusive rhythm, a fragment of lost words," that "uncommunicable forever" as they are, in fact the lost keys to his own lost innocence. Nick is deeply grateful for being inspired to even this elusive and fragmentary epiphany, and will soon acknowledge his debt to Gatsby in language which, in its uncharacteristic verve and diction, reveals something that Nick's propriety usually hides. It is a Gatsby from the right side of the tracks who tells the Gatz Gatsby, " 'You're worth the whole damn bunch put together'" (p. 154).

Like his father, Gatsby counts on photographs to validate his problematic history: " 'Here's another thing I always carry. A souvenir of Oxford days'" (p. 67). Even more convincing than the engraved medal from Montenegro, "it was a photograph of half a dozen young men in blazers loafing in an archway through which were visible a host of spires. There was Gatsby, looking a little, but not much, younger—with a cricket bat in his hand" (p. 67). We expect Nick to respond in the manner of Owl Eyes: " 'It's a bona-fide piece of printed matter. It fooled me. This fella's a regular Belasco'" (p. 46). But Nick is capable of deeper belief in the revelations of photography. He sees the picture and is satisfied. "Then it was all true," he says. "All" in this context includes Gatsby's statement earlier in this conversation. "I am the son of some wealthy people in the middle west—all dead now. I was brought up in America but educated at Oxford, because all my ancestors have been educated there for many years. It is a family tradition'" (p. 65). Nick, as he recalls this scene, knows that Gatsby's statement is not true,[11] but the snapshot, at least for the moment, carries great conviction, has the power to suspend disbelief.

On display in Gatsby's room are two additional photographs, a "large" one of Dan Cody—" 'He used to be my best friend years ago'" (p. 94)—and a smaller one of Gatsby looking about eighteen and dressed, as was Cody, in "yachting costume." When the paths of these two sailors intersected, James Gatz was reborn as Jay Gatsby. Like Myrtle Wilson who displays a photograph of her mother on her apartment wall, Gatsby exhibits his own "parents." Or if it is true that he "sprang from his Platonic conception of himself," the photographs are of his singular "parent" and his god-father *cum* midwife. The photographs record and preserve the essential myth, the rewriting of history. They can make visible truths which otherwise would be invisible and unknown, and they can present forceful evidence of propositions that are not true, not scientifically or historically true but true to the heart's desire and to its aspiring imagination.

The debate between these kinds of truth began long before the invention and development of photography, but that invention renewed and recast the question.[12] Fitzgerald's use of photography and photographic metaphors in *The Great Gatsby* is an advance over the decision of Delacroix in 1853: "Jusqu'ici, cet art à la machine ne nous a rendu qu'un détestable service: il nous gâte les chefs-d'oeuvre, sans nous satisfaire complètement."[13] The kinds of seeing and the kinds of truth seen and made newly see-able by the camera's new kind of eye can satisfy us completely, although they can also be, like McKee's works, meretricious and banal. In our century, photography does not compete with traditional arts so as to force fiction, or painting, to ape the photograph's needle-sharp accuracy and the completeness of its descriptive record. *The Great Gatsby* can be considered a work of social realism, but its prose style and narrative manner are very far removed from the typical nineteenth-century realists. Fitzgerald gives Nick a richly decorative, metaphoric and imaginative prose style. He has so assimilated photographic ways of seeing that he only rarely names the particular photographic techniques he is borrowing. Their distortions, particularly of time, are unobtrusive because of the large place photography has come to have in our visual consciousness. (One might say that Gatsby's insistence on repeating even recapturing the past, is the morbidly exaggerated result of seeing too many movies.)

Nick's photographic sensibility can be illustrated from almost any page of the novel:

> He smiled understandingly—much more than understandingly. It was one of those rare smiles with a quality of eternal reassurance in it, that you may come across four or five times in life. It faced—or seemed to face—the whole external world for an instant, and then concentrated on *you* with an irresistible prejudice in your favor. . . . Precisely at that point it vanished—and I was looking at an elegant young roughneck, a year or two over thirty, whose elaborate formality of speech just missed being absurd. (p. 48)

Thackeray or Scott, or even Dickens could not have written that, nor could their readers have read it in comfort. But the passage could be part of a screenplay. It directs, specifically, the cameraman and the film editor, and we, used to motion pictures, know how to read it and how to recreate the pictures in our minds.

The mind's eye, in another passage, moves with the silky, slow and carefully composed precision of an expert pan and dolly shot: "A wafer of a moon was shining over Gatsby's house, making the night fine as before, and surviving the laughter and the sound of his still glowing garden. A sudden emptiness seemed to flow now from the windows and the great doors, endowing with complete isolation the figure of the host, who stood on the porch, his hand up in a formal gesture of fare-well" (p. 56). The naked human eye does not move at that stately pace, nor does it come to rest so imperceptibly and completely. But the eye behind the camera does.

Any photographic technician would know how to put the following kind of distorted time onto film. And none of us would misread it as childish fantasy or metaphysical jest:

> The only completely stationary object in the room was an enormous couch on which two young women were buoyed up as though upon an anchored balloon. They were both in white, and their dresses were rippling and fluttering as if they had just been blown back in after a short flight around the house. . . . Then there was a boom as

Tom Buchanan shut the rear windows and the caught wind died out about the room, and the curtains and the rugs and the two young women ballooned slowly to the floor. (p. 8)

An extreme example of the imaginative liberties that photographic technology encourages in the prose writer, like Fitzgerald, is this startling scene of instantaneous change, a jump-cut:

Through the hall of the Buchanans' house blew a faint wind, carrying the sound of the telephone bell out to Gatsby and me as we waited at the door.
    "The master's body!" roared the butler into the mouthpiece. "I'm sorry, madame, but we can't furnish it—it's far too hot to touch this noon!"
    What he really said was: "Yes . . . Yes . . . I'll see." (p. 115)

One of the more memorable scenes in *The Great Gatsby*, and one Nick calls a "picture," is a distant cousin of the facetious art photograph, "*George B. Wilson at the Gasoline Pump*," a still picture of a mundane subject yet one which reveals, with great impact, a critical insight and the emotional jolt at the discovery of bitter knowledge:

Daisy and Tom were sitting opposite each other at the kitchen table, with a plate of cold fried chicken between them, and two bottles of ale. He was talking intently across the table at her, and in his earnestness his hand had fallen upon and covered her own. . . . They weren't happy, and neither of them had touched the chicken or the ale—and yet they weren't unhappy either. There was an unmistakable air of natural intimacy about the picture, and anybody would have said that they were conspiring together. (p. 146)

The passage could be said to be "Jamesian," comparable to corresponding tableaux in *The Ambassadors* and *The Portrait of a Lady*. The picture seals Gatsby's fate, and Nick's too: his doubts and his hopes are over now. "Jamesian" surely, but just as surely photographic.

Two years after the dismal aftermath of Gatsby's death, Nick remembers "only . . . an endless drill of police and photographers and newspaper men in and out of Gatsby's front door" (p. 164). He retreats to Gatsby's room, upstairs, to search for evidence of the existence of Gatsby's parents, and finds "nothing—only the picture of Dan Cody, a token of forgotten violence, staring down from the wall" (p. 166). Nobody came to the funeral, not even, for Nick's sake, Jordan Baker. There remains one last obligation for Nick, who wants "to leave things in order and not just trust that obliging and indifferent sea to sweep my refuse away" (p. 178). His affair with Jordan is over. He thought he had first seen her in a "picture" (p. 11), a photograph on the sports or social page, but he has come to know her and the moral carelessness of her world. He finds her, here at the end, "dressed to play golf, and I remember thinking she looked like a good illustration, her chin raised a little jaunt-ily, her hair the color of an autumn leaf, her face the same brown tint as the fingerless glove on her knee" (p. 178). The decisive judgment is made before the description of her person and dress: "She looked like a good illustration." For Nick, who knows the potential power of pho-tography, its ways of distorting time in the service of the timeless, who has seen Henry Gatz hold with "trembling fingers," a photograph of a house, and who has come to know the part photographs played in Gatsby's dream-life—to look like an "illustration," however "good," is to fall far short of "Great."

Notes

1. This is the emphasis of R. W. Stallman, "Gatsby and the Hole in Time," *Modern Fiction Studies*, 4 (1955), 2–16, and an important aspect of Richard Lehan's reading in *F. Scott Fitzgerald and the Craft of Fiction* (Carbondale: Southern Illinois Univ. Press, 1966), pp. 91–122.

2. This line of interpretation is commonplace today, but early reviewers would have found it as misguided as we now find them. Many superficial appraisals can be seen in Jackson R. Bryer, *The Critical Reputation of F. Scott Fitzgerald: A Biblio-graphical Study* (Hamden, Conn.: Archon, 1967).

3. The information in this paragraph was derived from "Photography," and "Photographic Art," *Encyclopaedia Britannica*, 1967.

4. Percy Y. Howe, "Preface," *The American Annual of Photography*, 1924, p. 3.

5. *Idylls of the King*, "Gareth and Lynette," ll. 272–74.

6. *The Romantic Egoists*, ed. Matthew J. Bruccoli, Scottie Fitzgerald Smith, and Joan P. Kerr (New York: Scribner's, 1974). See pp. 117.9.

7. Ibid., p. 165, labeled "March 1929."

8. Stallman, p. 13, refers to this scene as one of the few places in which "the rushing time-flow of the novel gets arrested." He writes of McKee's photography as a "fixing [of] space," p. 10.

9. I have based this generalization on the evidence of the many photographs reproduced in *The American Annual of Photography* from 1920 to 1927.

10. Edna Osborne Whitcomb, "Artistic Photography," *The American Annual of Photography*, 1924, p. 172.

11. Nick later says that Gatsby "never told me definitely that his parents were dead" (p. 160). I take this as a lapse on the author's part.

12. For an admirable, brief treatment of this, see Carl Woodring, "Nature and Art in the Nineteenth Century," *PMLA*, 2 (1977), 196–99.

13. Quoted by Woodring, p. 196, from Delacroix's *Journal*, ed. Andree Joubin (Paris: Plon, 1932), II, 59. I translate: "Up to now, this mechanical art has done us only wretched service; it spoils masterpieces for us without satisfying us completely."

Novel to Play to Film: Four
Versions of *The Great Gatsby*   Alan Margolies*

Although there have been three film versions and one major theatrical production of *The Great Gatsby* since 1925, none of those responsible for the adaptations has successfully transformed Fitzgerald's work to the screen or stage.[1] This is not because conversion to a second medium is not possible. Erich Von Stroheim's *Greed* (1923), based on Frank Norris' *McTeague*, John Ford's *Grapes of Wrath* (1940), and David Lean's *Great Expectations* (1946) are only three of a number of exceptional films that have been made from equally great novels. And many of those who saw the Royal Shakespeare Company's production of *Nicholas Nickleby* (1980) feel the same way about the metamorphosis of novel to the stage. Of course, not every novel can be successfully transformed to another medium. Perhaps *The Great Gatsby* is such a novel, but it is impossible to be certain, since the failure of the adaptations so far have clearly derived more from inferior writing, acting, and directing than from any lack of dramatic potential in the original work.

In late 1925, Owen Davis, an extremely prolific playwright, wrote the first adaptation, a stage production that opened in New York on February 2 of the following year with a cast that included James Rennie as Gatsby, Florence Eldridge and Elliot Cabot as Daisy and Tom Buchanan, and Edward H. Wever as Nick Carraway.

Critics of the time, for the most part, praised the play, although a number noted some problems. Brooks Atkinson in the *New York Times*, for example, began his review by stating that the play "retain[ed] most of the novel's peculiar glamour," but concluded by noting the "clumsiness in the ordering of material, occasional bare spots and frequent confusing shifts of mood."[2] Alexander Woollcott felt that Davis had "carried the book over on to the stage with almost the minimum of spilling. . . ."[3] And Edmund Wilson loyally supported the production, stating that while "it [had] the usual theatrical deficiencies of stories not originally conceived for the stage . . . Davis [had] adapted it very adroitly. . . ." Further, Wilson said, "What is most remarkable about *The Great Gatsby* is the extent to which Fitzgerald's characters have come to life on the stage."[4]

Audiences seemed to agree with the mainly favorable reviews and the play had a run of 112 performances on Broadway. Then, with some changes in cast, it had a successful road run, including performances that same year in Chicago from August 1 to October 2.[5]

Because of the exigencies of drama, Davis telescoped Fitzgerald's plot into a prologue in Daisy Fay's house in Louisville in 1917 and then

*This article, written especially for this volume, appears here for the first time.

three acts taking place over a seventeen day period in August, 1925, the first in Nick Carraway's cottage, the next two in Gatsby's library.

For his prologue, Davis wrote a scene not found in the novel. Here he integrated Jordan Baker's recollections of Daisy's early life—she tells them to Nick at the Plaza Hotel in chapter four—with what Gatsby tells Nick about the same period during World War I at the very end of chapter six and the beginning of chapter eight. To these recollections, Davis added new plot and three new characters; Daisy's mother, Mrs. Fay; Sally, the black maid, who opens the scene with dialect humor (Mrs. Fay enters asking "Sally! Is that you?" and Sally replies "Yes, yes, Miss Amy, dat am me."[6]); and a Dr. Carson, a middle aged army officer who provides Mrs. Fay with information about Gatsby's background.

In this version, Gatsby is still a man of mysterious beginnings, but here Dr. Carson has discovered that he comes with excellent recommendations from his fellow army officers despite the fact that he has a slightly different name from that of his parents. "That's common enough of course," Dr. Carson says, "as foreign names anglicized, and seems to have raised no question" (Prologue, p. 3). Mrs. Fay, however, is wary of her daughter's wartime flirtation. Further, she is afraid of Gatsby. "He's absurd, but he is dangerous!" she tells Dr. Carson. "He is as romantic as a gypsy, handsome, ambitious . . ." (Prologue, p. 3). Thus, the 1926 audience, already laughing at one minority group, was immediately made suspicious of Gatsby by associating him with the many middle and eastern Europeans with unpronounceable names entering the United States at that time.

As in the novel, Gatsby is in love with Daisy and, at the same time, fascinated with her upper class background. "[T]here was mystery here . . . a feeling of stepping into a world that was strange, and yet familiar [,] a hint of romances, of gaiety . . ." (Prologue, p. 4), he tells her in words similar to Nick's statement in chapter eight in the novel. But, in addition, by converting Nick's paraphrase at the end of chapter six into another speech for Gatsby, Davis placed even greater emphasis on the destructive possibilities of Gatsby's love for Daisy.

> The quiet lights of the house were humming out into the darkness and there seemed to be a stir and bustle among the stars [Gatsby tells Daisy], I could see, out of the corner of my eye, the blocks of the sidewalks in the moonlight and I had the fancy that they formed a ladder that mounted to a secret place above the trees. I knew that I could climb to it, if I climbed alone [,] but my arms were around you and my heart beat faster and faster as your white face came up to mine. I knew that when I kissed you all that I meant to live for should go, and just your image would take its place, and so I hesitated. (Prologue, p. 5)

Daisy, of course, is hurt by this statement, but Gatsby immediately makes amends by telling that this thought vanished when he kissed her.

Further, Davis added speeches clarifying why Daisy threw Gatsby over for Tom. Just before Gatsby leaves—he is going overseas—Daisy tells him that she is afraid of being alone, afraid of her mother, and that "people make [her] do things!" (Prologue, p. 6). But as soon as he exits, Daisy begins flirting with Tom Buchanan—also an officer in uniform—who has been waiting in the next room to court her. Daisy's unbelievable shift in behavior, again made necessary by the exigencies of the theatre, is underscored by her curtain line to Tom. "You silly old thing," she says. "Why didn't you come before?" (Prologue, p. 10).

While the major events of the novel occur in 1922, the remainder of the play was set three years later, making it contemporaneous for the audience. Act one combined much of the novel's opening scene in the Buchanan house with the scene in chapter five when Gatsby and Daisy, for the first time since the Louisville farewell, meet in Nick Carraway's cottage. Again Davis used much new material. As the curtain rises, Nick confronts Meyer Wolfsheim while the latter is crossing Nick's lawn to Gatsby's house. To parallel the maid's comic dialect at the beginning of the prologue, Davis once again relied on racial humor. Here Wolfsheim, whose role called for "a natural Jewish accent" (act one [p. 1]), was heard indistinctly as the curtain rose. Nick calls out, "What? Where's what? Speak English!" and Wolfsheim replies, "I vonted to know if somebody couldn't tell me the way to the Gatsby place" (act one, [p. 1]), a line that did nothing to reflect Wolfsheim's amoral qualities but presumably guaranteed another laugh, and, by association, once again suggested something unworthy about Gatsby's background.

To avoid portraying Fitzgerald's Valley of Ashes—the location in the novel of the Wilson garage—on stage, which would obviously have required a third set, and to telescope events even more, Myrtle Wilson's husband is introduced as the Buchanan's chauffeur. By the end of act one, however, he has been fired because Daisy suspects Tom's affair with Myrtle. To keep Wilson (here called "Buck") in the play, Nick immediately manages to get him a job with Gatsby. None of this, of course, was in Fitzgerald's book either, nor did the Buchanans in the novel have a replacement, a second chauffeur ironically named "Scott." The act ended with the confrontation in Nick's cottage between Gatsby and Daisy that occurs exactly in the middle of the novel, but here in a final symbolic gesture at the curtain, Gatsby picks up a flower, puts it in Daisy's lap, and "steps back adoring her" (act one, p. 28).

In acts two and three, Davis used underworld slang and emphasized Gatsby's criminal activities much more than Fitzgerald had. At one point, for example, Wolfsheim, in a speech only vaguely suggested by events in the novel, says to Gatsby, "Lots of the boys I know got a good start, not so good as yours, but nice, but they pushed their luck, and something broke, somebody squealed maybe, or maybe it was a woman butted in, and where are they, up the river there, or even worse in

Atlanta" (act two, p. 2). And, soon after using slang that Fitzgerald's Gatsby never uses, Gatsby says about a squealer, "Don't pay him a penny until he shuts his mouth. . . . We know too much about him, if he tries to threaten put the screws on" (act two, p. 2). Gatsby's evil qualities are further emphasized in other additions to Fitzgerald's plot. In act two, for example, Ryan, one of three new henchmen, forces Wilson to drive five hours to White Plains and back to deliver a suitcase filled with money. And in act three another henchman describes how the coast guard has captured a boat bringing in illegal alcohol.

> We stood off shore for three days because there was a moon [he says], and we had a hot tip they were looking for us; night before last I took a chance and started in a small boat to look the ground over, I hadn't got half way to shore when I heard a machine gun going. I turned back until I saw a cutter right alongside of us and the uniforms on our deck. They took her into Norfolk yesterday morning. (act three, p. 10)

Another major difference between the novel and the play reflected contemporary attitudes toward adultery and divorce. At the end of the second act, while her husband is meeting with Myrtle Wilson in the Wilson cottage, Daisy decides to gain revenge by sleeping with Gatsby. But Gatsby heroically refuses because he correctly understands Daisy's motive. Daisy, piqued, calls him a "romantic fool," but she refuses to divorce her husband. "I'm afraid of divorce," she tells Gatsby. "I don't like it" (act two, p. 25).

Davis also added a number of antifemale comments, all of which again presumably reflected the tastes of the time. Tom's excuse for his philandering, "What's the harm at taking a look at a pretty woman! What do you suppose they were made for?" (act two, p. 17) and Myrtle Wilson's friend's statement about Myrtle's husband, "I always said you'd marry him. I never saw a girl with pretty legs that had any brains" (act two, p. 10) only cheapened Fitzgerald's story. Even Gatsby's reflection on Jordan Baker's cheating at golf smacks of the same bias. "We can't quite expect real loyalty from women . . . ," he says. "You can't blame them too much for breaking faith." He believes that women do this more than men because "they get pushed around more . . . pushed in directions they never meant to go at all" (act one, p. 7).

Eventually, as in the novel, Tom Buchanan's deceit is responsible for Wilson shooting Gatsby, but no switch of cars here results in Myrtle Wilson's death. Instead Tom tells Wilson that the cigarette case he accidentally left in the Wilson cottage is Gatsby's. Thus, Gatsby is shot in his library (in the novel, of course, he dies in his pool), and Nick delivers the final line over his body, a restatement of Nick's comment to Gatsby in chapter eight, "He was the best of the whole damned crowd of us" (act three, p. 25).

In November, 1926, six months after the play closed in New York, a silent film version opened in that same city's Rivoli Theatre. The credits included director Herbert Brenon, who had just recently completed the successful *Beau Geste* (1926); Elizabeth Meehan, responsible for adapting the novel; and scriptwriter Becky Gardiner. Warner Baxter, who was later to gain fame in the role of the stage director in the film *Forty-second Street* (1933), was Gatsby; others in the cast included Lois Wilson and Hale Hamilton as Daisy and Tom Buchanan, Neil Hamilton as Nick Carraway, and Georgia Hale and William Powell (later known for the role of Nick Charles in the *Thin Man* film series) as Myrtle and George Wilson. This version seems not to have been influenced at all by Davis' play and, although much closer in plot to the novel, it too at times deviated widely. Here Gatsby's return after the war was portrayed as a threat to Daisy's marriage. In an early flashback, according to Meehan's treatment, she was seen in one scene in Louisville clutching her child and fearing Gatsby's return. But soon enough she falls for him. At the Plaza Hotel, however, when Tom reveals that Gatsby is a bootlegger, her feelings change once again and she coldly asks Gatsby to take her home. After Wilson kills Gatsby, Nick phones to tell the Buchanans of the murder, but they leave New York without answering the phone and without ever knowing of Gatsby's death. At this point, Daisy wants to confess to the police that she killed Myrtle, but doesn't. Finally, Tom and Daisy are reconciled, and, according to one reviewer, the last shot showed "Daisy and her husband Tom and their tot draped beautifully on the porch of their happy home. . . ."[7]

Hollywood had given Fitzgerald's novel a happy ending, and this was only one of the reasons that many reviewers of the time were not completely satisfied with the film. The reviewer in New York *Morning Telegraph*, for example, criticized all of the actors—with the exception of Lois Wilson and William Powell—and said of the film, "The production has everything, it would seem. Yet it doesn't ring true."[8] And while Mordaunt Hall of the *New York Times* called the film "quite a good entertainment," he then went on to criticize both the direction and at least some of the acting. "[I]t is obvious," he wrote "that [the film] would have benefitted by more imaginative direction. . . . Neither [Mr. Brenon] nor the players have succeeded in fully developing the characters."[9] A third reviewer, John S. Cohen, Jr., not only found the production "commonplace" and the film "half way dull, half way cold and uninteresting," but, in addition, he even found space to criticize this silent film's titles. Referring to one in particular, he wrote:

> In one respect, "The Great Gatsby" is unique. It boasts of the longest bit of reading matter in the history of the cinema. This is a title which comes along somewhere in the middle of the film, and it stretches from the top of the screen to the bottom. Of course, with

such wordy interruptions, &c., the picture has no visual flow whatsoever. It is about as smooth pictorially as sandpaper, and the individual composition[s] were unquestionably conceived by the office
boy.[10]

Apparently the public agreed with the majority of the critics.
After only two weeks the film was pulled from the Rivoli Theatre and
did little business elsewhere.

The second film version, released in 1949, also differed from Fitzgerald's concept, this time partly because of the Production Code of the
time. According to Richard Maibaum, co-author and producer, the novel
"dealt with unpunished adultery, unpunished manslaughter, and an unpunished moral accessory to a murder."[11] Thus, to satisfy Hollywood's
self-imposed rules, much moralizing was added.

This moralizing began with the very first scene. Here, twenty years
after Gatsby's funeral, Nick and Jordan have returned to the cemetery
where the camera shows us a tombstone inscribed "Jay Gatsby 1896–1928
Proverbs 14:12." Nick recites the biblical passage: "There is a way
which seemeth right unto a man but the end thereof are the ways of
death."[12] Thus, again according to Maibaum, the audience saw that Nick
and Jordan "like the country [had] come through the debacle to become
decent, humbled, and worthy."[13] Their eventual salvation and what
appears to be their eventual marriage obviously was crucial in this
version.

As in the novel, it takes Nick some time to fully appreciate the
Buchanans' true nature, but in the 1949 film he refuses to arrange the
meeting in his cottage between Daisy and Gatsby. This task is left to
Jordan who arranges the assignation only after forcing Gatsby to agree to
give her a Dusenberg automobile. Jordan's immoral attitude is also
made evident when she admits having told her caddy to move a ball
during a golf tournament, an act mentioned in the novel only by Nick.
"I thought I could get away with it. . . .," she says in the film. "Nowadays, everybody gets away with things." She voices similar statements
when she finally repents. "Nick, I'm a pretty sad lot. But so's the world
I'm in," she declaims in a speech that was repeated with variations in
a number of post World War II films. "It's all out of joint. Crazy, wild,
careless. Nothing to live for or believe in except yourself. Oh, I've lost,
Nick." But Nick, in love with her and wishing, of course, to share the
guilt, replies, "We all are."

In contrast, the young Gatsby is a highly moral individual in this
film when he is with Daisy in Louisville. Daisy wants to marry him
despite her family's desire for her to "marry right." Gatsby, whose small
legacy is being contested, tells her, "I [want to be] your husband. But the
right way. I want your family proud of me," and, as in all the other
versions, leaves for overseas still a bachelor.

After Gatsby returns, Daisy shows great willingness to go off with him, and, as opposed to the Daisy of the 1926 play, is obviously unconcerned about divorce. For the 1949 audience, walking out on one's husband might be condoned; on the other hand, child custody was still a great problem. "If you go with him, there isn't a court in the country would award the child to you," Tom warns her. But Daisy defiantly replies, "That's all I need, really it is. That's the final thing. And now you can do what you want and say what you want and try to take my baby if you think you can. But I'm leaving you and nothing in the world can force me back."

But Myrtle Wilson's death changes her plans. Daisy is deathly afraid of going to jail and permits Gatsby to selflessly volunteer to take the blame for her actions. As in the novel, Tom suggests to Wilson that Gatsby was driving the death car. But here, to make certain that the censors as well as the audience realized that Buchanan would be punished for his action, Daisy tells him: "If anything happens to [Gatsby], I'll never forgive you. I'll hate you as long as I live." Tom then tries to warn Gatsby but to no avail, since the latter is too busy moralizing to answer his phone.

In this final speech, Gatsby repents in words reminiscent of the many heroic statements in films of the 1930s and 1940s:

> I'm seeing it clear from here on. I'm going to pay up, Nick. I'm going to square myself. I've beat a lot of raps for my time but I'm going to take this one. I'll wait right here until the cops find that car— And if they don't find it, I'll call them. I owe that to a kid named Jimmy Gatz. Me— Nick— me. What's going to happen to kids like Jimmy Gatz if guys like me don't tell them we're wrong? Maybe after I do my time and start over again—

At this point Wilson shoots him, frustrating Gatsby's penitential desire.

The hoodlum language used by Gatsby and his henchmen in this film is only one of the many characteristics linking it to the other gangster films of the 1930s and '40s. Since the credits gave equal billing to Fitzgerald *and* Davis, it also seems likely that the adapters were influenced by the greater emphasis that Davis placed on Gatsby's nefarious acts. Further, Alan Ladd, who portrayed Gatsby, had played tough-guy roles in such films as *This Gun For Hire, The Glass Key*, and *Lucky Jordan* (all 1942), and two other actors who had played similar roles— Elisha Cook, Jr., the "gunsel" in *The Maltese Falcon* (1941) and Ed Begley the corrupt politician in *Boomerang* (1947)—were cast as Gatsby's associates.

Many other scenes, not in the novel, also contribute to Gatsby's tough-guy image. A series of brief scenes at the very beginning of the film, for example, ends with Gatsby in an automobile firing his pistol at a machine gun toting gangster in a second vehicle, a scene reminiscent of many Warner Brothers' gangster films of the previous decade. But this Gatsby is not always so threatening. Early in the film, when Nick's cottage is discovered to be on Gatsby's property, one of his associates suggests a way of dealing with the problem. "It's an eyesore," he says. "You could pick it up cheap, bounce this Carraway guy, and tear it down. If he squawks, throw a little business his way." Gatsby, however, demurs. "These people are high class around here," he points out. "They don't like to be bounced around."

How did Gatsby get this way in this film? As in the novel, he meets robber baron Dan Cody, played here by Henry Hull with make-up giving him a satanic appearance. The idealistic young Gatsby believes that he will achieve wealth through perseverance. But uttering sentiments that a post World War II audience would find abhorrent, Cody advises him otherwise:

> My boy, you've fallen for the old razzle-dazzle [he tells Gatsby]. All that stuff is to keep the suckers quiet while the wise people rake the chips in. There are special rules for smart people and if a smart man sees something he wants, he just stakes his claim to it and if somebody else is ahead of him—well—he just moves in anyway. Whatever your dream is, son, your first step is to get some money in the bank. Whatever you want, anything in the world, you got money, you just take it.

The 1949 film also differed in many other ways from the novel. Here, the major events took place in 1928, probably because the audience thought of the year just before the stock market crash as the height of prohibition and gangsterism. "Wild careless dances [beat] out the crazy rhythms of the jazz mad twenties" says a narrator at the beginning of the film. Thus, with this new chronology, Gatsby and Daisy meet once again here after *eleven* years. Another difference, for a less apparent reason, is the geographic reversal of Fitzgerald's two "eggs," with Gatsby and Nick living on *East* Egg and the Buchanans coming from *West* Egg. And Wolfsheim, who was a comical but threatening Jew in Davis' play, and then became "Charles Wolf" in the first film, is given the Latinized name of "Lupus" here and is played without an accent. Apparently, Fitzgerald's original portrayal had become too offensive for Hollywood, especially since the film was made soon after the Nazi horrors of the second World War.

While Maibaum used Fitzgerald's symbol of a wasteland god, he cheapened it despite its pictorial impact. At the beginning of the film, as Gatsby and his henchmen drive toward East Egg, they see the eyes of T.J. Eckleburg, a pair of eyeglasses painted on a billboard. Klipspringer asks, "Did you notice that thing? Them eyes. They get you." "Sees all, knows all, hey," Lupus responds. "Like God bought himself a pair of eyeglasses so he could watch us better. They follow you," replies Klipspringer. But Gatsby is not impressed. "It's painted that way," he says, "it's what they call an optical illusion." Later, after Myrtle Wilson's accident, we see T.J. Eckleburg's eyes again as Tom, Nick, and Jordan park directly under the billboard. And finally, when Nick and Jordan leave the cemetery after Gatsby's funeral, the last shot in the film shows the eyes of T. J. Eckleburg superimposed over the grave-diggers.

Once again, film critics were not generally pleased with the way Hollywood had transformed Fitzgerald's work. Bosley Crowther in the *New York Times* felt that the "flavor of the prohibition era [was] barely reflected" and suspected that Paramount Pictures had made the film "primarily as a standard conveyance for the image of its charm boy, Alan Ladd." Not only did Crowther pan Ladd's acting, but he placed the blame for the film's failure on Cyril Hume and Maibaum's script and Elliot Nugent's direction.[14] The *New Yorker* critic, John McCarten, felt that Ladd acted "with the stiffness of a pallbearer" and, in addition, criticized Betty Field's "jittery carryings-on" as Daisy Buchanan.[15] New York's *Cue* had a few kind words for this film, stating that it retained "a great deal of the atmosphere of the Delirious Twenties," but then it stated that "it [fell] down in developing the personalities of the central characters, and most particularly that of Gatsby himself."[16]

And yet, despite this well-deserved criticism, and despite the un-exceptional acting of Macdonald Carey as Nick, Ruth Hussey as Jordan Baker, and Barry Sullivan as Tom, the film holds interest for film buffs today mainly because of such character actors as Begley, Cook, and Hull, Howard da Silva as Wilson, and a youthful Shelley Winters as the doomed Myrtle Wilson.

Twenty-five years later, David Merrick produced the third film version, this time directed by Jack Clayton and with a script credited to Francis Ford Coppola. With the enormous sales of the novel during the 1960s and early 1970s, and with so many readers familiar with the plot, any radical adaptation probably would have produced howls of protest. Thus this version was much closer to the plot of the novel. And yet there were still differences. Here, for example, an embarrassed Gatsby does not walk out of Nick's cottage just before Daisy appears as he does in their reunion scene in the novel, nor is it raining outside; further, this is all taking place *eight* years since their Louisville separation.

In addition, this film made far greater use of the pictorial to convey Fitzgerald's themes than the 1949 *Gatsby*. For example, the differences between the economic classes is emphasized at the very beginning when Nick in a small boat with outboard motor crosses the bay to his cousin's house. In a voice-over he recites the opening passages of the novel, talking of the advantages that some people have. Suddenly a much larger sailboat cuts him off, knocking his hat momentarily into the water. When Nick arrives at his destination, this theme of rich versus poor is further visually emphasized when the athletic Tom Buchanan, in a riding outfit, coming directly toward the camera on one of his polo ponies, is juxtaposed with Nick standing by in his summer suit.

But too many of the cinematic effects were unsuccessful. Several seem to be metaphors used first during a much earlier period in the history of film and may have been used to evoke the feeling of the 1920s. A closeup of a white flower symbolizing Daisy's virginal beginnings in Louisville; a closeup of two birds nibbling bread while Daisy and Gatsby are in Nick's cottage and then a shot of Nick stubbing out a cigarette, showing his impatience; and a shot of a pool reflecting the images of Daisy and Gatsby kissing while a goldfish idly swims by are all extremely old-fashioned devices.

Other far too obvious scenes are those that suggest the erotic relationship between Daisy and Gatsby. These include shots of a water fountain spurting up in the distance behind the couple dancing at a party, another scene of their dancing around a candlestick on the floor, and, especially, a third scene in Gatsby's kitchen where Daisy first fondles a shiny copper mold and then fondles her lover's hand.

Although many sections of the script were adapted from Fitzgerald's novel without too much change, the dialogue, as in the previous version, was not completely satisfactory. Even Fitzgerald's own dialogue is disconcerting at times, particularly when Nick's narration is broken up and given to the other characters. Still more disturbing is the added dialogue, and there is a good amount of it. Some is clearly unnecessary, such as Daisy's "My, my, my" as the camera shows Jordan Baker cheating at golf, or her "Do you remember?" introducing a flashback. And Fitzgerald would never have abided such trite conversation as:

Gatsby: (to Daisy) I'll love you forever.
         (They kiss.)
Daisy: Be my lover; stay my lover.
Gatsby: Your husband.
Daisy: Husband, lover.
         (Fade out.)

Some of the actors played their parts extremely well, especially Howard de Silva (the Wilson of the 1949 film), whose worn pug face and expressive voice made for a marvellous Wolfsheim with fractured syntax but no perceptible accent; Tom Ewell, who was seen as Owl Eyes in some theatres in the United States, but whose scenes were eventually cut and never replaced; and possibly Bruce Dern, whose athletic body and gruff voice seemed to match Fitzgerald's portrait of Tom Buchanan. But one can quarrel with the casting of others. Sam Waterston and Lois Chiles were far too bland as Nick and Jordan; on the other hand, Karen Black's acting was far too broad for the role of

Myrtle Wilson, especially when after cutting herself in one scene, she licks the blood from her fingers as if it were melted chocolate. Mia Farrow's poorly disguised pregnancy in a number of scenes (note the furniture purposely placed in front of her once or twice as well as her *empire*-style dresses) resulted, for some viewers, in an unwelcome added dimension to her portrayal of Daisy and was as disconcerting as her uneven acting. And finally, Robert Redford's matinee-idol face, blonde hair, and far too even voice in no way fit Fitzgerald's description of "an elegant young roughneck, a year or two over thirty, whose elaborate formality of speech just missed being absurd."[17]

This slow-paced, approximately two hour and twenty minute film, the longest and most expensive of the four adaptations—it cost some $6.4 million dollars, a large sum for a movie in 1974—had a huge advertising campaign. The studio extensively publicized the fact that exteriors were being filmed both in New York and "in some of the most famous mansions in America" in Newport, Rhode Island.[18] But other exteriors as well as interiors were shot in Pinewood Studios, London, and far less publicity was given to this. There were many advertising tie-ins too, such as one for Ballantine Scotch—"Gatsby's parties . . . Ballantines was there"—and another for an E. I. du Pont product, a "new 'classic white' line of cookware."[19]

But despite the ballyhoo, critics intensely disliked this film, using such phrases as "a long, slow, sickening bore" (Stanley Kauffmann, *New Republic*),[20] "a disaster" (Stephen Darst, *New York Times Book Review*),[21] and "appalling" (Robert Hatch, *Nation*).[22] Even the headlines were disrespectful. These included "The great enigma"(*Sunday Times* [London]),[23] " 'The Great Gatsby' Not So Great—Despite Fanfare" (*Philadelphia Inquirer*),[24] and "They've Turned 'Gatsby' to Goo" (*New York Times*).[25] Penelope Gilliatt's extensive *New Yorker* review was the only major exception and even it had some objections to the film.[26] In short, the latest and longest adaptation of Fitzgerald's *Great Gatsby* had received the most negative reviews.

Thus to date Fitzgerald's novel has proven too much of a challenge for its adapters. None, for example, has successfully portrayed Fitzgerald's reflections on the death of the American dream, despite the obvious Horatio Alger parallels in all of the adaptations and despite the introduction, in the play and the 1974 film, of Gatsby's Hopalong Cassidy book with its list of Franklinian resolutions. In Davis' work, it is hurriedly introduced and even more quickly dropped in act three mainly for the purpose of contrasting the romantic Gatsby with the later prying, callous Daisy:

Nick: He wanted to get to the top, didn't he?
Daisy: I remember once he told me something about the cement blocks of the pavement in the moonlight making a ladder

for him, to take him up to the stars, or above the trees or somewhere, all bunk of course, but it made a terrible hit with me at the time. [act three, p. 25]

In the most recent film, Gatsby's father tells Nick of his son's early desires, reads from the old book, and laments, "If he lived he'd have helped build up the country." But this late scene is merely an afterthought in a film whose major theme is best exemplified by Daisy's sobbing explanation for her jilting of Gatsby in Louisville: "Rich girls don't marry poor boys."

Further, despite such obvious exceptions as the portrayal of Wolfsheim in the 1974 film, very little of Fitzgerald's incisive satire is found in any of the adaptations. One of the most glaring omissions is the lengthy list of metaphoric names of those who attended Gatsby's lavish parties. "Oh, I see the Chester Beckers are here," Tom tells Daisy in this last film. "And the Leeches. Oh, no. There's that man Benson. I knew him at Yale. . . ." He mentions a few others, but this is mainly for the purpose of impressing us with his pomposity, and to demonstrate too that some well-known people as well as some unsavory ones were in attendance. In no way does the scene reflect Fitzgerald's biting commentary on the class structure in this country.

Fitzgerald's scattered comments suggest that he would never have expected a version of *The Great Gatsby* that was a mirror image of his novel. His statement to Maxwell Perkins in 1939 about his work on the script of *Gone with the Wind*, for example, mocked producer David Selznick's rigid restrictions. "[D]o you know in that *Gone with the Wind* job," he wrote, "I was absolutely forbidden to use any words except those of Margaret Mitchell; that is, when new phrases had to be invented one had to thumb through as if it were Scripture and check out phrases of hers which would cover the situation!"[27]

Further, his film adaptations of his own work wandered far from the source. In his treatment of *Tender Is the Night* (written with the young Charles M. Warren, who much later achieved fame on television as the originator of the long-running *Gunsmoke*), the story was changed to the tale of a brain surgeon who marries a rich girl who suffers a mental disorder after a fall from a horse. The surgeon and his wife separate when she is attracted to another man, but the marriage is saved after he operates and cures her of a second illness, this time a brain disease. Sixteen years later, in his film script for "Babylon Revisited," the novelist once again deviated greatly from his original story. He shifted his point of view from the hero, Charles Wales, to Wales's young daughter who has run away from her aunt and uncle to be with her father in Switzerland. In this version, Wales has been swindled by his partner and his brother-in-law, and has gone to Switzerland for new financing. Here he is unsuccessful, but by exposing his partner's plot, he regains his daughter.[28]

Both adaptations were written while Fitzgerald was in need of money. Further, there can be no doubt that many of the changes in *Tender Is the Night* (especially the discussions of incest) were due to the restrictions of the Hollywood Production Code of 1934. And yet it seems likely that even if these had not been the circumstances, the results would not have been too different.

As he so deftly illustrated in the scenes between producer Stahr and writer George Boxley in *The Last Tycoon,* and as he indicated in his correspondence in 1938 with Mrs. Edwin Jarrett who had attempted a stage adaptation of *Tender Is the Night,* Fitzgerald was aware of the differences between film, theatre, and novel. To Mrs. Jarrett, for example, he wrote: "The play pleases me immensely. So faithful has been your following of my intentions that my only fear is that you have been *too* loyal. I hope you haven't—I hope that a measure of the novel's intention *can* be crammed into the two hours of the play."[29]

Undoubtedly there will be more adaptations of *The Great Gatsby.* One can only hope that with better scriptwriting, casting, and acting, those responsible will give us "a measure of the novel's intention. *Gatsby* is obviously much more than a gangster thriller and much more than a love story. Possibly some future adapter will recognize this and succeed in creating a satisfactory version of Fitzgerald's masterpiece.

Notes

1. Other adaptations of *Gatsby* have included at least two television dramas: 9 May 1955 on NBC's *Robert Montgomery Presents,* adaptation by Albert Sapinsley, and 6 June 1958 on CBS's *Playhouse 90,* adaptation by David Shaw; and at least one major university production, a musical produced by the Yale Dramatic Association in May and June, 1956, book by Aubrey L. Goodman, Jr., Yale '56, music by Robert E. Morgan, Yale '58.

2. "The Play: Careless People and Gatsby," *New York Times,* 3 February 1926, p. 22.

3. "The Stage: Great Scott," *New York World,* 3 February 1926, p. 13.

4. "Mürger and Wilde on the Screen," *New Republic,* 24 (March 1926), 145.

5. An extensive number of reviews and articles about Davis' play with corroborating statements about the run as well as other facts in this essay are in William A. Brady's scrapbook of clippings, 1926, in the Theatre Collection, New York Public Library, Lincoln Center. Reviews and articles about the play as well as the 1926 film are also in F. Scott Fitzgerald's scrapbooks in the F. Scott Fitzgerald Papers, Princeton University, Princeton, New Jersey.

6. Prologue, p. [1]. Quotations from the play are from the typescript in the Library of Congress.

7. At present there is no known extant print of the silent *Gatsby,* although periodically there have been rumors of its existence. It is possible, however, to

reconstruct the plot from Meehan's typed adaptation on file at the Theatre Arts Collection, UCLA, from Paramount's *Press Sheet* on file at the Library of Congress, and from reviews of the film. The quotation is from John S. Cohen, Jr., "Picture Plays and Players," *New York Sun*, 22 November 1926, p. 30.

8. "Herb" Cruikshank, "Impressions of New Pictures," *New York Morning Telegraph*, 22 November 1926, p. 3.

9. "The Screen: Gold and Cocktails," *New York Times*, 22 November 1926, p. 28.

10. "Picture Plays and Players," p. 30.

11. Richard Maibaum, "The Question They Faced With 'Gatsby': Would Scott Approve?" *New York Daily Compass*, 8 July 1949, p. 19.

12. Since at present no scripts of the 1949 and 1974 *Gatsby* films are available, quotations are based on transcriptions made while viewing these films. No corrections have been made of what seems at times to be the players' misreadings. Since some films are recut after release or for release in foreign countries (and this was true of the 1974 *Gatsby*), there are flaws to this method of quoting, but similar problems exist today when one quotes from any continuity script.

13. "The Question They Faced With 'Gatsby': Would Scott Approve?" p. 19.

14. "The Screen in Review," *New York Times*, 14 July 1949, p. 20.

15. "The Current Cinema: Not So Great Gatsby," *New Yorker*, 23 July 1949, p. 69.

16. Jesse Zunser, "New Films: F. Scott Fitzgerald's Jazz-Age Classic Comes to Paramount," *Cue*, 16 July 1949, p. 19.

17. *The Great Gatsby* (New York: Scribner's, 1925), p. 48.

18. Paramount Pictures, *Handbook of Production Information . . . "The Great Gatsby"* (New York: Paramount, [1974?], p. 3. Also see, e.g., Enid Nemy, "Those Extras on 'Gatsby' Set Weren't Doing It for the $20," *New York Times*, 11 July 1973, p. 36.

19. "Ready or Not, Here Comes *Gatsby*," *Time*, 18 March 1974, p. 87.

20. "On Films," 13 April 1974, p. 33.

21. "The Late Gatsby," 28 July 1974, p. 23.

22. "Films," 6 April 1974, p. 446.

23. 14 April 1974, p. 32.

24. 4 April 1974, p. 8-B.

25. 31 March 1974, Section 2, p. 1.

26. "The Current Cinema: Courtly Love's Last Throw of the Dice," *New Yorker*, 1 April 1974, pp. 93–98.

27. *The Letters of F. Scott Fitzgerald*, ed. Andrew Turnbull (New York: Charles Scribner's Sons, 1963), p. 284.

28. The movie treatment of *Tender Is the Night* is in Matthew J. Bruccoli, *Some Sort of Epic Grandeur: The Life of F. Scott Fitzgerald* (New York: Harcourt Brace Jovanovich, 1981), pp. 511–23. The script of "Babylon Revisited" (*Cosmopolitan*) is in the F. Scott Fitzgerald Papers, Princeton University Library, Princeton, New Jersey.

29. *The Letters of F. Scott Fitzgerald*, p. 566. Mrs. Jarrett co-authored the script with Kate Oglebay.

"A New World, Material Without Being Real": Fitzgerald's Critique of Capitalism in *The Great Gatsby*

Ross Posnock*

Although Fitzgerald's interest in Marxism has long been known, it has not often been taken seriously as a presence in his life or art.[1] But the enthralled if distrustful observer and occasional member of the leisure class was not glibly posturing when he stated late in life that his outlook was "essentially Marxian."[2] By taking Fitzgerald at his word one can locate his masterpiece, and particularly the much discussed theme of money's dehumanizing effects, in a significant new context: Marx's critique of capitalism. Juxtaposing *The Great Gatsby* with Marx's essay on "Money" in the 1844 *Economic and Philosophic Manuscripts*, his discussion of "commodity fetishism" in volume 1 of *Capital*, and Lukacs' seminal interpretation of Marx in *History and Class Consciousness* (1923) provides a deeper understanding of the novel's concern with the power of money upon human relations, and reveals that Fitzgerald's vision of capitalist social reality possesses a profounder intellectual coherence than previously recognized.[3] Like Brian Way in his recent book on Fitzgerald's "art of social fiction," this paper seeks to explode "one of the least questioned critical assumptions about his work": "his supposed intellectual inadequacy."[4]

What follows does not seek to discover proof of Marxism's direct influence upon Fitzgerald but to demonstrate how deeply Marx's critique is assimilated into the novel's imaginative life. And perhaps the very fact that Fitzgerald's Marxism was not the product of wide reading helped him fuse so organically a Marxist orientation with his own representation of life in the era of high capitalism.[5] The crucial distinction to be made in aligning Fitzgerald with Marx and Lukacs, of course, is that the novelist does not share their abhorrence of capitalism. Fitzgerald's notorious ambivalence towards the rich was vital to his artistic power, for his double consciousness permitted him not only to expose the hidden corruption of their society but to reveal the seductive allure of what he indicted.[6]

I

A year before publishing *The Great Gatsby* Fitzgerald stated that he was a "pessimist [and] a communist (with Nietzschean overtones)."[7] Although the statement initially puzzles by yoking together Marx's emphasis on collective experience and Nietzsche's celebration of the superman beyond good and evil, this disjunction is precisely what is most

*This article, written especially for this volume, appears here for the first time.

interesting about Fitzgerald's gnomic remark. What he seems to suggest here is a sense of the divided nature of man: the individual is at once defined and limited by social bonds and conventions, and possessed by the desire to be powerfully autonomous. Fitzgerald's oblique recognition of man's paradoxical status becomes more meaningful when we turn to his depiction of Gatsby's flagrantly contradictory identity. A figure at once exalted and impoverished, utterly rare and embarrassingly derivative, Gatsby is both "gorgeous" in his "heightened sensitivity" and "romantic readiness," and pitifully empty, less a man than an "advertisement," in Daisy's word.[8]

Gatsby risks incoherence (as does his creator's creed of Nietzschean communism) not simply from personal defect but because he is a product of a capitalist society that Fitzgerald reveals to be profoundly incoherent, founded on contradictions so irreconcilable that they must be ignored or carefully hidden. Contradictions belong "to the nature of capitalism," says Lukacs; and an awareness of them is not a "sign of the imperfect understanding of society," but rather the crucial step in penetrating the "illusions enveloping all phenomena in capitalist society."[9]

Strikingly, Fitzgerald's conflicting images of the individual suggested in his 1924 statement recall a central contradiction that Lukacs finds in capitalism: "the fact that the bourgeoisie endowed the individual with an unprecedented importance, but at the same time that same individuality was annihilated by the economic conditions to which it was subjected by the reification created by commodity production."[10] Lukacs' terms in the last part of his statement require some explication because of their Marxian context. But, more importantly, "reification" and "commodity production" demand discussion for they loom so importantly in *The Great Gatsby*, where Fitzgerald's famous declaration of interest "in the individual only in his relation to society" acquires a Marxian resonance. The novel's account of man's relation to society, we shall see, profoundly agrees with Marx's great discovery that it is social reality rather than individual consciousness that determines man's existence.

Lukacs' claim that "reification requires that a society learn to satisfy all its needs in terms of commodity exchange"[11] depends on the traditional distinction between a product's use-value and its exchange-value. Briefly, use-value is based on a means to fulfill a specific end; for instance, thirst determines the use-value of water. In contrast, exchange-value transforms the use-value of things from instruments of direct satisfaction of needs into commodities—things which are ends in themselves to be sold for profit. At the outset of his famous discussion of the character of commodities, Marx calls them "at first glance very trivial." But far from trivial, commodities are "mystical," because they originate as "the products of men's hands," yet "appear as independent beings endowed with life," Marx maintains. "This I call the Fetishism

which attaches itself to the products of labor, so soon as they are produced as commodities, and which is therefore inseparable from the
production of commodities."[12] Capitalism, since it is founded on commodity exchange and production, forces the worker himself to become a
thing to be bought and used. Yet not only the worker, Marx insists, but
"everything . . . is sold as objects of exchange . . . everything has been
transformed into a commercial commodity."[13]

Inevitably, then, in capitalism social relations acquire a commodified
character, as people become objects for each other, sized up as commodities to be bought or sold. This condition Lukacs calls *reification*; Marx's
term *alienation* designates the more general phenomenon of dehumaniza-
tion. Crucial in understanding reification is to recognize it as a process of
mystification invisible to the individual, who acts under the illusion of
being a wholly free and autonomous subject, while in fact existing more
as a manipulated object of larger economic and commercial powers.
Instead of seeming abnormal and dehumanized, reification always appears
natural, absolutely objective, and thus conceals the historically specific
form of capitalist social relations. In short, the condition of reification
imposes a "blanket ignorance upon anyone trying to understand capitalism."[14] Bourgeois society enforces a veil over all contradictions in an
effort to maintain the illusion that capitalism is "eternally valid . . . pre-
destined to eternal survival by the eternal laws of nature and reason."[15]
Thus the task of philosophy, according to Marx, is to demystify, to
"unmask human self-alienation" endemic to capitalism.

Lukacs enacted his project of demystification in 1923; two years
later Fitzgerald was engaged in an analogous effort to penetrate "the
veil of reification." The proximity of dates is particularly noteworthy
when we remark that at the outset of his discussion of reification,
Lukacs stresses the urgency and scope of the problem: "Commodity fetishism is a *specific* problem of our age, the age of modern capitalism . . .
it must not be considered in isolation or even regarded as the central
problem in economics, but as the central, structural problem of capitalist
society in all its aspects."[16] Lukacs' emphasis on the pervasive power of
commodity fetishism and reification, their ability to sink "definitively
into the consciousness of man," "permeating every expression of life,"
accounts for one reason his work is regarded as epochal. And in the
realm of fiction no American novelist, with the exception of Henry James,
has dramatized more vividly and subtly than Fitzgerald the insidious
extent to which money deforms human life.

Money, says Marx, "since it has the property of purchasing everything . . . is the object par excellence."[17] Money is the most mystifying,
fantastic commodity of all. Describing its magical powers, Marx, in the
1844 manuscripts, provides a most relevant frame of reference for understanding the "purposeless splendor" and "foul dust" of Gatsby's world.
One brief example from Marx's exuberant catalog of instances must

suffice. "I am ugly, but I can buy the most beautiful woman for myself. Consequently, I am not ugly, for the effect of my ugliness, its power to repel, is annulled by money. . . . Does not my money, therefore, transform all my incapacities into their opposites?"[18] This power to transform and invert is precisely what is terrifying for Marx, and a source of the incoherence of capitalist social reality. Because money "exchanges every quality and object for every other, even though they are contradictory," "it forces contraries to embrace": "It confounds and exchanges everything, it is the universal confusion and transposition of all things, the inverted world, the confusion and transposition of all natural and human qualities."[19] The moral, emotional, and spiritual chaos unleashed by money is at the center of *The Great Gatsby*.

II

The desperate gaiety and frenzied pursuit of happiness, the unappeasable, restless dissatisfaction of people being "rich together," the "ash-gray men" moving "dimly and already crumbling" in this "twilight universe," are a few of the signs and portents of an "inverted" world, "material without being real," where "the unreality of reality" reigns (pp. 23, 162, 100). These last two oxymoronic phrases can serve as Fitzgerald's most succinct descriptions of the contradictory, mystified world of the novel. At Gatsby's extravagant parties the "unreality of reality" is most flagrant, as anonymous hordes of uninvited guests come and go "like moths"; their "chatter and laughter" barely conceal the pseudo-intimacy and indifference of "introductions forgotten on the spot" and "enthusiastic meetings" between strangers. The "constantly changing light" reveals the endless and aimless procession of fashionable faces and voices, just as the parade of outlandishly artificial names that Nick will later catalog serves to diminish further any sense of the recognizably human. Inevitably, this "bizarre and tumultuous" partygoing, Nick's initiation into Gatsby's world, ends with the "harsh, discordant din" of a car crash and women "having fights with men said to be their husbands"; all of which "added to the already violent confusion of the scene" (pp. 40, 52, 54).

Confusion also characterizes Nick's (and the reader's) reaction to Gatsby's attempt to tell the "God's truth" about himself. Prior to the tête-à-tête Gatsby arranges, his identity has been built upon wildly "romantic speculation," "bizarre accusations." But in an effort to dispel the rumors, Gatsby's "elegant sentences" weave an absurdly fraudulent tale: "it was like skimming hastily through a dozen magazines," says Nick, expressing his disgust at Gatsby's patchwork self composed of the borrowed images of the advertising and fashion media. Listening to him recite his fabulous biography, Nick is reminded of a "turbaned 'character' leaking sawdust at every pore" (pp. 65–67).

But as soon as Nick is about to dismiss Gatsby as a mere fraud and con man, the latter offers seemingly incontestable proof of the authenticity of his claims—he produces two objects for Nick's inspection. One is a "piece of metal" commemorating war valor, the other a photograph, "a souvenir of Oxford days." "Then it was all true," notes an astonished Nick. But, as we later learn, it isn't all true; or rather, truth, exaggeration, and outright falsehood combined to baffling effect, creating what Nick will later recall as a "time of confusion, when I had reached the point of believing everything and nothing about him." This "confusion" is never to evaporate, but will cling to Gatsby's self-portrayal and to Nick's account of him. Gatsby essentially remains a "vague contour"; the mystery surrounding him is irreducible (p. 102).

This scene confirms that the use of language to establish or present one's identity to another tends toward the duplicitous, the indeterminate, and nowhere more so than in moments of supposedly sincere revelation, as Nick discovers earlier in his private chat with Daisy. Like Daisy's confession of weary sophistication, Gatsby's verbal narration of his life is made empty by lies, clichés, and sentimentality. His attempt at purely human communication fails. But if speech is precarious, an unstable means of creating a self, objects acquire an unmerited but unimpeachable authority. Gatsby's deft use of objects in this scene creates at once the illusion of his veracity and identity. Things, not human beings, seem to possess a nearly magical power of legitimation.

The mystique of "enchanted objects," as Nick calls them, is one of Gatsby's most cherished beliefs, and he surrounds himself with things, a preoccupation that, while fetishistic, is also the source of much of the novel's glamour. The extravagant abundance of "beautiful" shirts, the colossal mansion Gatsby doesn't live in so much as keep well-stocked, "always full of interesting people," the "white card" that liberates him from legal limits, as if he resides in his own private kingdom, and the "monstrous" car, an object "swollen" and stuffed with other objects, which seems to enclose its own world "terraced with a labyrinth of windshields that mirrored a dozen suns"; all of these things, in their sensuous palpability and disproportionate status, help comprise the "unreality of reality" (pp. 68, 64). The near autonomy of objects is established early on, even before Gatsby's entrance. In Nick's first description of Jordan and Daisy, the two are in white; "their dresses were rippling and fluttering as if they had just been blown back" after a flight around the house. In direct contrast to these weightless people (who will prove to be morally hollow as well) is the solid bulk of the "enormous couch": "the only completely stationary object in the room." With this seemingly minor detail we are shown that in this world objects are real, in the sense of being fully present and stable, while people seem unreal—less (or more) than human in their ethereal airiness (p. 8).

More significantly, the novel discloses that the most desired people are perceived as desirable objects: Daisy "gleaming like silver," her "voice full of money" (pp. 150, 120). She is never simply Daisy, but is inseparable from the objects that surround her. "She dressed in white and had a little white roadster," is Jordan's initial impression (p. 75). Daisy, of course, represents the "object par excellence," as Marx defined money. The first encounter between the prize object and the compulsive collector is momentous, and a close examination of their meeting can illuminate the origins of Gatsby's belief in "enchanted objects." Fitzgerald here reveals his profound grasp of how capitalism "penetrates the very depths of man's . . . psychic nature" (according to Lukacs) to shape his sexual desires.

Although Gatsby arrives in Louisville an aspiring capitalist, having been the factotum of a millionaire, his commodity fetishism has yet to be established. Indeed, in his "overwhelming self-absorption" he "took for granted" "things" that others "were hysterical about" (p. 99). Also unknown to him is strong sexual desire. He finds Daisy, "the first 'nice' girl he had ever known," "excitingly desirable," whereas his earlier experiences were with women he was "contemptuous of" "since they spoiled him." But Daisy, aloof, not easily available, must be competed for. "It excited him, too, that many men had already loved Daisy—it increased her value in his eyes." Made explicit here is the mediated nature of his desire for Daisy; Gatsby's interest in her is not simply spontaneous or self-generated but stimulated by others' desires. Fitzgerald goes on to make a crucial link: Gatsby feels the "presence" of others' desires "all about the house, pervading the air . . ." Daisy's home and the objects it contains become the repository of other men's desires. Thus he imagines a "ripe mystery about" the "beautiful house," "a hint of bedrooms upstairs more beautiful and cool than other bedrooms . . . of romances . . . fresh and breathing and redolent of this year's shining motor-cars . . ." Bedrooms and motor cars become fused (or confused) with the "still vibrant emotions" of other men's desires, and acquire a sexual resonance: "beautiful and cool," "fresh and breathing" and "shining." Fitzgerald describes Gatsby's now commodified consciousness: he "was overwhelmingly aware of the youth and mystery that wealth imprisons and preserves, of the freshness of many clothes . . ." With this, Gatsby's displacement of his desires onto objects becomes nearly explicit. The above passages blur the distinction between humans and objects because Gatsby invests both with the sensual urges of "many men," whose invisible presence establishes the prestige of what Gatsby sees (pp. 148, 150).

By splicing together Gatsby's initiations into sex and commodity fetishism, Fitzgerald brilliantly dramatizes how social existence (Gatsby's capitalist orientation) determines consciousness (he expresses his sexual desire by projecting it into things). Both desire and commodity fetishism, Fitzgerald implies, are governed by displacement and mediation and are inherently insatiable, perpetually deferring immediate gratification. In erecting other mens' desires as his standard of value, and negating the reality of his own impulses, Gatsby entraps himself in an endless pattern of imitation. This self-negation is the source of his conspicuous reliance on mediators—models of behavior—throughout his life. Ranging from Dan Cody to Wolfsheim to the man in England who buys him clothes, others continually shape Gatsby. His obsession with Daisy, his commitment "to the following of a grail," is founded on her mediated value, a value splendidly confirmed by her marriage to a multimillionaire. In short, Tom, Gatsby's hated rival, is also a model, a guarantee of Daisy's prestige. To become wealthy (like Tom) and take Daisy for himself becomes Gatsby's consuming strategy[20] (p. 149). And when Daisy first visits Gatsby her power as mediator is explicit: "he revalued everything in his house according to the measure of response it drew from her well-loved eyes" (p. 92).

The individual's suppression of spontaneous desire reflects the condition of capitalist culture, which reduces the immediate in favor of the tyranny of fashion. Be it the tapestry of "ladies swinging in the garden of Versailles" hanging in Myrtle's dismal apartment, the imported English oak in Gatsby's imitation Norman mansion, the predatory young Englishmen giving tone to Gatsby's party, the prevailing cultural fashion dictates the adoption of a European, aristocratic manner and taste (p. 29). Money has created this artificial, denatured world, "material without being real" for, as Marx reminds us, with the money to buy everything comes the power to change "reality into mere representation."[21] The transformation of reality into symbol defines the condition of commodity fetishism—the passionate chase after symbolic representations of other men's desires. Symbols, things embodying an excess of meaning, come to dominate consciousness. Nothing is valued in and for itself, as is evident when we note Gatsby's reactions during Daisy's first visit. Having succeeded in his quest, Gatsby's sense of the "colossal significance of" the green light at the end of her dock "now vanished forever." "Now it was again a green light on a dock." But this stripping away of the symbolic brings not elation but a sense of loss: "His count of enchanted objects had diminished by one." With Daisy in his arms at last, a "faint doubt," "an expression of bewilderment" soon comes over him, for to be face to face with an "actual and astounding presence" in this culture is a disorienting experience. And the rich irony here is that Daisy, that symbol "par excellence," in this scene serves as an emblem of unmediated presence (pp 94, 97).

Gatsby's feeling of being "overwhelmingly aware of the youth and mystery that wealth imprisons and preserves" betrays a profoundly deluded, reified consciousness. To believe that wealth can preserve youth—stop time—is to be thoroughly mystified by the power of money, to inhabit what Marx calls an "inverted world" where time is exchanged for its opposite—stasis. Gatsby's more famous remark about time— "Can't repeat the past? . . . Why of course you can!"—reveals the the same refusal to recognize and accept temporality. "I'm going to fix everything just the way it was before," he boasts (p. 111). Here Gatsby transforms time into a commodity, as if it was a clock he might simply repair and reset. Such an attitude towards time Lukacs finds typical of a commodified vision: "time sheds its . . . variable, flowing nature, it freezes . . . in short it becomes space."[22] Thus, for Gatsby, moving closer to Daisy in space (becoming her neighbor) is the way to recapture time. The "colossal vitality" of Gatsby's "illusion" succeeds, if not in repeating the past, at least in contriving a renewed affair with Daisy. In their first reunion scene Fitzgerald makes vivid the bewilderingly contradictory character of reified reality.

Appropriately their reunion is a near orgy of commodity celebration; indeed, Daisy and Gatsby communicate emotionally and sexually through the mediation of objects. After an initial unease both relax; "a new well-being" radiates from Gatsby, a sense of pleasure that increases when he shows Daisy his home and his store of "enchanted objects." The ostentatious artificiality of his "factual imitation of some Hotel de Ville in Normandy" is readily apparent as Gatsby conducts Daisy and Nick through the "Marie Antoinette music rooms and Restoration salons," and past the "Merton College Library" (p. 92). The eerie silence and emptiness of his usually chaotic showplace accentuate the pretentious, nearly surreal decor, with its slavish aping of European style. The climax of the tour and reunion (the two are nearly synonymous here) occurs when Gatsby, opening "two hulking" cabinets, begins throwing his gorgeous shirts, "piled . . . in stacks of a dozen high," one by one in front of his guests. Daisy responds with a sudden "strained sound, [she] bent her head into the shirts and began to cry stormily. 'They're such beautiful shirts,' she sobbed, her voice muffled in the thick folds. 'It makes me sad because I've never seen such—such beautiful shirts before.'" The intensity of feeling that the usually blasé Daisy reveals in this famous scene is more passionate and spontaneous than anything else she expresses in the novel. Her orgasmic response to Gatsby's shirts is also ironic and absurd, in that she shows more emotion for Gatsby's possessions than for Gatsby. But, in fact, Gatsby becomes his possessions here, and his display of clothing a symbolic sexual act; it is his means of arousing Daisy. And Daisy's excited response, her impulse to luxuriate in the "soft rich heap" of richly textured fabrics, reveals her intuitive sense of the erotic quality of the moment. That this intensity of emotion is generated by commodities is unsettling yet precisely Fitzgerald's point: in a reified world, objects, the repository of human desires, are the means of communication, of emotional and sexual exchange (pp. 93–94).

The scene's implicit sexual rhythm is suggested by the muted aftermath following the rapturous climax amidst the silken shirts. A melancholy sense of loss and confusion suffuses the scene, as Gatsby, having run down like a "overwound clock," sits with Daisy in "gloom." "The expression of bewilderment had come back into Gatsby's face, as though a faint doubt had occurred to him as to the quality of his present happiness." Although suspecting that the actual Daisy has "tumbled short" of Gatsby's dream, Nick leaves the couple convinced that they are "possessed by intense life." Colossal illusions and bewilderment have somehow produced "intense life," and this contradiction is only one of many in an episode where intimacy and emotion interact with florid ostentation and material excess, all testifying to the "unreality of reality" (pp. 93, 97).

The "possession of intense life" is not to last. Before long Gatsby's dream is "dead," "struggling unhappily" toward Daisy's "lost voice"; on that terrible day when Myrtle Wilson is killed, "Jay Gatsby" breaks "up like glass against Tom's hard malice" (pp. 135, 148). But Gatsby is granted one last experience of "intense life" minutes before his death. In a "transitory, enchanted moment" of epiphany he penetrates the veil of reification. Gatsby awakens to a new knowledge of reality: "he must have looked up at an unfamiliar sky through frightening leaves and shivered as he found what a grotesque thing a rose is and how raw the sunlight was upon the scarcely created grass." In this remarkable passage, Gatsby faces what is utterly strange and wholly other: unmediated nature. The sky is unfamiliar, leaves are frightening and a rose grotesque because they all are simply mortal. Wealth does not imprison and preserve them. In a society where authority derives from the atemporal stability of objects, nature's naked, vulnerable presence is indeed grotesque, and this sense of inverted values is captured in Fitzgerald's description of the moment as "material without being real." So powerful is capitalism's capacity to confound reality that an epiphany of demystification dissolves almost instantaneously into mystification. Analogously, Gatsby's experience here of "intense life" is most fragile, poised as it is on the verge of death. Lurking about is the "ashen, fantastic" figure of his killer (p. 162).

In this distinterested moment of contemplation, free of all desire to dominate or exploit, Gatsby glimpses a world of transparent immediacy where things are only and fully themselves. Perhaps for the first and last time his "relation to the world [is] a human one," an unalienated relation in Marx's sense. Indeed, Marx's celebrated vision of an unalienated world has a striking relevance to Gatsby:

> Let us assume man to be man and his relation to the world to be a human one. Then love can only be exchanged for love, trust for trust, etc. . . . . Everyone of your relations to man and to nature must be a specific expression . . . of your real individual life. If you love without evoking love in return, i.e., if you are not able,

by the manifestation of yourself as a loving person, to make yourself
a beloved person, then your love is impotent and a misfortune.[23]

Gatsby's love is "impotent and a misfortune" precisely because he
doesn't exchange love for love. Such a balanced, equal transaction is
nearly impossible in capitalism; which is founded on profit, created by
what Marx calls the "surplus-value" produced by "unequal exchange."
Gatsby is fatally enmeshed in the capitalist economy of profit and
commodity exchange, which, we have seen, creates a culture of surplus
meaning. The disorienting symbolization of reality that results makes
life "confused and disordered," as Nick describes Gatsby in the years
after Daisy's marriage (p. 111).

Although entrapped, Gatsby maintains his naive but compelling
"romantic readiness" to regain "the freshest and the best." That his
effort to escape the distortions of capitalist social reality is founded upon
the use of the most mystifying commodity of all—money—defines the
doomed character of his quest. Also doomed is his "extraordinary gift
for hope," which has been defined by that central capitalist paradigm
for success—Ben Franklin. Indebted to Franklin's strict, rational cal-
culation of time, Gatsby's "Schedule" and "General Resolves" survive
only in the ragged pages of a tawdry boyhood souvenir—*Hopalong Cassidy*—one of the "enchanted objects" in Mr. Gatz's own collection.

Inevitably one must consider whether Nick is immune from the
reification he reports upon. Though one of the "few honest people" that
he knows, Nick's account is conditioned by the inverted world he lives
in. Regardless of his various attempts to establish detachment and ob-
jectivity, Nick is implicated in the commodification of reality under
capitalism, a complicity revealed in his deeply divided evaluation of
Gatsby. In a brief aside in chapter six Nick indicates that his role is
to "clear . . . misconceptions away," which justifies his biographical
sketch of Gatsby's early years that opens the chapter. But far from dis-
pelling misconceptions, what Nick has "put down here" is an exceedingly
abstract, mythic rhapsody: "Jay Gatsby . . . sprang from his Platonic
conception of himself. He was a son of God . . . and he must be about
His Father's business, the service of a vast, vulgar, and meretricious
beauty." Instead of "exploding those first wild rumors" about Gatsby's
origins—his avowed purpose—Nick mystifies rather than demystifies
(pp. 102, 99). His attitude towards Gatsby is one of "aesthetic contemplation," a phrase he uses in his concluding summary, where Nick's
propensity for inflated, mythologizing rhetoric is most conspicuous.

Like his intentions in chapter six, Nick's lyrical conclusion is an
attempt to set matters straight, in this case by supplying an historical
context in which to place Gatsby. But, as earlier, his transcendental
language ("transitory, enchanted moment," "aesthetic contemplation,"
"capacity for wonder," "last and greatest of all human dreams") distorts

and veils the historical actuality he describes—the entry of the Dutch sailors into the new world. But Nick's romanticizing can't fully obscure the reality of exploitation. The "new world" is sexualized as a "fresh, green breast" which panders "in whispers," arousing the predatory Dutch sailors to rape the virgin forests that contained trees now "vanished," "the trees that had made way for Gatsby's house." What separates the sailors' discovery and the building of Gatsby's house is the advent and triumph of capitalism. And "that huge incoherent failure of a house" Nick laments can serve as the very image of modern capitalism's commodification of reality, which inevitably confounds and frustrates. Perhaps the essential confusion that capitalism breeds originates in the moment of "aesthetic contemplation" enjoyed by the sailors, who transform the "old island" into a nubile woman ripe for plunder and profit. The loss of distinction here between the human and the nonhuman constitutes the initial instance of reification. This moment is "enchanted" and a "wonder" only in the sense that a nearly magical transposition has occurred, a fusion of sexuality and objects that recalls Gatsby's Louisville encounter with Daisy and, later, his display of shirts to her, as he is "consumed with wonder" (p. 93).

Nick's "aesthetic contemplation" abstracts Gatsby from a human world and places him in an ideal realm. The account Nick offers of the transformation of James Gatz resembles nothing so much as one of those "grotesque and fantastic conceits" that allegedly "haunt" young Gatsby. Nick's adoration is evident from the outset. "Only Gatsby" is "exempt from" Nick's weariness with the role of confidante, only Gatsby is free of moral pollution, the pervasive "foul dust." An innocent victim of a predatory society, "Gatsby turned out all right at the end; it is what preyed on Gatsby, what foul dust floated in the wake of his dreams. . . ." (p. 2). Gatsby becomes just the sort of hero that a lonely, modestly successful thirty-year-old like Nick would be likely to invent. As Nick's invention, Gatsby, in effect, is transformed into a commodity that Nick sells the reader. The object Nick provides for our consumption is a version of a perenially marketable cultural myth—the romantic hero as passive sacrificial victim.

And yet, at the same time, Nick creates much more than a reified image. While he may worship and objectify Gatsby, Nick's portrayal is also informed by deep skepticism, for Gatsby represents "everything for which" Nick has an "unaffected scorn." "I disapproved of him from beginning to end," he reminds us near the conclusion, and his occasional exasperation with and distaste for Gatsby gives credence to his remark. Nick's critical stance imparts, no doubt, a richer complexity to his representation of Gatsby, even as it makes his ultimate attitude utterly ambivalent.

The blatant contradictions in Nick's response, like the contradictions in Gatsby and in the society they are part of, are not to be ignored or resolved, for they are the very source of the lasting authority of Fitzgerald's novel. These tensions, crucial in *The Great Gatsby* and in Fitzgerald's personal response to the rich, express not confusion but the profoundest understanding, at once penetrating and sympathetic. Only an understanding rooted in the acceptance of contradiction can defy the reductionism of reification and discover the "antagonistic whole" of life under capitalism, to use a phrase of the Marxist philosopher Theodor Adorno. In revealing the inescapable dialectic between Gatsby's "appalling sentimentality" and his heroism, between capitalism's grotesque inversion of human values and its power to endow "mobility and grace,"[24] Fitzgerald achieves in fiction something akin to what, says Adorno, only the most rigorous Marxist student of society can hope to attain: "totality . . . in and through contradiction."[25]

Far more than ever suspected, the man whose test of a first-rate intelligence was "the ability to hold two opposed ideas in the mind at the same time, and still retain the ability to function," knew just what he was about when he declared himself to be "essentially Marxian."[26]

Notes

I wish to thank Professor Walter Wenska for his penetrating reading of an earlier version of this essay.

1. A significant exception to this general attitude towards Fitzgerald's Marxism is Scott Donaldson's valuable and thorough essay on "The Political Development of F. Scott Fitzgerald" *Prospects*, VI, (1981), 313–55.

2. Quoted in Robert Sklar, *F. Scott Fitzgerald, the Last Laocoön* (New York: Oxford Univ. Press, 1967), p. 325.

3. A brief sampling of recent critical opinion concerning money and its dehumanizing effects should be noted here. The novel is a "criticism of American worship of success, the destructive effect of money." (Robert Emmet Long, *The Achieving of The Great Gatsby* [Lewisburg: Bucknell Univ. Press, 1978], pp. 172, 154.) Fitzgerald portrays a "society of accumulation" where "love becomes a commodity," as do women, who are perceived as "mere projections of class and wealth." (John Callahan, *The Illusions of A Nation* [Urbana: Univ. of Illinois Press, 1972], pp. 57, 21, 213.) Daisy has been described as "the ultimate object . . . in the magical world Gatsby inhabits. . . . She is for him symbolic rather than personal." (Judith Fetterley, *The Resisting Reader* [Bloomington: Indiana Univ. Press, 1978], pp. 74–75.) I take issue with none of the above; indeed their relevance and validity is assumed from the outset. What the present essay seeks to do is to probe and extend the implications of these observations and generate new insights by employing a Marxist framework.

4. Brian Way, *F. Scott Fitzgerald and the Art of Social Fiction* (New York: St. Martins, 1980), p. 147.

5. In 1931 and 1932 Fitzgerald did some reading in *Capital* and in a work concerning Russian communism. See Donaldson, footnote 1.

6. Way provides an excellent account of Fitzgerald's subtle use of ideas in fiction.

7. Quoted in Donaldson, p. 350, n. 33.

8. F. Scott Fitzgerald, *The Great Gatsby* (New York: Scribner's, 1925; rpt. 1953), pp. 2, 66, 119. All subsequent references in the text.

9. Georg Lukacs, *History and Class Consciousness* (Cambridge, Mass.: MIT Press, 1971), pp. 10, 14.

10. Lukacs, p. 62.

11. Lukacs, p. 91.

12. Karl Marx, *Capital*, vol. 1. (New York: International Publishers, 1967), p. 43.

13. Quoted in Joachim Israel, *Alienation: From Marx to Modern Sociology* (New Jersey: Humanities Press, 1979), p. 44. Israel's book is a lucid and thorough discussion of the subject.

14. Bertell Ollman, *Alienation* (Cambridge: Cambridge Univ. Press, 1971), p. 198.

15. Lukacs, p. 19.

16. Lukacs, pp. 84, 85.

17. Karl Marx, *Early Writings*, ed. T.B. Bottomore (New York: McGraw Hill, 1964), p. 189.

18. Marx, *Early Writings*, p. 191.

19. Marx, *Early Writings*, p. 193.

20. Patricia Bizzell notes that Tom is both a rival and model for Gatsby. See her article "Pecuniary Emulation of the Mediator in *The Great Gatsby*,"*MLN*, 97 (1979), 774–83.

21. Marx, *Early Writings*, p. 193.

22. Lukacs, p. 90.

23. Marx, *Early Writings*, pp. 193–94.

24. F. Scott Fitzgerald, "Handle With Care," *The Crack-Up* (New York: New Directions, 1945), p. 77.

25. Theodor Adorno, "Sociology and Psychology," *New Left Review*, 47 (1968), 67–81. See p. 74.

26. Fitzgerald, *The Crack-Up*, p. 69.

History-Myth-Meaning

The Great Gatsby: Fitzgerald's
Meditation on American History   Kermit W. Moyer*

In a letter to Maxwell Perkins written in April of 1924, Fitzgerald
said: "I feel I have an enormous power in me now, more than I've
ever had in a way . . ." He had just begun work on his third novel.
"This book," he told Perkins, "will be a consciously artistic achievement and must depend on that as the first books did not."[1] Some
four and a half months later, when he had nearly completed a first
draft, Fitzgerald wrote Perkins again: "I think my novel is about the
best American novel ever written," he said.[2] The only thing he was
really unsure of was a title, but by the time the book appeared in
April, 1925, Fitzgerald had decided to call it *The Great Gatsby.*

Gatsby has since become the Fitzgerald novel everyone agrees on—
the book that assures Fitzgerald his place in the first rank. It is the
novel that in 1925 T. S. Eliot called "the first step that American fiction
has taken since Henry James."[3] *Gatsby* is so good, in fact, that critics
tend to confront it with a hint of grateful incredulity: as if Fitzgerald
simply couldn't have gone *that* far in the five years that separate *Gatsby*
from *This Side of Paradise.*

There is also, among recent critics at least, a strong consensus that
The Great Gatsby must be understood as a meditation on American
history. As early as 1937, John Peale Bishop recognized in Jay Gatsby
"the Emersonian man brought to completion and eventually to failure."[4]
In an influential essay written less than a decade later, Lionel Trilling
maintained that "Gatsby, divided between power and dream, comes
inevitably to stand for America itself."[5] Trilling insisted that when Jay
Gatsby is described first as springing "from his Platonic conception of
himself" and then as a son of God whose business is "the service of
a vast, vulgar, and meretricious beauty," Fitzgerald's clear intention

*Reprinted from *Fitzgerald/Hemingway Annual 1972* (Washington, D.C.: NCR
Microcard Editions, 1973), pp. 43–57, by permission of the publisher.

215

is "that our mind should turn to the thought of the nation that has sprung from its 'Platonic conception' of itself."[6] A few years later Edwin Fussell based a strongly persuasive interpretation of the novel on the "connection between Gatsby's individual tragedy and the tragedy of American civilization."[7] Fussell claimed that "Roughly speaking Fitzgerald's basic plot is the history of the New World . . . more precisely, of the human imagination in the New World."[8] Fitzgerald's subject in *The Great Gatsby*, Fussell insisted, is not the Jazz Age or the Lost Generation, "but the whole of American civilization as it culminated in his own time."[9] This sort of historical approach to the novel has since become more or less standard. In 1954 Marius Bewley praised *Gatsby* as "an evocative and an exact description" of the violation of American "aspiration and vision" by "the conditions of American history."[10] Three years later, James E. Miller, Jr., talked about "the gradual expansion of the significance of Gatsby's dream," an expansion which Miller saw as finally encompassing "the dream of those who discovered and settled the American continent."[11] In 1958 another Fitzgerald scholar, John R. Kuehl, described *The Great Gatsby* as "a sort of cultural-historical allegory."[12] Still more recently, Richard Lehan has claimed that in *The Great Gatsby* "We move from a personal sphere (a story of unrequited love), to a historical level (the hope and idealism of the frontier and of democracy in conflict with a rapacious and destructive materialism).[13] Finally, Robert Sklar maintains that "the whole of American experience takes on the character of Gatsby's romantic quest and tragic failure; the history of a continent finds expression in the transcendent images of felicity man made from the beauty of its mocking nature."[14] But despite critical agreement on the profound importance of the historical perspective in *The Great Gatsby*, we still lack a reading of the novel which clearly and concisely articulates the way Fitzgerald has worked out his historical theme. This essay is an attempt at such a reading.[15]

Fitzgerald originally conceived of *Gatsby* as an historical novel set in the Gilded Age: "Its locale," he wrote Maxwell Perkins, "will be the middle west and New York of 1885 I think."[16] The story "Absolution" seems to derive from this first conception of the novel. Although the book that Fitzgerald finally wrote is contemporary in setting, the historical approach that seems to have informed his original conception was not discarded: *The Great Gatsby* is a profoundly historical novel.

Gatsby is really an extended flashback: events are narrated by Nick Carraway some two years after they have occurred. This technique gives the novel a formal circularity (starting at the end, we move to the beginning and proceed back to the end) which reflects structurally a series of circular movements within the story itself (circles of movement traced from West Egg to East Egg and back, from Long Island to

Manhattan and back, from East to West and back). The image of the circle is perhaps most obviously apparent in the egg-shaped geography (hence the name) of East and West Egg. Ultimately this circularity reiterates the novel's perspective upon American history; and since that perspective is contained in Gatsby's personal history, it is perhaps inevitable that in death Gatsby describe with his own life's blood "a thin red circle" in the water of his swimming pool.[17]

.Gatsby's romantic quest for Daisy Fay is circular in essence: his sustained and single-minded thrust into the future is an attempt to recapture, not merely Daisy, but *that moment of wonder which she had once inspired.* For Gatsby, the future has become simply an avenue leading back to the past—or, more specifically, leading back to the glittering possibilities the past once seemed to offer. It isn't enough that he have Daisy, he must have her as she was five years ago, before she married Tom Buchanan; he must recapture the romantic texture of that ecstatic instant when she suddenly embodied for him all of life's wonder and possibility, that moment when he exchanged forever the riotous tumult in his imagination for the vision of her white face and the enchantment of her silvery voice.

> "And she doesn't understand," he said. "She used to be able to understand. We'd sit for hours—"
> He broke off and began to walk up and down a desolate path of fruit rinds and discarded favors and crushed flowers.
> "I wouldn't ask too much of her," I ventured. "You can't repeat the past."
> "Can't repeat the past?" he cried incredulously. "Why of course you can!"
> He looked around him wildly, as if the past were lurking here in the shadow of his house, just out of reach of his hand.
> "I'm going to fix everything just the way it was before," he said, nodding determinedly. "She'll see."
> He talked a lot about the past, and I gathered that he wanted to recover something, some idea of himself perhaps, that had gone into loving Daisy. His life had been confused and disordered since then, but if he could once return to a certain starting place and go over it all slowly, he could find out what that thing was.... (pp. 111–12)

Gatsby's urge is transcendental: his vision of life acknowledges neither time nor limit. But throughout this passage an image of discarded favors and crushed flowers reminds us of the irrevocability of time and of the fatal materiality of the terms of Gatsby's transcendentalism. One autumn night five years before, he had "forever wed his unutterable visions to her *perishable* breath" (p. 112; my emphasis). He had kissed Daisy, and "At his lips' touch *she blossomed for him like a flower* and the incarnation was complete" (p. 112; my emphasis). Now the crushed flowers at his feet comment ironically upon the tragic terms of Gatsby's transcendental vision, and we suddenly realize why the girl who has given focus to that vision is named Daisy.

Throughout the novel, then, a flower metaphor reveals the essential materiality at the core of Gatsby's transcendentalism. In "Winter Dreams," a story universally recognized as a precursor to *The Great Gatsby*, Fitzgerald had also worked with this theme. Dexter Green's lavish dreams are also undermined by the mutability of their material terms (a mutability suggested by Dexter's surname and underscored by the seasonal emphasis of the title). The quality in Judy Jones upon which Dexter's dream of imaginative fulfillment depends is time-bound, transient; her particular beauty is characterized by "a sort of fluctuating and feverish warmth, so shaded that it seemed at any moment it would recede and disappear. This color and the mobility of her mouth gave a continual impression of flux, of intense life, of passionate vitality . . ."[18] When time destroys Judy's fragile beauty, Dexter's dreams dissolve too. The dreams were winter dreams after all—they were tied to time from the outset, as transient as any green bud, as fugitive as any daisy. Gatsby's transcendentalism, of course, is not only tainted by materialism, it is revealed as disastrously circular since it seeks by embracing the *future* to regain and freeze that instant in the *past* when Daisy seemed equal to the demands of Gatsby's transcendental imagination. In the meantime, the present doesn't count: the present is simply the ground upon which Gatsby stands while looking to the future where he sees the past; the present is carelessly exploited (serving also as a dumping ground for the detritus of that exploitation) in order to feed the impassioned thrust into the future. Appropriately, Gatsby first appears in the novel frozen in a pose which exactly represents this circular transcendentalism: facing the green light at the end of Daisy's dock, Gatsby stands with arms outstretched, as if by somehow embracing that green light and possessing the "orgastic future" it represents (p. 182), he could regain that time five years before when he had kissed Daisy and she had "blossomed for him like a flower."

Throughout the novel, Fitzgerald underscores the transcendental nature of Gatsby's love for Daisy. To repeat, it is not just Daisy Gatsby wants but something *beyond* her: he wants that moment when life seemed equal to his extraordinary capacity for wonder, and that moment is indissoluably wedded to Daisy herself, to materiality. When Gatsby explains to Nick that any love Daisy may have felt for her husband was "just personal," Nick realizes that Gatsby's conception of the affair possesses an intensity that can't be measured (p. 152). Like Braddock Washington in "The Diamond as Big as the Ritz," Gatsby combines transcendental imagination with time-enthralled materialism (both heroes also try to control the future by buying back the past); and like the story of Braddock Washington's family, Gatsby's story is a mirror which reflects an image of American history.

After Gatsby reveals to Carraway his astonishing belief that the past can be repeated, that one can retrieve and sustain that moment when reality promised to realize the ideal, Nick remarks:

> Through all he said, even through his appalling sentimentality, I was reminded of something—an elusive rhythm, a fragment of lost words, that I had heard somewhere a long time ago. For a moment a phrase tried to take shape in my mouth and my lips parted like a dumb man's, as though there was more struggling upon them than a wisp of startled air. But they made no sound, and what I had almost remembered was uncommunicable forever. (p. 112)

Gatsby's story, his peculiar and naive audacity, his intense idealism, have evoked a resonance that goes beyond himself. By the end of the novel it becomes clear that the elusive rhythm Nick is here unable to articulate is the rhythm of American history, a rhythm created by man's headlong pursuit of a dream all the way across a continent and back again. Fitzgerald makes this parallel between Gatsby's history and America's history explicit on the last page of the novel.

> Most of the big shore places were closed now and there were hardly any lights except the shadowy, moving glow of a ferryboat across the Sound. And as the moon rose higher the inessential houses began to melt away until gradually I became aware of the old island here *that flowered once for Dutch sailors' eyes*—a fresh, green breast of the new world. Its vanished trees, the trees that had made way for Gatsby's house, had once pandered in whispers to the last and greatest of all human dreams; for a transitory enchanted moment man must have held his breath in the presence of this continent, compelled into an aesthetic contemplation he neither understood nor desired, face to face for the last time in history with something commensurate to his capacity for wonder. (p. 182; my emphasis)

Just as Daisy flowered for Gatsby, so the new world flowered for the Europeans who touched her shore; in both cases, for one electric moment, the material world promised to fulfill the imagination's deepest long-ings. Fitzgerald goes on to link the wonder evoked by Daisy's green dock light with the wonder evoked by the green breast of the new world: "And as I sat there brooding on the old, unknown world, I thought of Gatsby's wonder when he first picked out the green light at the end of Daisy's dock (p. 182). By association with the green trees *which have now vanished,* the green light is included in the flower metaphor which Fitzgerald has used to underscore the essential transiency of the materiality which Gatsby and the Dutch sailors before him have invested with spiritual value. The parallel between the wonder evoked in Gatsby by Daisy and the wonder inspired by the new world is re-inforced through Fitzgerald's use of erotic imagery to describe the Dutch sailors' response to the new land: they are arrested by the "fresh, green *breast*" of America, and the trees *pander* to their insatiable dreams. The word "pandered" also suggests the essential meretriciousness of the new world's spiritual and imaginative appeal. We already know by this time that the promise embodied in Daisy is meretricious. The passage goes on to compete the link between Gatsby's pursuit of Daisy and America's historical pursuit of an ever-receding frontier:

> He had come a long way to this blue lawn, and his dream must have seemed so close that he could hardly fail to grasp it. He did not know that it was already behind him, somewhere back in that vast obscurity beyond the city, where the dark fields of the republic rolled on under the night. (p. 182)

Gatsby's dream, the dream inspired by Daisy, is here identified with the dream which pushed the frontier ever westward. The assumption contained in this identification is that, like Gatsby's history, American history has been the record of a futile attempt to retrieve and sustain a moment of imaginative intensity and promise. By reaching into the future, by pushing continually up against the receding frontier, we have tried to recapture that original sense of wonder evoked when the whole continent was a frontier—that original sense of wonder which soured because its evocation was essentially meretricious, a reading of spiritual, transcendental promise into mere materiality. So we struggle on against the current of time only to be "borne back ceaselessly into the past" (p. 182): our vain effort to seize the lost moment of promise by reaching for the future creates the fabric of our history.

This is an outline of the historical perspective which informs *The Great Gatsby* and which, to some extent, probably derived from Fitzgerald's discovery in Conrad of a kind of hero (Mr. Kurtz) who embraces cultural contradictions. But there are several other important aspects of the novel which must now be explored in terms of this perspective—specifically, Fitzgerald's treatment of Tom Buchanan and the Wilsons; his portrait of Gatsby's early mentor, Dan Cody; the significance of the "waste land" and the eyes of Doctor T. J. Eckleburg which preside over it; Nick Carraway's implicit contrast of East and West; and the role of World War I, which casts a kind of shadow over the events of the whole novel.

The Buchanans are obviously meant to represent an American class. When, at the end of the novel, Nick Carraway says, "They were careless people, Tom and Daisy—they smashed up things and creatures and then retreated back into their money or their vast carelessness, or whatever it was that kept them together, and let other people clean up the mess they had made" (pp. 180–81), we realize that Nick's judgment is generic rather than individual in application. Before moving to East Egg, the Buchanans "had spent a year in France for no particular reason, and then drifted here and there unrestfully wherever people played polo and were rich together" (p. 6). The Buchanans, standing for the modern American upper class, embody a materialism which is totally cynical, undirected by idealism or transcendental hope. Tom Buchanan's chief characteristic is his harsh *physicality*: his orientation is intensely physical at the expense of the mental, the spiritual, and the social. He is described as arrogant, aggressive, powerful: ". . . he seemed to fill those glistening boots until he strained the top lacing, and you could see a great pack of muscle shifting when his shoulder moved under his thin coat. It was a body capable of enormous leverage—a cruel body" (p. 7). Even his past accomplishments are physical: he had been one of the most powerful ends ever to play football at Yale, and Gatsby introduces Tom to his party guests as "the polo player" (p. 106). Jordan Baker, also a representative of this class, mirrors Tom's materialist orientation and consequent athleticism as well as his dishonesty: "She was incurably dishonest. She wasn't able to endure being at a disadvantage and, given this unwillingness, I suppose she had begun dealing in subterfuges when she was very young in order to keep that cool, insolent smile turned to the world and yet satisfy the demands of her hard, jaunty body" (pp. 58–59). Appropriately enough, Jordan is a tournament golfer who cheats. Daisy's role, as we have seen, is more complicated than either Jordan's or Tom's, but the imagery surrounding her is loaded with materialistic associations: she is described continually in terms of silver and gold and her magical voice is "full of money" (p. 120). Daisy represents the materialism of her class as well as the materialism at the core of Gatsby's transcendental idealism. The class to which Daisy and Tom and Jordan Baker belong, the class represented in somewhat broader terms by East Egg itself, has completely lost touch with the transcendental spirit which once shaped American history and which renders Gatsby's materialism tragic rather than shallow. Although Nick deeply disapproves of Gatsby, a sense of the transcendental emotion at the bottom of Gatsby's materialism makes Nick stop, turn, and call out: "They're a rotton crowd . . . You're worth the whole damn bunch put together" (p. 154). Even Daisy senses the tragic nature of Gatsby's impossible transcendental-materialism when he displays his shirts for her, heaping them in a luxurious pile until she cries because she has "never seen such—such beautiful shirts before" (p. 94), moved not so much by the shirts themselves as by the intense emotion with which Gatsby has invested them.

The Buchanans and their class represent an historical dead end. In his own inarticulate way, Tom Buchanan senses this. He clumsily recommends Nick to read " 'The Rise of the Colored Empires' by this man

Goddard" (p. 13), a reference—characteristic of Tom in its inaccuracy—to Theodore Lothrop Stoddard's *The Rising Tide of Color Against White World-Supremacy* (1920). "Civilization's going to pieces," Tom explains. "The idea is if we don't look out the white race will be—will be utterly submerged. It's all scientific stuff; it's been proved" (p. 13). Tom goes on: "This idea is that we're Nordics. . . . And we've produced all the things that go to make civilization—oh, science and art, and all that. Do you see?" (p. 14). Nick perceives that "Something was making [Tom] nibble at the edge of stale ideas as if his sturdy physical egotism no longer nourished his peremptory heart" (p. 21). Nick, of course, is right: Tom's panic over civilization's decay is symptomatic—standing at the end of an historical alley, Tom feels the wall against his back. In the light of Fitzgerald's historical perspective in this novel, the dead end was inevitable from the start: as the frontier disappeared, as the possibility of making the virgin land fulfill its first intense promise passed, American materialism increasingly became just that—simple, spiritless materialism, unregenerative and omnivorous. Gatsby (embodying the complete historical progression) inevitably arrives at this dead end himself. Near the close of the novel, Gatsby waits amidst shattered hopes for Daisy's telephone call, the call that never comes, and Carraway guesses that perhaps Gatsby no longer even cared.

> If that was true he must have felt that he had lost the old warm world, paid a high price for living too long with a single dream. He must have looked up at an unfamiliar sky through frightening leaves and shivered as he found what a grotesque thing a rose is and how raw the sunlight was upon the scarcely created grass. A new world, *material without being real.* . . . (p. 162; my emphasis)

This new world is mere materiality, no longer transformed by the transcendental vision which had given it its meaning and therefore its reality. Kismine Washington had felt the same sense of frightening materiality when, at the end of "The Diamond as Big as the Ritz," she could no longer think of the stars as "great big diamonds that belonged to some one."[19]

It was the American pioneer who carried the burden of this historical progression into the twentieth century. The American pioneer was the proper heir of those Dutch sailors; he inherited their transcendental spark and the promise of the frontier kept the spark alive; but after pursuing that promise all the way to the Pacific ocean, he discovered that it had somehow eluded him, and he was left with nothing but the material which had fed the flame. He was rich but that was all: direction was gone, meaning was gone; the dream began to turn back upon itself. Gatsby is the adoptive son of such a pioneer—a pioneer with the prototypal name of Dan Cody. The succession is almost apostolic, but (as in *The Beautiful and Damned*) the inheritance is essentially empty.[20] Cody has become "a gray, florid man with a hard, empty face" (p. 101) who continually circles the continent in his yacht, the *Tuolomee*, as though looking for something lost. Cody is a millionaire many times over, "a product of the Nevada silver fields, of the Yukon, of every rush for metal since seventy-five" (p. 100). His yacht is named after the gold fields of northern California—a name which manages to suggest both the frontier's end and the avid materialism to which the frontier gave way.[21] Jay Gatsby was born the moment James Gatz, idly searching for his destiny along the beaches of Lake Superior, saw Cody's yacht drop anchor in the dangerous waters of Little Girl Bay, a name which ironically foreshadows the direction of Gatsby's fate.

Given such a vision of American history, it is not surprising to find a theme of material and spiritual waste running through the novel. The famous description of the "valley of ashes" which opens Chapter II strongly echoes the description of the village of Fish which opens the second part of "The Diamond as Big as the Ritz." The barren little village and the valley of ashes are both rather obvious metaphors of American spiritual desiccation.[22] The waste land between West Egg and New York, in fact, comes to resemble a microcosm of America itself; it is a vision of an America made of dust:

> This is a valley of ashes—a fantastic farm where ashes grow like wheat into ridges and hills and grotesque gardens; where ashes take the forms of house and chimneys and rising smoke and, finally, with a transcendent effort, of men who move dimly and already crumbling through the powdery air. (p. 23)

It is a "gray land" and "spasms of bleak dust . . . drift endlessly over it." This description echoes a judgment Nick Carraway had made on the second page of the novel: "Gatsby turned out all right at the end; it is what preyed on Gatsby, *what foul dust floated in the wake of his dreams* that temporarily closed out my interest in the abortive sorrows and short-winded elations of men" (my emphasis). That dust actually becomes tangible toward the end of the novel. Wandering with Gatsby through the echoing emptiness of Gatsby's colossal mansion on the night of Myrtle Wilson's death and Daisy's defection, Nick had noticed that "There was an inexplicable amount of dust everywhere" (p. 147). The foul dust that floats in the wake of America's dreams: the waste of material resources exploited in a desperate effort to sustain that impossible and disastrously circular thrust into the future and the waste of spiritual resources exploited in "the service of a vast, vulgar, and meretricious beauty" (p. 99). The foul dust is the corruptive materialism, like a worm in an apple, at the center of the transcendental dream.

In the meantime, as though in eternal mourning, the gigantic billboard eyes of Doctor T. J. Eckleburg,[23] "dimmed a little by many paintless days, under sun and rain, brood on over the solemn dumping ground" (p. 23). George Wilson confuses those faded eyes with the eyes of God, a confusion which, like the desolate village of Fish with its twelve ghostly inhabitants, suggests that in twentieth-century America God has become a thing of cardboard, ineffectual and passive, robbed of power by a short-sighted, materialistic displacement of spiritual values. This displacement is only underscored by the fact that Eckleburg's enormous, spectacled eyes are in actuality an oculist's abandoned roadside advertisement.

George Wilson and his wife are themselves closely associated with this metaphor of waste and spiritual anemia. The Wilsons live in "a small block of yellow brick" which sits on the very edge of the waste land, "a sort of compact Main Street ministering to it, and contiguous to absolutely nothing" (p. 24). The image suggests the exploited and wasted character of the American middle class (or "Main Street") from which the Wilsons derive. The Wilsons represent the resources of human energy and hope that are drained in order to feed the materialistic orgy which American transcendentalism has inevitably become. George Wilson is already a wasted man. He works sporadically on a "dust-covered wreck of a Ford" and first appears "wiping his hands on a piece of waste" (p. 25). He is described as "a blond, spiritless man, anaemic, and faintly handsome" (p. 25), and his dark suit is veiled by "white ashen dust" (p. 26). Wilson owns a failing garage. In the course of the novel, the automobile becomes an important symbol for the superficial and dangerous beauty of materiality—dangerous because its glitter conceals a vast, destructive power.[24] So it is appropriate that Wilson spend his energy feeding the automobile of the wealthy, of those who make the circular journey from New York to East or West Egg and back again. One of those automobiles destroys his wife. If George Wilson is a man already wasted, Myrtle Wilson still possesses a great reservoir of vitality. Nick Carraway described her as a woman whose face "contained no facet or gleam of beauty, but there was an immediately perceptible vitality about her as if the nerves of her body were continually smouldering" (p. 25). It is Myrtle's vitality, of course, which attracts Tom Buchanan: the upper class, locked into its historical dead end, depends upon the energies of the aspiring middle class to sustain itself; the middle class, in turn, wastes its energy in fruitless pursuit of that materialistic and meretricious beauty embodied most completely in the upper class. Myrtle is killed in a desperately foolish attempt to intercept Gatsby's car; she is destroyed by the class (Daisy) and the materiality (the yellow car) she had so fervently pursued. Finally, Myrtle's death becomes a metaphor for human resources wasted in pursuit of and exploited by unregenerative materialism. Lying dead immediately adjacent to the valley of ashes, Myrtle mingles "her thick dark blood with the dust," her mouth "wide open and ripped at the corners, as though she had choked a little in giving up the tremendous vitality she had stored so long" (p. 138). Fitzgerald had used this theme before, of course: the decay of Gloria Gilbert's vitality in *The Beautiful and Damned* had also stood for the waste of human resources in America, and Gloria had also been identified with the middle class.[25]

The one character in the novel who is able to understand the historical process in which they are all trapped is Nick Carraway. Carraway has been called "the historical voice of the book"; he has a sense of history which separates him from everyone else.[26] This is not to say that Carraway has escaped the trap—he simply understands it. Like all the characters in the novel, Carraway has come from the Midwest to the East—an inversion of the earlier, westward movement. The total progression implied here is, once again, circular: beginning in the East, America pushed westward, pursuing the frontier to California, and then turned back upon itself. The ultimate dead end of that historical thrust lay not in California then but in East Egg, at the original point of departure: it is there that the circle closes. "[T]he pilgrimage eastward of the rare poisonous flower of his race," Fitzgerald once wrote, "was the end of the adventure which had started westward three hundred years ago . . ." And Fitzgerald compared that circular movement to a serpent turning back upon itself, "cramping its bowels, bursting its shining skin."[27] In line with this metaphor of reversed migration, of the East-as-inverted-frontier, Carraway, newly arrived in New York, thinks of himself as "a guide, a pathfinder, an original settler" (p. 4). Driving across Manhattan on a warm summer afternoon, Nick finds the atmosphere so pastoral that he "wouldn't have been surprised to see a great flock of white sheep turn the corner" (p. 28).

America's migratory pilgrimage had begun to really circle back upon itself during "that delayed Teutonic migration known as the Great War" (p. 3). Nick confesses that he had returned from the war feeling "restless":[28] "Instead of being the warm centre of the world, the Middle West now seemed like the ragged edge of the universe—so I decided to go East and learn the bond business" (p. 3). Gatsby had also been overseas during the war; in fact, Nick's first conversation with Gatsby concerns their having been in the same Division. This reverse migration, moving from the New World back to the Old World, is further suggested by Gatsby's having spent some time at Oxford after the war and by the fact that Gatsby's lavish West Egg mansion is "a factual imitation of some Hôtel de Ville in Normandy" (p. 5).

If the war stands as a fulcrum in this radical shift which has brought Nick Carraway to the East, Nick's nostalgia is not for any factual Midwest, but for the *pre-war* world of his childhood—a world as yet untouched by the moral anarchy and inarticulate panic Nick finds in the dead end of the East. "That's my Middle West." Nick says, "not the wheat or the prairies or the lost Swede towns, but the thrilling returning trains of my youth" (p. 177).

The novel concludes on this note of irretrievable loss, of inchoate nostalgia for a past which no longer exists. The wheel of American history has revolved full circle, and the end is in the beginning. It is as if Nick and Gatsby and America itself, carrying still a burden of tarnished wonder and languishing hope, had gone East in a last, tired effort to deposit the burden, to find a lodging place for the fevered imagination, and had found instead—a dead end, a wrong address. The East, Nick says, still figures in his dreams:

> I see it as a night scene by El Greco: a hundred houses, at once con-
> ventional and grotesque, crouching under a sullen, overhanging sky
> and a lustreless moon. In the foreground four solemn men in dress
> suits are walking along the sidewalk with a stretcher on which lies a
> drunken woman in a white evening dress. Her hand, which dangles
> over the side, sparkles cold with jewels. Gravely the men turn in at a
> house—the wrong house. But no one knows the woman's name, and
> no once cares. (p. 178)

Notes

1. F. Scott Fitzgerald, *The Letters of F. Scott Fitzgerald*, ed. Andrew Turnbull (New York: Scribner's, 1963), p. 163.

2. *Ibid.*, p. 166.

3. Reprinted in *The Crack-Up*, ed. Edmund Wilson (New York: New Directions, 1945), p. 310.

4. John Peale Bishop, "The Missing All," *Virginia Quarterly Review*, 13 (1937), 115.

5. Lionel Trilling, "F. Scott Fitzgerald," in his *The Liberal Imagination: Essays on Literature and Society* (New York: Viking, 1950), p. 251; appeared originally in Trilling's "Introduction" to *The Great Gatsby* (New York: New Directions, 1945).

6. *Ibid.*

7. Edwin S. Fussell, "Fitzgerald's Brave New World," in *F. Scott Fitzgerald: A Collection of Critical Essays*, ed., Arthur Mizener (Englewood Cliffs: Prentice-Hall, 1963), p. 48; appeared originally in slightly different form in *ELH*, 19 (1952), 297.

8. *Ibid.*, p. 43; original, 291.

9. *Ibid.*, p. 49; original, 297.

10. Marius Bewley, "Scott Fitzgerald's Criticism of America," *Sewanee Review*, 62 (1954), 225; reprinted in Bewley's "Scott Fitzgerald and the Collapse of the American Dream," in his *The Eccentric Design: Form in the Classic American Novel* (New York: Columbia University Press, 1959), p. 270.

11. James E. Miller, Jr., *The Fictional Technique of Scott Fitzgerald* (The Hague: M. Nijhoff, 1957), p. 105; reprinted in Miller's *F. Scott Fitzgerald: His Art and His Technique* (New York: New York University Press, 1964), pp. 122–23.

12. John R. Kuehl, "Scott Fitzgerald: Romantic and Realist," an unpublished dissertation (Columbia University, 1958), p. 144.

13. Richard Lehan, *F. Scott Fitzgerald and the Craft of Fiction* (Carbondale: Southern Illinois University Press, 1966), p. 118.

14. Robert Sklar, *F. Scott Fitzgerald: The Last Laocoön* (New York: Oxford University Press, 1967), p. 195.

15. Since finishing this essay, I have discovered that Milton R. Stern's long, informative, richly diffuse chapter on *The Great Gatsby* in his recently published *The Golden Moment; The Novels of F. Scott Fitzgerald* (Urbana: University of Illinois Press, 1970) confirms some of my conclusions. We have worked from similar assumptions about Fitzgerald's historical preoccupations; and this has led us, I think, to complementary, rather than identical, insights.

16. Fitzgerald in a letter to Maxwell Perkins, as quoted by Henry Dan Piper, *F. Scott Fitzgerald: A Critical Portrait* (New York: Holt, Rinehart and Winston, 1965), p. 101.

17. F. Scott Fitzgerald, *The Great Gatsby* (New York: Scribner's 1925), p. 163, hereafter cited in the text.

18. F. Scott Fitzgerald, *All the Sad Young Men* (New York: Scribner's, 1926), p. 66.

19. F. Scott Fitzgerald, *Tales of the Jazz Age* (New York: Scribner's, 1922). p. 191.

20. Frederick Hoffman notes that, in his role as Gatsby's mentor, Meyer Wolfsheim can be seen as Cody's successor and that "the difference between the two masters suggests clearly the story of several decades of exploitation and money-gathering in the American world" (*The Twenties: American Writing in the Post-War Decade* [New York: Viking, 1955], p. 115). Cody is not the only prototypal American figure to whom Gatsby is linked; he is also linked, through his childhood "Schedule" and "General Resolves," to Benjamin Franklin. See Floyd C. Watkins, "Fitzgerald's Jay Gatz and Young Ben Franklin," *New England Quarterly*, 27 (1954), 249–52.

21. Robert Emmet Long suggests a similar interpretation of *Tuolomee*: "Cody's yacht, the *Tuolomee*, is named after the gold fields in northern California, and underlies the idea of grandiose promise betrayed by brutalized reality" ("The Great Gatsby and the Tradition of Joseph Conrad—Part I," *Texas Studies in Literature and Language*, 8 [1966], 262).

22. Although T. S. Eliot's *The Waste Land* almost certainly influenced Fitzgerald's conception of "the valley of ashes," the fact that Fitzgerald had used a similar "waste land" metaphor in "The Diamond as Big as the Ritz" (published four months before *The Waste Land*) should caution us against interpreting *Gatsby* completely in terms of Eliot's poem. Nevertheless, it is possible to see *Gatsby* as a novel concerning "a grail quest in a waste land, over which presides a deity-like figure" (Wilfred Louis Guerin, "Christian Myth and Naturalistic Deity: The Great Gatsby," *Renascence*, 14 [1962], p. 80). In other words, Fitzgerald, like Eliot, may be working with a set of symbols deriving from the Fisher King/Grail legends described in Jessie L. Weston's *From Ritual to Romance* (1920). Besides Mr. Guerin's article, see John W. Bicknell, "The Waste Land of F. Scott Fitzgerald," *Virginia Quarterly Review*, 30 (1954), 556–72 and Philip Young, "Scott Fitzgerald's Waste Land," *Kansas Magazine*, 23 (1956), 73–77.

23. Lottie R. Crim and Neal B. Houston note that the name Eckleburg seems to be a play on two German words ("ekel" and "burg") which taken together suggest "loathsome town." It is therefore possible to see in the name an implicit judgment upon New York and, by extension, upon the East itself. See Crim and Houston, "The Catalogue of Names in *The Great Gatsby*," *Research Studies*, 36 (June 1968), p. 117.

24. The role of the automobile in *Gatsby* has been discussed elsewhere. See Sklar, *F. Scott Fitzgerald: The Last Laocoön*, pp. 180–82 and Leo Marx, *The Machine in the Garden* (New York: Oxford University Press, 1964), p. 358.

25. At a middle-class nightclub in New York—the sort of place frequented by "the little troubled men who are pictured in the comics as 'the Consumer' or 'the Public' " —Gloria murmurs "I belong here . . . I'm like these people" (F. Scott Fitzgerald, *The Beautiful and Damned* [New York Scribner's, 1922], pp. 69, 72).

26. Alan Trachtenberg, "The Journey Back: Myth and History in *Tender Is the Night*," in *Experience in the Novel: Selected Papers from the English Institute*, ed. Roy Harvey Pearce (New York: Columbia University Press, 1968), p. 136. Trachtenberg also notes that the lack of historical sense which underlies Gatsby's tragic attempt to recover the past is parodied in the novel's other characters:

> The frenzy in the life surrounding Gatsby enacts the quest for recovery as parody. Like its elegant roughneck hero, the book's world has deprived itself of conscious historical experience—it prefers the "sensation" of "Vladimir Tostoff's *Jazz History of the World*," or furniture like Myrtle's, tapestried with "scenes of ladies swinging in the garden of Versailles"—in order to pursue one or another debased version of the dream of incarnation. ("The Journey Back: Myth and History in *Tender Is the Night*," p. 138.)

Trachtenberg might have included here Carraway's sense that "Tom would drift on forever seeking, a little wistfully, for the dramatic turbulence of some irrecoverable football game." This lack of historical consciousness, of course, is a fundamental part of the circular transcendentalism I have already discussed.

27. Fitzgerald, "The Note-Books," in *The Crack-Up*, p. 199.

28. This restlessness is shared by all the novel's characters. The Buchanans drift "here and there unrestfully," Jordan Baker has a "wan, charming, discontented face" and a body that asserts itself with "a restless movement"; Gatsby's nervous physical energy is "continually breaking through his punctilious manner in the shape of restlessness."

F. Scott Fitzgerald's *Gatsby* and the Imagination of Wonder

Giles Gunn*

There are certain occasions, I believe, when it is useful, even necessary, to formulate an interpretation of a book which attempts to explain why we keep coming back to it, to suspend the usual critical apparatus and simply try to concentrate on those details, selective as they may sometimes be, which shape or determine the way a particular book reads us as well as we read it. I regard this, in fact, as an indispensable part of the critic's total job of work. For criticism does not end with explication, it only begins there. It ends, if at all, only with an account of how specific books, writers or traditions somehow reorder the mental, emo-

*Reprinted from the *Journal of the American Academy of Religion*, 41 (June 1973), 171–83, by permission of the publisher and the author.

tional and spiritual furniture of our lives, somehow move us, if ever so slightly, to accept new ideas of order, fresh reconceptions of what will suffice. In this, one of its furthest reaches, the act of criticism is very like the act of love. The critic finds himself in the paradoxical situation of seeking to preserve and enhance the memory of something he cherishes only to discover in the process that this response has been compelled almost from the very beginning by an odd sense that he is merely reciprocating in kind. Hence, as much as the critic should strive, in Matthew Arnold's words, "to see the object as in itself it really is," there comes a point in his negotiations with certain literary texts when his comprehension inevitably will, and necessarily should, be determined as well by how the object sees him.[1] Though few may wish to go quite as far as Leslie Fiedler, there is still a certain warrant to his confession that "the truth one tries to tell about literature is finally [no] different from the truth one tries to tell about the indignities and rewards of being the kind of man one is—an American, let's say, in the second half of the twentieth century, learning to read his country's books."[2] What Fiedler is suggesting has been beautifully expressed by Erich Heller where he claims that the ultimate business of the student, teacher and critic of literature is "not the avoidance of subjectivity, but its purification; not the shunning of what is disputable, but the cleansing and deepening of the dispute." To this degree, Heller maintains, there are no methods which completely and satisfactorily comprehend the critic's subject matter—"only methods, perhaps, that produce the intellectual pressure and temperature in which perception crystallizes into conviction and learning into a sense of value."[3]

This, I would argue, is how the critic tries, if he ever really can, to improve the quality of life. By assessing the actual in light of its own potential, that is, by seeking to comprehend a work not only for what it is in and of itself but also in terms of what it merely suggests but still elicits, he struggles not only to preserve a sense of value but also to increase it. Yet in a culture characterized chiefly by what Richard Gilman has described—and far too sanguinely, I believe—as a confusion of realms, he can afford no illusions about the heavy odds stacked against him. His position, like that of the writer's for whom he serves as an advocate, is always an embattled one; for he knows, or should know, that in the realm of cultural and spiritual values, as T. S. Eliot once remarked, "we fight rather to keep something alive than in the expectation that anything will triumph."[4]

It is no accident that F. Scott Fitzgerald could have said very nearly the same thing. For *The Great Gatsby* is nothing if not an attempt to keep something alive in the face of a certain conviction that it has no possibility of ultimate triumph. What is at issue, of course, is not the survival of Gatsby himself nor even the substance of his vision; the one is fatally vulnerable, the other hopelessly naive and corruptible. The novel is rather about the energy and quality of the imagination which propels both Gatsby *and* his vision, and which endures, if at all, only in the narrative strategies of Fitzgerald's art. Viewed as a story about Gatsby and his dream, the novel is merely an elegy, or, more specifically, a threnody sung over the death of one of our culture's most affecting but flawed innocents. Viewed instead as a story about Gatsby's poetry of desire, his imagination of wonder, the novel is an act of historical repossession, an attempt to release and preserve some of the unspent potential of our spiritual heritage as Americans.

I

Nonetheless, there is no blinking the distance which separates most of us from F. Scott Fitzgerald's *The Great Gatsby* and what I would call "the Imagination of Wonder." For in a world bounded on the one side by the agonies and atrocities of Vietnam or the American urban ghetto and on the other by televised moon landings, I would suggest that we wonder, if at all, only about what is left to wonder at or wonder about. The imaginative capacity for wonder—whether it takes the primitive form of awed and passive astonishment before the unexpected, or the more sophisticated form of active, imaginative penetration into modes of being other than our own—requires a special openness to the unanticipated, a certain susceptibility to surprise, and most of us can no longer allow ourselves to be so vulnerable. Instead of remaining receptive to novelty, we have become rotten-ripe with knowingness as the imagination's last defense in a world which, if experienced directly, might stun us back into the Stone Age. Having inured ourselves to strangeness with a surfeit of information, we are all but dead to those startling confrontations with otherness which have traditionally given shape and substance to the literature which has created as well as reflected our national experience.

The reason is not hard to find. In the shadows of a possible nuclear holocaust where we have now lived for more than a quarter of a century, reality takes on proportions of enormity simply too vast, too horrific, for the imagination to grasp. What we have made, what in fact we have it in our power to do, is now beyond our capacity to dream. Suddenly there seem to be no "others" more monstrous than the ones which, if Marshal McLuhan is to be believed, are mere extensions of ourselves, and this is something beyond the compass of even our darkest, our most diabolic, night thoughts.

Yet when morning finally comes and the shadows of disaster lift at least high enough for us to see the landscape about us, all we are still likely to perceive is what we have put there ourselves, something which in the daylight looks more like a metropolis than a mushroom cloud, but which, as Thomas Pynchon has suggested in *The Crying of*

Lot 49, is less identifiable as a city "than a grouping of concepts—census tracts, special purpose bond-issue districts, shopping nuclei, all overlaid with access roads to its own freeway."

To be sure, even in a world whose most discernible and meaningful patterns suggest nothing so much as the printed circuitry of a transistor radio, one may still, like Oedipa Maas, discover what appears to be "a heiroglyphic sense of concealed meaning, . . . an intent to communicate." The problem is that when the environment has become but an extension of man himself, there is no way of telling the difference between what Robert Frost calls "counter-love, original response" and "our own voice back in copy speech." Thus one is left yearning as Americans have always been, for "a world elsewhere"[5] beyond the self, yet suspicious that whatever traces of it are left constitute evidence of nothing but our own paranoia. In such circumstances as these, wonder gives way all too easily to cynicism, yearning to submission, and hope to the madness of boredom.

This is a prospect of which F. Scott Fitzgerald was acutely conscious. Had he foreseen it with any less clarity in his evocation of the world of Tom and Daisy Buchanan, he could not have written so compellingly of the marked contrast which Gatsby himself presents to it. For Gatsby's illusions have nothing whatsoever to do with the modern, secularized world of Tom and Daisy. As Fitzgerald makes clear on the last page of the novel, Gatsby's dream belongs to a historical order which has long since ceased to exist, to a vision of possibility which had almost died on the eyes of those first Dutch sailors to these shores who, paradoxically, were the last to look out upon the American landscape in innocence: "for a transitory enchanted moment," Fitzgerald writes, "man must have held his breath in the presence of this continent, compelled into an aesthetic contemplation he neither understood nor desired, face to face for the last time in history with something commensurate with his capacity for wonder" Fitzgerald describes this "capacity for wonder" as an "aesthetic contemplation," but for Jay Gatsby, in whom Fitzgerald invests it to such an extraordinary degree, it is clearly something more. "Out of the corner of his eye," Fitzgerald tells us at one point in the novel, "Gatsby saw that the blocks of the sidewalk really formed a ladder and mounted to a secret place above the trees—he could climb to it, if he climbed alone, and once there he could suck the pap of life, gulp down the incomparable milk of wonder."

There is, of course, an incredible garishness involved in Gatsby's capacity for wonder precisely because he attempts to make so transparent and gauche a religion out of it. What with all his gorgeous sacramental shirts, his splendid gestures of supplication, and his ornate West Egg mansion which functions throughout the novel as a kind of sacred shrine, Gatsby seems a grotesque parody of some high priest or shaman who is continually dispensing holy waters, consecrated food, and other elements of the sanctified life to whatever aspirants he can gather around him. And the fact that Gatsby's friends inevitably turn out to be "faithless" in the end only heightens the parody: it was never intended that he serve their illusions but rather that they serve his. Thus Gatsby remains ridiculously sentimental to the very end, a fool for, and ultimately a victim of, the faith he made out of his own unquenchable thirst for wonder.[6]

Part of the triumph of the novel is that Fitzgerald refuses to discount the vulgarity of it all and instead confronts it directly by employing as his narrator and chief spokesman, a character who, like one side of Fitzgerald himself possesses an "unaffected scorn" for everything that Gatsby represents. During the course of the novel, however, Nick Carraway undergoes what Melville would have called a "sea-change" as he is himself brought slowly face to face with something at once intransigently American and also universal which by the end of the novel somehow transcends and, to a point, even redeems the crude and sordid materials in terms of which it is expressed. I refer to Gatsby's marvelous capacity for wonder when viewed not as an inborn trait of character so much as a reflex response to life, and which issues in what Nick describes as his "extraordinary gift for hope," his "romantic readiness." If Gatsby's personality is no more than "an unbroken series of successful gestures," as Nick muses at the beginning, still there is what can only be described as "something gorgeous about him, some heightened sensitivity to the promises of life, as if he were related to one of those intricate machines that register earthquakes ten thousand miles away."

By the end of the novel, Nick is able to identify this responsive capacity with something the American continent once might have elicited in all men, but neither he nor Fitzgerald is under any illusions about what America offers now. Contemporary American society presents itself in *The Great Gatsby* as utterly devoid of any of those fresh and unexpected images which once astonished man into a new and original relation with the universe and which thus gave rise, whether in Jonathan Edwards or Ralph Waldo Emerson, in Walt Whitman or Hart Crane, to a new American imagination of wonder. The "fresh, green breast of the new world," which first presented itself to those unsuspecting Dutch sailors, has now diminished to the tiny, green light which burns all night on Daisy Buchanan's pier and which illumines little more than the desolate Valley of Ashes, that wasteland of frustrated desire and shattered hopes existing, so Fitzgerald would have us believe, at the end of every contemporary American rainbow.

Thus Jay Gatsby, "born of his Platonic conception of himself," as Nick tells us, and "elected to be about his Father's business" is left from the beginning without anything in twentieth-century America but "a vast, vulgar, and meretricious beauty for him to serve." The tragedy, however, is not his alone but also his society's for both seemed doomed by what they lack—Gatsby by his lack of any critical ability to distinguish his spiritual ideals from the material conditions in and through which he must realize them; American society by its lack of either substance or form commensurate with Gatsby's belief in them.[7] Yet if Gatsby's destruction by "the foul dust" which "floats in the wake of his illusions" is thus inevitable, his inexhaustible store of wonder and good will still confer upon the very actuality which eventually extinguish them whatever truth, beauty or goodness that American actuality ever fully attains. Fizgerald is thus able to celebrate Gatsby's veritable religion of wonder, while at the same time exposing its pathetic vulnerability and ultimate defilement. His tribute is part of his critique, a single act of judgment and love which proves that Fitzgerald knew what he was talking about when he remarked that "the test of a first-rate intelligence is the ability to hold two opposed ideas in the mind, at the same time, and still retain the ability to function."

II

Nick Carraway's first glimpse of Gatsby outlined in all his elemental loneliness against the sky as he makes his trembling gesture of acknowledgement and supplication to the green light which beckons to him from across the bay contains nearly the entire meaning of Gatsby's story. For, like Melville's Captain Ahab before him and Faulkner's Thomas Sutpen after him, Gatsby has committed his life to a pursuit in the future of what has already become a symbol of his own reinterpreted and idealized past. As a symbol, the green light is most clearly associated in Gatsby's mind with Daisy, but it represents much more than Daisy herself. As Gatsby's appropriately sexual substitute for "the fresh, green breast of the new world," the green light symbolizes to Gatsby all that Daisy once meant to him during their very brief but poignant love affair five years before, some idea of himself which went into his loving of her but which he irretrievably lost the moment he "forever wed his unutterable visions to her perishable breath." Once the incarnation was complete the vision began to wither, and Gatsby would henceforth be condemned to living in that country of American fantasy which is always located in the spiritual as well as historical wilderness between the "no longer" and the "not yet," or, to recall Klipspringer's song, "In the meantime, in between time" where all one asks is "Ain't we got fun?"

From the very beginning Gatsby's "unutterable visions" had served to convince him "that the rock of the world was founded securely on a fairy's wing," but they had not received human shaping until the day Dan Cody's yacht dropped anchor in the shallows of Lake Superior and the young Jimmie Gatz rowed out to have a look. To young James

Gatz—soon to become Jay Gatsby, but now only a recent drop-out from St. Olaf College—the appearance of Cody's yacht seemed as momentous as the arrival of the Nina, the Pinta, and the Santa Maria, and so he signed on to serve Cody in some vague personal capacity for what eventually turned out to be five years. When Cody died at the end of that time, Jimmie Gatz was cheated out of the $25,000 his mentor had left him, but Jay Gatsby had acquired something much more valuable— what Nick describes, with not a little irony, as an "appropriate education" from a man who was the "product of the Nevada silver fields, of the Yukon, of every rush for the metal since seventy-five" (p. 100). The historical allusion is perfect. At Gatsby's point of time in history, who but one of the fallen Sons of Leatherstocking could have transmitted to him what was left of that earlier American vision which now lives on only in the body of his corruption? Yet it was not until the now hardened but still adolescent Jay Gatsby of Minnesota met the beautiful but unstable Daisy Fay of Louisville during the Great War that his education was filled out. The myth of the Northern Yankee forever seek-ing the paradise of his dreams in the ever-vanishing world of the West had to be joined with what was left of the legend of the Southern Cavalier discovering a salvation of refinement in the gossamer world of midnight balls and late afternoon teas before Gatsby's vividly Amer-ican identity could be firmly fixed.

If Cody's world, as Nick speculates, is the world of "the pioneer debauchee, who during one phase of American life brought back to the Eastern seaboard the savage violence of the frontier brothel and saloon" Daisy's is the artificial, vapid and completely brittle world of the teenage socialite whose only real aim in life is to remain "gleaming, like silver, safe and proud above the hot struggles of the poor." Like so many before him, Gatsby was compelled into an attitude of absolute enchantment by the sense of "ripe mystery," of throbbing expectation, which seemed so much a part of Daisy's person, her house, her culture, and, particularly, her voice. There was "a singing compulsion" to it, "a whispered 'Listen,' a promise that she had done gay, exciting things just a while since and that there were gay, exciting things hovering in the next hour." It was a voice which held out to him the possibility of every promise's fulfillment, a future of unlimited beatitude and sexual felicity which was, to quote Howard Mumford Jones, "if not the kingdom of Prester John, the empire of the Great Kahn, or Asia heavy with the wealth of Ormuz and of Ind, then next door to it, or a passage toward it. . . ."[8] Only years later, in telling Nick of his poignant affair with Daisy five years before, would Gatsby be able to perceive that "the in-exhaustible charm that rose and fell in it, the jingle of it, the cymbals' song of it" was simply the sound of money. Gatsby and Daisy had, of course, fully intended to marry after the war, but before Gatsby could cut through the red tape delaying his return, Daisy's febrile will had collapsed and her letter arrived announcing her marriage to a mid-westerner named Tom Buchanan.

As so many critics have noted,[9] Tom exists in the novel as a kind of double to Gatsby, thus permitting Fitzgerald to point up by contrast Gatsby's incomparably greater stature. Tom strikes Nick from the moment he meets him as "one of those men who reach such an acute limited excellence at twenty-one that everything afterward savors of anti-climax." A Chicago boy from an enormously wealthy family, Tom had played end at Yale and ever after gave the impression that he "would drift on forever seeking, a little wistfully, for the dramatic turbulence of some irrecoverable football game." If Daisy's most striking attribute is the sound of her tinkling voice, Tom's is his "cruel body," "a body," Nick surmises, "capable of enormous leverage." Gatsby, by contrast, is all spirit. Far from creating the impression of power, Gatsby conveys the impression of desire. Nick acquires this impression the first time he meets Gatsby when he catches a glimpse of it in Gatsby's most characteristic attribute, his smile:

> It was one of those rare smiles with a quality of eternal reassurance in it, that you may come across four or five times in life. It faced—or seemed to face—the whole external world for an instant, and then concentrated on *you* with an irresistible prejudice in your favour. It understood you just as far as you wanted to be understood, believed in you as you would like to believe in yourself, and assured you that it had precisely the impression of you that, at your best, you hoped to convey. Precisely at that point it vanished—and I was looking at an elegant young roughneck, a year or two over thirty, whose elaborate formality of speech just missed being absurd. (p. 48)

This passage is brilliantly executed because, as Marius Bewley has suggested, "it presents Gatsby to us less as an individual than as a projection, or mirror of our ideal selves."[10] Gatsby's youthful impression, in fact, has nothing to do with youth at all: It is a quality of good will, of total willingness, which neither time can stale nor age wither—a prejudice, to paraphrase part of Alfred North Whitehead's definition of religion, that the facts of existence shall find their justification in the nature of existence. As a prejudice which has no concern for the facts as they are, it can, of course, become absurdly sentimental; but even here Gatsby is to be contrasted with Tom. For whereas Tom's sentimentality is decadent and wholly self-serving, Gatsby's is ebullient and wholly self-effacing. Tom is never more revealing than when he is brought to tears over the sight of a box of half-finished dog biscuits which constitute the final remains of a day of drunken philandering with his own dead mistress, a day which was finally brought to a close only after Tom, in a fit of adolescent pique, had broken her nose with his open hand in one "short deft movement." Gatsby's sentimentality, on the other hand, is revealed in his constant temptation to confer his essentially heroic capacity for faith and wonder upon objects which are decidedly unworthy of them, objects ultimately as dangerous as style, money, and class. The latter points only to a deficiency of mind, the former to a deficiency of heart. What Gatsby lacks is the critical ability to temper his generous, if also innocent, feelings, which are in turn responsible for the splendor and naivete of his illusions. What Tom lacks, by contrast, is the effective power to feel truly anything but pity for himself, which renders him depraved and inhuman.

In this, as in other ways, Tom and Gatsby reflect related but different strains in the development of American history and culture. Tom is a scion of the great robber barons of the Gilded Age who "seized the land, gutted the forests, laid the railroads,"[11] and turned the cities into vast urban fortresses for the purpose of protecting their own moneyed interests. Descendants of those early pioneers, frontiersman and later settlers who attempted to transform the Virgin Land into a New World Garden, these later empire-builders of the post-Civil War period who wanted to replace crops with machines set aside morality as easily and quickly as they attempted to buy up civilization. Men of single-minded purpose who were at once daring and perseverent, they, like Captain Ahab, allowed nothing to stand in their "iron way," and they assured themselves of Heaven's blessing—as Tom would if he could but remember the right words—by convincing themselves that they were doing Heaven's will.

Gatsby, by contrast, recalls an earlier generation of American worthies who originally journeyed to these shores in the hopes of establishing a kingdom on earth which might more nearly conform to the Kingdom of Heaven. But in the century and a half intervening between the first settlement and the establishment of the Republic, the dreams of the one had become intertangled with the success of the other. The original theocratic impulse to found a City upon a Hill to the greater glory of God had been displaced by the more secular desire to build a nation in the wilderness which testified instead to the inalienable rights of man. The seventeenth-century propulsion to know why had been reduced to the eighteenth- and nineteenth-century preoccupation with know how. The Calvinist belief in God as the maker of man's destiny had been supplanted by Benjamin Franklin's doctrine of self-help. To be sure, there were still traces of that earlier Puritan dream in its later, more pragmatic expression. As Perry Miller has noted, Benjamin Franklin pursued worldly success every bit as disinterestedly as Jonathan Edwards pursued the nature of true virtue, and both shared a similar conviction "that the universe is its own excuse for being."[12] But by the time Gatsby had got hold of it, American society, but for an hour on Sunday mornings, had long since abandoned the view Franklin strangely shared with Edwards, the view that life on earth could and should be, as it were, lifted up to Heaven. Instead, for a century or more, America had been telling the Jimmie Gatzes of this world that the Kingdom of God could be established right here in America, perhaps even on somebody's rented estate, and that, further, one could get away with populating this New World paradise with Daisy Fays, Tom Buchanans, and Meyer Wolfsheims, the latter being reputed to have fixed the World Series in 1919.

This is absurd, and Fitzgerald knew it was. Thus he shows that the plan Gatsby concocted to express it was doomed from the beginning, and he does not mince words as to the reason why. Gatsby's proposal to rectify what he considers the mistake of Daisy's marriage to Tom, by asking her to request a divorce so that she can marry him instead, is based upon his incredible belief that history doesn't matter, that the past can be repeated. This is the ultimate flaw at the heart of Gatsby's dream, and, with the dream itself, it shatters like glass against Tom and Daisy's brutal indifference.

That indifference is nowhere more apparent than when Daisy accidentally kills Myrtle Wilson, Tom's mistress, with Gatsby's car. The accident merely fulfills and completes the earlier act of violence which Tom committed against Myrtle himself and thus serves as a perfect expression of that reliance upon brute force, at once physical and material, which holds Tom and Daisy and their kind together. Hence when Gatsby magnanimously offers to protect Daisy from any possible recriminations from Tom, Tom and Daisy repay his generosity by insinuating to Myrtle's grief-crazed husband, George Wilson, that Gatsby was responsible instead. In deflecting Wilson's certain vengeance away from themselves out of a habit of self-protection it took their forbears several generations to perfect, Tom and Daisy make Gatsby the scapegoat of their own irresponsible pasts. Yet this is in character, Nick later surmises, for in spite of their wealth and glamor, perhaps even because of it, Tom and Daisy were simply "careless people" who "smashed up things and creatures and then retreated back into their money or their vast carelessness, or whatever it was that kept them together, and let other people clean up the mess they had made" (pp. 180–81).

Thus when George Wilson kills Gatsby and then himself, a strange circle of significance is completed. If Gatsby represents that irrepressible reaction of wonder and hope which once gave force to the vision of what the American reality might one day be, Wilson represents that spiritless desperation and hopelessness at the center of what the American reality, in this novel at least, has actually become. The only people who escape are ironically those who have done most to create the one out of the other, people like Tom and Daisy who have acquired enough money and shrewdness in the process to buy their way out of trouble.

III

But Gatsby's destruction at the end in no sense indicates a complete triumph of the forces, both from within and without, which have conspired against him. For Fitzgerald has so constructed his novel that Gatsby's true stature and significance can only be finally measured by his impact upon the narrator, and to Nick Carraway Gatsby's ultimate victory is absolutely assured.

As narrator Nick seems perfectly suited to his task. He describes himself on the very first page of the novel as one of those people who is "inclined to reserve all judgments, a habit that has opened up many curious natures to me and also made me the victim of not a few veteran bores. . . ." But Nick's tolerance is not without its limits; for he is concerned to live as he has been raised, according to "a sense of the fundamental decencies." And having returned from the East to tell his story, he confesses, "I felt that I wanted the world to be in uniform and at a sort of moral attention forever; I wanted no more riotous excursions with privileged glimpses into the human heart" (pp. 1–2).

Yet much as Nick tries to remain ambivalent and uninvolved throughout the book, "simultaneously enchanted and repelled by the inexhaustible variety of life," he cannot maintain the distance of a neutral observer as he becomes progressively more involved in Gatsby's incredible scheme to recapture Daisy. For if Nick is contemptuous of everything Gatsby represents, he still cannot resist admiring the intensity with which Gatsby represents it. And the more Nick uncovers the cynicism and corruption beneath Tom and Daisy's glamor, the more he grows to respect Gatsby's optimism and the essential incorruptibility not of his vision but of the desire it incarnates. Hence by the time Gatsby is murdered by the demented Wilson, Nick has come to think that Gatsby was "worth the whole damn bunch put together." But he also finds that, like Gatsby before him, he must pay the price of loneliness for his conviction. For it readily becomes apparent at the time of Gatsby's death that Gatsby's friends no longer have any use for him. And then it is that Nick realizes the nature of his own relationship to Gatsby: "it grew upon me that I was responsible, because no one else was interested—interested, I mean, with that intense personal interest to which everyone has some vague right in the end" (p. 165).

This feeling of genuine concern and sympathy for another human being emerges as one of the most important positive values of Gatsby's tragedy. If it does not seem capable of mitigating the pathos of Gatsby's destruction, much less preventing it, Nick's capacity for concern and love nonetheless enables him to see in the tragedy of Gatsby's own idealism a symbol for the tragedy of all human aspiration. Before Nick leaves the East permanently after Gatsby's death, he crosses his front yard to take one last look at Gatsby's house:

. . . as the moon rose higher the inessential houses began to melt away until gradually I became aware of the old island here that flowered once for Dutch sailors' eyes—a fresh, green breast of the new world. Its vanished trees, the trees that had made way for Gatsby's house, had once pandered in whispers to the last and greatest of all human dreams; for a transitory enchanted moment man must have held his breath in the presence of this continent, . . . face to face for the last time in history with something commensurate to his capacity for wonder. (p. 182)

Nick is able to give his words such a beautiful, haunting, evocative quality because he had himself been partially seduced by Gatsby's dream. Not only had he once felt the mysterious attraction in Daisy's voice; he had also fallen half in love with someone who suggested its rich ring of promise. But Nick had been able to discern the note of cynicism and emptiness behind the magic suggestiveness of Daisy's voice, just as he had also been able to perceive that Jordan Baker, his temporary lover, was basically a liar and a cheat.

At the end Nick can only surmise as to whether Gatsby was ever able to acknowledge the terrible disparity between his magnificent illusions and the coarse actuality which finally betrayed them. Nick can scarcely believe that Gatsby remained ignorant to the very end of "what a grotesque thing a rose is," but as for himself there is no question. The culture of the East, which once held out to him, as it always did to Gatsby, the promise of beginning all over again in a New World in the very next hour—the culture of the East now appears to Nick as a night scene from El Greco:

In the foreground four solemn men in dress suits are walking along the sidewalk with a stretcher on which lies a drunken woman in a white evening dress. Her hand, which dangles over the side, sparkles cold with jewels. Gravely the men turn in at the house—the wrong house. But no one knows the woman's name, and no one cares. (p. 178)

The only illumination which relieves Nick's otherwise dark and feral tableau is the absurd, little green light at the end of Daisy's pier which Gatsby so fervently believed in, "the orgiastic future that year by year recedes before us. . . ." ". . . but that's no matter," Nick assures us— "tomorrow we will run faster, stretch out our arms farther. . . . And one fine morning—"

"So we beat on," Nick concludes, "boats against the current, borne back ceaselessly into the past" (p. 182).

This image, with its perfect union of sexual and spiritual promise, arrests us with its terrible poignancy. Gatsby's capacity for wonder was doomed from the beginning. "He had come a long way to this blue lawn, and his dream must have seemed so close that he could hardly fail to grasp it," Nick muses. "He did not know that it was already behind him, somewhere back in that vast obscurity beyond the city, where the dark fields of the republic rolled on under the night." Yearning always forward to secure a future that was already lost to the past, Gatsby is borne ceaselessly backward in time until he becomes a sacrificial victim of the pasts of others, indeed, of the American Dream itself.

The pathos of the final image thus seems definitive: Gatsby's beautiful circuit of belief and desire is broken on the rack of America's cruel indifference; his generous "willingness of heart" is simply no match for Tom and Daisy's "hard malice." Committed to pure spirit in a world almost exclusively composed of mere matter, Gatsby is defeated by his inability to understand that the things of the spirit can exist only amidst the unavoidable conditions which the actual and the material make for them.[13]

Yet this is not the whole truth, either for Nick as narrator or for us as readers. Because if the coarse materials of Gatsby's world have refused to yield to the impulses of his spirit, if, indeed, Gatsby himself at the end "must have felt that he had lost the old warm world, paid a high price for living too long with a single dream," still the very intensity of his commitment to spirit has nonetheless transfigured, for however brief a time, the otherwise drab materials of existence. That Gatsby's imagination of wonder can never overcome the current, cannot even resist the current, is nothing to the point: It is the poetry of beating on that counts! As a reflex response to that most elemental, though not most profound, intimation of the sacred both within and beyond us, Gatsby's spontaneous act of resistance constitutes here, as in life generally, what might be described, in R. W. B. Lewis's fine phrase, as "the tug of the Transcendent."[14] Without it, life loses all of its energy and interest, all of its color and originality. With it, we recover a sense of that radiance which temporarily redeems life even as the flow of life itself bears it away.

But we do not have to settle or Fitzgerald's word alone on this subject. Robert Frost once used an image almost identical to Fitzgerald's boats beating on against the current and gave that image of primitive spiritual resistance one of its definitive religious expressions. Frost's image occurs in the poem "West-running Brook." Fred and his wife have been speaking of the meaning of contraries when suddenly an illuminating example presents itself to him: ". . . see how the brook," he remarks to his wife,

> In that white wave runs counter to itself.
> It is from that in water we were from
> Long, long before we were from any creature.
> Here we, in our impatience of the steps,
> Get back to the beginning of beginnings,
> The stream of everything that runs away
> . . . .

The universal cataract of death
That spends to nothingness—and unresisted,
Save by some strange resistance in itself,
Not just a swerving, but a throwing back,
As if regret were in it and were sacred.
It has this throwing backward on itself
So that the fall of most of it is always
Raising a little, sending up a little.
. . . .
It is this backward motion toward the source,
Against the stream, that most we see ourselves in,
The tribute of the current to the source.
It is from this in nature we are from.
It is most us.

Gatsby's abundant store of wonder, with its reflexive capacity to generate and sustain such marvelously radiant, if also deeply flawed, visions *is* "a throwing back,/ As if regret were in it and were sacred." So too, I would have to say, is Nick's whole narrative attempt to understand its meaning. Taken together, then, Nick's and Gatsby's "backward motion toward the source,/ Against the stream" constitute Fitzgerald's "tribute of the current to the source." And thus we say at the close of the novel, when we finally put the book down and begin to let it have its way with us:

It is from this in nature we are from.
It is most us.

Notes

1. Certain passages in this and the following paragraph are drawn from my "Reflections on My Ideal Critic," *Criterion* 2 (Spring 1972), 18–22.

2. Leslie Fiedler, *Love and Death in the American Novel* (New York: Criterion, 1960), p, xiv.

3. Erich Heller, *The Disinherited Mind: Essays in Modern German Literature and Thought* (Cleveland: World [Meridian Books], 1959), p. ix.

4. T. S. Eliot as quoted by F. O. Matthiessen, *The Achievement of T. S. Eliot* (New York: Oxford, 1935), p. 6.

5. The phrase is Emerson's, which Richard Poirier uses as the title of his fine *A World Elsewhere: The Place of Style in American Literature* (New York: Oxford, 1966).

6. In this there is, to be sure, a marked parallel between Gatsby and all those other devotees and avatars of something like an American religion of wonder—Emerson, Thoreau, Whitman, Twain, a certain side of James, Gertrude Stein, Sherwood Anderson, Hemingway, Salinger, and Walker Percy—whose idealization of an unencumbered simplicity of response Tony Tanner discusses in his *The Reign of Wonder: Naïveté and Reality in American Literature* (Cambridge University Press, 1965). But where Tanner is interested in wonder chiefly as a way of seeing, as "the cultivation of a naïve eye," I am more interested, as I think Fitzgerald was as well, in wonder as a mode of being, as something intrinsic to the very nature of life itself.

7. For this and several other insights in this paper, I am indebted to Marius Bewley's excellent chapter on the novel entitled "Scott Fitzgerald and the Collapse of the American Dream" in his *The Eccentric Design: Form in the Classic American Novel* (New York: Columbia, 1963), pp. 159–87.

8. Howard Mumford Jones, *O Strange New World* (New York: Viking, 1964), p. 41.

9. See, in particular, Bewley, pp. 283–85.

10. *Ibid.*, p. 284.

11. F. O. Mathiessen, *American Renaissance: Art and Expression in the Age of Emerson and Whitman* (New York: Oxford, 1941), p. 459. The reference is to Captain Ahab's descendants.

12. See Perry Miller, "Benjamin Franklin—Jonathan Edwards," in *Major Writers of America*, I, ed. Perry Miller (New York: Harcourt, Brace and World, 1962), p. 96.

13. I am here paraphrasing an idea expressed in Lionel Trilling's essay "Anna Karenina," reprinted in his *The Opposing Self* (New York: Viking [Compass Books], 1959), p. 75.

14. R. W. B. Lewis, *Trials of the Word: Essays in American Literature and the Humanistic Condition* (New Haven: Yale, 1965), p. vii.

Fitzgerald's *Gatsby:*
The World as Ash Heap   James E. Miller, Jr.*

It was about twenty-five years ago that I spent my days and nights writing a doctoral dissertation at the University of Chicago on F. Scott Fitzgerald. It is hard to remember that in those distant days, in the late 1940's, there wasn't much of a bibliography on Fitzgerald to read. I was working on his fictional craft, and there wasn't very much on fictional technique to digest either (the "new criticism" stuck pretty much to poetry). I spent a lot of time going through magazine files in Chicago and newspaper files in Minnesota. There were no paperback reprints, and even some of the hardcover editions were missing from the library. I picked up original editions in small second-hand bookstores in Chicago for around a dollar each, including (as it turned out) a first edition of *The Great Gatsby.*

I published my dissertation some years later (1957), and then revised and added to it slightly to make *F. Scott Fitzgerald: His Art and His Technique* (1964). In the meantime, articles and books on Fitzgerald poured forth in rich abundance, his work became widely read even in high school, and Fitzgerald was firmly lodged with Hemingway and Faulkner as one of the three "great" writers of the 1920's—and some bold critics today see even more in Fitzgerald than in Hemingway.

Fitzgerald now appears to be central, somehow, however vaguely,

*Reprinted from *The Twenties: Fiction, Poetry, Drama* (Deland, Fla.: Everett/ Edwards, 1975), pp. 181–202, by permission of the publisher.

to American self-conception (he has, perhaps, replaced Hemingway in this role), and *The Great Gatsby* appears to be central to Fitzgerald's meaning and significance. My work on Fitzgerald's *Gatsby* a quarter of a century ago was on craft, on technique, on art. It is time that I had my say on the book's meaning, its themes, its moral implications.

I
"the deeper psychology"

In a famous letter to Fitzgerald, T. S. Eliot wrote of *The Great Gatsby*: "In fact it seems to me to be the first step that American fiction has taken since Henry James. . . ." This statement must have seemed, at one time, a forgivable exaggeration, but by now serious critics begin to wonder whether it is indeed true. And if true, what it means. Unfortunately, Eliot never got around to explaining his meaning.

The more we stare at Eliot's letter, the more it seems to sound like another famous letter in American literature, Emerson to the unknown Whitman in 1855, saying: "I greet you at the beginning of a great career." Eliot said that he had read *The Great Gatsby* three times, and he added: ". . . it has interested and excited me more than any new novel I have seen, either English or American, for a number of years." It is possible that it has taken us as long (in the case of Fitzgerald) as it did Whitman's readers to catch up with that writer's first distinguished critic.

When Eliot wrote, his masterpiece, *The Waste Land*, lay three years behind him, and it is possible that he saw in *The Great Gatsby* a reflection of some of the kinds of images of the horror of modern life that he himself had given currency in his poem. And a review of the "waste land" images of *Gatsby* is in order. But it is worth dwelling briefly first on Eliot's invocation of the name of Henry James. F. Scott Fitzgerald and James? Who besides Eliot could link them so casually?

Eliot might have had in mind Fitzgerald's craft, but it is more likely that he was thinking of something in addition and beyond. And Eliot's 1918 essay on James, written for the special memorial issue of *The Little Review*, might provide some clues. It is in that famous essay that Eliot paid his notorious compliment to James: "He had a mind so fine that no idea could violate it." Eliot did, of course, make his meaning about "idea" clear by noting the universal tendency that destroyed art: ". . . instead of thinking with our feelings . . . we corrupt our feelings with ideas; we produce the political, the emotional idea, evading sensation and thought." James, Eliot contended, maintained a "viewpoint untouched by the parasite idea. He is the most intelligent man of his generation."

In a later part of his essay, Eliot linked James with Hawthorne, quoting James's compliment paid his compatriot in his book on the New

Englander: ". . . the fine thing in Hawthorne is that he cared for the deeper psychology." This "deeper psychology" (missing, says Eliot, in English contemporaries of the American writer such as Dickens and Thackeray) was central to the achievement of both James and Hawthorne: "The point is that Hawthorne . . . did grasp character through the relation of two or more persons to each other; and this is what no one else, except James, has done. Furthermore, he does establish, as James establishes, a solid atmosphere, and he does, in his quaint way, get New England, as James gets a larger part of America, and as none of their respective contemporaries get anything above a village or two, or a jungle." (It should be parenthetically noted that among the James titles that Eliot lists for his examples, perhaps the most relevant in a discussion of F. Scott Fitzgerald are *Daisy Miller* and *The American,* the one work a classic portrait of the uninhibited American girl, the other a portrait of a rich American entrepeneur.)

Clearly Eliot's hostility to "idea" in fiction (or art) does not hinder his appreciation for Hawthorne's "getting" New England and for James's "getting" America. It might be difficult to say just what the "solid atmosphere" is that enables these novelists to "get" the places they "get," but obviously such "getting" makes, in Eliot's view, for major achievement in fiction. And it is tempting to see Eliot's analysis thus: that, as James represented a step (or perhaps several steps) beyond Hawthorne, so Fitzgerald represents a step beyond James (or through him) in his avoidance of contamination of "idea," and his ability to "get" not only America but the modern age: that same modern age that Eliot "got" so brilliantly in *The Waste Land.*

It takes only a casual acquaintance with Eliot's work to know that his conception of James's term, "the deeper psychology," could not have implied protracted and direct psychological analysis by a novelist, nor could it have had reference to Freud and his followers. James used the term in a discussion, mostly unfavorable, of Hawthorne's tendency toward allegory (in his 1879 book on Hawthorne): in spite of this tendency, the "fine thing" about Hawthorne was that he cared for the "deeper psychology." Both James and Eliot, then, must hold in common the view that the "deeper psychology" is that which is revealed by the novelist through dramatized relationships among people and through the use of powerfully charged concrete images. In short, Eliot must have seen (as in the passage above) in the achieved "deeper psychology" of Hawthorne and particularly James something in the nature of a successfully realized "objective correlative"—a concept which he was shortly to elaborate in his essay on "Hamlet and His Problems" (1919).

We might translate Eliot's praise of *Gatsby* into a paraphrase of Eliot on James: *The Great Gatsby* is a book that has not been "violated" by an idea, but is one of the most "intelligent" books of Fitzgerald's generation. It "gets" America and the modern age, not through direct proclamation of a set of ideas (as in Sinclair Lewis, for example), but through dramatization of Gatsby's pursuit of Daisy, through dramatic presentation of a number of other intricately related characters (Tom, Nick, Jordan, Wolfsheim, Owl Eyes, Gatsby's father), and through a sequence of powerful, pervasive, and devastating images that force the reader to "think with his feelings" (as does the reader of *The Waste Land*). Thus without writing allegory, Fitzgerald has provided a commentary on his country, his time, and the contemporary era through his intuitive understanding of the "deeper psychology." And Fitzgerald's achievement is both a triumph of technique and a triumph of meaning or theme.

With the recent publication of the original version of *The Waste Land*, we are beginning to understand how stubbornly personal in its origins was that most impersonal poem of the twentieth century. We have long known that *Gatsby* also grew out of personal agonies of the spirit. Both poem and novel clearly transcended the personal not by ignoring it but by drawing on the instinctive wisdom it bestowed, and, through the "deeper psychology," discovering the universal malaise in the particular "sickness," the common darkness in the individual gloom.

Let us turn briefly to this "deeper psychology" (as defined above) in both Eliot and Fitzgerald. In Part II of *The Waste Land*, "A Game of Chess," we find what is in effect the juxtaposition of two dramatic scenes of sexual intrigue or malaise or conflict. The first scene is one of meaningless elegance and profound boredom, shot through with the echoing question—"What shall I do now? What shall I do?" and concluding,

> The hot water at ten.
> And if it rains, a closed car at four.
> And we shall play a game of chess,
> Pressing lidless eyes and waiting for a knock upon the door.

The next scene shifts to a lower class pub and tunes in on a conversation about Lil and her husband Albert—he recently "demobbed" and set on "a good time," she spending his money not on her teeth but on abortion pills (she has five children already, "and nearly died of young George"):

> The chemist said it would be all right, but I've never been the same.
> You *are* a proper fool, I said.
> Well, if Albert won't leave you alone, there it is, I said,
> What you get married for if you don't want children?

Several generations of Eliot interpreters have pointed out that these ingeniously juxtaposed scenes not only ring true in detail, idiom, rhythm, but they also suggest much about the sterility, aridity, vacuity of modern life: sexual relationships have been diminished, devitalized, debased, and thus life at its vital center has dwindled into meaninglessness and banality.

The first two chapters of *The Great Gatsby* similarly juxtapose two separate but intricately interrelated worlds, the rich and baroque world of the East Egg mansion of the Buchanans and the mean and grotesque world of the Myrtle Wilson—Tom Buchanan trysting apartment in New York. When Nick visits the Buchanans shortly after the novel opens, he walks in on a scene as filled with boredom and meaninglessness as that portrayed by Eliot described above:

> The only completely stationary object in the room was an enormous couch on which two young women [Daisy and Jordan] were buoyed up as though upon an anchored balloon. They were both in white, and their dresses were rippling and fluttering as if they had just been blown back in after a short flight around the house. I must have stood for a few moments listening to the whip and snap of the curtains and the groan of a picture on the wall. Then there was a boom as Tom Buchanan shut the rear windows and the caught wind died out about the room, and the curtains and the rugs and the two young women ballooned slowly to the floor. (p. 8)

The slow motion of the scene, together with super-sophisticated conversation about nothing at all and the suggestion of sexual intrigue in Tom's mysterious telephone conversations, reveal a life lived on meaningless and purposeless levels and surfaces in which sex is no more than a "game of chess."

In the chapter that immediately follows, we find ourselves in the apartment rendezvous of Tom and Myrtle:

> The apartment was on the top floor—a small living-room, a small dining-room, a small bedroom, and a bath. The living-room was crowded to the doors with a set of tapestried furniture entirely too large for it, so that to move about was to stumble continually over scenes of ladies swinging in the gardens of Versailles. The only picture was an over-enlarged photograph, apparently a hen sitting on a blurred rock. Looked at from a distance, however, the hen resolved itself into a bonnet, and the countenance of a stout old lady beamed down into the room. (p. 29)

In the drunken brawl that ensues, the conversation is as meaningless, and as revealing, as that in Eliot's pub scene: "I almost married a little kike who'd been after me for years. I knew he was below me. Everybody kept saying to me: 'Lucille, that man's 'way below you!' But if I hadn't met Chester, he'd of got me sure." (This from Mrs. McKee.) The scene concludes with Tom breaking Myrtle's nose for daring to mention his wife's name. Meaningless sex and meaningless conversation resolve into meaningless violence, in a life as empty and shallow and sterile as any described in *The Waste Land.*

II
"night scene by El Greco"

If my conjectures are right about Eliot's conception of "the deeper psychology," it involves not only characters but images, particularly as they might be assembled to "get" a place and time. In his own poem, *The Waste Land,* we encounter a great collage or assemblage of images only subterraneously connected but which are so powerful and so intricately orchestrated as to haunt the imagination for long after the encounter. Eliot's mind, too is so fine that it cannot be violated by an idea, but he thinks powerfully with his feelings and that means, surely, that he "thinks" in images and compels his readers to do likewise. And in *The Waste Land,* those images are most frequently of death—

> Unreal City,
> Under the brown fog of a winter dawn,
> A crowd flowed over London Bridge, so many,
> I had not thought death had undone so many.

The most horrible death in *The Waste Land* is, like that in these lines, a living death.

In a similar way, but without the concentration of poetry (though often with its ingenuity of language), *The Great Gatsby* progresses by images. At the opening of Chapter II, Fitzgerald reveals what might be called the controlling image of the book, the first of a series of subtly interrelated images of death in life, life in death:

> About half way between West Egg and New York the motor road hastily joins the railroad and runs beside it for a quarter of a mile, so as to shrink away from a certain desolate area of land. This is a valley of ashes—a fantastic farm where ashes grow like wheat into ridges and hills and grotesque gardens; where ashes take the forms of houses and chimneys and rising smoke and, finally, with a transcendent effort, of men who move dimly and already crumbling through the powdery air. Occasionally a line of gray cars crawls along an invisible track, gives out a ghastly creak, and comes to rest, and immediately the ash-gray men swarm up with leaden spades and stir up an impenetrable cloud, which screens their obscure operations from your sight. (p. 23)

The reader may hear himself murmur, as he reads, "I had not thought death had undone so many." Fitzgerald's waste land scene is clearly a scene of a living hell, an assemblage of "grotesque gardens" that parody in ashes the vital world of growing things; and it is peopled by living dead men who crumble away even as they rehearse their pointless activities, swallowed finally from view by the clouds of ash-dust raised by their meaningless movement. Over this bizarre scene stare the gigantic eyes of Dr. T. J. Eckleburg, the fading sign of a long-forgotten oculist. Those weather-dimmed eyes, as they "brood on over the solemn dumping ground," will reappear in the novel, coming to haunt it and the reader: the world as ash heap, presided over by the vacant stare of a billboard deity.

Though confined geographically to the area near the Wilson garage, the valley of ashes spreads like a contagious fungus psychically through all the novel, leaving in its wake a trail of images of death. They appear sometimes only on the periphery of vision, as on the drive to New York (Nick with Gatsby): "A dead man passed us in a hearse heaped with blooms, followed by two carriages with drawn blinds, and by more cheerful carriages for friends. The friends looked out at us with the tragic eyes and short upper lips of southeastern Europe, and I was glad that the sight of Gatsby's splendid car was included in their somber holiday" (p. 69). The hearse and its contents may serve as an omen for Gatsby's car, which in spite of its ministering so spectacularly to all the comforts of life (". . . bright with nickel, swollen here and there in its monstrous length with triumphant hat-boxes and supper-boxes and tool-boxes . . . terraced with a labyrinth of wind-shields that mirrored a dozen suns" [p. 64]) becomes the novel's chief vehicle of death, leading directly to Myrtle's. Her death, within easy view of the valley of ashes, is as grotesque and meaningless as her life, ripping asunder the body that was the repository of her cheap successes and minor ambitions: ". . . when they had torn open her shirtwaist, still damp with perspiration, they saw her left breast was swinging loose like a flap, and there was no need to listen for the heart beneath. The mouth was wide open and ripped at the corners, as though she had choked a little in giving up the tremendous vitality she had stored so long" (p. 138).

Gatsby's gorgeous cream-colored car is also the indirect cause of his own death, as it is the deep imprint of the fantastic car on his excited brain that enables Wilson (through Tom Buchanan) to track Gatsby down and to shoot him (erroneously, of course) for killing Myrtle. At this critical moment, Gatsby has gone to his pool for a swim, and Nick speculates that for Gatsby it might have been a moment of awareness—awareness that he had lost Daisy to Tom, and that he had lived "too long with a single dream." As Nick imaginatively recreates the scene, Gatsby is touched with terror at the discovery that the world is not a garden of delights but something of an ash-heap: "He must have looked up at an unfamiliar sky through frightening leaves and shivered as he found what a grotesque thing a rose is and how raw the sunlight was upon the scarcely created grass. A new world, material without being real, where poor ghosts, breathing dreams like air, drifted fortuitously about . . . like that ashen, fantastic figure gliding toward

him through the amorphous trees" (p. 162). *Ashen.* By now the signal
is unmistakable. Though driven by a dream of splendid life, Gatsby
plays out his role (like the others) on the dumping ground of ashes.
But in contrast with the violence of Myrtle's death, Gatsby's seems
hardly noticeable as his body floats silently on the swimming pool surface:

> There was a faint, barely perceptible movement of the water as
> the fresh flow from one end urged its way toward the drain at the
> other. With little ripples that were hardly the shadows of waves, the
> laden mattress moved irregularly down the pool. A small gust of
> wind that scarcely corrugated the surface was enough to disturb its
> accidental course with its accidental burden. The touch of a cluster
> of leaves revolved it slowly, tracing, like the leg of transit, a thin
> circle in the water. (pp. 162–63)

It is surely the vacuous eyes of Dr. T. J. Eckleburg with their uncom-
prehending and meaningless stare that preside over this scene of the
pneumatic mattress floating aimlessly on "its *accidental* course with its
accidental burden." In a world become ash-heap, one's fate has no
relevance to one's life: *accident* rules supreme.

As the valley of ashes is introduced early in the novel to become
a kind of pervasive presence, gradually becoming the psychic setting
for all the novel's action, so "the night scene by El Greco" in the last
chapter tends to take over the reader's memory of the novel and to
distort the action into a kind of surrealist dream. In trying to sum up,
finally, his inexplicable feelings about the East, Nick reports the way
it appears in his "more fantastic dreams": "I see it as a night scene by
El Greco: a hundred houses, at once conventional and grotesque, crouching under a sullen overhanding sky and a lustreless moon. In the foreground four solemn men in dress suits are walking along the sidewalk
with a stretcher on which lies a drunken woman in a white evening
dress. Her hand, which dangles over the side, sparkles cold with jewels.
Gravely the men turn in at a house—the wrong house. But no one knows
the woman's name, and no one cares" (p. 178). The "day scene" of
The Great Gatsby is surely the valley of ashes, and its night scene is this
El Greco dreamscape, with its meticulously dressed characters perform-
ing meaningless actions in a meaningless world. But there is, perhaps,
more connection between these two powerful images than is explicitly
stated. The night scene by El Greco seems to be the dark underside
of the valley of ashes, the night of its day, the nightmare of its reality.
The one posits the other. And there seems to be a continuity in the
gigantic, vacant oculist's eyes of the valley of ashes and the "sullen
overhanging sky and . . . lustreless moon" of the El Greco night scene.
The worlds merge and meld into each other. And in that world, if one
looks over his shoulder, he might well notice a scene out of *The Waste
Land*, Part V:

A woman drew her long black hair out tight
And fiddled whisper music on those strings
And bats and baby faces in the violet light
Whistled, and beat their wings
And crawled head downward down a blackened wall. . . .

III
"looking for a business gonnegtion"

Although *The Great Gatsby* conveys much of its meaning obliquely through its imagery, it still is filled with what Henry James called "solidity of specification" and what T. S. Eliot named "a solid atmosphere." Although *The Great Gatsby* is much more than a book about the 1920's, it remains solidly based in the era and place that gave it birth. But it is not only based there: it also provides, in some sense, a commentary on the times.

The 1920's saw the enshrinement of business as the religion of America, and at the same time saw some of the most pervasive business and governmental corruption the country had ever experienced. One president gave the country the Teapot Dome scandal, a rip-off of oil resources to stagger the imagination; another president proclaimed that "the business of America is business." The decade opened with a scandal of the "fixing" and "wheeling-dealing" that will never be wholly unravelled. It was the era of Al Capone in bootlegged booze and Harry Sinclair in Teapot Dome oil lands. For the first time in history, members of the presidential cabinet were jailed for bribery. With such national heroes for models, what more can a country ask for?

Fitzgerald's novel is a more powerful embodiment of the spirit of the times than the collected works of Sinclair Lewis, perhaps because Fitzgerald *dramatized* while Lewis *stated*. The corruption of the 1920's saturates *The Great Gatsby*. Gatsby's "greatness" is constructed in part on illegal activities that are never fully and clearly defined—bootlegging in a string of drug stores? the handling of bonds from governmental bribes? big-time gambling and gangster war-fare? No matter. Our imagination improves on the withheld reality (as in James's *Turn of the Screw* and *The Ambassadors*). Even the narrator Nick Carraway is infected with the "business ethic" of the time as he pursues his career as a bond salesman and confesses: "I bought a dozen volumes on banking and credit and investment securities, and they stood on my shelf in red and gold like new money from the mint, promising to unfold the shining secrets that only Midas and Morgan and Maecenas knew" (p. 4).

Tom Buchanan comes from the world of established wealth, which, though contemptuous of the blatant kinds of corruption represented by Gatsby and his associates, itself indulges quietly and discreetly in bribery, blackmail, and manipulation (preferably legal) to maintain and consolidate its power. It is a world that has lines into the more obviously corrupt world, as witness Tom's friend Walter Chase, a one-time associate of Gatsby, who is willing to spy on Gatsby for Tom (and no doubt for a price). In many ways Tom Buchanan is the most sinister character in *The Great Gatsby*, as he seems to typify the American business man (man of power) who remains the perpetual adolescent intellectually: "Tom would drift on forever seeking, a little wistfully, for the dramatic turbulence of some irrecoverable football game." "Something was making him nibble at the edge of stale ideas as if his sturdy physical egotism no longer nourished his peremptory heart." Tom is presented as circling around an idea that might provide the means for the application of his brute strength and financial power—racial suppression: "Civilization's going to pieces . . . I've gotten to be a terrible pessimist about things. Have you read 'The Rise of the Colored Empires' by this man Goddard? . . . The idea is if we don't look out the white race will be — will be utterly submerged. It's all scientific stuff; it's been proved" (pp. 6, 21, 13–14).

If Tom Buchanan appears sinister in all his respectability, Jordan Baker appears pathetic in her petty cheating at golf. But her corruption cannot be dismissed as minor, as it suggests the contagiousness of the 1920's disease (the disease is not, of course, confined to the 1920's, but it reached epidemic levels in that age). In a few swift strokes, Fitzgerald through Nick reveals her character and her world: "When we were on a house-party together up in Warwick, she left a borrowed car out in the rain with the top down, and then lied about it—and suddenly I remembered the story about her that had eluded me that night at Daisy's. At her first big golf tournament there was a row that nearly reached the newspapers—a suggestion that she had moved her ball from a bad lie in the semifinal round. The thing approached the proportions of a scandal—then died away. A caddy retracted his statement, and the only other witness admitted that he might have been mistaken" (p. 58). It is not surprising that, given her allies in the world of the rich, the unpleasant incident would be "fixed." But the point revealed in the novel is that however easily a cheating episode can be hushed-up, a debased spirit cannot so quickly be mended or fixed. Jordan Baker remains what she is, a product of the pervasive corruption of the period: she will cheat her way through life.

Meyer Wolfsheim is the most clear-cut figure of 1920's gangsterdom. He lurks in the shadows behind Gatsby throughout, and when he emerges briefly in the restaurant scene in New York to have lunch with Gatsby and Nick, we glimpse something of his career in his short and sweet tale of the "night they shot Rosy Rosenthal." It was at "the old metropole": "It was six of us at the table, and Rosy had eat and drunk a lot all evening. When it was almost morning the waiter came up to him with a funny look and says somebody wants to speak to him outside."

Over the protest of his friends, Rosy "went out on the sidewalk, and they shot him three times in his full belly and drove away." It is at his point that Wolfsheim turns to Nick and says, "I understand you're looking for a business gonnegtion." Later, Gatsby tells Nick: "Meyer Wolfsheim? . . . he's a gambler. . . . He's the man who fixed the World's Series back in 1919" (pp. 70–71, 74).

Although the foreground of *The Great Gatsby* is largely filled with the super-sophisticated life of the rich and pleasure-bound figures of the jazz age, the "roaring twenties," not far in the background are the Rosy Rosenthals, the Meyer Wolfsheims, the Walter Chases, in violent pursuit of money and the good, easy life. The two worlds share in common the universal desire for the right "business gonnegtion," and the reader may be sure that at the edges, where the two worlds meet in the shadows, such "gonnegtions" are negotiated and consummated continually.

IV
"a vast, vulgar, and meretricious beauty"

Gatsby's own "corrupted innocence" lies at the heart of the meaning of the novel. And although he is quite obviously a figure of the 1920's, he is also something more. Although *The Great Gatsby* is deeply rooted in its time, it is considerably more than a revelation of life in the jazz age. It transcends its time to reveal something about America, American character, and the American dream. Tom Buchanan and the others exploit the American "business ethic" (or "gangster ethic") for their own sordid advantage. But Gatsby is as much victim as exploiter. From the moment that we (with Nick) first set eyes on him, we sense that he is vulnerable in his innocence in some way that all the others are not. He is standing outside in the dark night, looking over the waters from West Egg to East Egg: ". . . he stretched out his arms toward the dark water in a curious way, and, far as I was from him, I could have sworn he was trembling. Involuntarily I glanced seaward– and distinguished nothing except a single green light, minute and far-away, that might have been the end of a dock. When I looked once more for Gatsby he had vanished, and I was alone again in the unquiet darkness" (p. 22).

Trembling? Gatsby is not the only character capable of *trembling* in the "unquiet darkness" of the novel, but surely he is the only character in pursuit of something transcendent and worthy of his own submission. And it is his tragedy that his vision of transcendence comes to focus on an object that is enchanting on the surface, rotten at the core.

To trace the origins of Gatsby's dream means beginning near the end of the novel and zig-zagging back and forth in order to piece together the broken pieces of his life. For example, it is only in the last chapter that we encounter (through his father come East for the funeral) Gatsby as a boy. And in that midwestern boyhood we discover the roots of Gatsby's transcendent vision. Gatsby's father shows Nick a tattered copy of an old *Hopalong Cassidy* book, and there on the flyleaf are the resolutions that the boy James Gatz made for his self-improvement and "getting ahead." They include such touching items as, "Practice elocution, poise and how to attain it . . . 5.00–6.00 p.m." and "Read one improving book or magazine per week" (p. 174). This schedule and list of "General Resolves" look as though they have been copied from the pages of Benjamin Franklin's *Autobiography* They constitute, of course, but ˙one of the many suggestions throughout the novel that Gatsby's dream is rooted deeply in the American dream, here manifested in its materialistic bias as it conjures up visions of crafty ånd thrifty Benjamin Franklin and his solemn advice on the "Way to Wealth."

From Gatsby's boyhood we must jump to his young manhood (and Chapter VII) for our next glimpse of the development of the dream. We learn only the bare outline of his life on Dan Cody's yacht, encountered on Lake Superior. It was at this time that Gatsby began the remaking of himself, beginning with the change of name from James Gatz to Jay Gatsby: "The truth was that Jay Gatsby of West Egg, Long Island, sprang from his Platonic conception of himself. He was a son of God—a phrase which, if it means anything, means just that—and he must be about his Father's business, the service of a vast, vulgar, and meretricious beauty. So he invented just the sort of Jay Gatsby that a seventeen-year-old boy would be likely to invent, and to this conception he was faithful to the end" (p. 99). Thus, even before the encounter with Daisy, the dream appears unworthy of the dedication of the dreamer, and curiously at odds with his astonishing innocence. The adventure on the Cody yacht concludes with Gatsby as victim (cheated of the money left him by his rich patron).

The next transformation in Gatsby takes place on his initial encounter, as a young officer in the army, with Daisy Fay in Louisville, and for this event we have only fragmentary accounts in scattered chapters. But from these it is clear that the vague, inchoate dream alights on Daisy, and romantically transfigures her into a creature of Gatsby's imagination: "He knew that when he kissed this girl, and forever wed his unutterable visions to her perishable breath, his mind would never romp again like the mind of God. So he waited, listening for a moment longer to the tuning-fork that had been struck upon a star. Then he kissed her. At his lips' touch she blossomed for him like a flower and the incarnation was complete" (p. 112). Whatever the "incarnation" is, we can be sure that it is not the real but a transcendent Daisy commensurate with the energy and compatible with the innocence of the dream creating her. Something of the nature of this transfigured Daisy is suggested in another passage (in Chapter VIII): Gatsby "had intended, probably, to take what he could and go—but now he found that he had committed himself to the following of a grail" (p. 149).

Gatsby's re-encounter with Daisy is, of course, the action represented in the foreground of the novel as constructed, but the fate of Gatsby's dream is not so fully delineated. We must speculate with Nick as to Gatsby's feelings and insights: "There must have been moments even that afternoon [their first rendezvous after five years] when Daisy tumbled short of his [Gatsby's] dreams—not through her own fault, but because of the colossal vitality of his illusion. It had gone beyond her, beyond everything. He had thrown himself into it with a creative passion, adding to it all the time, decking it out with every bright feather that drifted his way. No amount of fire or freshness can challenge what a man will store up in his ghostly heart" (p. 97).

In the confrontation scene between Gatsby and Tom, in the New York hotel room, when Tom reveals to Daisy what his spies have learned about Gatsby's activities, Gatsby appears to lose control as he begins to talk excitedly and irrationally, "defending his name against accusations that had not been made." At this critical turning point, we are told that "only the dead dream fought on as the afternoon slipped away, trying to touch what was no longer tangible, struggling unhappily, undespairingly, toward that lost voice across the room" (p. 135). Was the dream dead or dying for Gatsby at this point? Although he plays out the role he has assigned himself in relation to Daisy, there are hints that he might have developed some self-awareness. But there is suggestion too that he preserved his illusion intact. When Nick leaves him standing outside the Buchanan house, after Daisy has killed Myrtle Wilson with Gatsby's car, and after we have just glimpsed (with Nick) the cosy, conspiratorial scene of Tom and Daisy at a kitchen table holding cold fried chicken and bottles of ale—Gatsby appears to be devoted to the "sacredness of the vigil." But does he sense, on some level of consciousness, what Nick tells us and we know to be true—that he is "watching over nothing"?

The complexity of Gatsby's illusion, and his own complicated feelings about it, are suggested in a number of astounding remarks that he drops in off-hand manner in casual conversation. For example, as Nick at one point (before the New York confrontation scene) is trying to find the right description for Daisy's voice, Gatsby says: "Her voice is full of money," and Nick is overwhelmed with the aptness of the metaphor. In another instance, after the confrontation scene, as Nick and Gatsby are discussing the relation of Tom and Daisy, Gatsby suddenly says: "In any case, . . . it was just personal." And Nick asks the reader: "What could you make of that, except to suspect some intensity in his conception of the affair that couldn't be measured?" (pp. 120, 152)

It is no doubt this immeasurable and indefinable "intensity" of Gatsby's dream that induces Nick to call out to him, on their last meeting (when Gatsby is still waiting for the call from Daisy that will never come): "You're worth the whole damn bunch put together." Nick adds: "I've always been glad I said that. It was the only compliment I ever gave him, because I disapproved of him from beginning to end. First he nodded politely, and then his face broke into that radiant and understanding smile . . ." And as Nick senses something of Gatsby's embryonic awareness, he remembers his first encounter with Gatsby at his big parties: "The lawn and drive had been crowded with the faces of those who guessed at his corruption—and he had stood on those steps, concealing his incorruptible dream as he waved them goodby" (pp. 154–55). At Gatsby's death, we must again speculate with Nick as to the extent of Gatsby's self-knowledge: "I have an idea that Gatsby himself didn't believe it [the call from Daisy] would come, and perhaps he no longer cared. If that was true he must have felt that he had lost the old warm world, paid a high price for living too long with a single dream" (p. 162). But whatever the extent of Gatsby's final insight, Nick's judgment remains clear from the moment it is presented on the second page of the novel: "No—Gatsby turned out all right at the end; it is what preyed on Gatsby, what foul dust floated in the wake of his dreams that temporarily closed out my interest in the abortive sorrows and short-winded elations of men."

How can it be that Gatsby, surrounded by so much corruption, can remain innocent? We know something of the sordidness of the sources of his fortune, and we witness the moral shallowness of Daisy, about whom he has spun the gossamer foundations of his fantastic and colossal dream. We cannot even be sure that he has, in the face of defeat, achieved that kind of self-knowledge that would render his fate genuinely tragic. We can only speculate, as Nick speculates, on what he has learned in his obsessive pursuit of so unworthy an object. But Nick's judgment is clear in Gatsby's defense, and after all is said—it is only Nick's Gatsby that we come to know in the novel. But even as Nick asserts Gatsby's worth above all the others, he is compelled to add that he "disapproved of him from beginning to end." It is the moral awareness that Nick achieves in the progress of the action of the novel that enables him, in spite of Gatsby's "corruption," to affirm that he came out all right in the end. His ambivalent moral judgment is not unlike that of Owl Eyes, the party guest who earlier was startled to find the books in Gatsby's library real. He is the only one of the multitudinous party-goers to attend Gatsby's funeral, and says the final word at the graveside: "The poor son-of-a-bitch." It is moral sympathy for a victim whose innocence transcended his corruption.

Whatever the extent of Gatsby's moral awakening, it could not have embraced the totality of vision that Nick has at the close of the novel. As Nick sits on Gatsby's beach, his imagination reaches back into history: ". . . as the moon rose higher the inessential houses began to melt away until gradually I became aware of the old island here that flowered once for Dutch sailors' eyes—a fresh, green breast of the new world. Its vanished trees, the trees that had made way for Gatsby's house, had once pandered in whispers to the last and greatest of all human dreams; for a transitory enchanted moment man must have held his breath in the presence of this continent, compelled into an aesthetic contemplation he neither understood nor desired, face to face for the last time in history with something commensurate to his capacity for wonder" (p. 182). From Benjamin Franklin's plan for moral improvement, which incidentally showed the way to wealth, all the way to the "greatest of all human dreams," whose fulfillment seemed to require destruction of the very wilderness which inspired it (the "vanished trees")—Gatsby was as much the victim of his American heritage as he was of Tom, Daisy, and George Wilson. His innocence was his persistence in the belief in the American dream as he carried it with him deep in his psyche, unaware that it contained the seeds of its—and his—destruction. He could "tremble" in the unquiet darkness as he gazed at the beckoning green light, just as the settlers must have been caught up in overwhelming "wonder" at the sight of the new continent. He and they could submit themselves to a vision that was, however distorted with materialistic bias, touched with the ideal or transcendent. The others, the "foul dust that floated in the wake of his dreams," were incapable of comprehending dream or vision: "they smashed up things and creatures and then retreated back into their money or their vast carelessness . . ." (pp. 2, 180).

V
"borne back ceaselessly into the past"

Although *The Great Gatsby* is deeply rooted in the 1920's, and at the same time appears to provide a commentary on American character and the American dream, it is still something more—something reaching out beyond its time and beyond its place. In short, the novel embodies and expresses the simple, basic human desire and yearning, universal in nature, to snatch something precious from the ceaseless flux and flow of days and years and preserve it outside the ravages of time. This is obviously a theme that is not confined to the 1920's or to America. Although it may not win the designation of "archetypal," it is hard to imagine a time when human beings did not feel it deeply.

The Great Gatsby is a novel relentlessly devoted to the present, set, as it is, in its total action in the summer of 1922. But it is a novel that is haunted by the past—Gatsby's and America's—and it is the past which reaches into and shapes the present. Gatsby himself embodies in a grotesque way the desire to transcend time. When Nick repeats to him a truism, "You can't repeat the past," he astonishingly replies: "Can't repeat the past? . . . Why of course you can!" (p. 111) To Gatsby time appears as submissive to his will as wealth or power: "He looked around him wildly, as if the past were lurking here in the shadow of his house, just out of reach of his hand." And he cries out: "I'm going to fix everything just the way it was before." Gatsby's desire is not peculiarly American, but his stupendous self-assurance that he can recreate the past may well derive from the dark underside of the American dream. But time will run out on Gatsby, as it has on the American dream—and as it does on all human dreams and desires and aspirations.

It is this theme, more feeling than statement, that is evoked by the lyric style of *The Great Gatsby*. Throughout the novel, Nick responds in a deeply personal way to the events he witnesses, translating them into feelings that lie so deep as to defy precision of language. For example, at the end of Chapter VI, after Gatsby has tried to explain Daisy's meaning for him and the absolute necessity of recovering that lost past, Nick muses:

> Through all he said, even through his appalling sentimentality, I was reminded of something- an elusive rhythm, a fragment of lost words, that I had heard somewhere a long time ago. For a moment a phrase tried to take shape in my mouth and my lips parted like a dumb man's, as though there was more struggling upon them than a wisp of startled air. But they made no sound, and what I had almost remembered was uncommunicable forever. (p. 112)

"An elusive rhythm, a fragment of lost words"—we feel with Nick a sense of loss of the past that cannot be articulated. This sense of loss becomes acute and central in the closing lines of the novel, as Nick meditates on Gatsby's abortive dream: "He had come a long way to this blue lawn, and his dream must have seemed so close that he could hardly fail to grasp it. He did not know that it was already behind him, somewhere back in that vast obscurity beyond the city, where the dark fields of the republic rolled on under the night." Nick has come to realize that Gatsby's dream was lost before it was even dreamed, as the American dream itself had been frittered away, squandered in the past. But Nick's last thoughts move away from Gatsby to himself—and to "us"—as he meditates on time, and present, past, and future: "Gatsby believed in the green light, the orgiastic future that year by year recedes before us. It eluded us then, but that's no matter—tomorrow we will run faster, stretch out our arms farther . . . And one fine morning—" Nick here breaks off, the vision intercepted before it is launched, and speaks his last words on Gatsby's, his, the American, the human predicament: "So we beat on, boats against the current, borne back ceaselessly into the past."

With these closing words we find that we ourselves have become participants in the novel's meaning, as the action has broadened out to include us all. It is impossible to respond to those final words without being throw back into one's own past, in painful memory of those momentous events of purely personal meaning that have slipped away to be lost forever. We are all Gatsbys yearning to recreate the past;

we are all Nick Carraways lyrically regretting the rush of time swiftly past our grasp. And as we close the book and look about us, touched by an "elusive rhythm, a fragment of lost words," we may feel something of the impulse of the protagonist at the end of *The Waste Land*— to gather fragments to shore up against our ruin.

Letters

Editor's Note: The brief assemblage of letters below serves several functions. The correspondence with Perkins begins to indicate some of the care and craft that Fitzgerald put into composition of the novel. Letters from other professionals—editor and novelist Roger Burlingame, Edmund Wilson, H. L. Mencken, critic Gilbert Seldes, Edith Wharton, John Peale Bishop (who qualified his admiration with specific critical comments), and T. S. Eliot—reflect the immediate positive response. Other laudatory comments written some years after the book's publication— including previously unpublished ones from Jean Cocteau, Marjorie Kinnan Rawlings, and humorist Corey Ford—foreshadow the eventual acceptance of *The Great Gatsby* as a great American novel. Finally, Fitzgerald's June 1940 letter to his daughter makes it clear that in the last months of his life he understood his particular talent and was determined to practice it, just as Seldes counseled him to do in his *Dial* review.

Letters from F. Scott Fitzgerald to Moran Tudury, Edmund Wilson, and Frances Scott Fitzgerald are reprinted by permission of Frances F. Smith; excerpts from *Dear Scott/Dear Max: The Fitzgerald-Perkins Correspondence*, edited by John Kuehl and Jackson R. Bryer, are reprinted with the permission of Charles Scribner's Sons, © 1971 Charles Scribner's Sons; letters from Roger Burlingame and Edith Wharton to F. Scott Fitzgerald are reprinted with the permission of A. Watkins, Inc.; letters from Edmund Wilson to F. Scott Fitzgerald and Hamilton Basso are reprinted with the permission of Farrar, Straus & Giroux, Inc.; a letter from H. L. Mencken to F. Scott Fitzgerald is reprinted with the permission of the Enoch Pratt Free Library in accordance with the terms of the Henry L. Mencken bequest; a letter from Gilbert Seldes to F. Scott Fitzgerald and Seldes's review of *The Great Gatsby* in the *Dial*, 79 (August 1925), 162–64, are reprinted with the permission of Timothy Seldes; a letter from John Peale Bishop to F. Scott Fitzgerald is reprinted with the permission of Jonathan Bishop, and a letter from T. S. Eliot to F. Scott Fitzgerald is reprinted by permission of Mrs. Valerie Eliot and Faber and Faber Ltd.

F. Scott Fitzgerald to Moran Tudury   11 April 1924

I am so anxious for people to see my new novel which is a new thinking out of the idea of illusion (an idea which I suppose will dominate my more serious stuff) much more mature and much more romantic than This Side of Paradise. The B & D was a better book than the first but it was a false lead . . . a concession to Mencken . . . The business of creating illusion is much more to my taste and my talent.

F. Scott Fitzgerald to Maxwell Perkins   27 October 1924

Under separate cover I'm sending you my third novel, *The Great Gatsby*. (I think that at last I've done something really my own, but how good "my own" is remains to be seen). . . .

The book is only a little over fifty thousand words long but I believe, as you know, that Whitney Darrow has the wrong psychology about prices (and about what class constitute the book-buying public now that the lowbrows go to the movies) and I'm anxious to charge two dollars for it and have it a *full-size book*.

Of course I want the binding to be absolutely uniform with my other books—the stamping too—and the jacket we discussed before. This time I don't want any signed blurbs on the jacket—not Mencken's or Lewis' or Howard's or anyone's. I'm tired of being the author of *This Side of Paradise* and I want to start over. . . .

After you've read the book, let me know what you think about the title. Naturally I won't get a night's sleep until I hear from you, but do tell me the absolute truth, *your first impression of the book*, and tell me anything that bothers you in it.

Maxwell Perkins to F. Scott Fitzgerald   20 November 1924

I think you have every kind of right to be proud of this book. It is an extraordinary book, suggestive of all sorts of thoughts and moods. You adopted exactly the right method of telling it, that of employing a narrator who is more of a spectator than an actor: this puts the reader upon a point of observation on a higher level than that on which the characters stand and at a distance that gives perspective. In no other way could your irony have been so immensely effective, nor the reader have been enabled so strongly to feel at times the strangeness of human circumstance in a vast heedless universe. In the eyes of Dr. Eckleburg various readers will see different significances; but their presence gives a superb touch to the whole thing: great unblinking eyes, expressionless, looking down upon the human scene. It's magnificent!

I could go on praising the book and speculating on its various elements, and meanings, but points of criticism are more important now. I think you are right in feeling a certain slight sagging in chapters six and seven, and I don't know how to suggest a remedy. I hardly doubt that you will find one and I am only writing to say that I think it does need something to hold up here to the pace set, and ensuing. I have only two actual criticisms:—

One is that among a set of characters marvelously palpable and vital —I would know Tom Buchanan if I met him on the street and would avoid him—Gatsby is somewhat vague. The reader's eyes can never quite focus upon him, his outlines are dim. Now everything about Gatsby is more or less a mystery i.e. more or less vague, and this may be somewhat of an artistic intention, but I think it is mistaken. Couldn't *he* be physically described as distinctly as the others, and couldn't you add one or two characteristics like the use of that phrase "old sport,"—not verbal, but physical ones, perhaps. I think that for some reason or other a reader - this was true of Mr. Scribner and of Louise—gets an idea that Gatsby is a much older man than he is, although you have the writer say that he is little older than himself. But this would be avoided if on his first appearance he was seen as vividly as Daisy and Tom are, for instance;—and I do not think your scheme would be impaired if you made him so.

The other point is also about Gatsby: his career must remain mysterious, of course. But in the end you make it pretty clear that his wealth came through his connection with Wolfsheim. You also suggest this much earlier. Now almost all readers numerically are going to be puzzled by his having all this wealth and are going to feel entitled to an explanation. To give a distinct and definite one would be, of course, utterly absurd. It did occur to me though, that you might here and there interpolate some phrases, and possibly incidents, little touches of various kinds, that would suggest that he was in some active way mysteriously engaged. You do have him called on the telephone, but couldn't he be seen once or twice consulting at his parties with people of some sort of mysterious significance, from the political, the gambling, the sporting world, or whatever it may be. I know I am floundering, but that fact may help you to see what I mean. The *total* lack of an explanation through so large a part of the story does seem to me a defect;—or not of an explanation, but of the suggestion of an explanation. I wish you were here so I could talk about it to you for then I know I could at least make you understand what I mean. What Gatsby did ought never to be definitely imparted, even if it could be. Whether he was an innocent tool in the hands of somebody else, or to what degree he was this, ought not to be explained. But if some sort of business activity of his were simply adumbrated, it would lend further probability to that part of the story.

There is one other point: in giving deliberately Gatsby's biography when he gives it to the narrator you do depart from the method of the narrative in some degree, for otherwise almost everything is told, and beautifully told, in the regular flow of it,—in the succession of events or in accompaniment with them. But you can't avoid the biography altogether. I thought you might find ways to let the truth of some of his claims like "Oxford" and his army career come out bit by bit in the course of actual narrative. I mention the point anyway for consideration in this interval before I send the proofs.

The general brilliant quality of the book makes me ashamed to make even these criticisms. The amount of meaning you get into a sentence, the dimensions and intensity of the impression you make a paragraph carry, are most extraordinary. The manuscript is full of phrases which make a scene blaze with life. If one enjoyed a rapid railroad journey I would compare the number and vividness of pictures your living words suggest, to the living scenes disclosed in that way. It seems in reading a much shorter book than it is, but it carries the mind through a series of experiences that one would think would require a book of three times its length.

The presentation of Tom, his place, Daisy and Jordan, and the unfolding of their characters is unequalled so far as I know. The description of the valley of ashes adjacent to the lovely country, the conversation and the action in Myrtle's apartment, the marvelous catalogue of those who came to Gatsby's house—these are such things as make a man famous. And all these things, the whole pathetic episode, you have given a place in time and space, for with the help of T. J. Eckleburg and by an occasional glance at the sky, or the sea, or the city, you have imparted a sort of sense of eternity. You once told me you were not a *natural* writer—my God! You have plainly mastered the craft, of course; but you needed far more than craftsmanship for this.

F. Scott Fitzgerald to Maxwell Perkins
circa 20 December 1924

With the aid you've given me I can make *Gatsby* perfect. The Chapter 7 (the hotel scene) will never quite be up to mark—I've worried about it too long and I can't quite place Daisy's reaction. But I can improve it a lot. It isn't imaginative energy that's lacking—it's because I'm automatically prevented from thinking it out over again *because I must get all those characters to New York* in order to have the catastrophe on the road going back, and I must have it pretty much that way. So there's no chance of bringing the freshness to it that a new free conception sometimes gives.

The rest is easy and I see my way so clear that I even see the mental quirks that queered it before. Strange to say, my notion of Gatsby's vagueness was O.K. What you. . . found wanting was that:

I myself didn't know what Gatsby looked like or was engaged in and you felt it. If I'd known and kept it from you you'd have been *too impressed with my knowledge to protest.* This is a complicated idea but I'm sure you'll understand. But I know now—and as a penalty for not having known first, in other words to make sure, I'm going to tell more.

It seems of almost mystical significance to me that you thought he was older—the man I had in mind, half-consciously, *was* older (a specific individual) and evidently, without so much as a definite word, I conveyed the fact . . .

My first instinct after your letter was to let him go and have Tom Buchanan dominate the book (I suppose he's the best character I've ever done—I think he and the brother in *Salt* and Hurstwood in *Sister Carrie* are the three best characters in American fiction in the last twenty years, perhaps and perhaps not) but Gatsby sticks in my heart. I had him for awhile, then lost him, and now I know I have him again. I'm sorry Myrtle is better than Daisy. Jordan of course was a great idea . . . but she fades out. It's Chapter VII that's the trouble with Daisy and it may hurt the book's popularity that it's a *man's book.*

Anyhow I think (for the first time since *The Vegetable* failed) that I'm a wonderful writer and it's your always wonderful letters that help me to go on believing in myself.

F. Scott Fitzgerald to Maxwell Perkins
circa 18 February 1925

After six weeks of uninterrupted work the proof is finished and the last of it goes to you this afternoon. On the whole it's been very successful labor.

(1) I've brought Gatsby to life.

(2) I've accounted for his money.

(3) I've fixed up the two weak chapters (VI and VII).

(4) I've improved his first party.

(5) I've broken up his long narrative in Chapter VIII.

This morning I wired you to *hold up the galley of Chapter X.* The correction—and God! it's important because in my other revision I made Gatsby look too mean—is enclosed herewith. Also some corrections for the page proof. . . .

Do tell me if all corrections have been received. I'm worried.

I hope you're setting publication date at first possible moment.

Maxwell Perkins to F. Scott Fitzgerald   24 February 1925

Those [changes] you have made do wonders for Gatsby,—in making him visible and palpable. You're right about the danger of meddling with the high spots—instinct is the best guide there. I'll have the proofs read twice . . . and shall allow no change unless it is certain the printer has blundered. I know the whole book so well that I could hardly decide wrongly. But I won't decide anything if there is ground for doubt.

Roger Burlingame to F. Scott Fitzgerald
March or April 1925

I can't help writing you how grand I think the Gatsby is; I've read it twice now and I'm going to read it again and I've got to like a book something terrible to read it 3 times.

Of course I liked The Beautiful & D. & I suppose, in a way, that is a more substantial novel, but nowhere have you ever touched the warmth and living quality of this Gatsby; or its beauty or its strange nostalgia or its amazing color.

In . . . "For Daisy was young and her artificial world was redolent . . . etc.," you have done something that I think no one will ever do better. That's so damn beautiful it hurts & makes you cry out with pain. The one after too, is good but nothing in the book or any where that I know is so adequate for that particular thing. It does so much. It gives in 11 lines that whole phase of her life, of anyone's, of everyone's life. It's tremendous.

I could go on for a long time quoting things that delight me. The beginning of Ch. II, for instance, & that gorgeous place where she cried into the shirts, & the night "when we hunted through the great rooms for cigarettes."

Someone said once that the thing that was common to all real works of art was a nostalgic quality, often indefinable, not specific. If that is so then The Great Gatsby is surely one because it makes me want to be back somewhere as much, I think as anything I've ever read.

Edmund Wilson to F. Scott Fitzgerald   11 April 1925

Your book came yesterday and I read it last night. It is undoubtedly in some ways the best thing you have done—the best planned, the best sustained, the best written. In fact, it amounts to a complete new departure in your work. The only bad feature of it is that the characters are mostly so unpleasant in themselves that the story becomes rather a bitter dose before one has finished with it. However, the fact that you are able to get away with it is the proof of its brilliance. It is full of all sorts of happy touches—in fact, all the touches are happy—there is not a hole in it anywhere. I congratulate you—you have succeeded here in doing most of the things that people have always scolded you for not doing. . . .

H. L. Mencken to F. Scott Fitzgerald   16 April 1925

"The Great Gatsby" fills me with pleasant sentiments. I think it is incomparably the best piece of work you have done. Evidences of careful workmanship are on every page. The thing is well managed, and has a fine surface. My one complaint is that the basic story is somewhat trivial— that it reduces itself, in the end, to a sort of anecdote. But God will forgive you for that.

F. Scott Fitzgerald to Edmund Wilson   Spring 1925

Thanks for your letter about the book. I was awfully happy that you liked it and that you approved of the design. The worst fault in it, I think is a BIG FAULT: I gave no account (and had no feeling about or knowledge of) the emotional relations between Gatsby and Daisy from the time of their reunion to the catastrophe. However, the lack is so astutely concealed by the retrospect of Gatsby's past and by blankets of excellent prose that no one has noticed it—tho everyone has felt the lack and called it by another name. Mencken said (in a most enthusiastic letter received today) that the only fault was that the central story was trivial and a sort of anecdote (that is because he has forgotten his admiration for Conrad and adjusted himself to the sprawling novel) and I felt that what he really missed was the lack of any emotional backbone at the very height of it.

Without making any invidious comparisons between Class A and Class C, if my novel is an anecdote so is *The Brothers Karamazov*. From one angle the latter could be reduced into a detective story. However, the letters from you and Mencken have compensated me for the fact that of all the reviews, even the most enthusiastic, not one had the slightest idea what the book was about and for the even more depressing fact that it was, in comparison with the others, a financial failure (after I'd turned down fifteen thousand for the serial rights!).

Gilbert Seldes to F. Scott Fitzgerald   26 May 1925

Of course you know that you have written a fine book; but it may be news to you that we know it too. Amanda and I are madly enthusiastic about it, and some of that has gone into a very severely analytical boost of the truly great Gatsby for The Dial. (It probably won't be out for months, but I am doing a little propaganda elsewhere.) It's so good, Scott; so satisfying, and so rich in stuff. And written; and by the Lord, composed; it has structure and direction and an internal activity.

I'm told it's going well, but the reviews, apart from Mencken and Bill Benet have made me sour. Van Wyck Brooks and Paul Rosenfeld told me they admire it; from Bunny [Wilson] you've no doubt heard;

and your admirer, and the best critic hereabouts (Mrs. Mary Colum) is doing it for the New Republic so you'll have some sort of a press. For God's sake Scott, if it doesn't go well, don't be persuaded not to go on with this, your real line of genius. I hope you're writing another already, and that it is as good.

I trust I suggest, in a way, my enthusiasm.

Edith Wharton to F. Scott Fitzgerald   8 June 1925

I have been wandering for the last weeks and found your novel—with its friendly dedication—awaiting me here on my arrival, a few days ago.

I am touched at your sending me a copy, for I feel that to your generation, which has taken such a flying leap into the future, I must represent the literary equivalent of tufted furniture & gas chandeliers. So you will understand that it is in a spirit of sincere deprecation that I shall venture, in a few days, to offer you in return the last product of my manufactory.

Meanwhile, let me say at once how much I like Gatsby, or rather His Book, & how great a leap I think you have taken this time—in advance upon your previous work. My present quarrel with you is only this: that to make Gatsby really Great, you ought to have given us his early career (not from the cradle—but from his visit to the yacht, if not before) instead of a short résumé of it. That would have situated him, & made his final tragedy a tragedy instead of a "fait divers" for the morning papers.

But you'll tell me that's the old way, & consequently not *your* way; & meanwhile, it's enough to make this reader happy to have met your *perfect* Jew & the limp Wilson, & assisted at that seedy orgy in the Buchanan flat, with the dazed puppy looking on. Every bit of that is masterly. . . .

John Peale Bishop to F. Scott Fitzgerald   9 June 1925

As for myself, I think that you have definitely in this book, as you never did in its predecessors, crossed the line which distinguishes the artist from whatever you like, but not-artist. It has all the old fire, the instinctive gift of the novelist, which Godknows you've always had but it has also, what you never before showed, a fine and rigorous control, a clear sense of planning and an execution quite up to the plan. In brief you have got rid of your worst enemy, your ungodly facility . . . I could go on showering compliments on you quite as fervently as those you have already received and are about to receive . . . but I also think that having come over the aforementioned line into the artist class you have got to be taken seriously and scrupulously to task for short-comings which before were pardonable enough.

In the first place, I object to the inaccuracy of a great deal of the writing. For instance, in the paragraph in which you introduce the two girls buoyed up by the sofa, the first impression is a stroke of genius, but as you go on, you in one phrase add and in the next detract from that impression . . . This may seem like an amateur advising a professional, and it is. For there are a number of things which you can do already which no amount of note-taking will teach you or another. But I still think that you would gain by a very strict consideration of the elements which go into a description, whether of things only seen or of things felt. Different as they are, both Joyce and James are superbly accurate writers. The one is true to a visual, the other a nervous experience. Your own experience of things outside your self still seems to me a bit blurred, whether considered as a thing felt or a thing seen. . . .

I feel this lack of complete realization also in the broader aspects of the book—in the character of Gatsby and in his relation to the girl. What you have got is all right as far as it goes, but it does not, to my mind, go far enough. I grant of course that Gatsby should remain a vague mysterious person to the end, but though he is seen through a mist, always, one should feel his solidity behind that mist. And it's because you don't entirely "get" him, that the violent end seems abrupt. Emotionally it is beautifully prepared for, but it does to me seem in action just a little "willed." Everything of Gatsby is specified, but it as though you saw him in patches instead of getting casual glimpses of what is after all a complete man. . . .

I think too that the book is too short. I remember what you said to me in Paris about the excessive length of modern novels, and guess that you deliberately imposed the present length on your book. I grant the virtues you have gained by this; the impression of complete control, of nothing that is not strictly necessary, of the ultimate concision possible to your tale. Still I think the book would have gained by a greater elaboration and a slower tempo in the early portions. . . .

But you have done wonders both as a writer and as a social critic. And you have, a thing after all, very few novelists succeed in doing, broken new ground. Gatsby is a new character in fiction, and, as everybody is now saying, a most familiar one in life. You have everything ahead of you; Gatsby definitely admits you to importance. For god's sake take your new place seriously. Scrutinize your own impressions, distrusting your facility which will continue to work anyhow as far as it is needful, and cultivate the acquaintance of writers who are both subtle and accurate, especially those who are different in temper from yourself. A little more subtlety, a little more accuracy, and you'll have every living American novelist, and most of the dead ones, wiped off the critic's slate.

T. S. Eliot to F. Scott Fitzgerald   31 December 1925

The Great Gatsby with your charming and overpowering inscription arrived the very morning that I was leaving in some haste for a sea voyage advised by my doctor. I therefore left it behind and only read it on my return a few days ago. I have, however, now read it three times. I am not in the least influenced by your remark about myself when I say that it has interested and excited me more than any new novel I have seen, either English or American, for a number of years.

When I have time I should like to write to you more fully and tell you exactly why it seems to me such a remarkable book. In fact it seems to me to be the first step that American fiction has taken since Henry James. . . .

Victor Llona to F. Scott Fitzgerald   9 December 1928

Editor's Note: Llona, who translated *The Great Gatsby* into French, quoted a letter he'd received from Jean Cocteau, as follows:

"Voulez-vous faire savoir à F. Scott Fitzgerald que son livre m'a permis de passer de heures très dures (je suis dans une clinique). C'est un livre céleste: chose la plus rare du monde."*

*"Would you let Fitzgerald know that his book enabled me to pass some very difficult hours (I was in a clinic)? It's a heavenly book, the rarest thing in the world."

Edmund Wilson to Hamilton Basso   9 May 1929

I was rereading *The Great Gatsby* last night, after I had been going through my page proofs, and thinking with depression how much better Scott Fitzgerald's prose and dramatic sense were than mine. If I'd only been able to give my book the vividness and excitement, and the technical accuracy, of his! Have you ever read *Gatsby*? I think it's one of the best novels that any American of his age has done. Of course, he'd had to pass through several immature and amateurish phases before he arrived at that one, and writing, like everything else, is partly a matter of expertness. . . .

Marjorie Kinnan Rawlings to F. Scott Fitzgerald
Mid-1930s

You were wise so young—I'm only beginning to know some of the things you must have been born, knowing.

The book resolves itself into the strongest feeling of a crystal globe, or one of the immense soapbubbles we achieved as children, if it could hold its shape and color without breaking. It is so beautiful, it is so clairvoyant, it is so heart-breaking.

Corey Ford to F. Scott Fitzgerald   7 March 1937

This is the first damned fan letter I've ever tried, but I've just reread "Gatsby" for the first time in five years, and if that isn't the most memorable novel of our generation, then the hell with writing one.

F. Scott Fitzgerald to Frances Scott Fitzgerald
12 June 1940

. . . What little I've accomplished has been by the most laborious and uphill work, and I wish now I'd *never* relaxed or looked back—but said at the end of *The Great Gatsby*: "I've found my line—from now on this comes first. This is my immediate duty—without this I am nothing." . . .

Review

Spring Flight
Gilbert Seldes*

There has never been any question of the talents of F. Scott Fitz-gerald; there has been, justifiably until the publication of *The Great Gatsby*, a grave question as to what he was going to do with his gifts. The question has been answered in one of the finest of contemporary novels. Fitzgerald has more than matured; he has mastered his talents and gone soaring in a beautiful flight, leaving behind him everything dubious and tricky in his earlier work, and leaving even farther behind all the men of his own generation and most of his elders.

In all justice, let it be said that the talents are still his. The book is even more interesting, superficially, than his others; it has an intense life, it must be read, the first time, breathlessly; it is vivid and glittering and entertaining. Scenes of incredible difficulty are rendered with what seems an effortless precision, crowds and conversation and action and retrospects—everything comes naturally and persuasively. The minor people and events are threads of colour and strength, holding the principal things together. The technical virtuosity is extraordinary.

All this was true of Fitzgerald's first two novels, and even of those deplorable short stories which one feared were going to ruin him. *The Great Gatsby* adds many things, and two above all: the novel is composed as an artistic structure, and it exposes, again for the first time, an interesting temperament. "The vast juvenile intrigue" of *This Side of Paradise* is just as good subject-matter as the intensely private intrigue of *The Great Gatsby*; but Fitzgerald racing over the country, jotting down whatever was current in college circles, is not nearly as significant as Fitzgerald regarding a tiny section of life and reporting it with irony and pity and a consuming passion. . . .

The book is written as a series of scenes, the method which Fitz-gerald derived from Henry James through Mrs. Wharton, and these

*Reprinted from the *Dial*, 79 (August 1925), 162–64, by permission of Timothy Seldes.

scenes are reported by a narrator who was obviously intended to be much more significant than he is. The author's appetite for life is so violent that he found the personality of the narrator an obstacle, and simply ignored it once his actual people were in motion, but the narrator helps to give the feeling of an intense unit which the various characters around Gatsby form. Gatsby himself remains a mystery; you know him, but not by knowing about him, and even at the end you can guess, if you like, that he was a forger or a dealer in stolen bonds, or a rather mean type of bootlegger. He had dedicated himself to the accomplishment of a supreme object, to restore to himself an illusion he had lost; he set about it, in a pathetic American way, by becoming incredibly rich and spending his wealth in incredible ways, so that he might win back the girl he loved; and a "foul dust floated in the wake of his dreams." Adultery and drunkenness and thievery and murder make up this dust, but Gatsby's story remains poignant and beautiful.

This means that Fitzgerald has ceased to content himself with a satiric report on the outside of American life and has with considerable irony attacked the spirit underneath, and so has begun to report on life in its most general terms. His tactile apprehension remains so fine that his people and his settings are specifically of Long Island; but now he meditates upon their fate and they become universal also. He has now something of extreme importance to say; and it is good fortune for us that he knows how to say it.

The scenes are austere in their composition. There is one, the tawdry afternoon of the satyr, Tom Buchanan, and his cheap and "vital" mistress, which is alive by the strength of the lapses of time; another, the meeting between Gatsby and his love, takes place literally behind closed doors, the narrator telling us only the beginning and the end. The variety of treatment, the intermingling of dialogue and narrative, the use of a snatch of significant detail instead of a big scene, make the whole a superb impressionistic painting, vivid in colour, and sparkling with meaning. And the major composition is as just as the treatment of detail. There is a brief curve before Gatsby himself enters; a longer one in which he begins his movement toward Daisy; then a succession of carefully spaced shorter and longer movements until the climax is reached. The plot works out not like a puzzle with odd bits falling into place, but like a tragedy, with every part functioning in the completed organism.

Even now, with *The Great Gatsby* before me, I cannot find in the earlier Fitzgerald the artistic integrity and the passionate feeling which this book possesses. And perhaps analysing the one and praising the other, both fail to convey the sense of elation which one has in reading his new novel. Would it be better to say that even *The Great Gatsby* is full of faults, and that that doesn't matter in the slightest degree? The cadences borrowed from Conrad, the occasional smartness, the frequently startling, but ineffective adjective—at last they do not signify. Because for the most part you know that Fitzgerald has consciously put these bad and half-bad things behind him, that he trusts them no more to make him the white-headed boy of *The Saturday Evening Post,* and that he has recognized both his capacities and his obligations as a novelist.

INDEX